THE REPUBLICAN MOMENT

The Republican Moment

STRUGGLES FOR DEMOCRACY IN
NINETEENTH-CENTURY FRANCE

Philip Nord

Harvard University Press
Cambridge, Massachusetts
London, England

First Harvard University Press paperback edition, 1998

Library of Congress Cataloging-in-Publication Data

Nord, Philip G., 1950–
The republican moment : struggles for democracy in nineteenth-
century France / Philip Nord.
p.   cm.
Includes bibliographical references and index.
ISBN 0-674-76271-1 (cloth)
ISBN 0-674-76272-X (pbk.)
1. France—History—Third Republic, 1870–1940.   2. France—
Politics and government—1870–1940.   3. Republicanism—France—
History—19th century.   4. Middle class—France—Political
activity.   5. Elites (Social science)—France—Attitudes.
I. Title.
DC340.N67   1995
944.07—dc20
95-10445

for David

Contents

Figures

FIGURES

THE REPUBLICAN MOMENT

INTRODUCTION

Civil Society

FRANCE BECAME a republic in the 1870s, a parliamentary democracy endowed with the most generous franchise (universal manhood suffrage) in great-power Europe. The fact itself is not so remarkable. The nation had experimented twice before with republican government, in 1792 and again in 1848. But those regimes collapsed in short order whereas the Third Republic was destined to live for seventy years, a feat of longevity unmatched by any other postrevolutionary French regime. Why did democratic institutions take root in France in the 1870s? There are at least three explanations of the phenomenon.

The first is centered on problems of ideology, and in this domain the research of François Furet has been trend-setting. The Second Republic was snuffed out by Louis-Napoleon Bonaparte's coup in 1851. Driven underground or abroad, veterans of 1848 began to rethink the republican project. Furet has fastened attention on the figure of Edgar Quinet, a historian and lifelong republican who in 1865, from his exile in Switzerland, penned a forceful critique of the revolution of 1789, the Jacobin episode in particular. Quinet interpreted the terrorist practices of the First Republic as a throwback to the despotism of the old regime. His message to fellow republicans was clear: repudiate violent revolutionism or be forever condemned to repeat the self-destructive failures of the Jacobins. A new generation—young lawyers like Jules Ferry and Léon Gambetta—took Quinet's counsel to heart, eschewing the romantic posturing of yes-

① ideas

teryear in favor of a more practical approach to the science of politics. It was this "positivist generation" that shepherded the Third Republic into existence.[1]

The issue of how they assembled a working majority for the republic, a social coalition to underpin the regime, has prompted explanations of a second order, focused less on ideas than on alliance

② alliance building

building. Stanley Hoffmann, who experienced first hand the republic's dismal decline in the 1930s, was inclined to stress the brittleness of what he called "the republican synthesis." Ferry and Gambetta were spokesmen for a new middle class (Gambetta himself preferred to call it a "new social stratum") of businessmen and professionals. It was such men who in the 1870s rallied rural France to the republican banner. They wooed a countryside populated by small-holding peasants with a specific and welcome promise: material and moral improvement within a socioeconomic order anchored in the family enterprise. At base, then, the republican synthesis was conservative in orientation, wedded to a property regime that sustained such attitudes as an intense preoccupation with the preservation of family patrimony—inimical to the advance of entrepreneurial industrialism. The end result was a "stalemate society," resistant to change even when, as in the years between the two world wars, change was the price of survival.[2]

Eugen Weber puts a more positive gloss on the republicanization of the countryside, understood by him as the dissemination, through the seductions of the market and impositions of the state, of urban modes of thinking across a backward and fatalist peasant society. For Marxists like Sanford Elwitt, the entire operation has the look of a bourgeois scam. The Second Empire, after taking France into a disastrous war against Prussia in 1870, collapsed in the wake of stinging military defeat. On the ruins of the old imperial state, a new republic was constructed, which negotiated peace and promised a restoration of order. The eruption of the revolutionary Commune in Paris in March 1871 threatened to derail such plans, but the Commune was crushed, greatly simplifying the task of an emergent republican elite by eliminating a major competitor on the left. That elite took full advantage of the situation. Although representing the interests of property first and foremost, it contrived by means of artifice and material incentives to attract a wide swath of provincial opinion. The new governing class's democratic and reforming project, such as it was, was intended less to advance high-minded principle than to forge a citizenry respectful of the bourgeois republic, prepared to serve it in the military and resistant to the siren calls of socialism.[3] But whether the accent is placed on stalemate, urbanity, or manipulation, the conclusion remains the same: the republic rested on a social compact between a middle-class governing elite, on the one hand, and a rural and small-town populace, on the other, which might be counted upon to produce the requisite electoral majorities. The momentary silencing of the labor left in the aftermath of the Commune eased negotiation of a compact from which large portions of the working class felt excluded.

But what became of France's old governing elite, of the so-called notables who had managed public affairs in the half-century preceding the Third Republic? This question has prompted a third species of explanation, which emphasises the notion of compromise. New elites struck a bargain with the landlords and grands bourgeois of yesteryear. This is not to say that France's old notability embraced such a brokered outcome with enthusiasm. Indeed, much of the 1870s was spent resisting any such solution. In the winter of 1871, the fledgling republic organized its first national elections, which returned a conservative majority, nicknamed "the rurals" by Karl Marx. Hopes of a monarchical restoration flaired for a brief moment but foundered on the inability of the royalist factions, Bourbon and Orleanist, to reach agreement on how best to proceed. The republic survived, governed by men who felt only a minimal attachment to its institutions or principles.

Just how little was demonstrated during the so-called *seize mai* crisis (16 May 1877). Legislative elections in the preceding year had tipped the balance of power away from the old parties in favor of centrist republicans. The president of the republic, the reactionary Maréchal Maurice de MacMahon, maneuvered to reverse the trend, proroguing the Chamber of Deputies in May 1877. New elections were later ordered, and the executive used every strategem at its disposal to skew the results—but to no avail. A republican majority was returned once more; rumors of a military coup circulated; but then—and this is the important point—MacMahon backed down. For all that old elites resisted the rising tide of republican sentiment, or so the argument goes, they buckled in the end and opted for a negotiated settlement.

They exacted a price, however, for their compliance in the new order of things, although just how high the price is a matter of debate. On Furet's accounting, it was minimal. Republicans shucked off the Jacobin legacy bequeathed by the Great Revolution. Established elites, steeped in a liberalism that counted Tocqueville and Guizot among its progenitors, were reassured and made common cause with the likes of Ferry and Gambetta. From such union was born a new democratic parliamentarism. Christophe Charle tells a similar tale of compromise, but in less cheerful colors.[4] The coming of the republic delivered a setback to established administrative elites. The new regime purged politically unreliable oldtimers and pledged itself to the meritocratic recruitment of civil servants. But such changes, Charle points out, left the business sector intact. And old families contrived to find ways to reenter public administration, acquiring through private education the exam-taking skills necessary to a successful civil-service career. For a period, *la haute fonction publique* took on a more democratic cast, but over time, in social profile and to a lesser degree in political orientation, it reverted to type. A republicanized elite ruled in the Chamber and Senate, in the prefectoral corps, in the university, but the corporate business world and the senior civil service escaped its reforming grasp. Furet's happy compromise is recast here into a veiled competition for position, with the state apparatus itself as the object of contention. The uneasy division of spoils worked out between new and old takes on a more sinister look when politics is added to the mix. The republic's new men were in the main democrats, but not the corporate and civil service establishments, which were annoyed with the dithering of parliamentary politicians and pinned hopes for France's future on the managerial-administrative capacities of a competent few. They tolerated the new regime as the best option at the moment, but did not embrace it; they constituted a node of potential disloyalty at the republic's very heart.

For all that they differ in tone and focus, these accounts of the Third Republic's origins agree on one point: new elites are assigned a critical, catalytic role in the fashioning of democratic institutions. It is they who devise novel intellectual strategies; who maneuver to line up popular support; who negotiate deals with still powerful oldtimers. But where did these new men come from? The question is all the more compelling when placed in a comparative perspective.

The French, of course, held no monopoly on the democratizing impulse at midcentury. Mazzinians and Garibaldians dreamed of an Italy that would be not only unified but republican. In England, radical Dissent agitated for Church disestablishment, school reform, and an extension of the franchise. In Germany, partisans of genuine constitutionalism, such as Eugen Richter or the veteran 48er Rudolf

Virchow, rallied to the banner of an oppositional progressivism, distancing themselves from liberals who had with such disconcerting facility come to terms with Bismarck's blood-and-iron authoritarianism. But in all such instances, the democratizing thrusts were blunted or absorbed. Garibaldi and Mazzini, in the interests of national unity, submitted to Piedmontese policy, to the canny maneuverings of Count Cavour, who may have been a liberal monarchist but certainly no democrat. In England, a Liberal Party recast in the Gladstonian mold welcomed Dissent into its ranks, exacting in return submission to a party leadership composed of Whig grandees and Peelite administrators. German progressives retained a measure of independence, but found themselves in a squeeze that reduced them to ineffectuality. The gathering momentum of a socialist and working-class left tempered the progressives' democratic commitments and induced them to consider making peace with a liberalism they had once judged too compromised.

In France it was different. There, in the 1870s, the democratic movement broke through, giving rise to a new republican order. The monarchy and all its paraphernalia were banished. The restricted franchise so characteristic of aristocratic polities in the nineteenth century gave way to universal manhood suffrage. Cabinets were populated not by noblemen or landed gentry, but by bourgeois. It is not that the institutions of the republic were unmarked by compromise, far from it. But the terms were set by new men, not the old. Democratic elites did not have to bend themselves to the rules of a political order dominated by notables, but the other way around (although how far the notables were obliged to bend remains to be seen).

The problem under consideration may be reformulated as follows. At issue is not simply the origins of France's democratizing elites but the peculiar zeal they manifested, their capacity both to overcome resistance and, once in power, to make democratic institutions work. How is such exceptionalism to be accounted for? Democratic theory and an expanding social science literature on democratic transitions suggest where an answer might be looked for.

Democratic Transition

Theories of democratic transition fall into two principal categories. The first, rooted in modern cold-war battles against communism, accents the structural preconditions of participatory government.

Robert Dahl, Samuel Huntington, and others have worked this ground to exhaustion, identifying a wide range of variables said to be conducive to the consolidation of representative institutions: a high level of economic development, general literacy, a variegated social structure with a heavy middle-class ballast.[5] The policy implications of this line of argument are straightforward: finance growth and education, foster a native bourgeoisie, and democratic institutions will stabilize, enough so at least to withstand communist encroachments. But the international climate has changed in recent years, and a fresh angle of approach has been elaborated in response. The mid-1970s collapse of Iberian authoritarianism, the multiplying failures of military dictatorships in Latin America, and the "velvet" revolutions of 1989 in eastern Europe have inspired a rethinking of democratic transition. A new literature has taken shape that is centered less on structures than on voluntary action, on the dynamics by which democratic institutions can be made to sprout on the seemingly inhospitable ground of authoritarian rule.

Two distinct, but not contradictory, lines of inquiry have been pursued along these lines. The first, influenced by Latin American examples, hones in on the behavior of elites. The prospects of a democratic transition brighten, the argument goes, when elites, old and new, have learned from violent past experience to avoid confrontation. Bloody memories of former repressions can have a sobering effect on incumbent authorities. When faced with a new democratic challenge, the landlords, generals, and bureaucrats in power may hesitate to embark on yet another round of violence. Opposition elites too may have mulled over lessons of the past.[6] The experience of exile, prison, or enforced silence can work as a powerful solvent, eating away at the maximalist rigidity of former years in favor of a more flexible and reassuring pragmatism. In such circumstances a bargain becomes possible: the opposition is conceded the commanding heights of the state in exchange for no retaliation against erstwhile authorities; the outgoing elite, while obliged to abandon the political high ground, continues to exercise critical influence (thanks to its extensive property holdings) as well as an important, albeit reduced, measure of political power (thanks to control of certain institutional redoubts, such as the army). To students of the Third Republic's origins, such a scenario, focused as it is on problems of political learning and pact making, is bound to have a familiar ring. But whether it is France in the 1870s or Argentina in the 1980s, the

[6]

question remains: what is the source of the democratic challenge that enables elites to demonstrate the lessons they have learned in restraint and negotiation?

Transition theorists who address this problem have edged away from the study of high politics toward a discussion of what they call "civil society," the social and institutional settings in which new elites get their start. This avenue of inquiry, very promising in the French context, has a pedigree that reaches back to the early 1960s: to Gabriel Almond and Sidney Verba's work on "civic culture," to Jürgen Habermas' speculations on the rise and fall of the "public sphere."[7] To be sure, Almond and Verba on the one hand and Habermas on the other came to the problem from different perspectives. Almond and Verba, Anglo-American social scientists in the liberal mold, touted a democratic political culture as the surest antidote to the temptations of totalitarianism. Habermas, as a student of critical theory, worried less about fascist or communist threats than about the corrosive effects of consumer capitalism on free and rational discourse. But for all that they differ in point of departure, the two schools see eye to eye on one critical proposition: a strong and resilient public sphere is the sine qua non of a functioning democracy. There is agreement as well on what constitutes the building blocks of a vibrant civil society: first, dense and intertwined networks of communication and sociability (Habermas is more inclined to stress the importance of a critical-minded print culture, Almond and Verba the importance of a lively associational life); second, an informed citizenry, neither deferential nor defiant, which is committed to making public institutions work.

But missing in all this work is an account of origins: how does a democratic citizenry with all the requisite skills and attitudes arise in the first place? Almond and Verba take a well-developed civic culture as a given and never inquire into its genealogy. Habermas does offer a sketch of origins: the public sphere first took shape in the eighteenth century, expanded and democratized in the nineteenth, and is withering in the present. But few states, even in the great-power Europe from which Habermas' evidence is drawn, have followed a trajectory so smooth. Sharp alternations between moments of revolutionary possibility and more extended periods—post-1815, post-1848, post-1918—of reactionary closure, such is the more common experience. The apposite question for continental Europe (and for Third Republic France) is how this cycle of revolution and reaction was broken, how empires and monarchies were made to metamorphose into democratic states without subsequent backsliding.

It is on the issue of origins that society-centered transition theorists have struck out in new directions. Given that an articulated civil society is the bedrock of democracy, how does that society come to be? How was it built out of the debris of authoritarian government? The start of an answer is to be found in the destabilizing consequences of economic transformation. Dictatorships believe they want growth, but in fact make a serious mistake in fostering it. Development favors the "expansion of educated middle classes"; it engenders a "pluralistic infrastructure," a ramifying civil society ever more difficult to manage from above. Whether in response to pressures building within civil society or for tactical reasons of its own, the authoritarian state may opt at this juncture to relax its grip on public life. The decision is a fatal one, for into the openings created by liberalization pour accumulated discontents that, now articulated, take on the character of outright opposition.[8]

The hardening of opposition takes place at particular sites, certain institutional locales that enjoy or succeed in laying claim to a measure of autonomous activity. Autonomy may be an institutional tradition dating back to a nonauthoritarian moment in the past, as in the case of churches, bar associations, or even trade unions. Or it may be a goal aspired to by newcomers: organizations of businessmen, journalists, or human-rights activists determined to shake off state tutelage. Such institutions and organizations are important not only as "free zones" in which an independent public opinion begins to form itself, but also as arenas of democratic experiment and education. Here people might practice the electoral arts that in the wider polity have been tampered with and falsified.[9]

To the extent that such battles for autonomy are won, to the extent the state is driven out of a reawakening civil society, a new sphere of activity, a public sphere begins to form. Communication is all-important to the process. The various institutions, leagues, and clubs that constitute public opinion in formation make contact through informal networks of sociability, the print media, and, as the hold of dictatorship loosens, demonstrations out of doors. By such means, localized conflicts are woven into a widening movement of opposition.

Such a "resurrection of civil society," as it has been called,[10] presents dictatorships with a stark choice between repression or withdrawal. The decision might well be to cut a deal, opening the way to new elites and a new regime. But will the new democratic order survive? That depends in part on the kind of deal that has been cut. In much of the transition literature, there is a deep-seated anxiety that democratization will go too far. Oppositional elites that, on inheriting power, bear down on an outgoing authoritarian establishment invite a reactionary backlash. Better, therefore, that the new men not be too strong, that they treat the outgoing authorities with a gentle hand, sparing them purges, reprisals, and the like.[11] It helps too that incoming elites know how to use the existing institutional apparatus. At issue here is not just constitution making but the deployment of state power to legislate and police a civic order in which habits of citizenship can be learned.[12] Movement culture can in this way be transformed into official culture, acquiring a solidity that will make it all the more difficult to dislodge, whether by revolutionaries of the right or the left. But that civic order, however much the government may work to entrench it, cannot be legislated from scratch. It must be in place prior to the advent of democracy, having been worked out on the battlefield, so to speak, as part of the struggle against dictatorship. The conclusion of such a line of argument is evident: what makes possible a democratic transition is the prior elaboration, while dictatorship is still in place, of a counter-elite anchored in autonomous institutions and buoyed by an alternative political culture. The more articulated and coherent that culture and the institutional frame on which it rests, the more powerful the thrust toward democratization and, in the end, the more likely the endurance of a democratic transition.

[handwritten marginalia: Democ. possible when strong, private elite in place under dictatorship]

The Resurrection of Civil Society

Can such an outline help to explain France's precocious and, at least by national standards, long-lived transition to democracy in the mid-nineteenth century? It does not contradict existing interpretations that emphasize the political skills and determination of a new republican elite. But it does suggest that the analysis should be pressed further, that the republican elite be situated in the organizational and cultural web that first gave it life and strength. Pioneering research has been done on these lines, above all by Maurice Agulhon for the Second Republic.[13] But Agulhon's work also makes clear the extent to which Louis-Napoleon's 1851 coup shattered republican networks, which had to be rebuilt from the ground up on the basis of hard lessons learned in bitter defeat. As transition theory indicates, such building or rebuilding does not occur in a vacuum but unfolds in an institutional context that patterns the process in fundamental ways. The place to begin an analysis of France's democratic transition, then, is with a sketch of that context, of the character and structures of institutional life in the decades prior to the Third Republic.[14]

France's national elite at midcentury, a mixture of landed, mercantile, and industrial interests, was not a reactionary elite. The notables were not hostile to industrialization or to the Great Revolution. But they had been shaken and weakened by repeated bouts of popular upheaval and were determined to bring the revolutionary era to a close. To this end, over the course of the nineteenth century, they entrenched themselves in a network of state and para-statal institutions. The Institute and the University may be cited as examples.

The institute consisted of four state-chartered academies: the Académie Française, des Beaux-Arts, des Inscriptions et Belles Lettres, and des Sciences. A fifth was added in 1834, the Académie des Sciences Morales et Politiques, brainchild of the Orleanist François Guizot. The academies were conceived as ancillaries to the state. The Academy of Moral and Political Sciences, for example, functioned as a proto-policy institute, furnishing public officials with useful statistics and reports on issues of the day. The Academy of Fine Arts, in collaboration with the Ministry of Fine Arts, mounted the biannual and later annual *salons des arts,* until late in the century France's premier art exhibitions. The academies, though connected to the state by charter and function, enjoyed a measure of autonomy in that they were self-selecting bodies with a coopted membership.

The university (which in France encompasses secondary as well as higher public education) stood in a similar relationship to the state. Its constitution was dictated by the state; its highest official, the Grand Master, was a state appointee who answered on matters of policy to the minister of public instruction. Nonetheless, the institution conceived itself as an "independent corporation," attached but not subservient to public authority.[15] The minister and Grand Master were not the sole administrators of university affairs. They worked in tandem with the Conseil de l'Instruction Publique, which was in the majority an elective body composed of representatives of the university's multiple faculties.

CIVIL SOCIETY

In the days of the July Monarchy, in the 1830s and 1840s, relations between the central state apparatus and such institutions were cordial. Guizot, prime minister from 1840 to 1848, was himself a historian who counted numerous friends on the university faculty. He saw to it that the Academy of Moral and Political Sciences, his particular creation, was well stocked with men of enlightened views much like himself. In 1840 Guizot appointed a fellow *universitaire,* the philosopher and academician Victor Cousin, as minister of public instruction. Cousin, an able administrator, schemed with considerable success to pack the university with teachers and professors who shared his eclectic philosophy, a belief in transcendent ideals of truth and beauty that could be grasped through reason. The upper reaches of the state administration and of allied institutions were staffed by a small elite of accomplished but like-minded men. They used the accumulated and considerable institutional powers at their disposal to administer and, if need be, to discipline an unruly civil society in the name of order and progress.

With the coming of the Second Empire, institutional controls were tightened to an extraordinary degree. It is important not to exaggerate Louis-Napoleon's repressive intentions, which pale in comparison with the ruthless brutality displayed by would-be Bonapartes of our own era. There was, moreover, a liberal current in the Bonapartist camp, in sympathy with certain reform causes of the day, which seemed on the point of gaining the upper hand in the regime's closing years. But the empire, however restrained or "enlightened" at given moments, was always an authoritarian regime. It curtailed the right of free association and stiffened press censorship. It imposed a veritable straitjacket on civil society, annexing and breaking to its will all institutions that might breed independence of mind or action. Bonaparte at first had considered outright abolition of the university, but contented himself with appointing a tough-minded minister of public instruction, Hippolyte Fortoul, who in turn packed the once-autonomous Conseil de l'Instruction Publique with more pliable appointees. In like manner, the emperor debated suppressing the masonic Grand Orient of France, but ended by placing it under the tutelage of an appointee and close relative, Prince Lucien Murat. The Paris bar had in years preceding elected its governing council and presiding officer *(bâtonnier)* by direct and universal suffrage. The emperor maneuvered to reduce the bâtonnier's authority by tinkering with the electoral process. From 1852 on, it was the council and not the run of bar members who picked the bâtonnier, and they were obliged to choose one among themselves. The Paris Chamber of Commerce, which had a formal right to advise the government on matters of economic policy, was an elective body. In 1848 the suffrage was extended to all businessmen who met certain requirements of residence and probity. The emperor cut back the electorate to a mere 2,000 *notables-commerçants* and made admission to the ranks of the commercial notability contingent on the approval of a watchful prefect of the Seine.

Since the first Napoleon, France's minority religions—Protestant and Jewish—had been organized in consistories, bodies invested with a double mandate: to represent vis-à-vis the state the interests of the faithful and to perform vis-à-vis the faithful a variety of policing functions. Consistorial boards were mainly composed of lay representatives elected, in the Jewish case, by universal suffrage, in the Protestant by a more restricted franchise. Louis-Napoleon subjected both consistories to an institutional overhaul. The political motive was to strengthen those religious currents well disposed to the regime, or at least to weaken potential opponents. In the case of the Jewish consistory, such a policy translated into backing for its Rothschild-led, liberal-minded (in religious matters), and beleaguered governing elite, which communicated a willingness to deal with the empire in exchange for assistance against a menacing orthodox majority. Bonaparte responded positively to such overtures, imposing new restrictions on the consistorial suffrage in 1860, which in effect excluded from participation the poorest, and often most orthodox, sections of the Jewish community.

From the empire's point of view, the Reformed Church's governing elite represented a problem of a different sort. The Protestant church was run by a close-knit network of select families; its religious orientation was orthodox; and its dominant lay personality was none other than François Guizot, an Orleanist and determined enemy of the empire. The challenge in this instance was not to strengthen but to subvert elite authority. Louis-Napoleon accordingly curried favor with liberal, antiorthodox currents in the Reformed Church. At the same time, he imposed universal suffrage in consistorial elections in the hope of inciting a liberal Protestant groundswell to unseat the Guizot faction.[16]

On the whole, the abrasive institutional interventions of the imperial state irritated established elites accustomed, at least since the days of the July Monarchy, to an easy-going partnership with officialdom. The favored position of the Jewish consistorial elite may be counted an exception to the pattern. Notables dug in their heels and sealed off institutions like the institute or the Paris bar from Bonapartist interference. The Académie Française snubbed the regime time and again, rejecting candidates with imperial connections in favor of scions of the Orleanist notability.[17] The Paris bar in the 1850s elected governing councils of an oppositional complexion, who in turn elected a series of antiregime bâtonniers from Berryer on the legitimist right to Bethmont and Liouville on the republican left. So what remained in the wake of official efforts to close down public life was an extensive state apparatus, dominated by Bonapartists but, at strategic sites, colonized by notables who were cool to the new regime.

Bonaparte's rollback of the public sphere might have worked had it not coincided with a sustained economic boom. Economic growth, spurred on by the imperial regime itself, fed the expansion of a new middle class of businessmen and professionals. The institutional carapace Bonaparte had clamped on civil society proved too tight-fitting to absorb these new classes. They chafed against franchise arrangements that excluded them, against enforced silences, against arbitrary impositions from above. And the ferment that began under the empire persisted well beyond the regime's collapse. Louis-Napoleon left the scene in 1870, but he was succeeded by the centrist administration of the former Orleanist Adolphe Thiers (1871–1873) and then by the so-called regime of Moral Order (1873–1877), which was authoritarian and clerical-minded in its policies.[18] In the circumstances, middle-class discontent did not flag but even intensified.

That discontent, moreover, flared across a broad front: from the lodges of Freemasonry through the minority religious consistories and the Paris bar to the world of the arts. And an awakening republican opinion used any and all means to make its point. It dramatized its arguments through ritual and symbol.[19] It reworked public debate on family and gender roles into a double-edged polemic against the Catholic church and authoritarian state. No domain, public or private, was exempt from these politicizing efforts.

It was from such a general resurrection of civil society that the Third Republic was born. My task is to track republicanism's slow march through the institutions. There is no better place to begin than with Freemasonry and the university, for there the slow march turned into a veritable rout. A republican wave swept through the lodges, through the schools of the Latin Quarter, transforming them into democratic strongholds and, with the coming of the republic itself, into institutional pillars of the new regime.

[1]

Freemasonry

FRANCE'S EXTREME right from the very first reviled the Third Republic as a creature of Freemasonry, as the willing instrument of sinister plots hatched in the lodges. The regime was not ruled by a masonic conspiracy, of course, but its indebtedness to Masonry cannot be disputed. An estimated 40 percent of the republic's civilian ministers from 1877 to the outbreak of World War I were lodge members.[1] Whenever the regime fell into rough political waters, as at the time of the Dreyfus affair, Masonry was among the first to rally to its side. The affinities between the lodges and the regime were ideological as well, although the precise character of Masonry's moral legacy to the republic is a matter of some debate.

The lodges of the 1860s and 1870s, it is often argued, were nursery to an up-and-coming "positivist generation" that pushed aside an aging cohort of leaders, the *vieilles barbes* of 1848. The young positivists, sober-minded and legalistic, spurned the sentimental and fraternalist rhetoric of the old 48ers. They defined a different, pragmatic republicanism, drained of radical content; such reasonableness, it seems, paid off. The Second Republic, born of the revolution of 1848, survived less than four years. The Third Republic, the handiwork of the positivist generation, lasted almost seventy.

There is considerable truth to this description. A new generation did indeed enter the lodges at midcentury. Masonry experienced a veritable explosion of recruitment under the Second Empire. The number of ateliers, chapters, and the like affiliated to the Grand

Orient, France's largest masonic body, shot up from 244 in 1857 to 392 in 1870.[2] Many of the new recruits, moreover, were positivists, not least of all Emile Littré, Comte's most celebrated disciple in France, who became a member in 1875. That Jules Ferry was initiated at the very same ceremony stands in symbolic confirmation of the tightening bonds between Masonry, positivism, and liberal republicanism.[3]

In this chapter I want to endorse a different view of the evolution of Freemasonry and by implication a different assessment of the ideological currents that fed into the Third Republic. The Second Empire made a concerted effort to stifle public life in the 1850s, and Freemasonry did not escape the state's oppressive embrace. In 1854 the regime imposed a new and authoritarian constitution on the Grand Orient and undertook to fill the highest office of Freemasonry, the Grand Mastership, with a state appointee. Masons chafed under imperial tutelage, however. Dissident lodges mounted a campaign to reassert the order's institutional autonomy, and that campaign took on immediate political overtones, spilling over into an ill-concealed republican oppositionism.

The radicalization of the masonic opposition was in part a reaction to the weight of state oppression, but it was also propelled by elements within the order itself. The Bonapartist coup of 1851 had scattered the militants of France's democratic and socialist left. Many of these oldtimers—Saint-Simonians, Proudhonists, Fourierists, utopians and socialists of every hue and color—took refuge in the lodges. It was this older generation that helped to plot masonic strategy in the institutional battles of midcentury. The leadership they provided and the campaign they orchestrated gave shape to a distinctive current of masonic radicalism—federalist, anticlerical, ultrademocratic—which manifested itself through action in a knot of related progressive causes: pacifism, feminism, and the cooperative movement.

Generations and ideologies mingled in the lodges of the Second Empire, a simple observation that points to some general conclusions about the Third Republic itself. First, the regime's ideological inheritance was much richer than sometimes supposed. Liberal positivism as espoused by Ferry or Littré no doubt left a mark on the character of the new republic. Yet so too did a democratic utopianism that traced its origins back through the Second Republic to the 1830s and 1840s. From this perspective (and this is a second conclu-

sion), the regime appears less exclusively the work of pragmatists *not just*
bent on making a fresh start. Radicals and visionaries also had a hand *new generation*
in the framing of the republic, and to that extent the regime repre- *but old as*
sented not so much a rupture with as a consummation of republican- *well*
ism's revolutionary past.

The Grand Orient

Imperial authorities regarded Masonry with suspicion, not without
reason. In March 1848 a delegation of Masons paid a ceremonial call
on the provisional government to pledge Masonry's allegiance to the
fledgling Second Republic. Although lodges played only a minor
role in the democratic-socialist movement of 1849–1851, Masonry
retained a tinge of republicanism that made it noxious to the imperial regime born of the 1851 coup.[4] Louis-Napoleon in fact considered outright suppression of the order. The Grand Orient, apprised
of the danger, sought the protection of a member of the Bonaparte
family, Lucien Murat. Murat was acceptable to the regime, which
appointed him Grand Master in 1852. But Murat proved less a
patron than a disciplinarian. The state-imposed constitution of 1854
invested the Grand Master with extensive decision-making powers,
which Murat deployed to demolish or "put to sleep" well over one
hundred lodges.[5]

Provincial Masonry was hardest hit. In the first decade of Louis-
Napoleon's rule, more than half the lodges based in the departments
closed down, 120 out of 222. Masonry was mostly a Paris-centered
phenomenon, and even more so in the repressive climate of the
1850s. In 1858, some 40 of metropolitan France's 142 lodges were
headquartered in the capital. Little wonder that the first stirrings of
opposition to Murat's policies emanated from the Parisian wing of
the masonic movement. In the late 1860s, a reawakening provincial
Masonry weighed more heavily in the battle, but even then leadership remained in the Paris lodges.[6]

The antagonisms fanned by Murat's autocratic policies erupted in
1861. The constitution of 1854 fixed the Grand Master's term of
office at seven years, at which time the post was to be refilled not by
appointment but by a simple majority vote at the annual convent
(convention) of lodge representatives. Since 1861 was an election
year, dissidents intended to use the occasion to advantage. The first
signs of trouble appeared in early spring. Murat, also an imperial

senator, had cast a vote sanctioning the presence of French troops in Rome. Luc-Pierre Riche-Gardon, master (*vénérable*) of the Parisian lodge Le Temple des Familles, branded the prince an ally of papal obscurantism and was immediately suspended. Murat, who intended to run in the upcoming masonic elections, detected a cabal in the making. In mid-May, just weeks before the vote, he suspended a further half-dozen Masons accused of conspiratorial activities. Undeterred, the plotters gathered at the home of Charles Fauvety, venerable of La Renaissance par les Emules d'Hiram (also a Parisian lodge), and agreed to advance the candidacy of Prince Jérôme Bonaparte as an alternative to Murat. The decision made at least one brother uneasy, Jean-Marie Caubet of La Rose du Parfait Silence (a third Parisian lodge). "The Bonaparte dynasty," he later wrote, "had nothing to recommend itself to *la république maçonnique.*" But the strategy proved effective. By the time the convent met, Murat faced defeat. In desperation he decreed a postponement of the election. The dissidents met all the same. A furious Murat called in the police to break up the session, disciplined every Mason known to have taken part, and prorogued the convent until October. But fresh disturbances threatened in the fall, and the prefect of police acted to adjourn the convent sine die.[7] Murat's coup and the subsequent disorders persuaded the emperor himself to intervene. He imposed a new Grand Master on the order, the Maréchal Bernard Pierre Magnan, who took office in 1862. In a gesture of pacification, Magnan reinstated the suspended Masons.

Dissidents continued to agitate, however. Magnan proposed to petition imperial authorities to designate the Grand Orient an "institution of public utility." The measure promised Masonry financial advantages, and the Council of the Order, a twenty-one-member consultative body elected at the annual convention, endorsed Magnan's scheme. There was a lone dissenting voice on the council: André Rousselle stigmatized the measure as "a cause of servitude." The state, he warned, enjoyed particular rights of surveillance over institutions of public utility and would surely use those rights to inhibit Masonry's independence of action. Letters poured into the council from individual lodges, echoing Rousselle's objections. The commotion persuaded masonic officialdom to refer a final decision to the convent of 1863. There, the anti-Magnan forces were rallied by Jean-Claude Colfavru of L'Etoile Polaire and Alexandre Massol of La Renaissance par les Emules d'Hiram. Massol decried the public-utility project as an "alienation of our liberty," which threatened to shift the locus of sovereignty within the order upward, from the constituent lodges to the Grand Master and, indeed, to the state itself. Masonry was not a centralized body but "a confederation of lodges," a species of federal republic. Colfavru and Massol's exhortations carried the assembly, which rejected Magnan's proposal out of hand.[8]

The resistance generated by the Magnan project fed into a three-front assault on the constitution of 1854. Dissidents complained first that the document invested the Grand Master with autocratic and quasi-royal powers. Second, the opposition wanted to purge the constitution of "theologico-feudal language." Targeted specifically was article 1, which affirmed the existence of God and the immortality of the soul. Finally at issue were the privileges of the so-called senior grades—Brothers of the Rose Cross, Knights of Kadosch, and so on. Such high dignitaries enjoyed double membership, as initiates of "blue" lodges (to which all Masons belonged) and as coopted members of elite lodges (to which only men of the *hauts grades* might belong). Inasmuch as both blue and elite lodges were entitled to representation at the annual convent, senior-grade Masons were represented twice over. To dissidents, the system savored of an hierarchical spirit "contrary to the democratic essence of Masonry." They condemned the *hauts grades* as a foreign import of "catholico-feudal origin" and demanded their abolition.[9]

The dissidents' campaign met with success at first. The 1865 convent was declared constituent, but the new constitution worked out in debate proved a disappointment to reformers. True, the elective status of the Grand Mastership was reaffirmed; the chief executive's term was reduced from seven to five years; and, Magnan having died on the eve of the assembly, a new Grand Master, the relatively liberal General Emile Mellinet, was chosen. But the convent refused to expunge the reference to God in article 1 of the constitution. *Le Monde maçonnique,* principal organ of the opposition, blamed the setback on the senior grades, which had cast the deciding ballots. As for the *hauts grades* themselves, they were preserved from destruction, but only by the narrowest of margins, 86 votes to 83.[10]

The reverses of 1865, however, did not discourage reformers. Dissident lodges—La Renaissance par les Emules d'Hiram, Mars et les Arts, La Rose du Parfait Silence—conducted lecture series at which grievances on a wide range of issues were aired. Massol launched a new journal of opposition, *La Morale indépendante.* And new lodges were created that in short order became focal points of opposition, most notably the Parisian lodge, L'Ecole Mutuelle, headed by a series of able young lawyers: Rousselle, Jean-Jules Clamageran, Eugène Delattre, Amédée Dréo. Such efforts to mobilize opinion produced results.

The Grand Mastership fell first to the attacks of the opposition. Mellinet's term expired in 1870, and the convent of that year met in April to decide what to do. It voted in principle, to the surprise even of dissidents, to abolish the office of Grand Master altogether, pending consultation with the lodges. In the meantime it appointed to a one-year term Léonide Babaud-Laribière, an 1848 veteran and republican journalist. The democratic implications of Babaud's election were not lost on the candidate himself who, in a burst of exclamations, summed up the Grand Orient's recent political evolution: "A prince of the blood, Murat!—A maréchal of France, Magnan!—A general senator, Mellinet!—Finally, a simple journalist from the provinces." A new social stratum had risen to power in Masonry years before Gambetta invoked its "arrival and presence" on the national scene. Babaud was aware too that he was expected to act as a figurehead and, accordingly, deferred all important decisions to the Council of the Order. In due course, despite the disruptions of war and civil war, the lodges indicated strong preference for the suppression of the Grand Mastership. The convent of 1871 made the decision final, closing what one Mason called the order's "monarchical era" and completing its "evolution toward a genuinely democratic form of organization."[11]

The assault on the Grand Mastership was accompanied by sniping at the *hauts grades.* On the eve of the 1870 convent, one Brother Ratier presented a report to the Council of the Order calling for abolition of the elite lodges. "These noble and feudal titles," Ratier claimed, "offend the principles of equality and fraternity which are the rule of our institution" and subvert "our ambition to be the most perfect embodiment of democracy." The question was finally submitted to the 1872 convent. The assembly voted not to disband the so-called *ateliers supérieurs,* but to deny them representation at annual meetings, an outcome with immediate repercussions for the fate of article 1.[12]

Elite representatives, who had been an obstacle to revision of article 1, were now gone. The matter was settled once and for all at the convent of 1877, which met in the midst of the *seize mai* crisis. Pastor Frédéric Desmons of the Grand Orient of Nîmes reported on a motion to delete references to God in the constitution. The reform, he argued, was not aimed against believers who might still find a home in Freemasonry. At stake, rather, was "freedom of conscience." The old constitution, with its deist prescriptions, had discriminated against atheists. The convent passed Desmons' proposal by a crushing majority.[13]

The Grand Orient's embrace of secularism marked a turning point not only in its internal history but also in its relations with masonic movements abroad. The grand lodges of Ireland, England, and the Scandinavian countries immediately suspended all contacts with the French. French and German Masons had already had a falling out in the aftermath of the Franco-Prussian war when German lodges, abandoning all pretext of internationalism, had extended approval to Bismarck's annexation of Alsace and Lorraine. The Grand Orient's abandonment of deism hardened still further the anti-French feelings of the more religious and traditionalist Germans.[14]

The constitutional battles of the 1860s and 1870s turned on a demand for autonomy, but against whom were such claims pressed? Against the state, its servants and appointees, who responded in a spirit of resistance. In such an institutional context, the masonic dissidence inevitably took on an oppositional character. Demands for autonomy were couched in a language resonant with republicanism. The constitution of 1854, dissidents insinuated, smacked of the ancien régime. It sanctioned monarchical power; it recognized feudal rank; it abetted Catholic reaction. The reformist cause, by contrast, was democratic, egalitarian, and laic. Dissidents envisioned a Grand Orient purged of Bonapartist-royalist authoritarianism and reconstituted as a federation of self-governing lodges. Masons liked to think of themselves as a moral avant-garde. They had embarked on a course of republicanization in the 1860s, setting an example that the nation was destined to follow. Indeed, if France itself became republican, it was in part thanks to the efforts of militants like Rousselle and Delattre, both future deputies, who graduated from masonic politics to politics *tout court*.

Masonry's turn to republicanism in the 1860s was not an unnatural choice. The authoritarian character and conduct of the Bonapartist state pushed Masons in the direction of a republican commitment, but they were also drawn from within. What is striking about the cadre of militants who populated the lodges of the Second Empire is how many were republicans, and not just liberal republicans but radicals, utopians, and even mystics.[15]

Masonic Radicals

In the heat of the constitutional crisis of 1861–62, Murat's partisans ridiculed Riche-Gardon and his allies as "mystagogues and socialists," a charge that had some foundation.[16] A professor of philosophy and man of the left, Riche-Gardon had spent a lifetime in quest of the "definitive religion of humanity." He awaited, as harbinger of mankind's redemption, a "revelation of the universal law" and listened in particular to the voices of female prophets.[17]

Riche-Gardon's transcendental turn of mind was shared by Henri Carle and Charles Fauvety, both brothers active in the lodge La Renaissance. Carle, a one-time Icarian communist, wrote a tract, *Alliance religieuse universelle,* which argued for the creation of a United States of Thought.[18] In the 1860s he found a regular forum for such "theophilanthropic" elucubrations in the pages of *L'Opinion nationale,* a newspaper of freethinking views edited by Adolphe Guéroult, a former Saint-Simonian and fellow Mason. Fauvety's itinerary was similar. He had worked on Proudhon's *Représentant du peuple* in 1848 and then in the fifties moved on to coedit with Charles Lemonnier (like Guéroult, a Saint-Simonian turned Mason) a journal of moral and spiritual speculation, *La Revue philosophique et religieuse.* Fauvety was host as well to a salon that attracted a heterodox clientele: the feminists Jenny d'Héricourt and Juliette Lamber (later Juliette Adam), the Fourierist François Cantagrel (also a member of La Renaissance), the Kantian philosopher Charles Renouvier, and Eliphas Lévi, the magus of occultism.[19]

Nor were Riche-Gardon, Carle, and Fauvety that different from other masonic dissidents of the empire. Colfavru had been a club militant in 1848 and then a Proudhonist before taking up masonic activism. Like so many of the visionary socialists of his generation, he was drawn to Egypt, where he spent eight years from 1872 to 1880. Massol too had spent time in the Middle East. In the wake of the 1830 revolution, he had become a Saint-Simonian, loyal even in adversity. In 1833, when père Enfantin embarked on his ill-starred trip to Egypt in search of the female messiah, Massol was among the faithful few willing to follow.

It was men such as these—seekers of the absolute, legatees of utopian socialism, radical republicans—who ran the principal dissident lodges. Starting in 1862, Massol was the moving spirit behind La Renaissance par les Emules d'Hiram. At Mars et les Arts, the dominant figures were Montanier and Léon Richer, both veteran journalists at *L'Opinion nationale.* Montanier, a lifelong republican, wrote a science column for Guéroult. Richer penned a series of articles, later published in book form as *Lettres d'un libre-penseur à un curé de campagne,* which canvassed in sympathetic detail current efforts—among freethinkers, liberal Jews, and liberal Protestants—to negotiate the framework of a rational religión.[20] La Rose du Parfait Silence was Caubet's bailiwick. He was indeed a positivist, but also a *jacobin d'idées* and an intimate of Massol's.[21]

To the extent that Massol's *La Morale indépendante* can be taken as representative, the dissident press, no less than the dissident lodges, was run by freethinking radicals. A remarkable band of collaborators staffed the journal: Henri Brisson, François Coignet, Ange Guépin, and Frédéric Morin. Brisson, the youngest of the lot, was destined for a long career in republican politics: France's first Radical prime minister in 1885 and a founding member of the Parti Radical in 1901. Coignet and Guépin were comparative oldtimers, the former an ex-Fourierist, the latter an ex-Saint-Simonian. As for Morin, he was a professor of philosophy, cashiered by Bonaparte for refusing to swear loyalty to the empire. In his younger days, he had subscribed to the Christian socialism of Philippe Buchez but moved in the 1850s toward freethinking rationalism.

Utopian Vision

Many of the masonic dissidents were former utopians, like Morin, who had to temper their youthful idealism under the hammer blows of imperial repression. A scaling down of expectation, however, did not betoken a total abandonment of transcendental or religious impulses. Masons exalted reason, science, and rational education, but those earth-bound values held appeal for the service they might render the cause of a visionary humanitarianism.

Masons espoused a rationalist ethics partly as an antidote to Catholic theology and Cousinist eclecticism. The moral law, Massol argued, was inscribed in the hearts of men, and through the exercise of reason that law might be known. Men carried the springs of conscientious action within themselves and were capable of moral choice without the intercession of external authorities like the church or university.

But what was the precise ontological status of moral law? The men of *La Morale indépendante* answered the question with a profession of Kantian dualism. The moral realm existed apart from the material world; it functioned according to its own rules, which were fully intelligible. A science of morals was possible, but it would be a science closer to mathematics than to physiology or medicine. To many masonic moralists, however, the Kantian solution was unsatisfactory. To posit the autonomy of the moral realm did not, after all, answer the question of how that realm came into being. Proponents of rational religion like Riche-Gardon and Richer detected the hand of a benevolent deity at the origins of moral life. Masons of liberal Protestant background, Clamageran and Desmons for example, gave this line of argument a more explicitly denominational twist. Liberal Protestants understood conscience as "a kind of mysterious impression of the divine." In that conscience partook of the sacred, its workings were inaccessible to reason alone. The needed assistance came in the form of Scripture. Knowledge of the good was secured through a *libre examen* of the Bible, and by *libre examen* was meant not just a rational reading but a reading informed by "religious sentiment."[22] In the ranks of the masonic opposition, many voices—Kantian, deist, Protestant—joined in the moral debate. They all repudiated Catholic doctrine as an affront to the moral sovereignty of the individual, but that repudiation did not deter them from grounding individual conscience in a higher realm, whether metaphysical or religious in nature.

Masonic scientism was motivated by a similar blend of anticlericalism and transcendental aspiration. The doctrine of polygenesis challenged the biblical account of a single creation, maintaining that the human species had originated in several places. The church, of course, abominated the doctrine, but not Freemasonry. Indeed, the principal proponent of polygenesis, the Rouennais Protestant Félix Pouchet, was himself a Mason and a frequent speaker at lodge events.[23] The zeal of Masons to refute Catholic teachings at times led them to embrace theories that by present standards hardly merit the label of science at all. In an effort to uncover the material bases of intelligence and morality, Paul Broca, called the founder of modern physical anthropology, devised "scientific" methods of brain and skull measurement. Riche-Gardon's *Journal des initiés* heralded craniometry as a great scientific discovery, a step up from phrenology.

In 1870 Guépin, himself a youthful adept of phrenology and a lifelong believer in magnetist philosophy, drew up a list of Masonry's scientific heroes, which concluded with the names of Gall, Broussais, and Bernard.[24]

Masons took up the cause of science (and pseudo-science) as a weapon against Christian theology, but they also embraced it as, in Guépin's words, "a means of universal conciliation." Science taught that man was a natural being, a member of the animal kingdom, if a privileged one. Beasts were of a lower order but brothers nonetheless, "incomplete men" entitled to humane treatment. Science also taught lessons of brotherhood among men. Mankind, though diverse in origin, participated in a single moral universe. Masons were, in fact, warm partisans of black emancipation. Abraham Lincoln, himself a brother, was lionized as *une grande figure de l'humanité* who, "following the example of the Convention in France and of Wilberforce in England," had abolished the scourge of slavery. In the late sixties, in fact, relations between the Grand Orient and its counterpart in the United States were broken off precisely because of the refusal of American lodges to admit black men.[25]

The scientism professed by the masonic dissidents was redemptive in purpose, and the same may be said of its pedagogical philosophy. The commitment of Freemasons to rationalist education is well known. The 1860s witnessed a renewal of efforts in favor of secular and universal primary education, a campaign spearheaded by Jean Macé's Ligue de l'Enseignement, founded in 1866. The lodges lent early if not massive support to the Ligue. But there are some qualifications that need to be made here.

Catholic polemicists anathematized the Ligue de l'Enseignement as a masonic invention, but the Ligue at its beginning owed as much to utopians as to Masons and, indeed, the two strands are not always easy to disentangle. Macé was, of course, a Mason and former democratic socialist. But his first recruits came from the utopian camp—Guéroult, the Lyonnais textile broker François Arlès-Dufour, one of Enfantin's most loyal associates, and the "philanthropic utopian" Auguste Verdure. The Paris circle of the Ligue attracted a medley of personalities: Clamageran, Massol, Richer, all Masons, and Camille Flammarion, a science-fiction writer and aficionado of the occult.[26] When Masons enlisted in the campaign for universal education, they aligned themselves with men of utopian and, in some instances, mystical vision.

And Masons took the pledge of universal education with genuine seriousness. L'Ecole Mutuelle opened a night school in 1869. Staffed by lodge members, located in a *quartier populaire,* the Ecole Professionnelle de la Coopération undertook to educate workers in the principles of association and "social economy." This was not the first masonic venture into professional education. In 1862 Elisa Lemonnier and Mme. Adolphe Bertillon opened a day school, the Société Libre pour l'Enseignement Professionnel des Jeunes Filles, to teach practical skills to young women in the job market. The husbands of both Lemonnier and Bertillon were active Masons, which helps to explain *Le Monde maçonnique*'s claim that masonic ideas presided at the school's birth. The school, moreover, subscribed to a set of values—"tolerance, respect for oneself and for others, devotion, sincerity, fraternity, and above all hatred of *oisiveté*"—bound to hearten militants, so numerous in the dissident lodges, who harbored memories of a visionary past.[27]

Indeed, when it came to the teaching of such values, no institution was more suited or committed than Masonry itself. Dissidents conceived of their order as an *école mutuelle,* a school of democracy that inculcated principles of fellowship and solidarity. The society of lodges was Solomon's temple reconstructed, a beacon of light that, as it burned brighter, drove back the darkness and illuminated the path toward a new order of universal brotherhood.[28] Education, as Masons conceived it, was at once practical, moral, and regenerative.

The redemptive project of midcentury Masonry presupposed a vast settling of differences: between hostile nations, between men and women, between workers and bourgeois. But the prospect did not daunt the Masons, who were ready to work hard in the service of universal conciliation, and it is perhaps in such labors that Masonry's utopian inheritance was most evident.

The masonic commitment to human brotherhood entailed first and foremost an opposition to war, whether international or civil. From 1867 on, Switzerland was host to a series of international peace conferences. The conferences gave birth to a permanent body, the Ligue de la Paix et de la Liberté, and to a regular publication, *Les Etats-Unis d'Europe,* edited by Charles Lemonnier. In 1870, the Grand Orient expressed sorrow at the outbreak of hostilities between France and Prussia and pledged itself to succor the families of wounded or dead Masons "regardless of country of origin," not an easy gesture to make in the midst of national mobilization for war. During the

Commune, the lodges attempted to interpose themselves between the warring parties. A meeting was convened in April 1871 at Grand Orient headquarters, and the assembled brothers called on Versaillais and Communards, in the name of humanity, to abandon fratricidal struggle. After the Commune fell, Masons, led by Massol and Brisson, were among the first to raise funds for the victims of Versaillais repression.[29]

To Massol or Lemonnier, war was the consequence of militarism and authoritarian government. Standing armies and dictators went hand in hand, the two working in harness to impose despotism on the domestic front and to wage war abroad. To break the cycle, it was necessary to start at home, to abolish professional armies and replace them with citizens' militias, to dismantle imperial regimes and replace them with republican institutions. There would be no more war: differences, yes, but of the sort resolvable in a court of international arbitration. In place of a Europe of feuding dynasts there would emerge a United States of Europe, a federation of peoples, each living in concord with its neighbors.[30] Under the old Saint-Simonian dispensation, prospects for an internationalist future had hinged on the advance of industry. Utopian goals were not abandoned in the more sober-minded 1860s and 1870s, but now hopes were pinned not so much on economic progress as on the triumph of the republic.

In a similar manner, reworked utopian motifs can be detected in masonic debates on the role of women. Abandoned was the quest for the female messiah; the aspiration toward a reconciliation of genders was preserved, however, now to be worked out not in cosmic union but in the quotidian arrangements of married life. Masonic involvement in the feminist movement of the 1860s was extensive. Maria Deraismes, guiding spirit of the new feminism, made her speaking debut at the Grand Orient in 1866, an engagement arranged through the good offices of Richer. Richer himself launched a feminist weekly in 1869, *Le Droit des femmes,* and a year later founded a fundraising and propaganda organization, the Ligue Française pour le Droit des Femmes (LFDF). In 1866 feminist sympathizers formed a committee to promote marriage-law reform. Among the fifteen or so known participants, a half-dozen Masons can be counted: Brisson, Clamageran, Adolphe Clavel, Charles Floquet, Lemonnier, and Morin.[31]

But feminism was no more than a minor current in the lodges. When in 1868 the Le Travail lodge undertook to initiate a female candidate, the Council of the Order prohibited the move.[32] Maria

FREEMASONRY

Deraismes and Clémence Royer (the first translator of Darwin into French) had to join independent lodges unaffiliated to the Grand Orient. And not only the limits but also the peculiar thrust of masonic feminism should be kept in mind.

Masonic feminists were partisans of women's education. But they were inclined to conceive of school more as a training ground for a happy and virtuous domesticity than as a preparation for working life. A literate and knowledgeable spouse made for an understanding companion and a good mother. Rousselle urged fellow Masons to raise their daughters not to become beauteous courtesans, latter-day Phrynés, but modern Cornelias who, like the Roman matron of legend, would train their sons in the service of the republic. Education, in that it inoculated women against the poisons of obscurantism and coquetry, readied girls for a republican motherhood that would bear fruit in future generations of republican boys.[33]

A related mixture of concerns underlay masonic advocacy of marriage-law reform. Marriage, it was argued, should not be a relationship of subordination, lord ruling over serf, but an association of moral equals united by mutual respect and loving intimacy. Husbands and wives were by nature suited to different tasks, men for gainful employment, women for housework, but such a division of labor did not rule out cooperation in familial and social goals. Indeed, a marriage wanting in the spirit of cooperation had lost its raison d'être, and in such circumstances divorce was indicated. A home in which mutuality and affection prevailed uplifted and brought joy to its inhabitants: husbands, wives, and children. The existing civil code enshrined patriarchy, and the patriarchal family in turn bred authoritarian, monarchical attitudes. But rework the code, transform the home into a moral environment, and children would learn a new set of lessons: lessons of reciprocity and solidarity that would prepare them for republican citizenship.[34]

The reconciliation of genders envisioned by masonic feminists would lead to the emancipation of wives, the moralization of domestic life, and the fashioning of a republican home. The case for gender conciliation was made in a rhetoric punctuated with the catchwords of a lingering utopianism: association, mutuality, cooperation. And just as association held out the promise of more harmonious relations between the sexes, it also held out the promise of class reconciliation.

The masonic dissidents looked on a reawakening labor movement as kindred in spirit. The order also proclaimed the dignity of work. The tools of the mason's trade, the compass and right angle, were after all the very symbols of Masonry. If Masons warmed to working-class associationism, it was in part because they conceived of their order as itself an association, a temple of cooperation and mutuality. And if labor cherished visions of humanitarian internationalism, so too did Masonry. Masons wanted to make their order an examplar of brotherhood, the microcosm of a future social regime "where there will be no more war, no more castes . . . where the human race will proclaim its original unity."[35] Work, mutuality, brotherhood, such were Masonry's guiding principles, and such, it was believed, were labor's.

Masons acted to affirm a presumed commonality of principle through the patronage of working-class institutions. They applauded the formation of the First Internationale as "an application of the fundamental principles of Masonry." Fauvety was among the original shareholders in L'Association, a periodical first published in 1864 that styled itself the official organ of a renascent cooperative movement. In the same year, Lemonnier organized a credit union specializing in financial services for "workers and petty traders."[36]

French Masonry, over the course of its campaigns for institutional autonomy, carved out a distinctive position within the international masonic community. The Grand Orient's democratic and secularist policies, the seriousness of its commitment to the brotherhood of all men whether white or black, set it apart from masonic movements in much of northern Europe and the United States. But of far greater import were the domestic consequences of French Masonry's institutional battles.

The Grand Orient emerged from the struggles of midcentury as a bulwark of republicanism both in membership and in structure. Masonry's legacy to the republic was also double. It bequeathed a body of militants who went on to public service as deputies and, in Brisson's and Floquet's cases, prime ministers. The lodges, moreover, preserved and passed on a distinctive ideological heritage. They provided sanctuary to survivors of a more utopian era, and the Saint-Simonians, Fourierists, and seekers so numerous in their ranks left a lasting mark. The pacifist, feminist, and associationist impulses of the 1830s and 1840s were sustained and renewed in practical experiment.

These principles and preoccupations were relayed to the next generations. Richer and Deraismes militated in the feminist cause into the 1890s. Leadership of the LFDF then passed to younger militants: Maria Pognon, Marie Bonnevial, and Marguerite Durand.

Durand went on to found *La Fronde*, the semiofficial organ of republican feminism at the turn of the century. The paper also counted more than one oldtimer on its staff, most notably Richer and Deraismes' former companion-in-arms, Clémence Royer.[37]

Masonic associationism and pacifism lived on as well, finding an echo in the Solidarist movement of the 1890s, which preached class conciliation through social reform and world peace through international arbitration. Léon Bourgeois, Solidarism's founding father, was himself—it will come as no surprise—a masonic notable. Nor will it come as a surprise that Masons played a decisive role in the formation of the Radical Party, the Solidarist movement's main political patron. The party's founding congress convened in 1901. The impetus behind the event came in large part from the Grand Orient, then presided over by Desmons, and some 155 lodges declared immediate support for the new party.[38]

And what became of the commitment to the moral agency of the rational individual? In 1898, in the midst of the Dreyfus affair, members of the Ligue des Droits de l'Homme issued an appeal on behalf of Colonel Picquart, a pro-Dreyfus officer who had suffered persecution from his superiors. Among the signatories were Arthur Ranc and Clamageran, both members in the 1860s of Massol's La Renaissance par les Emules d'Hiram.[39] In fact, well over a third of the Ligue's first steering committee, including its president Ludovic Trarieux, were Masons, and the two movements remained intimately connected well through World War I.[40]

The Third Republic owed a great deal to the masonic movement. Its debt to the liberal positivists of the 1860s and 1870s has long been acknowledged, but less so its debt to masonic radicals. Men like Richer, Brisson, and Massol kept alive a visionary humanitarianism, tempering utopian impulse to serve republican ends. Such efforts at adaptation fed into movements and organizations—republican feminism, Solidarism, the Ligue des Droits de l'Homme—which, each in its own way, preserved a kernel of radical aspiration. From this angle, midcentury Masonry's achievement lay not in its fashioning of a deradicalized, positivist republicanism but, on the contrary, in its preservation and renewal of republicanism's radical legacy.

[2]

The Latin Quarter

THE UNIVERSITY, like the Grand Orient, was the target of republican insurgency in the decades of midcentury. But here republican agitation met with far stiffer official resistance. State and academic authorities expelled troublesome students, harassed dissident faculty, and closed down the schools with grinding regularity. The stakes were much higher than in the lodges: at issue was the control of a vast state enterprise that oversaw the operation of all institutions of public education. Authorities were not likely to cede so much terrain without a fight.

Yet the university, although connected to the state and under unceasing pressure to conform to official policy, retained a measure of institutional independence, which made it a difficult prize to keep, first for the Second Empire and in later years for the regime of Moral Order. Republican *universitaires* turned to advantage the margin of maneuver that such relative autonomy opened, organizing a student press, petition campaigns, and strikes. They came to such efforts equipped with superior organizational skills and with a bristling intellectual arsenal as well, with freethinking and scientific creeds corrosive of established belief. The progress of science, republicans claimed, had made possible the banishment of religious orthodoxy from the realm of human understanding. It was not just the natural world that might now be understood anew but the entire history of mankind, the physical and moral development of the species. Under such assault, organizational and intellectual, authorities gave ground.

Come the 1880s, and the Latin Quarter, home to so many of France's institutions of higher education, had become republican territory outright, a bastion of "republican legitimism."[1]

The conquest of *le pays latin* bequeathed the republic a rich but ambiguous intellectual legacy. It passed on first and foremost a cult of science, and the republic elevated that cult into a secular religion, reverencing scientists as men of progress, raising statues to them and extolling their virtues to the young. But mid-nineteenth-century science was a Janus-faced construction. It turned away religious and metaphysical obstacles to human autonomy, but at the same time sanctioned new hierarchies, imputing to European man a natural superiority over lesser breeds. The culture of the republic generated some strange intellectual hybrids—a scientific racism, a scientific misogyny—that flew in the face of the regime's more fundamental democratic strivings.

But the cult of science, however ambivalent a gift, was by no means the university's sole legacy to the republic. The new regime inherited from the academic struggles of midcentury a remarkable cadre of battle-hardened *universitaires:* scientists and teachers who were republican not only in the politics they espoused but in the kind of university they envisioned. When the republic emerged at last triumphant, it rewarded its partisans in the schools with institutional authority, and they used that authority to good advantage, democratizing the academy, hiring new personnel, and installing new disciplines. The university was remade into one of the regime's most reliable institutional supports, and so it became for that very reason a chief target of antirepublicans, who learned to revile the so-called new Sorbonne with the same fury they had earlier concentrated on Freemasonry.

The Awakening of the Quarter

The empire born of the 1851 coup debated a total dismantling of the university system. From Napoleon III's point of view, the institution presented a double inconvenience. It was first a *corporation indépendante,* a self-governing body.[2] The senior official of the university, the Grand Master, was a state appointee, but he undertook major decisions in conjunction with the Conseil de l'Instruction Publique, which was in the majority an elective body. Worse still, the reigning philosophy at the university was Victor Cousin's eclecticism, a doctrine which, for its reasoned liberalism, was antipathetic to a regime that in its early years chose to align itself with the party of Rome.

Cousin, first as director of the Ecole Normale (1835–1840) and then as Louis-Philippe's minister of public instruction (1840), had plotted with consummate skill to institutionalize the philosophical principles he espoused. Cousin asserted the primacy of metaphysical values. The good, the true, and the beautiful were conceived as timeless verities akin to Platonic forms. They might be apprehended by reason or, better, by a happy few who, after long years of training, had learned the proper use of the rational faculty. The political implications of such a doctrine were heartening to the liberal but by no means democratic notables who governed the July Monarchy. France was best ruled by an enlightened elite armed with the knowledge that its conventional wisdom was in fact eternal truth.

The university, in both its independence and philosophical orientation, posed a threat to Bonaparte. But he was persuaded by his first minister of public instruction, Hippolyte Fortoul, not to dissolve the institution, only to undermine its autonomy. Fortoul packed the Conseil de l'Instruction Publique with members of his choosing. He transferred responsibility for decisions on curriculum and promotions upward from the council to the ministry of public instruction. And he did everything in his power to root out rebellion and impose correct thinking. Morning and evening prayer was made obligatory in state-run high schools. The emphasis of lycée education was shifted from philosophy—the questions dealt with by philosophy, Fortoul claimed, "trouble the spirit"—to scientific subjects or to logic.[3] As for personnel, the most vexatious professors were fired. Others were driven to resign by the imposition of a loyalty oath.

But imperial academic policy could not remain frozen in this disciplinarian mold. The liberalization of the empire in the 1860s was accompanied by a liberalization of the university system. Victor Duruy's appointment in 1863 as minister of public instruction marked a turning point. Though not himself a so-called eclectic, Duruy reinstated Cousinist eclecticism as the university's official philosophy.[4] He did not, for all that, relax the state's grip on academic decision making.

Such an institutional setting inevitably bred opposition, but in an authoritarian environment how was opposition to be expressed? The turbulent reception accorded Victor Duruy's thesis (defended in 1855) provides the beginning of an answer. The thesis critically discussed the career of the Roman emperor Tiberius. Désiré Nisard, one of Duruy's examiners and considered to be "on over-good terms with the minister M. Fortoul," felt that the integrity of the present empire was at stake.[5] It was not fitting, Nisard claimed, for heads of state like Tiberius to be judged by the rules of common morality. The intimation that there might be two standards of moral conduct, one for the powerful and a second for the weak, raised an outcry in academic circles. When Nisard next attempted to teach a class, he was met with catcalls and whistles and was unable to continue.[6] It was not only students who stood against Nisard. A band of former professors—Jules Barni, Frédéric Morin, Etienne Vacherot—had founded a philosophical and literary review called L'Avenir. Barni, in the heat of the Nisard crisis, published an essay in its pages arguing the existence of a single morality based on Kant's categorical imperative. Given the political climate, professions of Kantianism carried an oppositional charge intolerable to the imperial censor, who ordered L'Avenir to be shut down.[7]

The Nisard incident set the pattern for subsequent Latin Quarter militancy. Dissidents assailed the imperial order obliquely through critiques of religion or philosophy. The regime responded with repression, which in turn provoked a new round of student and faculty attack. Opposition was not expressed in overt political criticism but by indirection, in an apolitical coded language.

To pick up the accents of that language, there is no better listening post than the burgeoning student press of the 1860s. The first Latin Quarter papers, La Jeune France (1861) and Le Travail (1861–62), made a simple claim: they spoke for "la jeunesse des écoles."[8] The students of today, they said, were neither pleasure seekers nor careerists but retained all the militancy of former years. Le Travail made its point by organizing a demonstration at the Bastille in February 1862 to commemorate the revolution of 1848. The incident resulted in the arrest and imprisonment of one of the paper's editors, a medical student named Georges Clemenceau.[9]

A spate of successor papers—Auguste Vermorel's and Gustave Isambert's Le Mouvement (1861–62), Charles Longuet's Les Ecoles de France (1864), and the longer-lived La Rive gauche (1864–1866), also edited by Longuet—spelled out in more detail the creed by which the new generation meant to live. A Latin Quarter veteran characterized the militants of the 1860s as "intrepid and sincere irregulars."[10] Sincerity was indeed a favored self-referent of the late empire's student radicals, and manliness too.[11] Youth, Longuet wrote, nursed "a virile hatred of servitude in all its forms"; it awaited the day when it would accede to political responsibility and don "the manly toga."[12] What sincerity and manliness amounted to in practice was demonstrated in 1862. In February, Ernest Renan delivered his inaugural lecture at the Collège de France, best remembered for its rationalist critique of the divinity of Christ. Catholic militants had come to shout Renan down, but they were met with a salvo of countercries—"Vive Michelet!" "Vive Quinet!"—from radical students, among them Isambert. The police were called in to restore order, and Duruy brought the incident to a swift close by suspending Renan.[13]

A new round of disturbances rocked the Latin Quarter in the mid-sixties. This time the catchphrase was "science." The young equated science with free thought, the positive method, and, in the most extreme instances, materialism; they contrasted the term not just with religious belief, as might be expected, but with "metaphysics," a short-hand for eclecticism.[14] Science then was the bluntest of instruments, a weapon with which to lay into academic authority, whether Catholic or Cousinist in orientation, and it proved effective. An international student congress gathered at Liège in October 1865. The French delegation consisted of experienced activists like Longuet as well as a raft of student newcomers: Paul Dubois, Victor Jaclard, Paul Lafargue, Aristide Rey. The French turned the event into a celebration of atheism and, at the conference's end, organized a private meeting with Brussels' social democrats. Those present pledged themselves to "the triumph of labor over capital," and none doubted ultimate success since, as Lafargue proclaimed, science was on their side.[15]

Events in Brussels did not go unnoticed in Paris. Two law students and five medical students were brought up on charges before the Conseil Académique in December. The council handed out a two-year suspension to one of the offenders and banished the rest from the Paris faculties altogether.[16] The Latin Quarter erupted. Students forced the dean of the medical school, Ambroise Tardieu, into virtual hiding. By the end of the month, with the Latin Quarter in a state of siege, it had become impossible to conduct classes.[17] The coming of winter recess and Tardieu's eventual resignation helped to quell student anger.[18]

Le Mouvement and *Les Ecoles de France* did not last long. The more durable *La Rive gauche* was driven into exile in 1865 in the midst of the Liège congress uproar. But such disruptions did not mark the climax of student journalism. One final batch of newspapers made an appearance: *La Libre Pensée* (1866–67) and its successor *La Pensée nouvelle* (1868–69). These journals also campaigned under the banner of free thought and science, but they deepened the notion. First, science was construed to embrace not just the physical and medical sciences but more broadly the study of man. *La Pensée nouvelle,* for example, boasted the collaboration of a remarkable band of up-and-coming social scientists: the demographer Adolphe Bertillon, Charles Letourneau, who was later to occupy France's first chair in sociology, and the anthropologist Gabriel de Mortillet.[19] The paper also made an effort to solicit the patronage of more established figures in the social sciences. *La Pensée nouvelle* organized a banquet in 1867 in honor of the German anthropologist Rudolf Virchow and invited Paul Broca, then at the faculty of medicine, to preside.[20] In extending the compass of science to include man and all his works, the newspapers saw themselves as completing the intellectual project begun by the Enlightenment. A. Coudereau, a pharmacology student and financier of *La Libre Pensée,* characterized the journal's collaborators as successors to the Encyclopedists.[21] Indeed, plans were laid in freethinking circles to launch a new encyclopedia, conceived, like its forebear, as "une oeuvre de combat." This time, though, the battle was joined not in the name of *les lumières* but of experimental science. The first volume of the so-called *Encyclopédie générale* appeared in 1869, with articles by Bertillon and Broca.[22]

The Latin Quarter newspapers of the 1860s give a fair indication of the slogans that stirred the young—sincerity, manliness, free thought, the experimental method, the *sciences humaines,* encyclopedism—and of how these slogans might be used against the regime. But the press constituted only one locus of student agitation. Trouble came from within the schools themselves and from two in particular, the Ecole Normale Supérieure and the Paris Ecole de Médécine. Here the issue was not just words and symbols but institutional autonomy, the right of students and faculty to resist intrusive appointments or unwanted interference in curricular matters.

Conditions at the Ecole Normale in the 1860s were repressive. The administration monitored when and for what reasons students, the *normaliens,* might leave the school grounds. Chapel attendance as well as fasting during Lent were mandatory. In charge of administering such a regimen were the school's director, since 1857, Désiré Nisard and Nisard's second-in-command, Louis Pasteur. Nisard was regarded as a creature of the imperial regime. As for Pasteur, he soon earned himself the reputation of a martinet who scolded students for lack of decorum at chapel and roamed study halls confiscating the works of such incendiary writers as Rabelais and Michelet.[23]

Students conducted a running battle against the Nisard-Pasteur regime, a battle they eventually won. The showdown came in 1867. The good citizens of Saint-Etienne had sent a petition to the Senate urging closure of a local *bibliothèque populaire* that stocked works by Voltaire, Rousseau, and Renan. The assembly debated the petition, and in the course of the debate, Senator Charles Sainte-Beuve made an unequivocal statement in favor of freedom of thought. A normalien named Lallier drafted a congratulatory letter to Sainte-Beuve, which 80 of the school's 101 undergraduates were persuaded to sign, including Emile Boutroux, Alfred Espinas, and Louis Liard, all future luminaries of republican academe. Two of the signatories, Henri Marion and Gaston Maspéro, passed the letter on to *L'Avenir national,* an opposition newspaper, where it was published. Nisard suspended Lallier and ejected both Marion and Maspéro. Students protested with a strike, and Duruy promptly suspended the entire student body.[24] In the long run, however, the affair led to a liberalization of the school. Duruy permitted most students to return to class without reprisal. Maspéro chose to quit and left for America, but Marion made sufficient amends to be allowed back in. Lallier, though not permitted to sit the agrégation for a period of years, was compensated with a teaching post in the provinces. On the administrative side, Nisard and Pasteur were sacked. Francisque Bouillier, a Cousinist philosopher, took Nisard's place as director.

The next time unrest flared at the school, the administration responded not with the stick as in 1867 but with conciliation.[25] Normaliens displayed a studied disrespect for religion, shambling into chapel wearing slippers, with copies of Voltaire tucked under arm. In 1870 the school's head boy, Georges Renard, drew up a petition calling for the abolition of compulsory mass and, with the backing of third-year student Alphonse Aulard, collected 83 signatures. The document was presented to Bouillier, who at first balked but then caved in when Renard threatened to go public. Thus, reminisced Renard in later years, "without commotion or hindrance, the separation of School and Church was consummated."[26]

Normaliens agitated in the name of free thought. At the Paris Ecole de Médecine, the rallying cry was science. The medical school, as we have seen, closed briefly in December 1865, but that was not the school's first or last brush with trouble. Tardieu's predecessor as dean of the medical faculty, Pierre Rayer (1862–1864), had also been driven from office. Rayer had two strikes against him from the students' point of view. He was the emperor's personal doctor and espoused the application of Cousinist principles to medical research. Students made their objections plain from the outset, greeting Dean Rayer's inaugural speech with "an infernal din." Such disruptions continued unabated until Rayer was forced to resign.[27]

Tardieu, who succeeded Rayer in 1864, hoped to get off to a better start. He proposed that medical students form a representative body, a "fraternal association." Tardieu's plan provided for an elected commission to draft the association's statutes. The more militant students, determined to escape administration tutelage, called a meeting to draw up an independent list of candidates. In the event, all but two members of the radical list were elected, and the commission chose as its president a well-known troublemaker, Clemenceau (fig. 1). Tardieu immediately dissolved the commission, and no more was heard of a fraternal association.[28]

Tardieu's departure in 1866 did much to pacify student militancy. The new dean Charles Wurtz, while no radical, was uncompromised by close ties to the imperial administration.[29] But still there was trouble, although this time not from the young but from *bien-pensant* outsiders who accused the faculty of purveying materialist atheism. The histologist Charles Robin was the first target of attack. In a lecture to students in 1866, it was said, he had made a profession of materialism. Although the charge was exaggerated—Robin, a positivist, never professed the kind of extreme materialism championed by the *Pensée nouvelle* circle—Duruy administered Robin a rebuke.[30] The appointment of Germain Sée, a specialist in therapeutics, to the faculty in 1867 occasioned another round of protest. Sée also had a reputation as a materialist, which prompted religious students to organize a ruckus at his inaugural lecture. A counterdemonstration, led by Jaclard, silenced the opposition. Sée was able to speak but was later reproached in the Senate for placing himself under the protection of troublemakers.[31]

1. Edouard Manet, *Portrait of Clemenceau,* 1879–80

Outside sniping against the Paris medical faculty erupted into a full-scale assault in 1868. The catalyst was P. J. Grenier's dissertation defense. Grenier's thesis denied the existence of free will, an argument with an anticlerical bite, for the notion of free will was central to Catholic doctrine of the fall. It did not help that the supervising professor, Alexandre Axenfeld, was a notorious freethinker.[32] Catholic critics of the medical faculty lobbied to have Grenier's thesis revoked and forwarded petitions to the Senate, charging the medical faculty as a whole with materialism. In the ensuing debate, Cardinal de Bonnechose spoke on behalf of the petitioners: "Go to the lectures of Mm. Vulpian,[33] Sée, Broca, Axenfeld, Robin, and others, and look at the jammed hall: 1500 young men eagerly listening . . . all determined adepts and defenders of science, i.e. materialism."[34] The Senate refused to censure the medical faculty, but Duruy, acknowledging the regime's duty to combat materialist doctrine, annulled Grenier's thesis.[35]

Only two years later the Paris medical school once again became the object of the regime's repressive attentions. In early 1870 a member of the imperial family, Pierre Bonaparte, shot to death the republican journalist Victor Noir. Expert testimony in Bonaparte's defense was delivered by the former dean and now professor of forensic medicine, Ambroise Tardieu. Tardieu's students began a campaign of disruption, interrupting lectures with shouts of "Vive Victor Noir!" The uproar was such that authorities decided to close down the whole faculty for a month.[36]

The medical school's battle against officialdom raged on into the mid-1870s, clericalism becoming ever more the main bone of contention. The empire was now gone, only to be replaced by the monarchist and clerical regime of Moral Order. In 1874, Minister of Public Instruction Arthur de Cumont, a devout Catholic, took steps to break up the phalanx of freethinkers at the medical school. He promoted professor of pathology Emile Chauffard to inspector-general of schools of medicine. Chauffard was a Catholic and in philosophy an opponent of materialism. It was further rumored that Cumont intended to replace an aging Dean Wurtz with a Chauffard confederate. The medical school rose in opposition. Students cheered Robin in class with the acclamation "Hats off before science!" while bawling anticlerical slogans at Chauffard. Amid the tumult, classes were suspended. When they resumed, Chauffard's lecture hall, if peaceful, was nearly empty. Wurtz was indeed retired, but it was the freethinking Alfred Vulpian, not a Catholic antimaterialist, who replaced him.[37]

The confrontations of midcentury made it plain where the battle lines were drawn in the Latin Quarter. On the one side stood the imperial state and the regime of Moral Order, seconded by Cousinist and clerical interests; on the other were sincere and manly youth, partisans of science and free thought who fought against constraints dictated from above. By the mid-1870s, the nexus of state and altar had all but lost the institutional battle. A separation of school and church had been effected at the Ecole Normale. Efforts to break down the freethinking bloc at the Ecole de Médecine had collapsed. On the intellectual front, too, the freethinking camp had seized the initiative, deploying a powerful battery of new disciplines and approaches to hammer away at entrenched orthodox scholarship.

The Human Sciences

Kantian philosophy in its French variant was conceived in critical opposition to Cousinist and Catholic orthodoxies. In the 1850s it had been a marginal phenomenon, professed by former *universitaires* like Barni or outsiders to the university like Charles Renouvier. But in 1864 one of Renouvier's disciples, Jules Lachelier, won a teaching post at the Ecole Normale where he initiated a new generation, Boutroux among them, into Kantian doctrine. Boutroux's appointment to the Ecole's faculty in 1877 sealed its conversion into a neo-Kantian bastion.[38]

Positivism had also begun as a minority faith, the creation of a visionary outsider, Auguste Comte. Under the empire, Comte's heirs had stripped away the creed's utopian trappings, leaving a hard, scientist kernel. The new positivist sought truth not in idle speculation but through the experimental method and a critical analysis of sources. In this form and championed by Charles Robin, positivism swept through the Paris medical faculty. It made inroads into the historical sciences as well, as the careers of Aulard and Maspéro attest. Aulard spent a lifetime editing and analyzing documents of the French revolution, exertions that earned him a chair at the Sorbonne in 1885. But as a compiler of texts and sifter of facts, Aulard was outdone by the Egyptologist Maspéro who, though he never finished the Ecole Normale, ended up at the Collège de France. In addition to writing more than a score of books, Maspéro published thousands of pyramid inscriptions and catalogued, in fifty volumes, the contents of the Cairo museum.

The materialist school, with a few exceptions, had less success in penetrating the inner sancta of academe. In 1876 Broca and Mortillet founded the Ecole d'Anthropologie. Broca was not a materialist, but the two men recruited a teaching staff—Abel Hovelacque, André Lefèvre, Letourneau—with a definite materialist bias. Broca belonged to the faculty of medicine; the school's professor of demography Adolphe Bertillon taught a course at the Sorbonne; but otherwise there were few formal links between the Ecole d'Anthropologie and the university. Yet for all its institutional marginality, Broca's school left a potent, if deeply equivocal, intellectual legacy.

The Ecole d'Anthropologie set itself a task of extraordinary ambition: the construction of a scientific history of man. The new history began with a refutation of the biblical account of human origins. God did not create humankind. The first cells, from which all later life sprang, were generated from inanimate matter, from a mineral soup cooking under intense pressure and heat.[39] The Bible sited the dawn of humanity in the garden of Eden; the Broca group were polygenists firmly persuaded that the human species had originated in multiple locales. The church, on the evidence of Scripture, claimed that humankind was not much over 6,000 years old. Broca and his colleagues cited the fossil record to demonstrate the profound antiquity of man.[40]

But if humanity was not a divine creation, what demarcated the human from other forms of life? Certain species-specific traits had evolved in the course of time, came the reply. Mortillet stressed toolmaking as the critical acquisition, Hovelacque stressed speech.[41] Man had ascended through the ages to a position of superiority among animals.

In similar fashion, certain races and civilizations of men had ascended through time to a position of superiority. Broca and his colleagues conceptualized human evolution as a series of interlocking narratives, each narrative corresponding to one of the new science's principal subdisciplines. Broca, France's leading practitioner of craniometry, situated men on the evolutionary scale according to the size and shape of the brain. The larger the brain, he argued, the more evolved and intelligent the subject. Broca, moreover, had amassed considerable evidence to demonstrate the localization of speech capacity in the forward left portion of the brain. Extrapolating from such findings, he concluded that a well-developed frontal lobe constituted proof of a superior, more advanced nature.[42] Mortillet picked up the evolutionary process at this juncture, tracking the upward progress of prehistoric European man through the tools he used, from stone implements to bronze to iron.[43] Language too was used as an indicator of progress. Hovelacque stressed the superiority of inflected as against monosyllabic or agglutinated tongues.[44] To Lefèvre, the key to European dominance in science lay in possession of an alphabet equipped with a full panoply of vowels.[45] Letourneau brought the narrative of human progress down to the present moment. He applied the evolutionary paradigm to social institutions, establishing the superiority of monogamous over polygamous marriage, of commercial over military civilization.[46] The story, begun by the physical anthropologist Broca, spun out by archaeologists and comparative linguists like Mortillet and Hovelacque, was at last brought up to date by the sociologist Letourneau.

The human sciences had more than a tale to tell, however. As conceived by the Broca school, anthropology and its ancillary disciplines fit into a project of immediate practical consequence: the application of science to the advancement of humanity's physical and moral hygiene. Bertillon compiled extensive statistics on birth and mortality rates and on the incidence of disease in Paris. His research demonstrated a clear correlation between good health and sanitary conditions in the surrounding environment. Cleanliness was a near obsession with midcentury freethinkers.[47] Progressive schoolteachers worried about the bathing habits of pupils, and doctors worried about diet and sanitation. Such concerns found expression in 1877 in formation of a policy-oriented hygienic association, the Société de Médecine Publique et d'Hygiène Professionnelle. Doctors, among them Bertillon and a half-dozen members of the Paris faculty of medicine, constituted the group's main clientele.[48]

On the moral front as well, the new science had policy implications. With important exceptions, the faculty at the Ecole d'Anthropologie were neo-Lamarckians. Circumstances, it was believed, shaped the intelligence, and one generation's gains in cerebral capacity might be passed on to future generations. It was necessary only to shape the environment with skill, and a man (or woman) might jump a rung on the evolutionary ladder. But was not environment shaping what good teaching was all about? On this account, pedagogy was elevated, in Letourneau's phrase, to the first of the sciences, for it did not only illumine the path of human progress but had the potential to deliver humankind an evolutionary push forward.[49] As Broca put it, "not only does education make a man superior . . . it even has the wonderful power of raising him above himself, of enlarging his brain, of perfecting its shape."[50]

The new science of man sanctioned a program of physical and moral hygiene administered by qualified experts. It made quite plain, moreover, the particular populations among which such experts were likely to be found, the success stories of evolutionary progress: whites, Europeans, males. Shed the neo-Lamarckian frame that most

Broca acolytes subscribed to, and it was the shortest of steps from there to scientific racism. There was indeed, as noted, a minority in the Broca camp prepared to take the step, persuaded that differences among races, genders, and civilizations were fixed and genetic. Broca himself, although a neo-Lamarckian by inclination, wondered if blacks were ever capable of perfectibility.[51] Such thinking fed directly into the pseudo-scientific misogyny of Gustave Le Bon or the biological racism of Jules Soury (who was in fact a graduate of the era's freethinking circles). The new science of man, whether in its optimistic neo-Lamarckian or hardened biogenetic mold, invites and merits accusations of racism, sexism, and imperialism.[52]

That is not, of course, how the Broca school understood what it was about. Mortillet and Letourneau thought of themselves as practitioners of a liberating science, as devotees of reason, progress, and the brotherhood of man. They styled themselves freethinkers—and not just in intellectual matters. Mortillet was a veteran democratic socialist who had spent much of the 1850s abroad as a refugee. In 1871 Letourneau, though not himself an insurrectionary, lent medical assistance to wounded communards and was driven into exile.[53] The new science of man was, at its origins, a science of the left.

Latin Quarter Politics

There was indeed a political dimension to the institutional and intellectual battles of the midcentury Latin Quarter. The struggle against imperial interventionism, against Cousinist and religious orthodoxies, was in the final analysis a struggle for the republic—but which one?

To the most militant, it was the revolutionary republic, the "universal Republic," that was at stake.[54] Would-be revolutionaries and socialists were numerous among the student journalists of the mid-1860s. Dubois and Jaclard were Blanquists. Staffers at *La Rive gauche* made repeated professions of a practical, Proudhonist socialism.[55] The Blanquist-Proudhonist current fed largely but not exclusively into the Commune. Driven underground in the Commune's aftermath, it resurfaced again in the 1880s. Some remained Blanquist die-hards, but a number, notably Karl Marx's sons-in-law Lafargue and Longuet, had moved on, converting the materialist scientism of medical schooldays into scientific socialism.

An electoral republicanism also had its place in the Latin Quarter of the 1860s. In 1869 Jules Ferry's electoral committee included not only Latin Quarter oldtimers like Michelet and Vacherot, but also the comparative youngster Gustave Isambert. Ferry had a following as well among Left Bank doctors: Axenfeld, Broca, and the Salpêtrière alienist and former 48er, Ulysse Trélat. The Ecole Normale was located in Paris' seventh electoral district. Normaliens in 1869 plumped by a wide margin for the republican opposition, but the preferred candidate was not the radical journalist Henri Rochefort but the moderate lawyer Jules Favre.[56]

And in 1871 the Latin Quarter sided less with the Commune than with the so-called Party of Conciliation, which attempted to negotiate a middle path between Versaillais reaction and communard revolution. On 24 March, less than a week after the uprising had begun, a meeting of faculty and students was convened at the Ecole de Médecine. The assembly, sanctioned by Dean Wurtz and chaired by Trélat, chided the insurrectionaries, said to have "struck a blow against universal suffrage," while at the same time repudiating "reaction in all its forms."[57] On 7 April citizens of the fifth, sixth, and seventh arrondissements issued a public letter calling on the National Assembly to affirm the sanctity of republican institutions. Such a gesture, the letter explained, was needed to reassure the people of Paris, who "right or wrong" suspected the assembly of monarchist designs. Only with such reassurance might the Commune agree to withdraw and the civil war be brought to an end. The letter bore sixteen signatures topped by the names of Charles Pajot, a professor at the faculty of medicine, and Louis Delasiauve, Trélat's colleague at the Salpêtrière.[58]

Latin Quarter conciliationism found its most consequential expression in the activities of the Ligue d'Union Républicaine des Droits de Paris. The Ligue was formed in the first week of April just as the Versaillais bombardment of Paris got under way. Ligueurs in the subsequent weeks shuttled between Paris and Versailles, attempting vainly to arbitrate a settlement. The group was perhaps less remarkable for its achievement than for its membership, a cross-section of lawyers, journalists, and, above all, Latin Quarter activists: Bertillon, Clemenceau, Coudereau, Dubois, Isambert, Lefèvre, Letourneau, Morin.[59]

In the decades that followed, the quarter backed away from revolutionism altogether. The favored creed of normaliens in the mid-eighties, it was said, was Gambettism. An 1876 police report characterized student opinion at the Paris medical school as moderate republican: "They are no longer the radicals of the late Empire."[60] In 1884, the Association Générale des Etudiants was formed, the first undergraduate body to survive beyond a few years. In the next decade and a half, upwards of 20,000 students passed through its ranks. And chosen as the association's first honorary president was Ernest Lavisse, never much of a republican himself, but a partisan of the new positivist history and an able academic politician well connected in official circles.[61] The militancy of the 1860s had settled into a firm if temperate republicanism, but not without leaving a radical trace. The midcentury Latin Quarter produced its fair share of republican politicians. Robin, a Ferry acolyte, won a Senate seat in 1876. Broca was elected to the Senate on the Gambettist ticket in 1880. For much of the 1880s, Paris' fifth arrondissment was represented in the Chamber by Désiré Bourneville, a Gambetta protégé, militant freethinker, and former student of the Salpêtrière psychiatrist Jean-Martin Charcot (himself a Gambettist).[62] But a knot of Latin Quarter veterans also graduated into radical republican politics: Dubois, Lefèvre, and Rey served on the Paris municipal council; Clemenceau and Hovelacque sat in the Chamber.

The republic had good reason to be grateful to its Latin Quarter constituency, and it acknowledged its debt in a variety of ways. The Paris municipal council paid for Aulard's chair at the Sorbonne. The council also subsidized the Ecole d'Anthropologie, which in 1878 became the recipient of state aid as well. Marion was awarded the first chair in the science of education at the Sorbonne (eventually succeeded in the position by Emile Durkheim). Ferry promoted Lachelier to inspector of public instruction in 1880 and Liard to director of higher education in 1884. Espinas was elevated to the deanship at Bordeaux three years later and, with Liard's help, engineered Durkheim's appointment to the faculty.[63] In addition to a renewal of faculty and administrative personnel, the regime undertook an overhaul of academic institutions. Ferry, in 1880, secured passage of legislation making the Conseil de l'Instruction Publique once more a largely elective body. Five years later, Liard shepherded a bill through parliament conceding the university a further measure of autonomy. In the new academe of Liard's design, the state retained its position as ultimate arbiter of university affairs but granted authority over appointments and curriculum to elected faculty councils.[64]

The republicanization of academic life, as far as it would go, was essentially complete by the mid-1880s. No moment made more manifest the symbiosis of regime and university than the Dreyfus affair, when so many academics rallied to the republic's defense. But the university came under increasing fire after the turn of the century. The right, as the work of Le Bon and Soury attests, had begun to remold republican science in the service of elitist and racist ends. Even the university's own progeny contested its philosophic under-pinnings. Durkheim, a true product of republican academe, threw over the positivist-materialist assumptions so dear to social scientists like Broca and Letourneau, positing the existence of a social reality beyond the individual, a *conscience collective* beyond the material.

But in the 1880s such critiques were still the stuff of future debate. For the moment, republicans could take satisfaction. They had wrested the university from entrenched Cousinism, transformed it into a bulwark of positivist science and Kantian philosophy, and in the process remade the institution into a pillar of the new regime. And so it was to remain into the interwar decades.

[3]

Commercial Politics

IN A SPEECH AT Grenoble in 1872, Léon Gambetta welcomed "the arrival and presence in political life of a new social stratum *(nouvelle couche sociale)."* A generation of new men had arisen to displace an aging elite of notables.[1] To Gambetta, as to many of his contemporaries, the confrontation of notables and new social strata involved more than a competition for place between ins and outs. It was a conflict underpinned by profound social and political differences. Gambetta spoke of the divide that at midcentury had separated "the liberal party from the republican party, the haute bourgeoisie from a more middling bourgeoisie."[2] The same analysis was elaborated by a conservative observer:

> There is not a cantonal capital where what is called *society* . . . has not had to compete against a stratum of fresh-minted bourgeois, lawyers, doctors, newly rich merchants, who expect in their turn to constitute *society* and to dominate local affairs. To sum up, almost everywhere the struggle of the Republic against conservatism is symbolized by the rivalry between the *Cercle de l'union,* in which nobility and old bourgeoisie are fused, and the *Cercle du commerce,* instinctively liberal and republican because here are concentrated all elements of the new bourgeoisie.[3]

The 1870s witnessed a growing social struggle, and its dividing line ran right down the middle of the bourgeoisie. The struggle was not merely over office but over political forms as well, a new "middling bourgeoisie" championing the republic against an haute bourgeoisie attached to dynastic tradition.

Such an interpretation of events, assimilated with remarkable speed into the republic's mythology about its own origins, raises a comparative issue. A groundswell of middle-class activism billowed over all of mid-nineteenth-century Europe, but in France it took a democratic course. How did this happen? How did social differences come to be constructed as political differences? I propose to cut into this problem by way of a study of commercial interest-group politics in the 1860s and 1870s, with a focus on a dissident institutional newcomer, the Union Nationale du Commerce et de l'Industrie (UNCI).

The choice of the UNCI is apt. At its foundation in 1858 it had a mere twenty members.[4] By 1872 membership had risen to 6,195 grouped in seventy constituent *chambres syndicales*. And that membership was middle class, consisting mostly of merchants and manufacturers in the Paris textile, garment, and luxury trades.[5] The UNCI may fairly be counted an organ of Gambetta's new social strata, an institutional product of the middle-class mobilization of the 1860s and 1870s. Not only that, but the UNCI was republican in political orientation, although not at the outset. It began as a nonpartisan organization designed to protect the integrity of Parisian manufactures against cheap foreign imitations.[6] But in the seventies the group shed its nonpartisanship, so much so that by decade's end it had become a bastion of Gambettism. In 1879 Gambetta's most loyal lieutenant, Eugène Spuller, put in an appearance at UNCI headquarters to speak on the virtues of association.[7] In March 1881 Gambetta himself was guest of honor at the union's gala first annual banquet. He arrived flanked by UNCI president Charles-Léon Hiélard and by one M. Nicole who, in the postprandial speechifying and to the delight of the 650 businessmen in attendance, sang the praises of that "great patriot Gambetta."[8] The politicization of Gambetta's famed *nouvelle couche* is well illustrated by tracking the UNCI's trajectory from nonpartisan pressure group to republican auxiliary.

The Paris Chamber of Commerce

The UNCI's institutional identity was fashioned in conflict. Three debates disturbed the moneymaking bustle of the midcentury business community in Paris. The first touched on the proper organization of the Chamber of Commerce, the second on the question of protectionism, the third on the rights of voluntary associations. On each issue the UNCI adopted a position that brought it into confrontation with the *notables-commerçants* who administered the Chamber of Commerce.

A peculiar process governed election to the Paris Chamber of Commerce in the 1860s. Not all businessmen were entitled to the vote, but only a small fraction of notables. Nor was it easy for the upwardly mobile merchant or manufacturer to gain access to this select group. He had first to sign up at the local mayor's office, submitting proofs of probity and good character. Arrondissement lists were then forwarded to the prefect, who in turn drew up a short list subject to the final approval of the minister of the interior.[9]

Most UNCI members were disenfranchised under the existing system, but the organization found a way to make its influence felt nonetheless. In 1867 the UNCI formed a committee to contest the Chamber of Commerce elections of that year. The committee drew up a slate of approved candidates and urged those UNCI members entitled to vote to back the slate. The Union Nationale, in a word, attempted to control the elections, and the results were not altogether disappointing. The move earned the UNCI the enmity of Chamber of Commerce incumbents. The then-sitting Chamber denounced the organization as "an assortment of envious and ambitious types."[10] On the question of commercial representation, the body issued a ringing endorsement of the existing system. The time had not yet come, it made plain, to expand the ranks of the *notabilité commerciale.*[11]

Chamber of Commerce resistance provoked the UNCI to broaden its attack. In March 1870 the organization sponsored a mass meeting at the Alcazar, which attracted the participation of an estimated twelve hundred businessmen. The assembly agreed on the abolition of the commercial notability and on the extension of the commercial franchise to all merchants or manufacturers who had paid the business tax *(patente)* for at least one year.[12] At that very moment, in fact, a bill to establish universal suffrage in matters of commercial representation was under debate in the legislature.

This combination of public and parliamentary agitation prompted a prudent Chamber of Commerce to revise its position. The Chamber adopted the principle of universal suffrage but within certain limits: only businessmen who had paid the business tax for five years could be admitted to the franchise; the voting population should include board members of corporate enterprises (a move designed to enfranchise insurance and railroad executives); and all voters should pay a special poll tax. In short, the Chamber accepted franchise reform but so structured as to assure a preponderant influence to "citizens of the elite with an interest in the defense of order."[13] And the Chamber of Commerce was successful in its effort to finesse the question of commercial democracy. In 1872 this franchise scheme, minus the poll tax, was imposed by prefectoral decree.

The question of commercial representation set the Union Nationale and Chamber of Commerce on a collision course. On the matter of tariff reform, however, differences were not so extreme. The Union Nationale was a passionate partisan of the open market. It applauded the Cobden-Chevalier treaty of 1860, which lowered trade barriers between Britain and France, and when the issue of treaty renewal came up for debate at the end of the 1860s, the union came out strongly in favor. Fifty-three member *chambres syndicales* pronounced on the question, 42 for renewal and 7 against with 4 abstentions. The UNCI's fight for free trade at the end of the Second Empire was led by Ernest Levallois, owner of a yard-goods and woolens business on the rue du Sentier. Levallois acted as spokesman for the Chambre Syndicale de la Nouveauté and the Chambre Syndicale de la Draperie, both export-oriented organizations. Indeed, dominant interests within the Union Nationale—the garment trade of Paris' second arrondissement and the luxury industries based in the third and tenth—were similarly export-oriented. Material advantage explains to no small degree the UNCI's free-trade partisanship.[14]

It also explains the ambivalence of the Chamber of Commerce. The range of trades represented in the Chamber was too diverse to permit the emergence of a unified stance on tariff revision. Wine wholesalers favored free trade; businessmen in metals and *tissus* favored protection. When the question of treaty renewal came up for formal discussion in the Chamber in 1869, the organization sidestepped the issue: "in Paris, unlike Rouen, Bordeaux, Mulhouse or Lyon, no single interest dominates. . . . It is impossible to sum up in a word prevailing opinion in Paris as to the impact [favorable or unfavorable] of the commercial treaty." The Chamber of Commerce did draw up a list of delegates authorized to testify on the tariff question, but they were empowered to speak not for the body as a whole, but only for the particular industries they represented.[15]

Finally, on the question of associational rights, the differences between the UNCI and Chamber of Commerce touched not only on the employer's right to organize but also, and above all, on the worker's. The Paris Chamber of Commerce was a quasi-official body. The state as a matter of course solicited its opinion in the formulation of economic policy; indeed, the Chamber was entitled to pronounce on all matters touching the organization of economic life. The group naturally was jealous of its prerogatives and its special relationship to the state.

The UNCI's legal status, by contrast, was tenuous at best. The Le Chapelier law of 1791 prohibited professional coalitions of any kind, whether trade unions or employer groups. The Union Nationale, as an organization of businessmen, by its very existence stood in violation of the law. It functioned of course, but it relied on the state's sufferance, which was by no means assured. In the wake of the UNCI's intervention in the 1867 Chamber of Commerce elections, the imperial police tore off a portion of the sign hanging at UNCI headquarters. The portion contained the words "chambres syndicales," and the gesture was a reminder to the Union Nationale of its legal vulnerability.[16] Little wonder that a liberalization of the law on associations figured so prominently on the UNCI program. Little wonder too that UNCI militants were so prickly about guarding the organization's independence from the state. In 1870 a UNCI official, Clémencet, was awarded the Légion d'Honneur. His colleagues were outraged. A founding member of the Union Nationale published a letter in the radical press:

> The government has for some time cast a covetous eye on our numerous, powerful and free organization. It has entered into our midst through a back door, through a flattery, through a decoration . . . In enriching ourselves with a ribbon, we lose our prestige and alienate our liberty.

Nine UNCI members formed a delegation to ask for Clémencet's resignation. Sixty-three signed a petition protesting the decoration.[17] If the Chamber of Commerce was protective of its state-conferred privileges, the UNCI was proud of its autonomy.

The UNCI's commitment to associational life translated into a hedged defense of labor's organizational rights. Strikes were legalized in 1864. A wave of work stoppages in the late sixties opened a debate in UNCI ranks on the wisdom of the 1864 legislation. An antistrike faction, led by J. Allain of the Chambre Syndicale des Cuirs et Peaux, regretted the law.[18] But other UNCI militants—Naud and Notelle of the Chambre Syndicale des Industries Diverses and Hippolyte Marestaing—were inclined to adopt a conciliatory, if paternalist, posture. The workers' movement was prone to violence, but it was young. With time and experience, labor would abandon confrontational tactics and turn to management in a spirit of cooperation.[19]

The conciliationist position gained the upper hand in the UNCI in the 1870s, thanks largely to the efforts of Joseph-Louis Havard.[20] Havard, a paper wholesaler, had involved himself in the cooperative movement in the late empire and then in the 1870s developed an interest in trade unionism. He and like-minded UNCI militants made the rounds of Paris' working-class *chambres syndicales,* urging cooperation between labor and business. Havard was a partisan of the *commission mixte,* a joint labor-management commission to settle wage disputes and strikes. Such commissions, most of them short-lived, were established in the paper, jewelry, lace, and glove industries.[21]

The UNCI, after debate, opted for conciliation, but the Chamber of Commerce assumed a consistently punitive stance. Workers had no notion of how to make good use of organization:

> Down to the present moment, in effect, they have not wanted nor have they known how to turn association to account; they have failed to create vital centers of activity. Exigent and despotic, they have disturbed the regular operation of labor, weakened industry and contributed to the decline of production standards.

Given the fecklessness of the working class, it had no right to organize. "[Strike] coalitions," one Chamber of Commerce member remonstrated, were "a misdemeanor and ought to be punished as such." A majority found such arguments persuasive. In 1872, by a tally of 8 to 5, the Chamber's steering committee voted to recommend abrogation of the 1864 strike law.[22]

Across a range of issues, then, the UNCI and the Chamber of Commerce were at odds. The institutional conflict between the two bodies brought into focus the underlying social tensions between *nouvelles couches* and notables. The question remains, however: how did such differences feed into republican politics?

Material Interest and Republican Principle

At first glance, it is interest alone that appears to divide the UNCI and the Chamber of Commerce. The Union Nationale gathered to itself the men who were excluded from established commercial institutions and wanted to gain access. Membership was concentrated in free-trade industries, and accordingly the organization embraced laissez-faire. As for the UNCI's opposition to the Le Chapelier law, the Union Nationale was itself a voluntary body with a vested interest in promoting the right of free association. No doubt self-interest was critical in shaping the UNCI's agenda, but it must also be recognized that interest and moral conviction are not always easy to distinguish. Questions of material advantage can spill over into matters of principle, and so it was with the UNCI.

Take the case of Chamber of Commerce organization. The UNCI-sponsored public assembly of 1870 voted an extension of the commercial franchise. Havard elaborated a defense of the decision, but he did not speak the language of interest. Instead he drew an analogy between commercial and political democracy. He was himself, after all, a republican who had refused to swear an oath of loyalty to the empire. In the political sphere, Havard argued, the *régime censitaire* had given way to universal suffrage; in the commercial world as well, privilege ought to cede to democracy and free competition.[23] Havard's argument struck a resonant chord. The Union Nationale looked on itself not just as a pressure group, but as the vanguard of Paris' vast "commercial democracy."[24] The UNCI's democratic pretensions were underscored by the presence of two republican deputies at the March 1870 rally: Alexandre Glais-Bizoin and Adolphe Crémieux.[25] A dispute over admission to the commercial franchise was thus translated into a confrontation between imperial privilege and republican democracy.

The issue of tariff reform lent itself to similar transmutations. Free trade was sound economic policy, but it was also sound international politics. Commerce created bonds between nations, bonds of interest, of course, but other kinds of bonds as well. The free play of the market permitted the exchange of ideas along with commodities. Such material and moral interpenetration generated sentiments of reciprocity. Aggressive impulses were tempered. Indeed, in a world governed by free trade, what cause would there be for war? A UNCI militant addressed the question to the arch-protectionist Thiers: "And war, will it not be abolished or at least contained by liberty of exchange?"[26] In place of a Europe divided into armed camps would emerge a fraternal Europe, a "grand family" of free peoples.[27] Free trade was an antidote to militarism and an agent of international concord.

Even more fundamentally, it was a sine qua non of democracy. Economic and political liberty were inseparable; they went hand in hand: "commercial liberty, under modern circumstances, being of necessity the source and guarantee of all others."[28] It was thus no coincidence that the enemies of free trade and of political democracy turned out to be one and the same. The great protectionist inter-ests—mining, metals, northern and Norman textiles—were repre-sented in the Corps Législatif by the likes of Thiers, Henri Schneider, Jules Brame, and Augustin Pouyer-Quertier, all magnates of indus-try and finance with close ties to the nation's Orleanist and Bonapar-tist establishments.[29] Supporting free trade was to strike a blow for democracy against bourgeois oligarchs and dynastic elites.

What about supporting the right of association? The "syndical idea," as Hiélard called it, had two principal virtues. Association was the bedrock of liberty. Unlike the corporations of yesteryear, *chambres syndicales* were voluntary; they exercised no exclusive powers, and monopoly was the very antithesis of freedom and individuality. The association introduced an element of order and decorum into business life but not at the expense of liberty.[30] On the contrary, where the right to associate was guaranteed, there political liberty was most secure. Gambetta made the point in his 1881 speech to the UNCI. In February 1848 he explained:

> one saw reborn, alas, for but a moment, freedom of association, and in an instant, with an almost spontaneous energy . . . association surged forward . . . had not those who at the time controlled the destinies of *la patrie* allowed a cunning reaction to take them by surprise, association might have spread across France, and not only would it have assured the national prosperity, it would have, in founding a truly republican liberty, protected the nation against the return of bloody despotisms.[31]

In a nation so bonded by a rich associational life, Bonapartism, indeed despotisms of any color, could make no headway. The UNCI audience greeted Gambetta's remarks with a roar of applause and acclamation.

Association was not only a bulwark of liberty, but—and this was its second virtue—it was also a vehicle of moral improvement. It was above all the "moralization" of the working classes that UNCI businessmen had in mind.[32] In its present state, labor was not "mature."[33] But it was hoped that the experience of responsible trade unionism would teach workers useful lessons of discipline and self-control. Participation in cooperatives, in arbitration commissions, in profit-sharing schemes, was bound to elevate the working man's intelligence and character. So argued Hiélard, and in the same article he also spoke up for free and obligatory education.[34] Association, like the school, was conceived as a pedagogical instrument, a device for the instruction of working men and women in the habits of good citizenship.

The interests the UNCI represented, the conflicts in which it was embroiled, the complex of forces arrayed against it, predisposed militants to express themselves in a special idiom. From the Union Nationale's campaigns for commercial reform there emerged a set of principled commitments: to democracy, to a Europe of nations, to liberty, and, more remotely, to free and compulsory education. The process by which the UNCI transmuted interest into conviction entailed more than an elaboration of positive commitments; villains were also identified—privilege, militarism, monopoly. The distinctive mix of positive and negative commitments that structured UNCI rhetoric is not hard to identify. The peculiar idiom business militants spoke was a variant of republican discourse.

So how can the UNCI's conversion to republicanism be explained? The union contained a minority of committed republicans within its ranks from the outset. France's repeated bouts of revolution had kept republican discourse vital and current, and the republican cause had its acolytes in the ranks of organized business. But I would argue that the particular milieu in which the UNCI was rooted had a definite susceptibility to the republican message. Business militants, at odds with established authority, turned to republicanism not only because it was the principal language of opposition available, but also because republican rhetoric made sense of UNCI experience and lent conviction to business demands. Republican militants made an appeal to the Union Nationale, but the union, for its own reasons, was prepared to listen.

Politics and the UNCI

It is easy enough to suggest that the Union Nationale was republican in orientation, but what brand of republicanism did it espouse? Over the course of the seventies, the group oscillated between radical and Thiersist poles before coming to rest at decade's end in the Gambettist camp.

It was during the turbulent months of April–May 1871, during the Commune, that the UNCI's radical wing was most active. More conservative members, Allain for example, had abandoned Paris, leaving the organization in the hands of radicals like Levallois and Marestaing. On 4 April, two days after Thiers' first bombardment of Paris, Levallois and others called an open meeting at UNCI headquarters to discuss their response to the civil war. The assembly drafted an address unmistakably biased in the Commune's favor. "Paris," the address began:

> has made a revolution as worthy of acceptance as any of the others. And, for many, it is the greatest revolution she has ever undertaken, for it represents an affirmation of the Republic and of the will to defend it . . .
>
> Why not give a serious try to these new institutions sanctioned by the votes of our fellow citizens? [The reference here is to the elections of 28 March which had led to the creation of the Commune.]
>
> Whatever happens, France will never have to pay what the old order of things has just cost us.[35]

As for the "monarchical assembly" sitting at Versailles, it was called upon to write a new law vouchsafing municipal liberties, to arrange for the election of a *constituante* and to disperse forthwith. To press home the demands contained in the April address, the UNCI appointed a commission of conciliation. The committee included Levallois and Marestaing, who were joined by UNCI counsel Joseph Camps (the owner of a dye business), Charles Loiseau-Pinson, and two businessmen from the third arrondissement: Adolphe Lhuillier, a lace dealer, and the so-called radical hosier, Charles Rault.

The committee undertook to mediate a peaceful resolution to the civil war. It enlisted the support of sympathetic workers' *chambres syndicales;* it met twice with the Commune; it was granted two interviews with Thiers and had scheduled a third in late May when

Versaillais troops breached Paris' fortifications, mooting the possibility of a negotiated settlement. Nothing came of the UNCI's effort at conciliation, but the effort itself attests to the presence of a radical faction within Union Nationale ranks, a faction prepared to make the claim that its program "apart from questions of nuance and degree . . . was the same as that of the Commune."[36]

The destruction of the Commune signaled an abrupt return to order in UNCI politics. Allain and like-minded hardliners returned, reviling the Commune as "that execrable insurrection." They faulted the commission of conciliation's conduct and opened a counteroffensive against the radical wing.[37] The attack on the conciliators stalled at first. The UNCI as a body refused to repudiate the commission's peace initiatives. The commission drafted a report in June 1871 on its April-May activities. An UNCI assembly debated whether to publish the report. Hardliners adamantly opposed publication but were outvoted.[38] They lost on this issue, but did in subsequent weeks succeed in persuading the Union Nationale to adopt a pro-Thiers line in the legislative byelections of July 1871.

It was a stunning victory for moderate businessmen, all the more so since the UNCI had at first appeared inclined to follow a radical lead. On 16 June, the UNCI election commission voted out a three-plank platform. Keeping the republic figured at the top of the list, but it was followed by two more radical demands: reorganization of the army, "service for all," and free and compulsory education.[39] In a week's time, though, the UNCI's tone changed. Loiseau-Pinson came away from a 23 June meeting disheartened: "The assembly . . . recognizes the necessity . . . of the Republic," he observed, but "it will go no further."[40] His reading of the situation was perfectly correct.

The UNCI's official electoral program, published on 1 July, declared a double commitment to the republic and "to the program of M. Thiers." The Union Nationale's shift toward the center extended to the backing of particular candidates. The UNCI endorsed an electoral slate worked out in collaboration with the so-called Union de la Presse, a slate that included reliable but well-bred republicans such as Emile Deschanel and Ferdinand Hérold.[41] Candidates elected on the Union de la Presse list signed on either to Thiers' parliamentary group, the Center Left, or to the Left, which was the group of the three Jules: Ferry, Grévy, and Simon.[42] In the aftermath of the Commune, under pressure from a reinvigorated hardline faction, the UNCI threw its support behind Thiers' "conservative republic."

During the 16 May crisis of 1877, however, the Union Nationale played a more daring role, one that contributed materially to the affirmation of a Gambettist republic purged of old notables. In May 1877 President MacMahon dismissed the short-lived republican ministry of Jules Simon and appointed in its place a ministry led by the Orleanist Duc de Broglie. MacMahon at the same time prorogued the republican-dominated parliament and made arrangements to hold new legislative elections in October. The Broglie ministry proceeded to dismiss uncooperative prefects and to apply official pressure on behalf of ministry candidates. To Broglie's dismay, the elections returned a new, if reduced, republican majority. Broglie withdrew from the fight, but a still defiant MacMahon replaced him with a yet more tough-minded Orleanist, General Gaëtan de Rochebouët.

It was at this juncture that business opposition to the *seize mai* coup bubbled over. In late November, UNCI president Hiélard, seconded by Levallois, organized a petition urging MacMahon to accord "a complete and sincere satisfaction to the will so clearly and so loudly expressed in the last elections by the majority of our fellow citizens." Ninety-seven Paris businessmen, well over half from the Sentier district of the second arrondissement, signed the document. The gesture, however modest, infuriated authorities, who resorted to the crudest of antisemitic and red-baiting tactics. The petitioners were attacked as "almost every one a member of the Israelite sect" and branded adventurers as well. Sentier businessmen, police sources insinuated, had a long history of political recklessness. Had they not militated in the Paris byelection of 1873 in favor of the radical Barodet against Thiers' candidate Rémusat? Had they not rejoiced at Thiers' subsequent ouster from office?[43] Police officials were, of course, exaggerating. The majority of garment-district militants were not Barodet radicals at all (although, as we have seen, a radical current did exist within the business community) but, rather, aggrieved citizens provoked into action by the antidemocratic behavior of reactionary authorities.

The November petition was met with official resistance. To redouble the pressure on an obstinate MacMahon, Hiélard called a public protest meeting. On 3 December an estimated 1,800 businessmen gathered at the Salle Frascati. The audience acclaimed yet one more petition calling on the maréchal to bend to the people's will, and a delegation was appointed to deliver the document in person to the president. The police thought they recognized the names on the December petition, republican troublemakers all: men like Jules Maumy, an UNCI officer with ties to Gambetta's newspaper *La République française*, and the textile *négociant* Koechlin, "an acquaintance and near relative of M. C. Floquet."[44] As for the delegation itself, it included Hiélard and at least one additional UNCI member, Alexandre Hatet of the Chambre Syndicale de la Draperie.[45]

But even so substantial a demonstration of business militancy left MacMahon unmoved. The maréchal refused to meet the Salle Frascati delegation and instructed it to hand its petition over to the minister of commerce, the Vicomte d'Harcourt. Worse, having snubbed the Hiélard delegation, MacMahon reportedly turned to the presidents of the Tribunal and Chamber of Commerce for advice. Angry businessmen drew the natural conclusion: the maréchal listened only to "princes, dukes, bishops, monks, lawyers, regents and governors of the Banque de France and *gros commerçants* like M. Baudelot [president of the Tribunal of Commerce] and M. Houette [president of the Chamber]." Even the police wondered what wisdom the maréchal expected to glean from such "princes of commerce."[46] The reform of the Chamber of Commerce franchise in 1872 had initiated a gradual rapprochement between UNCI militants and business notables, but in a moment of crisis, such as the 16 May coup, deep-seated antagonisms and rhetoric reasserted themselves, demonstrating just how far the process of reconciliation had yet to go.

MacMahon had imprudently offended the democratic sensibilities of business militants, and the situation now began to spin out of control. The fury of the Salle Frascati delegation was communicated to republican representatives who, it appears, counseled moderation. Business circles hoped at least that sympathetic deputies, the Gambettist Pierre Tirard for example, might be persuaded to interpellate the government.[47] In the meantime, the petition campaign was stepped up. The UNCI and the affiliated Chambre Syndicale des Tissus circulated anticoup petitions among members. But now not just the signatures of well-known *négociants* were solicited but also those of small shopkeepers and even employees. Police began to worry about the maintenance of public order.[48] Of no less concern to authorities, the anticoup agitation was spreading beyond the capital. By 5–6 December, petitions had begun to pour in from the provinces. Textile towns—Elbeuf, Lille, Lyon, Saint-Etienne—took the lead, but in a matter of days the petition campaign had engulfed the entire nation.[49] Only now, after having considered and rejected plans for military action, did MacMahon capitulate. A republican ministry under Dufaure was appointed on 13 December.

The UNCI's role in the *seize mai* episode points to three conclusions. That year of 1877 witnessed, it is said, "the real foundation of the Third Republic."[50] What has not been sufficiently acknowledged is the critical role played by organized business and by the UNCI in particular in the republican victory. Contemporaries were more astute. In an 1881 speech to the Chambre Syndicale de la Draperie et des Tissus (an UNCI affiliate), Gambetta remembered the struggles of 1877:

> *Eh bien,* from what quarter did help come, whose intervention weighed decisively in the struggle against a return of the combined forces of reaction? Gentlemen, it was the intervention of business. The day it was seen that men of commerce, men of industry, men of affairs stood on the side of the Republic . . . on that selfsame day, the 16 May coup was defeated.[51]

The events of 1877 marked the consolidation of an emergent republican democracy. And they dramatized critical transformations in the character and operation of business institutions. The UNCI, a voluntary body, had achieved a considerable triumph, and its role in business affairs increased in subsequent years, in no small part because of its powerful political connections. The Paris Chamber of Commerce, by contrast, was not the institution it had once been. It retained certain prerogatives, still had a representative function to perform vis-à-vis the state. But it was no more the oligarchical redoubt of former years; it was less secretive in its operations (since the early seventies it had begun to circulate among interested parties a record of its internal proceedings); and most important of all, it now had to share the institutional limelight with upstarts like the UNCI. The bright glare of 1877 brought into sharp relief a process that had been gathering momentum since the late Second Empire: the rise of independent voluntary associations like the Union Nationale and the retreat of constituted bodies like the Chamber of Commerce. "The end of the notables," the arrival of a "new stratum of bourgeoisie"[52]—such notions had a particular meaning to Paris business militants; they signaled a shift in the balance of institutional power in the world of commerce.

Last of all, the 16 May episode revealed just how Gambettist in political orientation the UNCI had become. Officialdom tried time and again to smear business militants as extremists, but the accusation fell wide of the mark.[53] To be sure, genuine radicals like Levallois were to be found in UNCI ranks but, with far greater and increasing frequency, business activists nurtured ties to Gambettism—to Gambettist papers like *La République française,* to Opportunist politicians like Tirard, and indeed to Gambetta himself. Gambetta's appearance at the Union Nationale's 1881 banquet sealed a compact that had been gaining in strength at least since *seize mai.*

From an interest group in the 1860s, the Union Nationale had evolved into a Gambettist satellite. It was a clash of interests with established commercial authority that had set the process of transformation in motion. The businessmen of the UNCI confronted a legal code that placed restrictions on the right of association; they faced a Chamber of Commerce vested by law with special privileges and dominated by *notables-commerçants.* Institutions in place encoded a particular set of power relations, and it was in confrontation with those relations that a new social stratum defined itself.

The UNCI's invocations of democracy, liberty, and international brotherhood, its condemnations of privilege, monopoly, and militarism, predisposed it to cast its identity in the language of republicanism. Republican ideology imparted coherence and power to UNCI demands, and across a decade of political experimentation, the organization evolved toward a form of moderate republicanism that both served its interests and affirmed its principles. A local squabble between an institutional newcomer and *notables-commerçants* was thus politicized and then absorbed into a wider struggle between an emergent republican middle class and entrenched elites tarred with antidemocratic attitudes.

In the case of the UNCI, however, confrontation in the end gave way to reconciliation. In 1884, the Third Republic legalized employer as well as worker trade unionism, removing one bone of contention between the UNCI and Chamber of Commerce. But it was the 1872 voting-rights decree that did most to dissipate tensions. The enfranchisement of much of the UNCI's membership increased the organization's electoral leverage, and in the face of such power, the attitude of many Chamber of Commerce incumbents was more forthcoming. To be sure, well into the seventies, elements of Paris' business elite, often stiffened by assurances of official backing, continued to oppose UNCI efforts to organize commercial elections.[54] And in 1877, as we have seen, old hostilities between newcomers and notables flared once again. By the 1880s, however, Chamber of Commerce resistance had collapsed once and for all. Thenceforth, acrimonious battles were avoided as the UNCI, in collaboration with other interested business associations, worked out common and essentially uncontested slates for the Chamber and Tribunal of Commerce elections.

The coming of the Third Republic resolved critical issues that had once divided Paris' business community. New lines of cleavage would emerge in short order, but for a brief moment in the 1880s, commercial Paris was again at peace with itself and more democratic in its constitution: more accepting of universal suffrage, more accommodating to freedom of association. The Jewish consistory in the 1860s and 1870s confronted an institutional insurgency like that posed by the UNCI, and with a similar conciliatory outcome.

[4]

Jewish Republicanism

THE DECADES OF midcentury constituted a formative period, a critical moment of mobility and reappraisal, in the history of modern French Jewry.[1] French Jewish life, as never before, was centered on Paris. The number of Jews in the capital quintupled from 8,000 in 1841 to 40,000 in 1880. The Ecole Rabbinique, France's sole seminary for the training of Jewish clergy, was moved from Metz to Paris in 1859. An expanding community financed construction of two spacious synagogues, both completed in the 1870s. Not only was the community growing, but it was growing richer.[2] Jews remained concentrated in the ranks of petty commerce, but an increasing number, buoyed by good times, lifted themselves into the more respectable strata of business *(le négoce)* and the liberal professions. There was movement even at the top. Péreires, Bischoffsheims, Camondos, and a host of newcomers scaled the narrow heights of Jewish finance, for so long the privileged roost of the Rothschild family.

The growth and embourgeoisement of the Paris community prompted members to self-reflection and debate, to a new understanding of what it meant to be Jewish and of the Jews' place in French life. In many accounts, such endeavors to shape a new consciousness are construed as part of a more general process of modernization or assimilation,[3] but this interpretation misses two points. First, Jewish self-making was mediated through politics. The community fashioned in the debates of the 1860s and 1870s was, indeed, more "French", but it was also (in constitution, philosophical orientation, and politics) more republican. Jews, in search of a new identity, edged toward what one historian has called a "Jewish republicanism,"[4] toward a conception of Jewish selfhood that embraced the republic as a secular incarnation of values embedded in Jewish tradition. Jewish republicanism, moreover, was elaborated in dynamic exchange with the wider republican movement. Jews joined in republican philosophical debate; they participated in a range of ancillary organizations from the Ligue de la Paix to the Ligue de l'Enseignement; and they campaigned for republican candidates if they did not themselves stand as republicans. Jews made a mark on a movement that, when it acceded to power, opened public life to them with a latitude unknown elsewhere in Europe. Assimilation implies a conformity to institutions and values that the assimilated had no hand in shaping. In midcentury France, Jews accommodated more than they were accommodated to, but the movement was not all one way.

In searching for identity, Jews turn to Repub. as place that provides them a place to act

The Consistory

The principal administrative organism in nineteenth-century Jewish life was the consistory. Napoleon Bonaparte, ever in search of mechanisms to manage an unruly civil society, prevailed upon Jews to organize a system of *corps constitués* invested with a double mandate: to represent the interests of the Jewish community to the state and to perform within the community a variety of policing functions. Seven local consistories were formed in France proper, the Paris consistory over time acquiring the status of primus inter pares. The locals in turn selected delegates to serve on the Paris-based central consistory, which occupied the top rung of the administrative hierarchy.

As was characteristic of such constituted bodies, the consistorial regime tended to elitist rule. Through the July Monarchy, the right to vote in consistory elections was restricted to a propertied few. An 1844 ordinance extended the franchise to certain *capacités,* but even then the electorate was minuscule. In the Paris consistory elections of 1845, a mere 233 voters were inscribed on the electoral rolls. The Second Republic, in Jewish affairs as in other domains, inaugurated the practice of universal suffrage, but the change was more formal than substantive. The Paris consistory electorate, it is true, shot up to 2,295 in 1850, but rates of participation remained low. Just over 500 voted in the elections of 1857. The orchestrated character of the electoral process does much to account for the sparse turnout. In Paris, for example, on the eve of a vote, sitting members of the consistory typically would compose an ad hoc committee, draw up a slate of candidates, and then convoke an open meeting to present the list for public approval.[5] There was little debate or choice; elections were decided in advance; and the same kinds of candidate, if not the same individuals, were elected time after time. Despite three changes of political regime, the social profile of the central consistory varied little from the 1830s to the 1850s. The inevitable Rothschild sat, flanked by lesser lights in the banking world and by one or two renowned recruits from the liberal professions: the magistrate Philippe Anspach, for example, who was Gustave de Rothschild's father-in-law, or the kabbalist and Collège de France philosopher Adolphe Franck.[6]

The "community of notables"[7] who administered Jewish affairs were wary of efforts to democratize consistorial procedures or open them to public scrutiny, and for good reason. The disenfranchised or unregistered were often religiously conservative; such insurgencies as there were in the Jewish community (until 1860) were led by men like Abraham Créhange, an orthodox Jew who was at the same time an 1848 veteran, devoted equally to the democratization of France and of the consistory. The consistory hierarchy was, by contrast, liberal in its religious leanings and worried that mass participation would set back the cause of religious reform. It did what lay in its power to shut out orthodoxy and assert consistorial control over a widening terrain, from the education of rabbis to the authorization of new congregations.[8]

What species of liberalism was it that prompted institutional practices at once elitist and centralizing? It is tempting to understand liberal Judaism as a variant of Cousinist eclecticism, all the more so since one of liberal Judaism's principal advocates, Franck, was himself a student of Cousin's.[9] Certainly the initial assumptions of liberal Judaism have a familiar eclectic ring to them. When shorn of medieval trappings, liberal Jews believed, Jewish law and liturgy disclosed a rational kernel. But so it was with all civilized religious creeds: pare away the accretions of dogma, and a hard core of universalist ethical prescription is revealed. At the present moment, however, at least in the ranks of the Jewish faithful, only a select few had arrived at an enlightened understanding of religion. It was fitting for such an elite to govern, duty-bound over time to regenerate and raise to citizenship the mass of their ignorant brethren.

Liberal Judaism labored hard to translate its commitments into practice. Reformers envisioned a religious service trimmed down but uplifting and decorous. Simplification meant the elimination of minor hymns *(piyyutim)* and increased liturgical use of French. The rabbi, dressed in sober and uniform clerical garb, was to provide the element of uplift, sermonizing on moral rather than legalist or dogmatic themes. As for decorum, reformers frowned on the noisy comings and goings characteristic of orthodox observance. In the modern synagogue, congregants should maintain an attitude of propriety, listening attentively to the rabbi and to the organ music that reformers believed imparted a note of dignity to services. The consistory in fact convened a rabbinic conference in 1856 to take up the question of liturgical reform, and the participants cooperated up to a point, sanctioning organ music on the sabbath and a cutback on hymns.[10]

How to demonstrate the essential sameness between a reformed Judaism and the enlightened civilization of postrevolutionary France was a more delicate problem. Much might be done in matters of appearance. The liberal laity gave over the wearing of the yarmulke in daily life. Rabbis were encouraged to dress in clothes that in cut and design were scarcely distinguishable from the robes of a priest or minister. Language too had a part to play. Liberals preferred the appellation of Israelite, a term that erased all hint of aspirations to nationhood: "A *Jewish* nation has often been spoken of, but never an *Israelite* nation."[11] There came moments, of course, when Jews were obliged to act as Jews, but if difference had to be asserted, at least it might be without fanfare. The central consistory made a point of not publicizing its proceedings. In 1858 the ultramontane journalist Louis Veuillot published a blood-libel charge against French Jewry in the pages of *L'Univers.* The consistory did not stand idly by, but it acted with discretion, inviting imperial authorities to file suit against Veuillot and, when the authorities demurred, opting to let the matter drop.[12]

But when it came to enlightening the unenlightened among one's own, liberal Judaism knew no such hesitation. The Paris consistory helped to maintain a full complement of communal schools. Albert Cohn, a Rothschild family confidant, organized a vocational training program for Jewish youth in 1846, the Société pour l'Apprentissage des Jeunes Garçons (later renamed the Société des Jeunes Garçons Israélites). A combination of philanthropy and education, it was hoped, would pull Jews out of poverty, steer them away from degrading forms of street commerce, and recast them as industrious and productive citizens.[13]

It would be excessive to affix a definite political label to liberal Judaism. What can be said is that the consistory felt most comfortable with regimes that shared in some degree its own enlightened and centralizing tendencies. The Jewish establishment had, of course, maintained cordial and, in the case of the Rothschilds, more than cordial relations with the July Monarchy. With the advent of the Second Empire, a liberal Bonapartist element crept into consistorial ranks. Léopold Javal, a banker and imperial deputy, was elected to the central consistory in 1853. Franck took to frequenting the empress' entourage at Compiègne.[14] The consistorial world was a select one that had hollowed out a niche for itself at the cusp of France's notability. By virtue of its institutional and social position and of its liberal political orientation, the Jewish elite enjoyed ongoing and friendly relations with established political authority.

The Alliance and the Consistory

In the 1860s, however, the cloistered peace of the consistorial hierarchy was disturbed by an institutional newcomer, the Alliance Israélite Universelle (AIU). The Alliance, in program and personnel, represented a democratic alternative to the consistory, but more than that. AIU members lobbied the consistory for more aggressive action on behalf of Jewish interests; they contested consistorial elections, managing even to win a majority on the Paris board. But the AIU's challenge to the consistorial status quo did not lead to rupture, for the consistorial elite, despite initial resistance, ceded ground. The Alliance and consistory over the long term managed to negotiate a modus vivendi. In the process, though, a democratic note was sounded, and the institutional practices of Jewish life took a leftward turn.

The origins of the Alliance are well known. Edgar Mortara, a Jew born in the Papal States, was baptized in infancy by a family servant. Mortara's parents were unaware of these proceedings but not so the papal authorities, who in 1858 claimed Mortara as a Catholic convert, wrested the child from his family, and sequestered him in a convent. Jewish communities across the continent denounced what amounted to a state-sanctioned kidnapping.[15] In France the loudest voice of protest was that of Isidore Cahen, son of the editor of the

Archives israélites, an independent Jewish periodical of liberal leanings. Adding to Cahen's fury was the central consistory's cautious handling of the affair and its disapproval of Cahen's own clamor. He riposted in December 1858 with a call for the constitution of "une représentation libre" mandated to operate outside consistory channels, goading Jewish officialdom to action.[16] A little over a year later, in the spring of 1860, a group of seventeen, including Cahen, gathered at the home of businessman Charles Netter. The assembly authorized six of its number—Aristide Astruc, Jules Carvallo, Narcisse Leven, Eugène Manuel, along with Cahen and Netter—to organize a so-called Alliance Israélite Universelle. In short order, the six published a bulletin, a manifesto, and an "Appel aux israélites" subsequently translated into four languages.[17]

The AIU made plain from the outset its differences with the consistory. The consistory operated behind the scenes. The AIU disdained the backroom, arming itself for open battle with "the avenging burin" of publicity. The Alliance, Cahen wrote, "will have neither armies, nor navies, nor diplomats, nor congresses at its disposal." Its strength lay in its willingness to "set in motion that great lever of the modern era, public opinion."[18] Opinion was to be mobilized not just to expose wrongs perpetrated against Jews, but also to nurture "a fraternity, a sentiment of family" among Jewish populations the world over. The AIU claimed for itself a global jurisdiction that extended well beyond the consistory's national field of action, and it did so in the name of cementing solidarity from country to country, "a fecund mutuality" among all Jews regardless of nationality.[19] AIU rhetoric, as such solidarist invocations suggest, was suffused with utopian idealism, in marked contrast to the *bien-pensant* rationalism of the consistorial elite. The Alliance claimed to speak for a new generation of Jews "nourished on the modern sciences" and the "principles of '89."[20] The new Jew was at the same time "sincerely, *modernly* Israelite," practicing an ancient religion that, because of its monotheism, the simplicity of its theology, and the economy of its ethical code, retained a full measure of vitality in a secularizing century. Fortified with the "invincible power of right and reason," the Alliance shouldered the task of vindicating and redeeming brethren across the globe.[21] The enterprise was of critical importance to Jews, but not just to Jews. The AIU laid out to its audience the wider implications of success in a sequence of more and more expansive claims: "an honor to your religion, a lesson to the peoples of the world, a step forward for humanity, a triumph for truth and universal reason."[22] The redemption of Jewry was a stepping stone in the emancipation of humankind, in the eventual fusion of all peoples and religions in a fraternity of reason.[23]

Publicity, solidarity, humanity, universal reason: such vocabulary outlined an agenda, if not at odds, then at least distinct from that of the consistory. But the originality of the Alliance lay not only in matters of program. The AIU's appearance served notice of the presence in Jewish life of a new social stratum—and a new politics.

The Alliance's first members were young, born in the 1820s or 1830s, and were recruited from the middling ranks of Jewish society. Cahen and Manuel had graduated from the Ecole Normale, Carvallo from the Ecole Polytechnique. Leven practiced law. Astruc was a rabbi and Netter a merchant *(négociant.)* The occupational profile of the AIU's seventeen original members was little different: five current or former *universitaires*, three *négociants*, two doctors, one rabbi, one engineer, one artist, one lawyer, one engraver, and two of unknown profession. The liberal professions and the trades predominated.[24]

There is, moreover, a distinct republican and freethinking tinge to the cohort, above all to the core six. "Youth ardent for liberty," which had "witnessed the revolution of 1848 and learned from it": such was Leven's characterization of the AIU's founders,[25] and it contained a kernel of truth. Manuel had studied at the Ecole Normale with Jules Simon and Vacherot and in 1848 backed Cavaignac's bid for the presidency of the Second Republic.[26] Leven had begun professional life at the Palais de Justice as a secretary in Adolphe Crémieux's law office. When, in 1870, Crémieux left legal practice to become minister of the interior, Leven followed in the capacity of Crémieux's *chef du cabinet.*[27]

Astruc may well have been a republican, but evidence bearing out such a claim is hard to come by. What is incontestable is that he conducted himself as an independent freethinker. He first drew attention to himself in the late 1850s as the author of an impassioned rebuttal to Veuillot's antisemitic diatribes. Serving briefly as assistant to the Grand Rabbi of Paris, he earned a rebuke from the central consistory for sermons lacking in moderation. Astruc left Paris in the mid-1860s to become Grand Rabbi of Belgium, but remained a source of controversy in France. In 1866 he delivered a eulogy at the funeral of Michel Berend, a Jew who had taken up freethinking and

Freemasonry (Astruc was himself a Mason). The event drew reproof from religious authorities in Paris, but the response was mild compared to the trouble stirred by Astruc's publication in 1869 of *L'Histoire abrégée des juifs.* The book made a point of excising the miraculous from biblical and postbiblical Jewish history, reinterpreting instances of divine intervention as metaphoric representations of states of mind or as poetic renderings of natural occurrences. The *Histoire* was doubly offensive because intended for children, and the Grand Rabbi of France, Lazare Isidor (1866–1888), was moved to condemn the book and prohibit its use in Jewish schools.[28]

Carvallo can also be situated on the freethinking left. He was a veteran Saint-Simonian and one of five founders of *L'Opinion nationale,* a paper of progressive views edited by Adolphe Guéroult, which proved itself one of the AIU's most stalwart champions outside the Jewish community.[29]

Netter and Cahen defy easy classification, whether as republicans or as ecumenical freethinkers. In Netter's case, there is no evidence of political or freethinking affiliation of any sort.[30] As for Cahen, he too studied with Simon and Vacherot at the Ecole Normale. Had he been able to pursue a university career, he might well have sought the patronage of a powerful republican sponsor, but antisemitic prejudice drove him out of the teaching profession. He turned instead to journalism, first as second-in-command at the *Archives israélites* and then from 1860 as editor-in-chief. Cahen opened the pages of the journal to an assortment of freethinking types—Marx's former comrade-in-arms Moses Hess, the one-time utopian socialist Alexandre Weill—but he himself remained a partisan of liberal Judaism. The *Archives israélites,* under Cahen's direction, took a republican turn in the late empire, but in 1860, at the time of the AIU's founding, neither the journal nor its editor made much show of republican conviction.[31]

A republican tint there was to the AIU, but it blurred into Saint-Simonianism and an independent liberalism. The picture grows more nuanced still when the composition of the Alliance's first steering committee, constituted in 1862, is taken into account.[32] Of the twenty men listed, five belonged to the original group of six. Netter had been called away from Paris on business and was listed only as a corresponding member. Many of the fifteen newcomers were democrats: Créhange, Crémieux, Edouard Horn (a naturalized Frenchman of Hungarian origin who served as Jewish chaplain to

Kossuth's army in 1848), and Ernest Lévy-Alvarès (a professor and future inspector of secondary schools in the Third Republic).[33] But there was also a contingent of liberal Jews with connections to the consistorial establishment—Rabbi Mayer Charleville, the orientalist scholar Salomon Munk, and the banker Bénédict Allegri. The new committee even included a liberal Bonapartist element in the persons of Javal and perhaps also Louis Koenigswarter, whose brother Maximilien had sat in the Corps Législatif since 1852. Yet no matter how much the AIU flirted with power, whether consistorial or imperial, its center of gravity remained within the republican camp. For almost the entire span of its first twenty years, from 1863 to 1880, the organization was headed by a lawyer-politician of unimpeachable republican credentials, an 1848 veteran and masonic official: Adolphe Crémieux.

But it was no doubt the AIU's conduct, more than its look or rhetoric, that caused most consternation in consistorial circles. In July 1860 Salomon Ulmann, Grand Rabbi of France (1853–1866), wrote a letter to the Alliance, distancing himself from an organization he judged, however praiseworthy in principle, too militant in behavior.[34] But what, from the central consistory's point of view, was so militant about the Alliance?

In mid-1860 the AIU sought out Cavour's help in resolving the Mortara affair. The initiative elicited a burst of irritation from one unidentified central consistory member, who regretted the Alliance's manifest lack of prudence, its "ill-considered démarches" which were potentially harmful "to the true interests of Judaism."[35] In November the Alliance addressed a letter to the central consistory soliciting its cooperation on projects unspecified. There was some positive response to the invitation, but it was not uniform. The objectives of the two organizations, pointed out a member, were not at all the same. A second complained about the AIU's name, which he found too pompous. The upshot was a letter to the Alliance amicable in tone but promising nothing.[36] The AIU petitioned the central consistory for help again in March 1861, this time on a variety of concrete issues, foreign and domestic. The Alliance's pushiness and manifest intention to intervene not just abroad but in internal French affairs were galling to the consistory, which believed it knew its duty and had "no need of counsel" from upstarts. What standing did the AIU have after all? It had "no legal existence, nor raison d'être, above all in France given the activities, authority and influence of the consistories, bodies legally recognized as the representatives and defenders of the religious interests of the Israelite community." The incident caused sufficient aggravation that Franck, the sole consistory official who had taken out membership in the AIU, was moved to draft a letter of resignation.[37] Such rebuffs did not deter the AIU from persisting in its requests for aid—on behalf of Algerian, Rumanian, and French Jews—but right through 1864 the central consistory remained unyielding.[38] It is clear enough from these incidents what the consistory objected to in the Alliance's behavior: the AIU lacked both decorum and a sense of limits, acting rashly and without due consideration for the established interests represented by the consistory itself.

The AIU's relations with the Paris consistory were even more tormented. Here the conflict turned upon the Alliance's electoral efforts to win consistorial representation. Incumbents put up a fight, and election campaigns, once peaceful affairs, grew more and more agitated until officialdom was either swept out of office or forced to back down.

Carvallo was the first AIU member to sit on the consistory. How he got elected illuminates both consistorial electoral practice and the pressures that might be brought to change it. Four consistory positions were scheduled to be filled in the elections of 1860. In three cases, there were incumbents who intended to run again; the fourth position, opened by virtue of a death on the consistory, was unspoken for. Sitting members, as was the custom, convened a public meeting to discuss a possible list of candidates. The three incumbents were in due course nominated, but who was to occupy the fourth slot? Isidore Cahen from the audience proposed Carvallo's name, and almost by inadvertence it was accepted. The consistory then circularized the community, in effect conferring its official imprimatur on the four. Cahen's *Archives israélites* added its voice to the consistory's in support of Carvallo's candidacy. That there might be "a sincere and thorough discussion" of outstanding issues, an unidentified "man of good character" took it upon himself to organize a second public meeting, which turned out to be tumultuous. The consistory came under fire from the audience for indifference and inaction. In the meantime, a proliferating number of opposition candidates showered voters with electoral propaganda. The official candidates, as was then standard practice, did not bother to campaign, with the exception of Carvallo who issued a circular calling for "the publication of consistorial proceedings." Observers were struck by "the eagerness, the ardor" that characterized the elections in contrast to the usual indifference. Voter turnout proved to be heavier than usual. All the excitement did not, however, alter the expected outcome. The consistorial list passed in its entirety with the name of Gustave de Rothschild at the top. Still Carvallo—who was more outsider than insider—finished a decisive second, a victory, declared the *Archives israélites,* for the AIU.[39] The elections indicated a certain public discontent with consistorial administration; they gave evidence too of how discontent might be mobilized—by independent public meeting, press endorsements, and electoral propaganda.

All these techniques were deployed to greater effect in the consistorial elections of 1863. At the behest of the central consistory, the empire had tinkered with the Jewish suffrage. To qualify to vote, a Jew now had to contribute at least one franc per year to a consistory or an affiliated institution. The new regime at one stroke disenfranchised both the indifferent and the poorest Jews. At the same time, it extended the suffrage to foreign Jews able to demonstrate three years' residence in a consistorial circumscription. In consequence of the change in electoral regime, the Paris consistory decided to resign en masse, putting all seats up for grabs. For one incumbent, Carvallo, the situation was more complicated still. As an engineer at the Ponts et Chaussées, he had embroiled himself in a series of dubious business deals. He was stricken from the corps, and word of his troubles crept into the press. The Paris consistory pressured Carvallo to resign, but he dragged his feet until obliged to join in the mass resignation of 1863. The consistory pressed him not to run for reelection, but Carvallo would not stand aside.[40]

The elections turned out to be the most animated in recent memory. The Jewish press commented on the "unaccustomed agitation" and the "febrile excitement" that accompanied the event. Twenty-four candidates presented themselves and buried the electorate under an avalanche of circulars. A clamorous meeting at the Salle Bonne-Nouvelle pulled in a crowd of two to three hundred, and almost 1,600 persons descended on the polls at the rue des Blancs-Manteaux. The outcome of the elections, moreover, came as a surprise to many. Of the six seats at issue, four went to dignitaries of the Jewish establishment, but Créhange, an orthodox Jew and a democrat, was likewise returned, and so was, despite the consistory's sullen opposition, Carvallo. The latter's success so fired up the consistory that it insisted on his withdrawal. After some procrastination, Carvallo finally gave in, submitting a letter of resignation full of bitter reproach.[41]

The Paris consistory scheduled an election in late 1865 to fill the vacancy left by Carvallo's departure. A half-dozen candidates took the field. One of them was Carvallo himself. It seems that he had struck a bargain with the Corps des Ponts et Chaussées. It agreed to reinstate him; he agreed to resign forthwith, making it appear that he had not been fired. The outcome, to Carvallo's mind, cleared him of charges of misconduct. He considered himself a worthy candidate once again and proceeded to mount an aggressive campaign, touting himself as an AIU founder and a true democrat. Carvallo exhorted voters that the consistory exercised "an authority without limits" inconsistent with the Jewish faith's democratic essence. Over the course of centuries, intoned one Carvallo circular, while Christians had groaned under feudal oppression, the Jewish community "in the shadows of the iron gates that enclosed it," had organized itself "on an eminently democratic, egalitarian and fraternal basis," but now that birthright was at risk.[42]

But Carvallo was not the only candidate who styled himself an AIU man. Paul Saint-Victor, an ex-banker and current member of the consistory's charity board, entered the competition, circulating a leaflet that advertised his affiliation to the AIU. The Paris consistory, worried about Carvallo's vote-getting appeal, promoted Saint-Victor as the best choice in a bad situation.[43] It published an official endorsement, a ham-fisted maneuver that almost backfired. Carvallo assumed the posture of injured democrat. He proclaimed his devotion to the sanctity of "Israelite universal suffrage," at the same time likening the consistory, with its preference for official candidates, to the Bonapartist regime. Carvallo's protestations found an echo in the Jewish press. The *Archives israélites* deplored the consistory's "extraordinary pressure," and the conservative *L'Univers israélite* characterized its conduct as a threat to liberty.[44]

The election turned out to be quite close. Saint-Victor won by a narrow plurality, with Carvallo placing second. The events of 1865 made it clear that the consistory could rid itself of a troublemaker like Carvallo but not of the AIU or, for that matter, of an aroused public opinion that had shown itself responsive to democratic appeals.

Yet another tumultuous election in 1867 drove the point home. Three seats on the consistory were contested. Carvallo, ever the bad penny, joined in the fray, canvassing hard for democratic reform. The consistory, speaking through the authoritative voice of Gustave de Rothschild, made known its intention to resign "in its entirety" in the event of Carvallo's election.[45] When the vote was taken, the turnout proved too low, less than the one third of registered voters required by law.[46] New elections were scheduled, and this time voters came out in sufficient numbers. Carvallo was elected, and the consistory, true to its word, resigned, leaving the minister of cults in a quandary whether to accept the resignation. There matters stood from April until November 1867, when the minister decided in favor of acceptance and ordered a new vote to fill all six slots on the board. The consistory decided against an overt anti-Carvallo campaign. A chastened Carvallo had, in any event, determined not to run. In the ensuing elections, the AIU fared extremely well. Créhange, Michel Erlanger, and Lazare Lévy-Bing, all Alliance members, captured seats. Leven finished just out of the running. The Jewish press had no difficulty interpreting the result. "The electors of Paris," observed the Archives israélites, fed up with "consistorial absolutism," had demonstrated they were no longer prepared to tolerate the status quo.[47]

The old consistory had given way, and the next elections in March 1873 were conducted in a much different climate. The electoral regime had been twice modified in the interim. In 1870 the republican Government of National Defense, which had acceded to power in the wake of the empire's collapse, reintroduced universal suffrage; in 1872, Thiers' administration restored the more selective franchise of the 1860s. Such upheavals persuaded the consistory that it needed a total renewal, and all six lay members resigned. Electioneering there was in the campaign that followed, but it took place in an atmosphere of relative calm. In the actual balloting, five Alliance members—Créhange, Erlanger, Leven, Lévy-Bing, and Joseph Derenbourg—were returned, the sixth seat going to the inevitable Rothschild.[48]

The AIU's persistent prodding and its electoral activities in Paris laid bare critical cleavages within France's Jewish community, but the fissures did not run so deep that an eventual reconciliation proved impossible. The consistorial elite's first response to the Alliance challenge had been one of obstructive condescension, but in the face of the AIU's evident success—its burgeoning membership, which had rocketed by 1870 to over 13,000[49] and its evident appeal to consistorial voters—official attitudes began to soften. First there was a concession of recognition. The central consistory sent observers to the Alliance's annual meeting in 1863. Grand Rabbi Isidor attended in 1864, accompanied by the president of the central consistory, Colonel Max Cerfbeer. By 1868 the AIU central committee counted among its numbers two of the more exalted representatives of official Judaism, Albert Cohn and Grand Rabbi Isidor.[50]

The path toward reconciliation was also eased by a common commitment to the poor and uneducated.[51] Alliance members had been interested in charitable work from the very first. Leven and Manuel had taught for years in an apprenticeship program that in 1853 was folded into Cohn's Société des Jeunes Garçons Israélites. As the rapprochement between Alliance and consistory proceeded, Leven, Manuel, and the others were drawn still further into the establishment's charitable network. Louis-Raphael Bischoffsheim had founded a trade school for girls in 1862. Slots on the Institut Bischoffsheim's governing board were reserved for the wives of community dignitaries: Mme. Zadoc Kahn (wife of the Grand Rabbi of Paris), Mme. Cahen d'Anvers, Mme. Bischoffsheim. In 1872 the roster of board members included as well the name of Mme. Eugène Manuel.[52] The indefatigable Cohn played a central role in the mid-seventies in the formation of a Comité Spécial des Ecoles to oversee the operation of Jewish communal schools. A Bischoffsheim, a Camondo, and a Cahen d'Anvers were invited to sit on the committee, but so too was a trio of Alliance men: Leven, Manuel, and Cohn's own son-in-law, the lawyer Ernest Hendlé.[53]

At the same time that AIU veterans were absorbed into official Judaism's charitable operations, members of the Jewish elite extended increasing support to the AIU's regenerative enterprise. In 1862 the Alliance opened a primary school in Morocco to expose the benighted Jews of the Orient to the wonders of western civilization. This was the first of a vast network of Alliance schools that spread across the entire Mediterranean basin. To staff such an apparatus, the AIU in 1867 organized a teachers' training college for men, the Ecole Normale Israélite Orientale (ENIO), and then in 1872 an equivalent institution for women. The financing of pedagogical operations on such a grand scale was beyond the AIU's means, and over the years it had to depend more and more on Jewish philanthropy. The Institut Bischoffsheim provided space for the women's normal school. Salomon Goldschmidt, who was Louis-Raphael Bischoffsheim's business partner and brother-in-law, bankrolled an Alliance school in Istanbul. But the AIU's breakthrough to financial solvency came in 1873, thanks to a one-million-franc donation from Baron Maurice de Hirsch (Goldchmidt's nephew). The AIU's links to the close-knit world of Jewish philanthropy were more than financial. An 1865 Alliance communiqué listed a Camondo as a corresponding member. Bischoffsheim for a period sat on the AIU central committee, as did Goldschmidt, who succeeded Crémieux as Alliance president in 1881.[54]

Tensions between Alliance and consistory dissipated in the late Second Empire. By the 1870s a compromise had been elaborated, a partnership sustained by a tight-woven lattice of personal, institutional, and financial connections. But did such a compromise entail a blunting of the democratic impulse that had animated the Alliance? Not entirely, for the AIU's coming had worked some permanent changes in the constitution of Jewish institutional life. "Official Judaism" had not been displaced, but it was now obliged to share power with a leaven of middle-class types. It would be too much to claim that the consistorial regime had been democratized. On the other hand, consistorial elections now looked more like the real thing with competing candidates, press endorsements, meetings, speeches, and campaign literature. Until 1860, never more than a few hundred had taken part in Paris consistorial elections; after 1860, voter turnout invariably surpassed the one-thousand mark.

The governing principles of Jewish institutional practice had also begun to change. Officialdom still preferred to act with discretion. But at the same time, the Paris consistory now published a periodic *compte-rendu* of its activities. The Alliance made representations to the French government; it sent representatives to international diplomatic congresses. Publicity was seen to have its uses. As for solidarity, the Jewish elite, as evidenced by the generosity of Hirsch and Bischoffsheim, had come to acknowledge an obligation to fellow Jews not just in France but the world over.

Republican Judaism

Whether the Alliance's visionary fraternalism left an equally lasting imprint is more difficult to say. What is certain is that the Alliance, as it skirmished its way toward the center of Jewish life, not only retained its utopian aspirations but cast them more and more frankly in republican form.

Cahen made explicit the connection between democratic politics and a regenerated Judaism. Without citizens, he argued, there could be no republican government; a responsible citizenship in turn, as the examples of Switzerland and the United States attested, was inconceivable without religion. Not all religions, of course, were suited to the task of molding citizens, but Judaism was. In fact Cahen, echoing the claims of Carvallo's 1867 consistorial campaign, portrayed the synagogue as a species of minirepublic. Congregations were just so many voluntary associations "each independent the one from the other." Rabbis exercised a certain authority, but, as Astruc pointed out, that authority depended on "the good will of the congregants, the suffrage of the community," which reserved to itself the right to interpret Scripture. Judaism recognized no "infallible authority," no "pontiff or sovereign," "nothing which resembles a monarchical or feudal mode of organization."[55] The publication of Astruc's *Histoire abrégée* stirred demands for sanctions against the author. Grand Rabbi Isidor, who might have been expected to pronounce punishment, refused. The "spirit of exclusion," he explained, was alien to Judaism. Cahen replied to Astruc's anathematizers with an anathema of his own: "We have no sacerdotal caste . . . individuals who, without title, proscribe and excommunicate have no place in our community: they are so many Veuillots who have wandered into the synagogue."[56]

The structure of authority in the modern synagogue taught congregants lessons in self-government. Services also had a pedagogical dimension both in the way they were conducted and in the overt message they communicated. AIU men were partisans of a purification of ritual observance, but when they wrote of "épuration," it was inevitably in a vocabulary shot through with republican codewords: *la morale, le foyer,* manliness, sincerity, simplicity. Since midcentury, religious instruction for girls culminating in a public confirmation ceremony had become standard practice in enlightened synagogues. The *Archives israélites* approved the innovation. *La morale du foyer,* it said, depended on women; the better educated the mother, the sounder and more virtuous the household.[57] Republicanizing Jews in like manner conceived of the rabbi as a "professor of morals and of religion," hence their emphasis on the centrality of homiletics. A well-made sermon should open with a bible selection chosen for its edifying moral rigor. On the whole, a rabbi did well to avoid Talmud with its dry scholarly debate and legalist reasoning, but a sermon might be enlivened by citations from Midrash, the collected sermons of the early sages, with their artful mix of interpretation, anecdote, and poetry. Delivery in a good sermon was considered almost as important as content. The Paris consistory promoted Zadoc Kahn when he was only thirty to Grand Rabbi precisely because he possessed exceptional speaking skills. The *Archives israélites* praised Zadoc Kahn's "manly and energetic eloquence," which stirred emotion and conviction in the listener's heart.[58] But in the moral drama of the service, more was expected of the faithful than a decorous receptivity. Hippolyte Rodrigues, an AIU member and a prodigal albeit quirky religious commentator, exhorted all congregants to engage in a "sincere and interior examination" of self. Of all the sacred days on the Jewish calendar, none was more wholly given over to such soul searching than Yom Kippur, the Day of Atonement. On that day of utmost simplicity, as Cahen described it, Jews abstained from work and food, shucking off the cares and pleasures of the world. They submitted themselves to the most intense self-scrutiny and, appearing alone before God, "without the intermediaries other religions believe necessary," supplicated for divine forgiveness.[59]

Jews like Cahen gave a republican twist not only to the forms of ritual observance but to their content as well. Cahen compared the contemporary synagogue to a school.[60] And what was taught in such a school? Mosaic law? But was not the animating spirit of Mosaic law the same as that of the French revolution? Weill, the former Fourierist turned Mason and Alliance member, made the parallel explicit, boiling down the essential tenets of Mosaism to a familiar three: liberty, equality, and humanity.[61] A Jew, by virtue of the faith he professed as a son of the Covenant, was no less bound in filial devotion to "our immortal Revolution"—and to all its present-day derivatives, whether the Polish struggle for national independence or the Italian wars of national unification.[62] To be a Jew meant to be a citizen and a patriot. Private faith and public personality flowed the one into the other. Or as Zadoc Kahn put it, speaking at the inauguration of the Rue de la Victoire synagogue in 1874: "Faithful children of Judaism, we are by that fact alone good citizens on whom the country can count whatever the circumstances."[63]

Republicanizing Jews conceived the practice of Judaism as a form of moral training that prepared congregants for citizenship. "The republican organization of consciences," such was Cahen's description of modern synagogue life.[64] But the temple was not the sole site of Jewish civic education. The AIU ran a primary school system which in philosophy and curriculum paralleled and in certain respects anticipated that of the republic itself. This should not come as a complete surprise given the overlap in personnel between the Alliance's and republic's school administrations. The ENIO's first director was Isaïe Levaillant, a committed pacifist who was active in the Ligue de la Paix.[65] It was likely through pacifist connections that Levaillant had made the acquaintance of the Protestant educator Ferdinand Buisson, a founding member of the Ligue and a voluntary exile who had spent the late sixties teaching in Switzerland. Buisson was recruited to teach at the ENIO as professor of French, ethics, and pedagogy, before moving on to serve the republic as its longest-sitting director of primary education (1879–1896). Irénée Carré, also a gentile, joined the ENIO faculty in its early years before going on to a career in the republic's educational bureaucracy. He ended as a school inspector, as did two of the three members of the ENIO's curriculum committee: Lévy-Alvarès and Manuel.[66]

The republican affiliations of the ENIO staff patterned the curriculum taught in Alliance schools.[67] AIU teachers posted to Mediterranean lands understood themselves as apostles of progress engaged in a battle against oriental backwardness. They taught western standards of industriousness and personal hygiene; and they discouraged the speaking of traditional Jewish tongues, Yiddish and Ladino, in favor of French, "the genius of the country that has done the most for freedom of conscience."[68] These were nonetheless Jewish schools, and some Jewish subjects had to be taught. But the Jewish curriculum was focused less on the Talmud than on Hebrew and the Bible, and the postbiblical history of the Jews was, until the end of the century, ignored. What history was taught, such as the history of the Great Revolution, had a distinct French bias. As in the metropole, Alliance-school curriculum made different provisions for boys and girls. Boys were instructed in useful artisanal or commercial skills. Girls were given training in needlework, but it was judged more important that they be taught a sense of self-worth: they should eschew oriental baubles in favor of modest dress, they should refuse precocious and arranged marriages, they should assert against overbearing husbands an autonomous presence in the household.

In questions of synagogue organization, ritual observance, and pedagogical philosophy, Jews were coming to see themselves as a republican people and the republic as an extension of Jewish life. But was there not a providential aspect to such an intermingling of destinies, Jewish and republican? The creator had charged the Jews with a mission: to sow the seeds of monotheism, to bring word of

God's justice to the peoples of the world. A new age had dawned with the advent of the French revolution, "our admirable and messianic revolution of 1789" as Cahen called it. The missionary burden, once borne alone by the Jews, was now shared by France, which had become in its turn an "initiator of the human race."[69] In the modern era, Jew and Frenchman, the Alliance and the Republic, labored shoulder to shoulder in the service of a divinely ordained *mission civilisatrice.*[70]

Republican Jews in fact so identified themselves with the fate of revolutionary France that they tended to see the history of the democratizing present in terms of the biblical past. Grand Rabbi Isidor described the French as modern-day children of Israel who, like "the people of God in days gone by," had worked "one of those great moral revolutions that change the face of the world."[71] The republicans of 1870, analogized Crémieux, stood in the same relationship to *les grands ancêtres* of 1789 as David and Solomon had to the patriarchs Abraham, Isaac, and Jacob.[72] Indeed, had not the present witnessed Father Abraham's spiritual return in the righteous if fleeting life of Lincoln, "that Abraham, that just man," as the assassinated president was eulogized in 1865?[73] Five years later, in December 1870 with Paris under siege, the congregants of the Rue Notre-Dame-de-Nazareth synagogue gathered to celebrate the first night of Hannukah. A single emotion-charged memory, it was reported, gripped the assembled faithful: as the besieged Maccabees had once battled the Syrians, so now the French were locked in combat with the Prussian invaders.[74]

Jews in the Republican Movement

The recasting of French Jewry's destiny in republican terms had one obvious and practical consequence: a deepening Jewish involvement in the republican movement itself, in its philosophical debates, associational life, and electoral activities.

In moral debate, Jews staked out a position that attempted a middle way between religious orthodoxy on the one hand and an unbelieving rationalism on the other. The modern Jew had faith in the power of a purifying reason to strip away dogmatic superfluities, to pare down liturgy and doctrine in accordance with "the growing exigencies of human intelligence."[75] It was in this spirit that Astruc spurned the supernatural and Cahen proclaimed himself a partisan of laicity.[76] But such commitments did not signal a slide into faithless secularism; God still spoke to the world but through conscience and prophecy, not dogma or miracle.

An enlightened Jew, according to Rodrigues, believed in the unity of God and *la morale vraie*.[77] To the one God and the ten commandments, Cahen was anxious to add a third article of faith: the immortality of the soul. Two avenues were identified through which knowledge of morality might be gained: through the decalogue, "foundation of all human law," and through the workings of conscience, "that manifestation of God—living in each of us."[78] Astruc conjured away the miraculous, but he believed nonetheless that the course of human history gave evidence of "the constant working, the permanent inspiration of a being."[79] That being did not work its will through external and arbitrary intervention. It dwelt instead in the heart of every person, murmuring counsel and consolation to all who cared to listen. The task of religion, of modern Judaism, was to turn the soul toward God's voice within, to appeal through poetry and emotion to an innermost religious sentiment, to the "intimate convictions that the heart nourishes." A "dissolvent positivism," let alone an atheistic materialism, had no place in such a scheme, but there was room for a reason prepared to admit the truth-affirming power of conscience.[80]

The imprint of God's will might also be detected in the conduct of great men, the prophets and philosophers who lighted mankind's way. Weill foretold the coming of universal reason. He believed himself to be a genuine prophet, moved by God, and heir to an illustrious tradition that originated in Moses and Isaiah and passed down through Plato and Philo to Descartes, Spinoza, Kant, and Voltaire.[81] Rodrigues made no claim to prophetic voice, but he did believe that God revealed himself in the workings of great souls. Rodrigues envisioned a future reconciliation of the great biblical religions, *les trois filles de la Bible* as he called them, and constructed a prophetic lineage to suit the purpose: Moses, Jesus, Mohammed, Arius, Wycliffe, Hus, Luther, Servetus.[82] Cahen also had a vision of history's design, conceived as a progressive ingathering of humanity "in a more truly felt and purer worship of the Creator." The process was mediated through great men who had been touched by the divine hand. Moses was one such, but so too was Jesus, understood not as the son of God but as a superior nature, a disciple of the Mosaic faith, "inspired by God."[83]

Republicanizing Jews tried to reconcile reason and religious sentiment. They professed devotion to liberty of conscience, to the cult of great men, and to an ecumenicism that admitted the essential truth of competing faiths. Other participants in republican moral debate, freethinkers and liberal Protestants in particular, were bound to take notice of a position that had so many obvious affinities to their own.

Henri Carle, a masonic freethinker and champion of natural religion, founded the Alliance Religieuse Universelle in 1865. Freethinking spirits who shared his devotion to the "universal conciliation of souls"—the Kantian Jules Barni, for example, or the mystic philosopher Charles Fauvety—were drawn to the enterprise, which soon began publication of a review. The point of interest here is the welcome Carle extended to Jews with a similar interest in universal conciliation. The ARU bulletin consented to publish an "Appel aux israélites," penned by Levaillant, who took out membership in the ARU, as did Carvallo and one Dr. Rabbinowicz, an occasional contributor to the pages of *Archives israélites*.[84]

Liberal Protestants, even more than freethinkers, took an interest in the doings of republican Judaism. By the end of the 1860s, relations between the AIU and the liberal wing of the Reformed Church had matured into a friendly partnership. In 1863 the Alliance expressed public sympathy for the plight of persecuted Spanish Protestants. In a gesture of reciprocity, Etienne Coquerel, the younger son of liberal Protestantism's most prominent spokesman, Athanase Coquerel, chided the Swiss canton of Argovie for its refusal to grant citizenship to residents of Jewish descent. And in 1866 one of Paris' senior liberal Protestant pastors, Joseph Martin-Paschoud, made an appearance at the Alliance's annual convention. He was there again the following year, accompanied by a second liberal Protestant minister, Auguste-Laurent Montandon. Such generous ecumenicism prompted Crémieux, the assembly's keynote speaker, to an exordium on the solidarity that conjoined Protestant and Jew in France, a solidarity born of a common experience of persecution.[85] But it was not victimization alone that bound the two religious communities. Zadoc Kahn succeeded Isidor as Grand Rabbi of Paris in 1869. Martin-Paschoud attended the investiture ceremony, as did Théophile Rives, pastor of an independent congregation at Neuilly. Isidor, now Grand Rabbi of France, addressed words of counsel to Kahn, expounding a creed that struck a startled Rives as identical in all essentials to the faith he himself professed. Were Jesus' teachings, he wondered, anything more than a distillation of rabbinic tradition: "The one God, respect for human life and conscience, the immortality of the soul and future reconciliation of all men and all races, is that not what M. Isidor invites his successor to teach at all times? And is that not, Christian teachers, what you preach yourselves?"[86]

Judaism, through such exchanges with freethinkers and liberal Protestants, added its distinctive voice to the din of philosophical and moral debate that accompanied the republican revival of the 1860s. Jews made a contribution as well to the constellation of progressive associations and causes that clustered on the republican movement's periphery.

No doubt it would be a mistake to overestimate the extent of the dialogue between Jews and Masons, but it cannot be dismissed. Allegri joined the Scottish rite as did Crémieux, who served in the post of Grand Master for over a decade and hosted what one biographer has called "a Masonic salon." The reform faction within the Grand Orient counted a knot of Jews among its numbers. Weill was a regular at the Fauvety salon in the 1850s and an early collaborator on Louis Ulbach's *Monde maçonnique.* Astruc, Hess, and Weill at one time or another all belonged to Massol's Renassisance par les Emules d'Hiram, and Hendlé was active in L'Ecole Mutuelle.[87] What made Masonry attractive to republicanizing Jews was first its material commitment to freedom of conscience. In 1868 a Metz lodge contributed to a rescue fund for Rumanian Jews, a gesture that summoned a warm expression of gratitude from the president of the local AIU chapter. The next year, much to the delight of the *Archives israélites,* a masonic congress published a manifesto against German lodges that refused initiation to Jews.[88]

The language of human brotherhood constituted a second bond between Jews and Masons. The lodges, like the AIU in France or the B'nai Brith in the United States, were pledged to the principle of "universal human fraternity."[89] Brother Veil-Picard, a Jewish Mason, explained how profound was the appeal to Jews of Masonry's temple imagery. To Masons, as to Jews, the temple represented an original unity, an architectonic harmony now lost but recoverable through a common reconstructive effort. Such humanitarian impulses found practical expression during the siege of Paris in 1870. Grand Rabbi Astruc and former Grand Master Mellinet joined hands in the organization of an ambulance service, a "fraternal effort" commemorated in a serene double portrait painted by Degas (fig. 2).[90]

2. Edgar Degas, *Rabbi Astruc and General Mellinet*, c. 1871

It was this commitment to an enlightened and fraternalist univer-
salism that motivated Jewish participation in the Ligue de la Paix
and the Ligue de l'Enseignement. Acollas, Hendlé, Naquet, and
Levaillant belonged to the former; Cahen, Hendlé once again, and
Javal to the latter. Carvallo saluted the public-library movement as a
work of civilization. As God, in a "column of light," had led the
Israelites of old through the desert, so now the *bibliothèque communale*
might lead Jews from "that solitude in which the middle ages had
shut them up."[91] Hendlé took part in the cooperative revival as well.
In 1868 he convened a meeting at the offices of the movement's
semiofficial newspaper *La Coopération* to organize an Ecole Professionnelle de la Coopération. The school opened a year later with a staff of
six, among them Amédée Dréo (a gentile and one of Hendlé's colleagues at the Palais de Justice), Edouard Horn, and Hendlé himself.[92]

Only a small gap separated such associational activism from politics as such, and more and more Jews in the 1860s and 1870s proved
willing to take the step. Under the empire, Crémieux apart, it was
rare indeed for a Jew to win election to parliament as a professed
republican. Yet if Jews shunned the lead in electoral politics, they

contrived to play an active supporting role. A young Ferdinand Dreyfus, a contributor to *Le Siècle* and a future deputy himself, wrote speeches for Favre's 1869 Latin Quarter campaign. Favre's *profession de foi* was postered all over the quarter thanks to Albert Cohn's son Léon.[93] Crémieux's candidacy in the Sentier district was, of course, seconded by the loyal Leven. Nor will it come as a surprise that Jewish voters, so numerous along the Rue du Sentier and Boulevard de Sébastopol, made it a point of honor to cast ballots for Crémieux who, it was said, owed them his election.[94] The year 1870–71 represented a breakthrough for republican Jews intent on public service. Naquet, through the fall of 1870, occupied a minor post on a government-appointed defense committee. Camille Sée, the nephew of central-consistory member Germain Sée, entered the ministry of the interior as secretary-general. Leven was appointed Crémieux's cabinet head in 1870, and Manuel was appointed Simon's in 1871. Hendlé served briefly as Favre's secretary before joining the prefectoral corps, which he did not leave until the collapse of the Thiers government in 1873.[95]

The regime of Moral Order that acceded to office in May 1873 drove the likes of Hendlé out of state service, but a less hospitable political climate did not deter Jews from rendering what service they could to the republican cause. In the wake of the crisis that led to Thiers' fall, Ernest Feray, a Protestant businessman and deputy of the Seine-et-Oise, made a frank public declaration of republican loyalties, a gesture that elicited a warm letter "conceived in a republican spirit" from 160 Paris businessmen. Veuillot spotted a Jewish plot in the letter. The *Archives israélites* took the trouble to count the actual number of Jewish signatories, arriving at the figure of 31. The tally was small enough to refute Veuillot, but sufficiently large to intimate a definite Jewish presence in opposition ranks.[96] The regime did indeed look with suspicion on its Jewish constituents. The new Rue de la Victoire synagogue opened in 1874. The republican-dominated municipal council sent a representative to the inauguration ceremony, but the government, as the *Archives israélites* pointedly observed, "shone . . . by its absence."[97] The *seize mai* crisis caused tensions to surface once again. David Schornstein, one of the AIU's original seventeen, characterized the fall elections, which were expected to resolve the crisis, as a "struggle by the past against the conquests of the modern spirit." The elections returned a republican majority, which had a sprinkling of Jews, including Eugène Lisbonne, Naquet, and Camille Sée. President MacMahon, however, balked at appointing a republican prime minister. In November, as we have seen, the Paris business community petitioned the maréchal to back down. Again the right sensed a "judaico-political intrigue," and again the *Archives israélites* tabulated the actual number of Jewish petitioners, 10 out of 96 by its count. Jews were a minority in the republican business opposition, but not an insignificant one.[98]

An important section of the Jewish community had implicated its fate in that of the republican movement. They had good reason to savor the Third Republic's triumph in 1877, all the more so when the republic returned the favor, opening the gates of public life to Jewish participation more widely than any preceding regime. Gambetta, in particular, extended himself on behalf of aspiring Jewish politicians.[99] He campaigned hard for David Raynal in the Gironde in 1876. Joseph Reinach and Paul Strauss, both destined for long parliamentary careers, entered politics as Gambettist protégés. In the case of Ferdinand Dreyfus, deputy of the Seine-et-Oise, patronage over the years evolved into real friendship. Even Leven, who had spent so many years in Crémieux's orbit, was moved, as a Paris municipal councillor in the 1880s, to switch into Gambetta's.

But more remarkable than the success of Jewish candidates at the polls was the willingness of republican officialdom to admit Jews into state service. As soon as MacMahon backed down in 1877, four Jews, Léon Cohn and Hendlé among them, were appointed prefects. Levaillant, at that time named a subprefect, won a quick promotion to full prefect and by 1885 had been made director of the Sûreté Générale.[100] The place of Protestants in the reconstruction of France's education system is well known, but Jews also played a part in the enterprise. The ENIO faculty, as we have seen, graduated three of its number, two Jews and one non-Jew, into the school inspectorate. Plans to overhaul the university were first mooted in the Société de l'Enseignement Supérieur founded in 1878. Funding for the operation came in the main from Jewish financiers like Maurice de Hirsch, Salomon Goldschmidt, and Raphael Bischoffsheim (Louis-Raphael's son). The society itself included at least one active AIU member, professor of philology at the Collège de France Michel Bréal. It was in consultation with a small circle of senior academics, Bréal included, that Liard drafted the university reform bill of 1885.[101]

In the world of business, an insurgent voluntary association, the Union Nationale du Commerce et de l'Industrie, had confronted

Paris' commercial elite, entrenched in the Chamber of Commerce, with a democratic challenge. So in the Jewish community, the AIU's creation posed a democratic challenge to the consistory system. In both instances, after an initial clash, terms of compromise were worked out. The net result was a community still united, but more democratic in its constitution and more republican in its politics. It is at the same time important not to exaggerate the extent of this leftward turn. The republicanizing Jews of the AIU, all utopian and fraternalist rhetoric notwithstanding, were never firebrands. They sought the patronage of solid 48ers like Crémieux or of the great lawyers and normaliens of midcentury like Favre and Simon, who were yet more moderate. In the late 1870s and 1880s, as those men retired from public life, Jewish loyalties, still republican, evolved in the direction of Gambettist Opportunism. There were always radicals of Jewish origin like Naquet, but on the whole such men did not practice their faith or involve themselves in the internal affairs of their community.

In the decades of midcentury, a relationship of dynamic and fruitful exchange was worked out between Jews and the republic. Jews played a part in the making of the Third Republic and remained in later years one of the regime's most loyal constituencies. The republic in its turn bestowed recognition and honors both on individual Jews and on the community as a whole. But such a relationship, however gratifying, was not without its dangers. The alliance of republic and Jews cemented a counteralliance of antidemocrats and antisemites, which first displayed its strength at the time of the Dreyfus affair. To the extent that Jews tied their destiny to that of the republic, they suffered when the regime suffered, as during the affair or again in the 1930s. When in 1940 the regime fell, France's Jewish community fell with it.

[5]

Liberal Protestantism

THE PROTESTANT ELITE, like the Jewish consistory, was shaken by an institutional insurgency in the 1860s and 1870s. The terms and outcome of the battle were not the same, however. In the Jewish community, the dominance of a liberal-leaning consistory was disputed by a republican-oriented upstart, the AIU. The contest ended in a negotiated modus vivendi and a definite if limited shift to the left in communal orientation. In the Reformed Church, on the other hand, the sitting consistory was orthodox; it was the insurgents who defined themselves as liberals. And no matter how vigorously liberal Protestantism prosecuted its cause, it never managed to muster majority support within the church. AIU successes obliged Jewish elites to cede ground. Liberal Protestant reverses only stiffened orthodox resistance, and the confrontation resulted not in compromise but in schism.

Prevailing interpretation disavows any link between Protestant ecclesiastical politics and debates within the wider political community. Liberal Protestants, it is said, espoused no single political position. If they did, they inclined more to the Bonapartist than to the liberal or republican side. The structure of the Reformed Church was overhauled by fiat in the wake of Bonaparte's 1851 coup; the man who drafted the new statute was a liberal Protestant, Charles Read. In the 1860s, as the orthodox-liberal conflict heated up, the liberal side profited from the patronage of the minister of justice and cults, Jules Baroche. But, it is asked, should such connections come as a surprise? Bonapartists were a modernizing minority disdainful of parliamentary elites. So too were liberal Protestants, who espoused a theological modernism and fretted against notable rule in church affairs.[1]

No one disputes that, with the advent of the Third Republic, Protestants went in growing numbers into public service, but it is denied that the conversion of Protestants to the republican cause had any relationship to the liberal-orthodox split. To be sure, some one-time liberal Protestants occupied prominent positions in the republic's educational establishment. Jules Ferry appointed Ferdinand Buisson director of primary education in 1879. In the following year the former pastor Félix Pécaut was made general inspector of studies at Fontenay-aux-Roses, the first teachers' training college for women. Jules Steeg, another former pastor and liberal Protestant militant, was made the school's director in 1896. But for every liberal Protestant who entered the Third Republic's service, there was an orthodox Protestant who did the same.[2] In any event, how religious were those erstwhile liberals who devoted themselves to the republic's interests? They may once have been churchgoers, but, so the argument goes, the more closely they bound themselves to the new regime, the more distant they grew from the faith that bred them, careening down "the agnostic slope" and ending as little better than renegades.[3]

Now I want to advance a different point of view. First, the institutional battles of the 1860s and 1870s, not at the outset but over time, acquired a definite political cast, at least in the eyes of Paris-based liberals. They understood themselves to be embarked on a campaign to advance church democracy and lashed out at the stubborn orthodox as crypto-papists and authoritarians. I do not suggest that the liberal characterization of the orthodox party was correct. What I will argue, though, is the growing affinity between theological liberalism and republican political commitment. Second, while it is true that liberal Protestants in the 1880s tended to shift out of church politics into politics *tout court,* this does not mean that they abandoned religion in the process. Quite the contrary. They thought they had conceived a new Christianity, a modern faith that reconciled the equally exacting demands of science and moral conscience. Stripped of its confessional and dogmatic trappings, that faith might serve as a kind of civic or lay religion, a sustaining creed for a nation in the throes of democratization. From this perspective, the pedagogical activities of Buisson and Pécaut are to be understood not as a full retreat from faith, but as so many endeavors under the name of laicity to disseminate to the nation as a whole what has been called "diluted Protestantism" *(protestantisme dilué)*.[4] The republic profited doubly from the confessional battles of midcentury. It inherited personnel practiced at institutional infighting and, perhaps more important, a religious-cum-pedagogical vision that grasped a fledgling democracy's need for an informing mystique.

The Consistory

The Protestant consistorial regime dated back to the First Empire.[5] By a decree of 1802 Napoleon sanctioned the creation of one local consistory for every 6,000 Protestant believers. Responsibility for consistory administration was divided between the local pastorate and a board of lay notables chosen by a propertied electorate. The narrow franchise skewed elections in favor of established elites. The Protestant consistory in Paris, like the Jewish central consistory, was dominated by a predictable mix of financial grandees and men of mark who had made reputations in the professions or in politics. At the time of the 1848 revolution, the Paris consistory included members of the André, Delessert, and Mallet banking families, who sat alongside France's most famous Protestant, the historian and political helmsman of the July Monarchy, François Guizot. As the names suggest, this was a select world, and an Orleanist one.

The Protestant and Jewish consistories, for all that they resembled one another in electoral constitution, social profile, and politics, did differ in two critical respects. The Reformed Church had no equivalent to the Jewish central consistory. Not that such an equivalent was lacking in Protestant tradition. Prior to the Napoleonic era, the Reformed Church had convened periodic national synods to settle disputes on doctrine and ecclesiastical organization, but under the new dispensation no provision was made for such events. Bible societies and pastoral conferences constituted the chief, almost sole, sites of interconsistorial exchange, but neither was invested with the necessary authority to resolve accumulating conflicts. A second point of difference: the Jewish elite was liberal in its religious convictions, but not so the Protestant.

In France, as elsewhere in Europe and North America in the first decades of the nineteenth century, Protestant communities had been "burned over" by a rekindling of religious zeal. *Le Réveil,* as the phenomenon was known, preached a return to the demanding orthodoxy of the Reformation fathers. The new orthodox thought of themselves as evangelicals. It is not that they were Bible-thumping proselytizers, as the term might suggest to some. Rather, they espoused a rigorous and fervent piety that defined itself in opposition to the relaxed, rationalist Protestantism of Enlightenment liberals, such as Pastor Athanase Coquerel père. Liberal Protestants had edged away from strict observance and interpretation of doctrine. Orthodox or, as they preferred to be called, evangelicals were determined to reverse course, and they found a ready hearing not just among humble churchgoers but in higher circles. The majority on the Paris consistory in 1848, including Ernest André, François Delessert, and Guizot, was evangelical in its theology, however liberal it might have been in its politics.[6]

But for all the disagreements between evangelicals and liberals, church politics in the 1850s remained calm. This is all the more surprising given the overhaul of the consistory's constitution in the wake of the 1851 coup. Louis-Napoleon's takeover was paralleled by what one historian has called an ecclesiastical coup d'état within the Reformed Church.[7] A decree of March 1852, drafted by Charles Read and promulgated by imperial authorities, reconstructed the consistorial regime from top to bottom. The new statute provided for the creation of a Paris-based Conseil Central, a quasi-central consistory, except that its members were in the majority appointed, not elected. When the imperial administration made its first nominations, it excluded by design the most prominent members of the old Orleanist notability. Such naked partisanship raised an outcry, and in the end the Conseil Central project had to be scrapped. More consequential was the administration's scheme to revamp church elections. The state now extended legal recognition to individual congregations, which were authorized to elect presbyteral councils. Each council delegated a lay representative to the local consistory, which recruited the balance of its membership from a variety of sources and by a variety of means. The scheme was innovative because it shifted the principal locus of electoral activity from the consistorial level down to the presbyteral council and, of yet greater importance, introduced the principle of universal suffrage.

In the short term, though, the shift to universal suffrage had little effect. In Paris, the presbyteral elections of the 1850s were quiet affairs. Only a minority of potential voters bothered to register. In 1852 less than 1,100 were inscribed on the rolls, a third of the levels achieved in the succeeding decade, and of those registered, well under half took the trouble to participate. But what was there to interest them? After a disappointing showing in the 1852 presbyteral elections, liberal Protestants decided to withdraw from the field. Evangelicals now ran uncontested, and voters, with no real choice to make, opted to stay home.[8] After a decade of universal suffrage, the evangelical faction's dominance in Paris church affairs had ripened into a virtual monopoly.

The imperial regime and liberal Protestants like Read struck a bargain in 1852. Both wanted to outflank or unseat the Reformed Church's notable elite—Bonaparte by way of an appointed central council, Read and others through democratic elections. As of 1860 that bargain proved a signal failure.

Schism

In 1874 *La Renaissance,* the major journal of the liberal Protestant camp, declared the Reformed Church to be in schism.[9] The relative calm of the 1850s had, in the space of little over a decade, given way to rupture and recriminations. How this happened can be explained partly in terms of the politicization of church affairs. Liberals in the 1860s organized into a party and behaved as such at election time. Evangelicals responded in kind, exploiting all the advantages of incumbency. In the 1870s both parties turned to the state, not just for a redress of grievances but for a resolution to the church's internal crisis. That the evangelical party found its staunchest backer in the regime of Moral Order and the liberal party in the republic after 16 May poisoned relations beyond hope of reconciliation. What had begun as a dispute about theology and church organization ended as a bitterly partisan contest for power, an affair of parties, elections, and state policy.

The 1850s may have been a decade of comparative political tranquillity for the Reformed Church, but on the spiritual front trouble was looming. Pastor Edouard Reuss at the Strasbourg faculty of theology introduced students to the findings of German higher criticism. One of Reuss's students, Timothée Colani, started up a review in 1850, the *Revue de Strasbourg,* to pursue in more detail the application of scientific methods to biblical scholarship. The enterprise attracted the participation of a band of young liberals: Théophile Bost, Michel Nicolas, Albert Réville, Edmond Schérer, and others. Colani's circle, the *jeune école* as it was sometimes called,[10] found a good ally in a sister periodical, the *Revue germanique,* founded in 1858 by Charles Dollfus and Auguste Nefftzer. Both were liberal Protestants and serious students of German theological debate, who collaborated on a revised, popular translation of D. F. Strauss's *Das Leben Jesu* (1864).[11]

For obvious reasons, the gathering wave of new critical scholarship rankled the evangelicals. Their creed sanctified the Bible as God's true word and celebrated in Jesus the divine redeemer who sacrificed himself and was resurrected so that humankind might be saved. But liberals now questioned the inerrancy of Scripture and worried about the veracity of Christ's miracles. The more extreme even cast doubt on the mysteries of the incarnation and resurrection. Paris' annexation of the old *banlieue* (suburbs) in 1860 provided evangelicals an occasion to vent their mounting indignation. Because of the annexation, the Paris presbyteral council had two new pulpits to fill. It shifted a center-city pastor, the liberal Auguste-Laurent Montandon, out to one of the new suburban slots, turned the other over to an evangelical, and filled Montandon's old post with a second evangelical. The reshuffling resulted in a net gain of two for the evangelical pastorate, and in the course of its deliberations the council passed over altogether the darling of the liberal camp, Athanase Coquerel fils, who had been stuck for over a decade as suffragan (assistant) to the ailing Pastor Martin-Paschoud.

Liberals, as might be expected, felt aggrieved and debated how best to respond. Jean-Jules Clamageran, a lawyer well connected among the liberal laity, urged self-organization. He helped to raise 25,000 francs and gathered a committee of eighteen; in January 1861 the formation of the Union Protestante Libérale (UPL) was announced. The UPL issued a series of circulars enumerating its complaints against the establishment and making plain its determination to contest the upcoming 1862 presbyteral elections. Six positions were scheduled to be filled that year. The union endorsed a trio of incumbents and advanced three new candidates of its own, Léon Say's name topping the list. The UPL slate was swept aside. Evangelical voters, the elections made clear, outnumbered liberals by a margin of two to one. But what was remarkable about the contest was not so much the outcome as the level of participation.

Over 1,500 voters cast ballots, three times the number in the elections of 1859.[12]

The UPL took encouragement from the 1862 elections and stepped up its activities. Liberals lobbied the church's Société Biblique to sanction distribution of a New Testament translation, known as the Geneva version. The text rendered with some ambiguity those passages that in the standard translations by Martin and Ostervald made clear reference to Christ's divinity. Evangelicals detected in the liberal faction's machinations a taint of Socinian heresy. Though a minority on the Société Biblique, they managed for some time, thanks to Guizot's exertions, to block dissemination of the new translation. The UPL entered the conflict at this juncture, taking upon itself the task of printing and distributing copies of the Geneva version. It was aided in the enterprise by the union's newly formed women's auxiliary, which, in addition to running a variety of charitable ventures, helped to circulate a cheap edition of the contested text.[13]

So many acts of defiance were galling to an evangelical majority used to having its own way. Worse still was the favorable publicity that UPL agitation stirred. The union, of course, ran its own newspaper, *Le Protestant libéral,* but the real press villain, from the evangelical point of view, was *Le Temps.* The paper's liberal partisanship is not hard to explain. Its founder, backers, and much of its staff were of liberal Protestant background. *Le Temps* was launched in 1861 by Nefftzer with monies collected from the great Alsatian textile clans such as the Dollfuses and the Koechlins. Schérer worked on the paper, specializing in political reportage. Responsibility for features was divided between Pastor Ernest Fontanès (a Clamageran confidant), Nicolas and Réville (with occasional help from Isidore Cahen and Frédéric Morin, the former a liberal Jew, the latter a lapsed Catholic).[14]

Liberals had sinned on three counts: they introduced into consistory affairs the agonistic practices of party politics; they dabbled in theological heresy; and they brought the church's private problems to public attention. Such nonconformity merited punishment, and it was not long in coming. In February 1864 the Paris presbyteral council, over the protests of Martin-Paschoud, voted not to renew Coquerel fils's suffraganship, in effect sacking him. The council report, read by Frédéric Mettetal, a division chief at the prefecture of police, lodged multiple charges against the young Coquerel.[15] First, he had shared his pulpit with such notorious theological extremists as Colani and Réville. Second, and no less grave, he had penned what was judged an overly generous review of Renan's *Vie de Jésus.* Evangelical Protestants, no less than Catholics, reviled the book. They dismissed Renan's aestheticized Jesus as little better than a fashionable Christ suited to amuse "a profane public on the steps of the temple" and no more.[16] But it was not just Coquerel's theological and critical failings that were at issue. As Jean Pédézert, editor of the evangelical periodical *L'Espérance,* recalled later: the presbyteral council may have struck the blow, but it was the UPL that forced its hand. Coquerel had aligned himself with that body, and for many evangelicals this constituted the young minister's most serious offense. Indeed, by hint and innuendo, liberals were made to understand that if they dissolved the UPL, Coquerel might yet hope to be reinstated.[17]

But the UPL did not back down, and the Paris presbyteral council pressed its assault against the liberal pastorate. In 1863 an ageing Coquerel père petitioned the council to appoint a suffragan. The council conceded the principle, but in the envenomed aftermath of the Coquerel fils affair rejected all the old man's nominees on doctrinal grounds. Martin-Paschoud was at the same time subjected to even more intensive harassment. He refused to give up on Coquerel fils, doggedly petitioning the presbyteral council for the young man's reinstatement. The council in January 1866 retaliated by attempting to force Martin-Paschoud into retirement. When Minister of Cults Baroche refused to authorize the maneuver, the council fired the unfortunate minister, saddling Baroche with the spiny decision of whether to accept the revocation. The final blow to the liberal pastorate came in 1868. Coquerel père, who had preached for decades at the Oratoire chapel in central Paris, died, and the question arose how to replace him. The presbyteral council selected an evangelical, Henri Paumier. It simultaneously created an additional tenured post at the Oratoire and also awarded that position to an evangelical.[18] By 1868, of the six pastors ministering to the three central parishes in Paris, all but one (Martin-Paschoud) belonged to the evangelical party.[19]

Liberals still found ways to make themselves heard. Denied access to the pulpit, they held public meetings. During Easter season of 1868, Coquerel fils, assisted by Auguste Dide and Charles Grawitz, conducted services in lecture halls rented at UPL expense. A series of public conferences was organized at the same time, which attracted the participation of the more controversial liberal Protestant polemicists of the day: Clamageran, Pécaut, Steeg, and Coquerel fils himself.[20] But it was council elections, more than the sermon or public conference, that afforded liberals the opportunity to demonstrate their presence, indeed, their growing strength. In Paris the campaigns of 1865, 1868, and 1872 turned out to be spectacular confrontations that riveted the attention not only of Protestants but of state officialdom and the cultivated public at large.

In the aftermath of the 1862 elections, the UPL embarked on an intensive voter-registration drive. In 1864 alone, 1,200 new names were inscribed on the rolls.[21] Standard registration practice required voters to sign up in person and to show proof at the time of Protestant affiliation. Liberals wanted to relax procedures and, in particular, favored registration by mail. Paul Broca, who had been married by a pastor from the Coquerel family, made several unsuccessful attempts to post his registration. He attended a UPL meeting to explain his situation and forwarded to Baroche a private note on the matter, which Coquerel fils's paper *Le Lien* later made public.[22] The agitation prompted the presbyteral council to preemptive action. In July 1864 it issued a set of electoral guidelines, which did not only maintain existing policy but made registration more difficult. Would-be voters were now required to appear alone and in private before the parish electoral bureau and to answer inquiries about church attendance. Imperial officialdom, after long deliberation, decided not to obstruct application of the new rules.

Liberals howled in protest. *Le Temps, L'Opinion nationale,* and *Le Siècle* weighed in on the liberal side,[23] and the elections became a minor cause célèbre. Turnout was higher than ever before. Of the 3,000 voters registered, 2,630 cast ballots. The liberals, running a full slate of six candidates, did not win a single seat, but for the first time in recent memory an evangelical candidate failed to win an absolute majority in the first round and was forced into a runoff. The identity of the failed candidate, François Guizot, was an added source of satisfaction to liberals. Guizot did win in the second round, but by a mere ten votes, 1,298 to 1,288, and against a candidate who was comparatively unknown, the ironmaster Henri Barbezat. To Pédézert, such an outcome represented less a success than a humiliation.[24]

The year 1868 was in most respects a replay of 1865 but with more disappointing results for liberals. The UPL amassed a huge campaign fund, an estimated 100,000 francs, from which it met the expenses of an electoral agent and four subagents. The registration drive continued, pumping up the number of registered voters to over 3,600. A half-dozen leading lights of the Paris business world—including Charles-Frédéric Dietz-Monnin, Jean-Jules Dubochet, and Jules Koechlin—signed on to the liberal campaign, publishing an endorsement of the UPL slate. But in the actual balloting, the union ticket did not fare well. Its strongest candidate, retired businessman Charles Fabre, garnered 1,467 votes to 1,596 for the leading evangelical, Delessert. Some solace was taken in the geographical distribution of votes. In the core parishes of the Oratoire, Penthemont, and Sainte-Marie, Fabre outpolled Delessert by a margin of 211. It was the overwhelming evangelical vote in the newly annexed outer parishes which tipped the balance the other way.[25] Liberals consoled themselves that at least the heart of Protestant Paris belonged to them.

The elections of 1872 raised hopes that, with patience, the majority might come around too. Circumstances were not propitious for the UPL. The disruptions of *l'année terrible* had caused the number of registered voters to fall off, down to just over 3,000. Actual voter turnout dropped from 85 percent in 1868 to 70 percent in 1872. But the UPL had assembled a strong list of candidates, a mix of veterans like Clamageran, Fabre, and Georges Wickham and well-known newcomers like Dietz-Monnin and Colonel Denfert-Rochereau, the hero of the siege of Belfort. This time, two evangelicals failed to win first-round majorities, a certain Girod and, once again, Guizot. The presbyteral council invalidated eleven ballots written on unofficial paper, which enabled Girod to make it through without a runoff. As for Guizot, he squeaked by in the second round with a thirty-vote margin.[26] Liberals believed themselves in a position to win at least one council spot in the next election, but before the opportunity presented itself, a massive state intervention in church affairs shifted the balance of power decisively to the evangelical side.

Evangelicals had for a number of years advocated the convocation of a national synod to settle the Reformed Church's political crisis. Only a synod had the authority to speak on doctrinal matters, to formulate a profession of faith that, however minimal, might oblige dissidents to conform or leave the church. The evangelical party got its way thanks to critical shifts in government personnel. Emile Ollivier became prime minister in January 1870; he reserved for himself the portfolio of the ministry of justice and cults, the post Baroche had once occupied; in April, Guizot's son Guillaume received an appointment to the post of assistant director of non-Catholic cults. The new team granted the evangelical request for a synod, but the outbreak of war adjourned the matter sine die. No sooner had peace been restored than Guizot père renewed evangelical entreaties for a synod. In November 1871 Thiers, "as a favor to M. Guizot," gave the go-ahead, and the following year a national synod was at last convened.[27] The assembly owed its existence to the combined efforts of Ollivier, the Guizots, and Thiers. As attested by the names of its patrons, partisans all of constitutional liberalism, the synod was meant to signal a return to parliamentary practice in church affairs.

But liberal Protestants had ample reason to find fault with the new parliamentarism. As partisans of direct, universal suffrage, they objected first to the many-tiered procedure by which synod representatives were chosen.[28] Sitting consistories were asked to elect a delegation the size of which varied not with the number of congregants but with the number of local pastors. Consistory delegations then met in regional assemblies, and it was here that the actual selection of synod representatives was made. Such a scheme guaranteed evangelicals, who controlled most consistory boards, an eventual majority at the synod itself.[29] Liberals were even more distressed by how that majority conducted itself. The 1872 synod voted to apply more stringent religious qualifications to the presbyteral electorate. When implemented in Paris, for example, the measure resulted in a near halving of the number of registered voters.[30] But most upsetting of all was the evangelical majority's decision by a 61 to 45 margin to impose a declaration of faith. The new confession proclaimed "the sovereign authority of Holy Scripture in matters of faith" and reaffirmed received dogma on Christ's divinity, the resurrection, and so on. The synod did not insist that the existing pastoral corps subscribe to the declaration, but it did make such a requirement of all future ministers.[31] And to enforce its will, the synodal majority appealed to the state for help.

Thiers' government fell in May 1873, and the regime of Moral Order that succeeded it proved amenable to evangelical lobbying. The 1872 synod had set up a permanent commission chaired by Mettetal to oversee execution of its resolutions. In November 1873 the commission solicited the Broglie administration's consent to a second meeting of the synod. The consent was given; liberals refused to participate; a synodal rump parliament met just the same and went on to petition civil authorities to issue an official promulgation of the decisions taken the preceding year. In February 1874 Broglie promulgated the Reformed Church's new declaration of faith. In presbyteral elections that spring, Minister Cumont intervened to invalidate all elections not conducted in conformity with the new regulations. It was liberal elections, of course, that were invalidated, leaving few doubts that evangelicals and the regime of Moral Order had struck up a partnership. That the minister of the interior at the time was François de Chabaud-Latour, the evangelical third in command after Guizot père and Mettetal, did little to dispel the liberals' suspicions.[32]

But recourse to state sanction was a double-edged sword. With the passing of the regime of Moral Order and the advent of *la République républicaine*, state intervention in Protestant affairs took a new turn. After the Franco-Prussian war, the Strasbourg faculty of theology was moved to Paris. Two new professors, both liberals, were named to the faculty in 1879 by Minister of Public Instruction Jules Ferry. In mid-1880 a Conseil d'Etat purged of antirepublican elements spoke against further application of the electoral regulations of 1872. And in 1882 the Freycinet cabinet decreed a measure long demanded by liberals: the breakup of the Paris church into multiple parishes each empowered to elect its own council. At the next presbyteral elections, held later in the year, liberals won control in the Oratoire. In a matter of months, the parish appointed its first liberal clergyman in more than a decade, Ariste Viguié.[33]

The republic's liberal tilt unsettled evangelicals. In 1879 and again in 1881, they convened synods at which plans to formalize the split in the Reformed Church were discussed. The liberal camp organized a national assembly of its own in 1882, which made a final and failed effort at reconciliation.[34] In the 1850s, the terms liberal and evangelical had described contesting currents of opinion within the Reformed Church. Under the Second Empire, that clash of opinion had hardened into partisan warfare, and by 1882 partisan warfare, superheated by repeated blasts of state intervention, had erupted into schism.

Protestants and Politics

It may well have been serendipity that successive governments of Moral Order took the part of the evangelical party. But that republican administrations were drawn to the liberal side cannot be chalked up to personality or accident. Liberal Protestants were engaged in an institutional battle conducted along parallel lines to the institutional battles waged by dissident Masons, the UNCI, and the AIU. The same techniques were employed—voter registration, electioneering, printed propaganda—and the same rhetoric too. In the case of the liberal Protestant, no less than in those of the radical Mason, the Sentier businessman, and the Alliance Jew, that rhetoric came out with a distinct republican inflection, and for good reason. Liberal Protestants were more often than not republicans themselves, acolytes of republican associational life and republican electoral politics.

From the outset, liberals denounced the evangelical party as "a retrograde oligarchy."[35] The accusation had particular bite in Paris where a handful of families, such as the Andrés and the Delesserts, seemed to have a stranglehold on church administration. Positions on the presbyteral council, it was claimed, were passed on from generation to generation. Alfred André succeeded his uncle Ernest upon the latter's death. "It's the law of heredity," commented *Le Protestant libéral* snidely, "guardian of aristocracies."[36] And these various dynasties were often interrelated, Mettetal to Guizot, council member Henri de Triqueti to the Delesserts. The Paris church, insinuated the UPL, had become "infeudated" to "a sort of hereditary peerage."[37] As for the liberals, they styled themselves a party of the middle, squeezed between the "orthodox oligarchy of the eighth arrondissement" and the "little churches of the *banlieue*."[38] The UPL fielded candidates like Say, Fabre, and Barbezat who had made a mark in business. It was run by lawyers like Clamageran or *propriétaires* like Wickham. The social cut of the union's electoral constituency was more modest but still distinctly middle-class. Pédézert summed up the results of the 1868 council elections in these terms: "The workers and haute bourgeoisie for the evangelicals; petty commerce and the middling bourgeoisie for the liberals."[39]

But liberal militants wanted to believe that the two parties represented not just distinct milieux but opposed sets of principles. The evangelicals, whom liberals always preferred to label orthodox, were castigated as would-be papists. A UPL circular in 1865 exhorted electors to vote against "these men who set themselves up as infallible arbiters of religion and of salvation." Dide inveighed against the Paris presbyteral council as a bastion of "infallible orthodoxy." Delessert was derided as "our pope" and Guizot likened to a Protestant Veuillot: "he should go to Rome . . . to kiss the Pope's slippers!" wrote an embittered Clamageran in 1861. "He is worthy of the privilege."[40]

Such name calling was reciprocated by evangelicals, who tarred liberals as extremists and freethinkers.[41] Freethinkers some of them may have been, but liberals preferred to conceive of themselves not as fervent radicals but as partisans of "freedom of conscience."[42] When in 1867 *Le Siècle* opened a subscription drive to erect a statue in Voltaire's honor, liberals endorsed the enterprise wholeheartedly. The statue would stand, asserted Dide, "as a lesson in tolerance." Coquerel fils served on the fundraising committee, alongside of Quinet, Crémieux, and Sainte-Beuve. Evangelicals, on the other hand, did not approve of the Voltaire memorial, an attitude that liberals were quick to publicize. *Le Protestant libéral* reported that evangelical Pastor Louis Rognon, chaplain at the Lycée Louis-le-Grand, had attacked Voltaire from the pulpit. The student congregation, the paper went on, had replied with murmurs of protest and, proof positive of evangelical intolerance, were punished for insubordination.[43]

The future of the church, claimed liberals, lay not with such a close-minded orthodoxy but with a "public opinion duly instructed." The UPL believed itself to be the mouthpiece for that Protestant public, a public much abused, at least in Paris, by a presbyteral council that kept its proceedings secret, tinkered with voting qualifications, and imposed pastors of orthodox views on liberal congregations. An offended citizenry cried out to be heard, and the UPL responded to the call. "Liberty, publicity, light, that is what we demand," intoned a union brochure published in the midst of the Coquerel fils imbroglio.[44] But the UPL fancied itself more than just a simple transmitter of opinion; it aspired to be an agent of enlightenment. And there was no more efficacious means to educate opinion, to work a revolution of souls, than through "the action of the book." The UPL organized the Société des Publications Religieuses Populaires in 1868, characterized by Dide as "a kind of intellectual cooperative society," a religious Ligue de l'Enseignement. In its first year, the society turned out a bargain edition of Steeg's *Lectures bibliques* and discussed the future publication of titles by Buisson, Coquerel fils, and Réville.[45]

The liberal camp conceived its conflict with the evangelicals as a series of oppositions: privileged aristocracy versus enlightened middle, infallibilist orthodoxy against freedom of conscience, and so on. Implicit in such pairings was a political accusation: that evangelicals constituted an authoritarian oligarchy stubbornly hostile to democratic government. Nor did the accusation always remain implicit. Despotism, absolutism, tyranny, no epithet was too strong to blacken the political character of the evangelical majority. In public life Guizot had opposed universal suffrage. Was it any wonder that he brought the same high-handed attitudes to ecclesiastical politics?[46] Mettetal had helped to organize Louis-Napoleon's coup d'état in 1851. It could be no surprise, with such leadership, that the evangelical party played fast and loose at election time, that the presbyteral council, like the Bonapartist regime, designated "official candidates."[47] At the fall of the empire, Coquerel fils expected evangelical rule to fall with it. "In reality," he wrote to Martin-Paschoud in October 1870, "the two are the same: same ways of proceeding, same usurpation of legitimate right, same scorn for the law."[48]

Evangelical dominance, however, did not end, nor did the evangelical party ever mend its imperial ways. In 1871 a report circulated that the Paris presbyteral council was contemplating imposition of a profession of faith on prospective voters. The liberal press, playing on anti-Bonapartist sentiment in liberal ranks, condemned the maneuver as "a veritable coup d'état, an ecclesiastical 2nd of December."[49] The same rhetorical tack was taken in response to evangelical efforts to arrange state promulgation of the synod rulings of 1872. As France had been not long ago, so today, declared Coquerel's newspaper, was the Reformed Church governed by an "administration *à poigne.*"[50] The subsequent rapprochement between evangelicals and the regime of Moral Order drove liberals to a fresh outburst of vituperation. Wasn't such an "edifying alliance" all too fitting? Didn't "the orthodox and the men of moral order" share a common commitment to authoritarian rule and religious obscurantism? The "clerical party" that now reigned in public affairs had found a most suitable partner in "the extreme right of Protestant orthodoxy."[51]

Liberals time and again conflated "orthodoxy" and the political right, indicting the evangelical party for importing Bonapartist practices and clericalist intolerance into Protestant affairs. By the same token, liberals liked to think of themselves as true sons of democracy. Catholicism, wrote Réville in *Le Protestant libéral,* was monarchical in its constitution but not so the Protestant Church founded, as it was on the principle of popular sovereignty.[52] "Scripture," declared Coquerel père in lapidary tones, "is profoundly republican." The first Christians had all been democrats, but only Protestants remained true to Christianity's original spirit.[53] They could never cringe in humility. As Réville put it, "the Protestant maintains a certain pride and dignity before all men . . . there is never an abdication of self."[54]

Such uprightness expressed itself in the believer's deportment in church. Congregants bowed to no man, clerical or lay; they prayed standing and addressed God with a loving *Tu*; and, as good citizens of a free country, they felt it a sacred duty to take part as equals in church governance. The body of the faithful in effect constituted a species of minirepublic, a religious democracy.[55]

But Protestant democracy, like all democracies, was susceptible to corruption from within. A slaveholding caste, remarked *Le Protestant libéral,* had propelled the American republic into civil war; so in France, an orthodox clique sowed fratricidal hatred in the Reformed Church.[56] But that clique, it was believed, might be dislodged before hatred actually turned into schism. Liberals pinned hopes on a frank and loyal application of the principle of universal suffrage.[57] They had from time to time despaired of the Protestant public, complaining of its indifference and pliability. But in the 1860s, as voters registered in unprecedented number and rates of participation shot up, doubts about the efficacy of the ballot gave way to enthusiasm. Through the vote, one of the UPL's first manifestoes declared, "fraternal union, a free faith, and the rights of all" might yet prevail. At decade's end, encouraged by near successes in council elections, buoyed by "the rising tide of religious democracy," the liberal party had made itself into a party of universal suffrage.[58]

Liberals had a clear sense of where the battle lines in the Reformed Church were drawn. On the one side stood an aggrieved public composed of enlightened middle-class democrats; arrayed against them was a coterie of aristocratic dynasts, dogmatic in their thinking and authoritarian in their politics. The republican bias of such a reading is evident. Why liberals harbored such a bias admits of a simple explanation: almost without exception, the leading personalities in the liberal camp were already republicans, a leavening presence in the burgeoning associational life of the republican revival.

Dynastic government, Coquerel fils wrote in the midst of the siege of Paris, only leads to war. But he saw a new era of peace and progress on the horizon, a France reborn, a republican France without conscription or standing armies.[59] Such a pacifism fueled liberal Protestant interest both in the international peace movement and, during the Commune, in the cause of conciliation. In the empire's closing years, Buisson of course but also Clamageran and Dide worked in the ranks of the Ligue de la Paix.[60] In 1871 the Coquerel family newspaper *La Renaissance* was among a handful to extend public support to the conciliationist efforts of the Ligue d'Union Républicaine. In the Commune's aftermath, brandishing the slogan "JUSTICE, NO RE-ACTION," the paper in vain exhorted the victorious Versaillais to restraint.[61]

In the repertory of midcentury republican causes, peace and con-ciliation figured as but one ingredient in a rich mix that included masonic fraternalism and popular education. And so it was with liberal Protestantism. It is not that liberal Protestants played a domi-nant role in masonic reform, but they did occupy within the move-ment some positions of strategic importance. The ubiquitous Clamageran, as we have seen, was a sometime venerable at one of the leading activist lodges, L'Ecole Mutuelle. Nefftzer belonged to Mas-sol's Renaissance par les Emules d'Hiram and was said to employ several brothers on the staff of Le Temps.[62] And it was liberal Protes-tant Pastor Frédéric Desmons who in 1877 proposed striking the deistic invocation from article 1 of the Grand Orient's constitution. Desmons did not belong to the UPL, but he did deliver the closing prayer at the organization's third annual assembly in 1867, and he attended the synod of 1872 as an alternate in a Nîmes delegation led by Coquerel fils.[63]

Protestants are known as the people of the book. Add to this liberal Protestantism's special preoccupation with molding an en-lightened public, and it will come as no surprise to encounter so many liberals in the vanguard of the education movement. Georges Wickham was treasurer of the Ligue de l'Enseignement's Paris circle. Clamageran belonged as well, and at least three women of liberal views can be identified in the ranks of the circle's Comité des Dames: one-time Fourierist, Clarisse Coignet, Mme. Paul Broca, and Mme. Jules Siegfried.[64] The Société Franklin, a driving force behind the public library movement, was founded in 1862 by what one source has described as "republicans, often Protestants." The society was in fact more a liberal than a republican enterprise (its president in 1870 was the liberal Bonapartist Marquis de Chasseloup-Laubat), but it did in fact count a sizeable Protestant contingent: Fernand Schickler, UPL candidate in the 1868 presbyteral elections; Jean Dollfus, brother of Charles and a major source of the society's initial funding; and Thierry-Mieg, himself an early and important con-tributor who was related to the Dollfus family by marriage.[65] Mid-century republicans made a specialty of churning out inexpensive editions of texts—classics, scientific primers, and the like—which were intended for the edification of a general reading public. One such enterprise, the *Bibliothèque démocratique*, specialized in reprinting tracts and speeches from the 1789 revolution. In the 1870s, Coquerel fils, already on record as a partisan of "a lay and broadly liberal education," joined the society's roster of patrons, which included the cream of republican society: Gambetta, Michelet, Quinet, and the rest.[66]

It is difficult not to understand the liberal Protestant insurgency of midcentury, given the republican accents of its rhetoric, given its connections to the leagues and lodges that structured republican associational life, as part of an encompassing republican revival. That most Protestant activists can be identified as committed republicans would seem to clinch the argument. Take the case of the Coquerels, the first family of liberal Protestantism. Coquerel père was an 1848 veteran, a Cavaignac republican of distinctly nonrevolutionary views. Of the son Etienne's politics, little can be said with precision except that he was, as the *Le Temps* obituary put it, "attached since childhood to the Republic." Athanase Coquerel fils, like his father, was a moderate republican but not quite so temperate. He ran for the National Assembly in 1871 on the so-called Comité Turbigo list, which featured solid republican party stalwarts like Barni, Broca, and Havard. At the same time, Coquerel's *La Renaissance* regretted that Gambetta was not also on the ticket, and this at a moment when Gambetta's name still conjured up images of firebrand radicalism.[67]

Nor were the Coquerels exceptional among liberal Protestants in their republican convictions. Denfert-Rochereau was elected to the National Assembly in 1871 as a radical and might have gone on to a successful political career had he not died so young. The cases of Clamageran, a future minister in the Brisson cabinet of 1885, and of Broca, a future senator of Gambettist persuasion, have been discussed in preceding chapters. But Buisson's lifetime accomplishment needs fuller mention. The two decades he spent as the Third Republic's director of primary education was only the beginning of a remarkable career, which included seventeen years of service as a Radical deputy, shorter stints first as president of the Ligue des Droits de l'Homme and then as president of the Ligue de l'Enseignement, and eventual award in 1924 of the Nobel Peace Prize. Buisson was by no means the sole liberal Protestant activist connected to the Ligue des Droits de l'Homme. Clamageran, as we have seen, was a charter member.[68] So too was Charles Seignobos, a Protestant of *echt* liberal pedigree, better remembered as a historian of the Third Republic and professor of positivist historical methodology at the "new Sorbonne." Seignobos' father, Charles-André, had played a minor role in the Reformed Church's institutional battles, attending the synod of 1872 as an alternate member of the liberal delegation.[69]

The republic had supporters as well among the businessmen who played such a large role in the Protestant insurgency. Elections were held in the fall of 1877 in the midst of the 16 May crisis. A huge contribution from Dubochet, himself a former carbonaro, helped to finance the republicans' successful campaign.[70] In the election aftermath, it may be remembered, UNCI militants organized a petition urging President MacMahon to appoint a prime minister acceptable to the republican majority. A meeting of 1,800 businessmen gathered at the Salle Frascati in December to acclaim the petition. Dietz-Monnin spoke, pleading with MacMahon to give in. The assembly then nominated a small delegation, including representatives from liberal Protestant firms such as Koechlin and Dollfus, Mieg, to pay a visit to the Elysée. Dietz-Monnin was elected to the National Assembly in 1871 as a moderate republican. Jules Koechlin was well known to the police as a close associate of Charles Floquet's. After the defeat of the 16 May coup, republicans in increasing number acceded to positions of authority. The advent of the Waddington administration in 1879 constituted a critical turning point in the process. Waddington's cabinet included Ferry, serving his first tenure at the ministry of public instruction, as well five Protestants, among them at least one liberal veteran, Léon Say.[71]

The liberal pastorate also fed its share of recruits into republican activism. Colani eventually left the ministry and, in the 1870s, joined the staff of Gambetta's *La République française.*[72] Desmons abandoned the pastorate in 1881 en route to a career in politics, entering the Chamber of Deputies in the 1880s, where he took up a seat on the radical benches alongside Clemenceau and Camille Pelletan. Dide boasted a political past that stretched back at least to 1858, when he had served a prison term for republican agitation. He spent much of the 1860s in exile and, on return to France, pursued a double career in scholarship as editor of the review *La Révolution française* and in politics as senator from the Gard.[73] Pécaut and Steeg, as we have seen, became senior officials in the republic's educational establishment. As for Réville, he renounced theological speculation in favor of a scientific approach to religious questions. Such a secularizing itinerary endeared him to freethinkers and to the republican regime, which created a special chair for him at the Collège de France in the history of religions.[74]

To liberals, theology and politics did not occupy distinct compartments. The fight against the evangelical party may not have begun as a republican fight, but it became one. Liberal Protestants over the course of two decades became skilled in the ways and idiom of democratic electoral politics. But more: they came to value the underlying principles of democratic practice—associational activism, publicity, electoral participation. For liberals at least, the Reformed Church's internal battles provided good experience, training them to public life in a democratizing France. Little wonder that, when at last the ecclesiastical battle seemed lost, so many graduated from church politics into republican public service, whether as parliamentarians, educational administrators, or university officials. But it was not only personnel that the republic inherited from liberal Protestantism.

Laicity

The idea of laicity, what Buisson called *la foi laïque,* had many sources, but liberal Protestants played a disproportionately large part in its codification and dissemination. What I will suggest here in fact is that laicity—a blend of rationalism, moral purposefulness, and humanitarian vision—was a form of secularized Protestantism. The men and women who made the transition from church to republican politics brought with them into public life a quasi-religious vision that left an enduring mark above all on the republic's pedagogical system.

Liberal Protestants had little doubt of the connection between a vital Protestant faith and the institutionalization of democracy in public life. The American republic, Etienne Coquerel pointed out to readers of *Le Lien,* owed its peculiar strength to "the Protestant faith of its founders."[75] Clamageran, as a UPL militant, wanted to liberalize the church, but as a republican he dreamed of making France free, of "founding liberty through Protestantism."[76] Such sentiments were widespread in republican circles and not only among Protestants. Edgar Quinet, though baptized a Catholic, flirted with Unitarianism. His monumental *La Révolution* (1865) may be seen as a critique of the revolution from a Protestant point of view. France in 1789 failed to break with Catholicism, to complete the spiritual renewal begun in the Reformation. That failure fed the forces of counterrevolution; the men of 1789, without a proper moral compass to guide them, fell back into the old ways, resorting to terror to silence their enemies, plunging France into decades of self-rending war and civil war. The message in Quinet's text was clear: a democratic France required a democratic faith to sustain it, and the source of that faith was found in Protestantism.[77] The Kantian philosopher Charles Renouvier came to a similar position, starting a periodical in 1879, *Critique religieuse,* in which he extolled the civic virtues of Protestant belief.[78]

Then there is the case of Jules Ferry, himself a freethinker but married to a Protestant. To him, Protestantism was "a friendly power, a necessary ally,"[79] and he acted on that presumption. As minister of public instruction, it was he who oversaw the first influx of Protestants—Buisson and Pécaut among them—into the Third Republic's pedagogical establishment. Nor were Buisson and Pécaut isolated cases. The director of the Ecole Normale de Sèvres, after Fontenay-aux-Roses the principal teachers' training college for women, was Mme. Jules Favre, daughter of a Protestant minister. Protestant women, indeed, distinguished themselves in the service of the new *école laïque* in a variety of capacities: as propagandists (Clarisse Coignet, Mme. Henry Gréville), school inspectors (Pauline Kergomard, née Reclus), and school administrators. At the turn of the century, a full quarter of all the principals of public secondary schools for girls were of Protestant origin.[80]

The republic turned to Protestantism as a source of democratic inspiration. What the regime got in return was a distinctive program that enjoined instruction in *la morale* understood as "obedience to God's laws as revealed by conscience and reason."[81] Such a vision, religious but not explicitly Christian, has been characterized as a form of religious freethinking; Buisson called it religious laicity.[82] But what do such oxymorons mean? A quick review of the position staked out by liberal Protestants in the theological debates of mid-century will provide a clue.

Liberal Protestants saw themselves engaged in a grand project of conciliation. They were heirs to a sacred patrimony—Scripture, the teachings and example of Christ—but they were at the same time men of the nineteenth century, who believed in reason and "the imperishable rights of science and conscience."[83] Liberals wanted to rethink Christianity, to reconcile faith and scientific modernity. This was no simple task. The natural sciences had demonstrated that, in

Pécaut's words, "the unchanging order of nature" was "incompatible with miracles." No reasonable person still believed that Joshua's trumpet brought down the walls of Jericho or that, as taught in the Apostle's Creed, Christ had descended to hell just prior to his resurrection.[84] And in the face of the new biblical scholarship, what thinking person still accepted the literal truth of Scripture? It was all too evident that the Bible had been authored not by God but by men who, like the apostle John, were not always reliable witnesses.[85] Conscience also had a quarrel to pick with Scripture. The Old Testament contained scenes of savagery and massacre revolting to Christians of tender heart. Was it credible that a merciful God ordained or condoned such barbarism?[86]

The inerrancy of Scripture melted away before the corrosive fires of reason and conscience. Graver still, so did the hard rock of dogma. Once science had driven the miraculous from the temple of faith, what room remained for the supernatural, for a god-man who had died to expiate humanity's sins, for a heavenly father who reigned in the skies above? The hardier souls in the liberal camp pushed such questioning to the limit. Pécaut abandoned belief in Christ's divinity altogether. Réville, unable to accept the supernatural but unwilling to foreswear the divine, took a pantheist turn, interpreting God as a presiding spirit, an immanence in all things. Not all liberals, of course, went to extremes, not Coquerel fils, for example, who maintained an enduring faith in the existence of a divine order. Nor should we think that liberals who made the break with received dogma did so with light hearts. Elise de Pressensé, wife of the evangelical pastor Edmond de Pressensé, came to doubt Christ's resurrection. Did a loving God, she reflected, require a blood sacrifice to persuade Him to forgive a repentant humanity? Pressensé's probing took place over a decade of spiritual struggle marked by self-doubt and loneliness. "How difficult it is," she confided in her diary in 1857, "to be sincere."[87] But whether the doubter's intentions were sincere or not, the result was the same: the sharp edges of critical intellect cut a wide swath through the inherited truths of Christianity. Even so, faith itself was not destroyed.

Liberals remained believers, if not in the mysteries of dogma, then at least in the abiding human aspiration toward a "perfect, living, conscious Infinite."[88] That aspiration, that religious sentiment whispering of the divine, was the surest guide to genuine religiosity. True piety lay not in obedience to ritual formulas but in attuning the inward ear to the "quivering of the soul beneath the divine breath." A searching plunge into the self revealed God's presence; and it revealed God's law too, imprinted on the conscience of every man and woman. The believer had but to listen to hear the voice of right conduct and, most wondrous of all, that voice spoke with such authority that reason could only bow its head in assent. An active intelligence was not the enemy of faith but its complement, ratifying by light of reason truths that welled up from the depths of the well-tempered soul.[89]

Liberals acknowledged the difficulties of self-searching, but Christians were doubly blessed in that they had two helpmates—Scripture and Christ—to illuminate the path. Not every word of the Bible was true, but when pondered in silence, the book's "astonishing religious power" imposed itself on every sincere spirit, on every sensible heart. God was present in the whole, in the Gospels above all, which could waken the stirring soul and enlighten the conscience.[90] Christ's life, indeed, was the surest guide to conscientious action. The figure cherished by liberals, of course, was not the so-called metaphysical Jesus of theological imagining, but the living, human Jesus who brought word of a loving God and who set the standard of human possibility. "La morale existe" trumpeted *Le Protestant libéral*—"it shows itself to us in the features of the martyr of Golgotha."[91] Learned commentary was superfluous to the genuine Christian, who had only to look and listen to understand Christ's message of moral progress and brotherly love.[92]

As that message spread from conscience to conscience, binding souls in loving communion, mankind approached the promised land of what Coignet called "universal liberation, the reconstruction of a *single* humanity in *Christ* and in *God*." An informing providence directed mankind's wanderings, bringing it step by step closer, elevating it progressively in liberty and union, "toward the higher spheres of a superior harmony."[93] Great spiritual revolutions there had been along the way—the Reformation, 1789—and humanity now stood once again at the crossroads, tempted on the one side by a decadent materialism and on the other by orthodoxies, Protestant and Cousinist, which had aligned themselves with the authoritarian status quo.[94]

Discerning the true path was hard indeed, but liberals took comfort that they were not alone on the road. Looking across the Atlantic to the United States, they discovered welcome fellow travelers among

Unitarians and abolitionists. Unitarian minister William Ellery Channing was a particular favorite of the French. Edouard Laboulaye, Channing's French translator, frequented the Coquerel fils salon. So too did Eugène Pelletan, who celebrated the Boston pastor as "the greatest Christian man of our time." American Unitarians returned the favor. When Athanase Coquerel fils died in 1875, he was eulogized in Unitarian services at Newport as "a Channing among the French."[95] And French liberals were also fervently against slavery. Etienne Coquerel welcomed Lincoln's election as a coup, and his circle of friends included Charles Sumner, one of the Republican Party's staunchest abolitionists. After the American civil war, Laboulaye formed a committee to funnel French contributions to American relief efforts for ex-slaves. Elise de Pressensé chaired the committee's women's auxiliary, and Clarisse Coignet served as secretary.[96]

The theological debates of midcentury drove liberal Protestants in the direction of a faith with a unitarian cast. Humankind yearned for the transcendent, and God was immanent in the human soul and in human history. Sincere Christians had only to read the Bible with an open heart to know the good. They had only to examine the course of history to detect the providential mainspring driving humanity toward fraternal union. There was nothing in such a creed, liberal Protestants believed, incompatible with reason's dictates or the findings of modern science.

The distance separating this position from the lay ideal was not too great. It was necessary only to tone down the Christian content, reducing Christ to one great man among many and the Bible to an inspired melange of legend, poetry, and moral uplift. The turn to laicity did not represent a dramatic break with Protestant belief, but its reworking into a civic creed. The result was a lay religion that might lack the metaphysical ballast craved by mystics or traditionalists, but it was suitable for citizens in the making who came from a variety of religious backgrounds.

A new regime, whatever its coloration, inevitably confronts problems of staffing, of where to find loyal bodies to run the institutions of state. The Third Republic, in the field of education above all, turned to liberal Protestants, who responded with alacrity to the call. The choice was an apt one. Republican sentiment ran strong in liberal Protestant circles. And liberals had evolved a modern faith that, while acknowledging the claims of science, placed primary stress on moral action and human brotherhood. With a little tinkering, such a creed might be applied to the fashioning of a conscientious and public-spirited citizenry.

What I have tried to show here is not only why the Republic took an interest in liberal Protestantism, but why liberal Protestants came to have such an investment in the republic and the lay ideal. Those commitments evolved in large measure out of conflicts, institutional and theological, within the Reformed Church. Liberals, in the heat of battle, worked slowly toward what they believed to be a democratic ecclesiology and a unitarian faith that could tolerate both the questioning intellect and transcendental aspiration. The final step from church politics to republican politics, from unitarian faith to *la foi laïque,* was an easy one.

The point is not whether those liberals who traveled the full distance ceased to be Protestants. Some remained faithful, others abandoned the church altogether. But churchgoing or not, liberals who entered the republic's service carried with them a vestige of the faith they were born in, and often much more. From such materials was the republic's lay mystique constructed. That mystique sustained the regime through its first uncertain years and, once institutionalized in the educational system, enabled it to replicate itself across generations.

[6]

The Republic
of Lawyers

THE CRITICAL ROLE played by lawyers in the public life of the Third Republic is well known. The regime has been dubbed "la république des avocats," and for good reason. Under the Second Empire, lawyers represented less than a fifth of the membership of the Corps Législatif. In the assemblies of the Third Republic, that percentage shot up to a full third. But some caveats are in order. First, lawyerly influence did not exert itself evenly across the republic's history. In the regime's first years, landlords and senior civil servants retained a grip not only on positions of bureaucratic power but also on elected offices. The great age of the lawyer-turned-deputy did not begin until after 1877. It lasted throughout the republic, but with a falling off after World War I as schoolteachers in increasing numbers entered the Chamber of Deputies. It was the period 1877–1914 that constituted the heyday of the lawyers' republic. This republic, moreover, had a distinct political coloration. The typical jurist in parliament avoided extremes and affiliated himself with the governing party. In 1881 some 45 percent of Ferry's Gauche Républicaine and 52 percent of Gambetta's Union Républicaine were recruited from the legal profession. It is little wonder that lawyers figured so prominently in ministerial ranks, accounting for over one minister in three between 1877 and the outbreak of the world war.[1]

The generation of lawyers who acceded to power after 1877 had reached maturity under the empire and, as they came of age, worked out for themselves a distinct political identity. They were republicans and, as such, were locked in battle with an imperial regime that had closed down public life and snuffed out political liberty. They were also young men in a hurry, fretting under the mentorship of a senior cohort of jurists who dominated both the bar and republican politics. These were not, of course, conflicts of equal intensity. The young reviled the empire but were only impatient with the old men, with Alexandre Marie or Jules Favre, who spoke in the romantic, high-falutin tones of a bygone age, who were burdened with memories of a failed republic (the second) when it was now time to construct a new one. It was against such foils, against the detested empire and the heavy hand of the old bar, that the new generation defined its agenda and style of politics: an agenda centered on the restoration of liberties, a style of politics attuned to the down-to-earth realities of getting votes. They arrived at a particular understanding of what politics was all about, and once in power, by law or example, they did what they could to turn that conception into standard practice. In the process they gave a particular and, for better or worse, lasting shape to the political culture of the Third Republic.

The Paris Bar

The Paris bar, at the time of Bonaparte's coup, had a well-merited reputation for liberalism. A dozen members had seen action in 1848 as ministers of the Second Republic. The provisional government of February counted a trio of lawyers in its ranks: Crémieux at Justice, Ledru-Rollin at the Interior, and Marie at Public Works. Lawyers were just as plentiful in the Cavaignac cabinets of June-December. The justice portfolio was assigned first to Eugène Bethmont, who was later replaced by Marie. Jules Sénard took over at the ministry of the interior and was succeeded in turn by the former Orleanist Armand Dufaure. All four belonged or were soon to belong to the Paris bar. The 1851 coup prompted a "reflux vers le barreau."[2] Lawyers left public life in droves, flooding back into private practice. From the new regime's point of view, the Palais de Justice threatened to become a viper's nest of republican dissidence, however moderate in tone that dissidence might be. Worse still, the bar, like the university, had pretensions to a self-governing independence. It claimed exclusive right to decide on admission to its ranks and to punish members who violated its code of ethics. Oversight on such matters as admissions and professional discipline was handled by a twenty-man Conseil de Discipline and a presiding officer known as the *bâtonnier*. Council members and bâtonniers alike were elected directly by all bar members in good standing.

It is no wonder that Louis-Napoleon targeted the bar for overhaul, an institution so jealous of its autonomy and packed with veteran 48ers. The emperor contemplated making council membership and the office of bâtonnier appointive. Jules Baroche, Claude Delangle, and Charles Troplong, imperial loyalists all but also legal men (Baroche was a former bâtonnier, Delangle and Troplong were senior magistrates), managed to persuade him to reconsider. The decree, which was at last worked out and promulgated in March 1852, was less drastic in its provisions but still intrusive. A minimum of ten years' affiliation was required of bar members who wished to stand in council elections; it was stipulated in addition that the bâtonnier be designated not in public election but by the council choosing from among its own members. The latter provision was intended to reduce the bâtonnier's stature, the former to exclude from office certain lawyers of well-known liberal views, such as Sénard and Dufaure, who had practiced in the provinces and come to the Paris bar only recently.[3]

But Bonaparte's half-hearted efforts to tame the legal profession proved a singular failure. It was not only that the Palais de Justice remained a haven to many individuals of liberal conviction, but that a liberal bias was built into the bar's very constitution, into its conception of itself and its place in the life of the nation.

The order of lawyers styled itself a school of liberal statesmanship.[4] There was no better preparation for a career in parliamentary politics than a stint at the Palais. The virtues essential to a life in public service, it was claimed, could be learned at the bar: independence of mind, eloquence in defense of principle, devotion to self-government.

Even the most cursory perusal of the bar's code of professional conduct reveals a persistent concern with preserving at least the appearance of disinterestedness. A true lawyer argued a case on principle, not because he owed a favor or had a fee to earn. For just such reasons, aspirants to the bar were paid a visit by a member of the Conseil de Discipline, who checked on the candidate's probity of character and financial status. Once enrolled, lawyers were forbidden to engage in a whole range of commercial practices that might compromise the integrity of the profession. They could not advertise, hang out a shingle, or even use letterhead stationery with an office address. As for money matters, bar members were instructed not to discuss fees with clients; the billing of customers was frowned upon; and in case of failure to pay, lawyers were forbidden to have recourse to the courts. A grateful client might offer an honorarium at the conclusion of a case, but such remuneration was considered a free gift. And the actual transfer of monies was never to occur on Palais premises, above all when counsel were dressed in robes. Such prescriptions, to be sure, were not honored all the time, but the council was prepared to enforce the code, to discipline and to strike from the lists any lawyer who strayed too far from the code of fit behavior. The bar did not consider the law a trade or a service, and it rankled deeply that the state obliged barristers to pay the business tax.[5]

Lawyers dealt not in cash but in *la parole,* in words well crafted and uplifting. Good-conduct manuals advised barristers against intemperant language or vulgar notoriety in the press.[6] A lawyer worthy of the name cleaved to the Palais and perfected the arts of eloquence. That, of course, came in many forms. It might be Demosthenian or Ciceronian, accenting impassioned delivery or good form and erudition. Connoisseurs of midcentury oratory touted the maverick legitimist Antoine Berryer (Crémieux also got a mention) as the most illustrious practitioner of the emotive or romantic style. Berryer was said to be ardent, sublime. He knew how to "subjugate," to move an audience.[7] Favre, on the other hand, was an exemplar of the Ciceronian school, an orator more cerebral than impetuous. He did not deny the value of performance but was above all a stickler for *le beau style.* A speaker's task, Favre explained, was to instruct, stir, charm. But, more, he had to make himself an example, to realize in word and gesture "the ideal type of the true and the beautiful."[8] There is no mistaking the Cousinian resonance of such an injunction, but Favre after all was a Cousin disciple and successor to the master's chair at the Académie Française.[9]

All genuine devotees of eloquence, whether they spoke in the Attic or the Roman manner, shared certain traits. They were philosophers who could elevate the humble facts of a legal dispute into a grand clash of principle. And they were wordspinners, happy to ramble on at length in the most high-flown language. A skilled barrister's opening plea, from exordium to peroration, might well last a full five hours. But there was more to eloquence than logorrheic high-mindedness. Oratory, at its best, was an exercise in moral virtue. Berryer,

Favre, and Marie were all judged "manly" speakers, a description that denoted both strength of character and physical presence. Lawyers revered the classics, quoting from Cicero, Tacitus, or Juvenal with abandon. The choice of authors—commentators on ancient Rome's plunge from liberty into despotism—was not arbitrary. The true lawyer aspired to Roman *virtù*. He was a man of high character, a noble soul, and, above all else, a lover of liberty.[10]

Liberty was the legal profession's life blood. Without it, no effective defense was possible. A barrister's duty was to contradict, to bring to light, to claim redress, and so he was the natural enemy of despotic regimes living in dread of public exposure. And in the unequal battle against the depredations of latter-day Caesars, the lawyer's most potent weapon was eloquence, "the greatest instrument of civilization and liberty known to peoples," as one legal commentator put it.[11] It was a cliché of the day that the Palais de Justice was but a step from the Palais Bourbon. Today's lawyer pleading at the bar was tomorrow's deputy orating in parliament. But whatever the venue, the speaker's task remained the same: the exercise of eloquence to address and avert the public, to protect its rights against the state.[12]

The bar staked a claim to special status as guardian of the nation's liberties: in part because it was France's premier "school of eloquence," a forum of free speech in the most censorious of times, but in part too because of its own liberal constitution.[13] Legal manuals referred to the bar as "our little republic."[14] It was after all a community of free citizens "administered by temporary governors chosen from within its own ranks."[15] The bâtonnier was regarded by senior members of the bar as dean of the order and by junior members as a benevolent paterfamilias.[16] He was less a disciplinarian than a helmsman who kept a liberty-loving order afloat in authoritarian times.

A republic *in petto* populated by independent would-be Ciceros: such was the institution Louis-Napoleon imagined he might subdue. He soon learned how mistaken he was. In 1853 the emperor invited the council of the order to attend an official reception, but it refused.[17] Indeed, throughout the 1850s, it elected a series of bâtonniers calculated to offend the regime. Berryer was chosen in 1852, served the standard two-year term, and then was replaced by Bethmont. In 1856 the council turned to Félix Liouville, founder in 1848 of the Association Républicaine du Barreau. Liouville was succeeded by Plocque, a one-time Blanquist turned republican, who was in turn succeeded by Favre.[18] The first opposition deputies, five in all, were elected in 1857. As might be expected, three of them were members of the Paris bar: Favre, Emile Ollivier, and Liouville's nephew Ernest Picard.[19]

Le Jeune Barreau

The new generation of lawyers began to make their presence felt at the Palais de Justice in the 1860s. They needed and were grateful for the patronage of *vieilles barbes* like Crémieux and Liouville, but they were also eager to make a mark, to affirm an individual personality more in tune with the times. It is not accurate to speak of a break between the generations, but tensions there were. The *jeune barreau* made the bar's constitutional traditions its own, but recast them in the process. What emerged was an updated liberalism, pragmatic and business-oriented, adapted to the rough-and-tumble of electoral politics, and quite at home with democratic practice.

Many of the young lawyers who enrolled at the bar in the decades of midcentury had, in student days, a brush with Latin Quarter radicalism, which took years to forget and, in certain cases, was never outgrown at all. The example of Léon Gambetta comes to mind. In the late 1850s he was a habitué of Left Bank cafés, a regular first at the Voltaire and then at the Procope, rubbing shoulders and swapping debating points with future communards like Jules Vallès and Auguste Vermorel. For many years he retained the bearded and unkempt look of the student. There was even some concern when he entered the Palais that he might be tossed out of court by strait-laced judges like Delangle, who disapproved of facial hair.[20] Emile Acollas, a professor of more or less the same vintage as Gambetta, ran a private Left Bank legal-studies forum in the fifties. He was himself a notorious troublemaker—a vocal critic of the civil code and later a founder of the Ligue de la Paix. During the Commune, he was offered but did not accept the deanship of the Ecole de Droit. More than a little of Acollas' radicalism rubbed off on the students he taught, among them Jules Méline. Méline is best remembered as an Opportunist prime minister, the apostle of protectionist conservatism in the 1890s, but in student days it was otherwise. He was a dabbler in Left Bank journalism, writing the occasional piece for *Le Travail,* and for a time was drawn to Proudhonism.[21]

A lawyer's political education did not end when he left the Latin Quarter for the bar. At the Palais, however, there was much less room for the freewheeling of student days. Professional advancement required a period of apprenticeship at the knee of a senior barrister. It is remarkable how many later officials of the Third Republic trained with veterans of the Second. Georges Coulon, a prefect of the Government of National Defense, worked under Favre; Georges Le Chevalier, also made a prefect in 1870, worked under Sénard; Waldeck-Rousseau, one of the republic's more illustrious prime ministers, got a start in Dufaure's *étude*.

A battery of future politicians graduated from Liouville's office. Ernest Cresson became Paris prefect of police in 1870; Georges Desmarest was elected on the republican ticket to the National Assembly in July 1871; Ernest Picard became minister of finance in the Government of National Defense. Crémieux also trained a portion of the up-and-coming republican elite: Leven, of course, but also Clément Laurier, a core member of the Gambettist circle. Of all Crémieux's former junior associates, none earned a reputation to equal Gambetta's. Gambetta had worked in the office of Jules de Jouy, a respected but not stellar figure, better known as an uncle of the Manets: Gustave (himself a lawyer), Eugène (husband of painter Berthe Morisot), and Edouard (who needs no introduction). Gambetta soon left Jouy's employ and, in 1863, found a spot in the Crémieux offices.[22]

Employment in the office of a barrister with a notorious republican past may or may not be counted a form of political education. More certain is the pedagogical and political function served by the *conférences* or debating societies that proliferated around the Palais in the Second Empire. The bar itself ran an official *conférence de stage*.[23] All newly enrolled lawyers, so-called *stagiaires*, were required to attend weekly meetings chaired by the bâtonnier, where legal issues of the day were mooted. The 600-odd stagiaires elected from among themselves a dozen secretaries. From that twelve, in turn, the council, in consultation with the bâtonnier, designated two who were invited to deliver the annual *discours de rentrée* at the opening session. The conference functioned as a kind of parliament. Debaters, like legislators, deployed what oratorical talents they had to argue a case. Whether they had been persuasive was decided at the debate's end by vote of the assembled stagiaires. Success here was judged a good augury of success in the future, especially for those who had set their sights on a career in politics. "It's at the conference of lawyers," as one commentator put it, "that all the celebrated politicians of the day got their start."[24] As in a real parliament, so in the conference, speakers who enjoyed the confidence of the majority were elevated to offices of authority. The secretaries were ministers in the making and considered as such by their peers, a notion not so far-fetched when one considers that Ferry, Floquet, Gambetta, Grévy, and Méline (the list could be longer) had all served as conference secretaries.[25] But all this was pretended politics. It was not permitted in conference session to engage in the genuine article, but on occasion clever speakers managed to score political points by innuendo. Ferry in 1855 delivered one of the two *discours de rentrée*. He spoke on Enlightenment influences on the eighteenth-century bar and used the occasion to take a dig or two at the empire.[26]

Such circumspection did not have to be observed at the numerous unofficial conferences that met sometimes in Palais chambers, sometimes in the homes of senior barristers. The Conférence Marie may be cited as a minor but not unimportant illustration of the genre. It was founded in 1852 by Marie, Desmarest, and Antoine Avond (Crémieux's *chef du cabinet* in 1848) and convened regularly at Marie's apartments. Twenty to twenty-five lawyers belonged. Marie conceived of the association as more than a debating society and hinted as much in an 1853 letter to conference members:

> in a time such as our own, when all beliefs are veiled or hide themselves, scientific activity remains, for the mind as for the heart, a worthy and consoling refuge . . . through such endeavors, you prepare and fecundate the future: that is better than compromising or disgracing yourself in the present.[27]

The Conférence Marie was intended as a retreat for the opposition, a sanctuary where it might sharpen its wits before the moment came to reemerge. There can be no mistaking the precise political orientation of this opposition. Marie and Desmarest were among the conference founders; Bethmont, Clamageran, Floquet, Grévy, and Manuel were rank-and-file members. The Conférence Marie, as such a roster of names indicates, was in effect a republican conclave operating under the cover of a professional association.[28]

By far the most prestigious and venerable of the private conferences was the Conférence Molé, which dated back to July Monarchy days. The Molé was also more than a professional association. It styled itself a kind of shadow parliament in which all shades of opinion were represented. No doubt the conference had its share of Bonapartists and royalists, but over time it was the republican opposition that set the tone. Candidates for conference membership were admitted by cooptation, but the standards of admission were not too strict. In the mid-1860s, 400 or so lawyers, stagiaires, and special invitees belonged, this at a time when the total number enrolled at the Paris bar hovered in the vicinity of 700. Special invitees, few in number, were outsiders to the Palais de Justice who had a specific interest in legal debate. Jules Castagnary, admitted to the conference in 1863, is typical of the category: a law-school graduate, journalist, and art critic who ended a varied career as a councillor of state. For members of the *jeune barreau,* the conference afforded a double opportunity. It was a social occasion, a place to make connections and exchange ideas. Ferry, it is said, was converted to positivism by a companion at the Molé, Philémon Deroisin, a future collaborator on Littré's monumental *Dictionnaire de la langue française.* But the Conférence Molé was above all a debating society, a forum in which speaking skills might be polished and powers of persuasion put to the test. Only here, at the Molé, the political dimension was more explicit. Gambetta, admitted in 1861, wrote home to his father an exultant description: "It is no mere lawyers' club, but a veritable political assembly with a left, a right, a center; legislative proposals are the sole subject of discussion. It is there that are formed all the political men of France; it is a veritable training ground for the tribune."[29] Gambetta, of course, seated himself on the conference left in the company of a familiar cast: Méline, Ferry, and the rest. And it was a left on the rise, as shown by Ferry's election to the presidency of the conference in 1864 and by Gambetta's in 1869 and 1870.[30]

The empire had good cause to look with suspicion on private conferences like Marie's and the Molé. Free speech was practiced with unwelcome gusto at these "little republics." In 1857 the prefect of the Seine declared Palais courtrooms off limits to private conferences. The bâtonnier placed the premises of the Palais library at the disposal of the homeless conferences. Others moved over to the Ecole de Droit, where they met under the probing eye of a police commissary. The prefect's prohibition took a toll nonetheless. Twenty-nine conferences had been operating in 1851–52; as of 1858, there were only ten. The vigorous protestations of a whole series of bâtonniers, from Liouville to Dufaure, pressured the imperial regime to relent, at least in part. In the early sixties, the prefect made two rooms at the Palais available for conference use; the number of conferences shot up in a twinkling, reaching twenty-two in 1863.[31]

At the conference as at the office, young members of the bar learned political no less than professional lessons, all under the scrutiny of their elders. Such tutelage extended into private life. Picard's mother held a salon that attracted a mix of oldtimers like Liouville and comparative youngsters like Ferry. Amédée Dréo recruited a host of young lawyer friends—Ferry and Floquet among them—to attend gatherings at the home of his father-in-law, Louis Antoine Garnier-Pagès, former minister of finance in the provisional government of 1848. Gambetta's social graces were refined at Juliette Adam's salon, started in the 1860s with the express purpose of bridging the gap between old and young, between the men of 1848 and the generation coming of age.[32]

But occasionally it was youth that set the tone, when the tutelary presence of older men was pared to a minimum. The Morisot household was frequented by fledgling painters like Manet and Alfred Stevens, come to call on Berthe Morisot. Yet, in the sixties, the Ferry brothers came calling as well. Jules in particular took a passing fancy to the young woman painter. At the same time, he ingratiated himself with Papa Morisot, a senior official at the Cour des Comptes. Indeed, it is said that Ferry's celebrated exposé of the imperial regime's financial finaglings, *Les Comptes fantastiques d'Haussmann,* was based on information culled in conversation with the old man.[33] Artists and lawyers mixed as well at the Hérold salon. Mme. Hérold, widow of composer François-Joseph, kept a weekly Sunday in the 1850s. Musician friends of the deceased were invited, but so too were the likes of Ollivier and Picard, who were acquainted with the children of the house: the son Ferdinand Hérold and the son-in-law Jean-Jules Clamageran, both lawyers. It was in such "intimate milieux," as the republican party stalwart Marcellin Berthelot recalled in later years, that "the sacred flame of liberty was kept alight" through the dark night of the empire's first years.[34]

The political bias of the Ferry and Clément Laurier salons was more pronounced still, not to mention the masculine character and youthfulness of the company. In the mid-fifties, the Ferry brothers, Jules and Charles, hosted legal gatherings attended by the cream of the young bar: Clamageran, Dréo, future councillor of state Paul Dupré, and above all Ollivier. Jules Ferry counted Ollivier a particular friend. When Ollivier was elected to parliament in 1859, Ferry (in the company of Dréo, Hérold, and Floquet) made a point of going to debates to cheer on the bar's fastest-rising star.[35] The Laurier salon was of a later vintage, getting its start in the sixties, but the crowd was similar in composition. Allain-Targé, Henri Brisson, Challemel-Lacour, and Gambetta were regulars. All were future dignitaries of the republic, and all, with the exception of Challemel, were lawyers.[36]

At the palace and in debating societies, young lawyers had to pick their way under the critical supervision of senior men. But at the Procope or Voltaire, at the Ferry "cenacle" or the maison Laurier, it was different. Here the new generation found some breathing room in which, amid friends and peers, the rites of youth could be celebrated and a distinctive personality worked out.

The Young Bar at the Palais de Justice

That "personality" had an impact on how the Paris bar itself operated. From midcentury on, observers of the legal scene began to remark on a sea change in oratorical practice. Case presentations were becoming more concise and businesslike. The contemporary barrister rejected the soaring rhetoric of more romantic times in favor of an everyday language that resembled conversational speech. The old bar had made a cult of formal elegance; the new was more improvisational. Citations from the classics remained a learned counsel's stock-in-trade, but the modern school preferred the Roman style to all else. Commentators appreciated the simplicity, the naturalness, and the unaffected character of what they called the realist manner. But they worried at the same time about what was being lost: passion, enthusiasm, a certain splendor of language and depth of allusion.[37]

Whether the change in oratory was to be praised or regretted, all observers agreed on one point: it was the growing incidence of business cases that inspired the change.[38] The presentation in terms comprehensible to the layman of detailed corporate, financial, or real-estate transactions—such was the challenge barristers faced. Little wonder that they aimed at a logical exposition of fact, uncluttered by rhetorical flights.

But what became of the barrister's Ciceronian commitment to public liberties if he turned down this realist road? Maurice Joly, a Palais gadfly who held the romantic oratory of old in high esteem, worried that the new lawyer had become too professional. He cited Laurier, who made a specialty of business cases, as a prime example of the strengths and shortcomings of what Joly called the "école des affaires." Laurier was clear but dry, less a public man who roused audiences than a dispassionate expert.[39] But, still, a few were prepared to dismiss the old oratory as so much verbiage. A lawyer's task, after all, was not to roll over juries in sonorous periods but to enlighten them with a solid narration of the facts. A narrative approach did not rule out improvisational appeals to the listener's emotions. Such appeals, however, were to be undertaken not "according to the rules of rhetoric, but following the promptings of good sense."[40] At its best, the new oratory represented an exhilarating amalgam of narration and improvisation, of plainspeaking and inspiration. No speaker better exemplified the new style than Léon Gambetta. He appreciated the importance of business, and he knew how to address juries in accessible accents. But when Gambetta spoke, he could make the mundane soar. Vulgar commerce became a civilizing influence that brought nations into peaceful communion.[41] Humble jurors became Citizens, competent to make sense of complex legal proceedings and to sit in judgment.[42]

The new oratory could degenerate into cramped legalism, focused on ownership and material interests. Or it could rise, when practiced by the likes of Gambetta, to a "manly and substantial eloquence"[43] that translated the practicalities of everyday life into civic discourse. When the young lawyers abandoned the courtroom for the hustings, that was the speaking style they brought with them: narrow and expansive by turns, spanning the poles of property and citizenship. And such, when they acceded to political office, was the style they bequeathed to the republic.

The new generation may have left an enduring mark on legal oratory, but not so on the bar's institutional modus operandi. To be sure, an attempt was made in the 1860s to democratize the bar, to publicize its internal workings. Such efforts were squelched. The Palais de Justice remained the same closed and corporate milieu it had always been. However many lawyers went on to public service under the republic, the bar itself never became one of the regime's institutional bulwarks.

There was a quiet routine to council elections in the 1850s. Candidates were in the main incumbents, older barristers of established reputation. Given the stature they enjoyed in the profession and their record of service, they were more or less assured of reelection. In practice, council seats went to the top twenty-one votegetters, provided each winning candidate tallied a majority of the ballots cast. Such majorities, it seems, were not hard to come by. Election of a new council did not require more than one round of balloting. In the circumstances the legal public showed but a modest interest in the process. In 1860, 327 voters took part; in 1861, 326.[44]

The next year, however, the calm was disturbed by a rapid-fire burst of reform agitation. In May 1862 some 182 lawyers, "members of the Bar militant" as one colleague characterized them, submitted a petition to the council, urging a substantial alteration in electoral procedure. The signatories proposed two changes: the council should be renewed on an annual basis by a third and not in toto; and incumbents should not be allowed to run for the slots. The petitioners, it was clear, wanted to open council ranks to new men so that the institution might function as it should, not as a privileged caste or "self-perpetuating house of peers," but as a "chamber of deputies" representing the interests of all. The council declined to act on the proposal but at the same time reminded all bar members that they were free to vote as they pleased. Turning out an incumbent did not constitute a breach of etiquette and was the elector's right.[45]

The petitioners took the advice to heart when the next council elections came around in August. Lists of preferred candidates were printed up and circulated in Palais cloakrooms. The object of the exercise was simple: "put in new men in order to put in new ideas." Foremost among the ideas touted by the young Turks, as their spokesman Frédéric Thomas later explained in Le Siècle, was the publication of an annual report on council proceedings.[46] Thomas, as the Siècle connection implies, was a man of republican convictions, one of the multitude of former legal associates whom Gambetta appointed to the prefectoral corps in 1870.[47] Was there a whiff, then, of oppositional politics in the 1862 campaign?

The election results point to just such a conclusion. Over 400 voters took part in the first round of balloting. Three additional votes were required before all twenty-one council slots could be filled. And the electorate, in a startling break with tradition, rejected nine incumbents. Among the newcomers were a trio of republican notables—Grévy, Nicolet, and Sénard—, as well as one of Louis-Napoleon's particular bugbears, Armand Dufaure (who had just then completed the eligibility requirement of ten years' membership at the bar). Dufaure was indeed made bâtonnier by the new council in an unmistakable gesture of defiance toward the regime. The unexpected outcome of the elections, not to mention the way in which they were conducted, prompted observers to speak of a "révolution du Palais."[48]

But a genuine revolution was not forthcoming. The new council declared in November that it would not sanction the distribution of printed election circulars.[49] Such official condemnations notwithstanding, the militant bar took to the stump again in August 1863. Fliers were sent around and voters canvassed. The turnout (389 votes cast in the first round) remained high, and as in 1862 it took four ballots before the requisite twenty-one councillors were elected.[50] In the end, only one new face was added to the sitting council, which had in no way tempered its antipathy to so-called electoral maneuvers. Quite the contrary. A council order of 11 August announced a formal inquiry into what were referred to as "instances of blameworthy competition." No formal charges issued from the investigation, but it had had the desired effect, chilling the electoral fervor of would-be reformers.[51] Candidates identified with the new bar, Nicolet for one, did stand for election in 1864 and again in 1865, but no overt campaign was conducted. Voter turnout tumbled, and erstwhile zealots like Thomas did not conceal their mounting disappointment. Apart from a few changes in personnel, the corporate practices of old remained intact.[52] The second edition of François Mollot's *Règles de la profession d'avocat* appeared in 1866. It laid out in the plainest terms that politicking had no place in the bar's internal affairs. "Avoid above all," he counseled, "imparting a political coloration to our elections; we are among family here."[53]

Entering the Public Domain

The *jeune barreau* made its professional debut in the late 1850s and early 1860s. Not all denizens of the Palais de Justice welcomed the event. Aficionados of the old order fussed about the realist turn in courtroom oratory and dug in to defend the decorum of yesteryear. It may have been frustration with a professional cadre so slow to change, or it may have been the goad of ambition, but as the 1860s wore on, the young and now not-so-young sought out wider fields of action. Institutional politics were abandoned for the real thing. Ferry, who in 1859 had contented himself with applauding Ollivier from the visitors' box, by 1869 had become a deputy himself. Graduates of the young bar, as they made the transition into public life, put to good use the oratorical and organizational skills first exercised in conference debate and palace elections. In so doing, they began to fashion a new style of politics, with its own forms and practices, which would enable them to mold a public just beginning to stir itself from the state-imposed slumbers of the 1850s.

It was in the Seine elections of 1863–64 that the new generation first distinguished itself. In the early months of 1863 a manual was published, detailing registration and voting procedures to would-be electors. It was printed in quantity and bore the imprimatur of the opposition's greatest legal talents. Deputies Favre, Ollivier, and Picard had signed on, as had Desmarest (a council member), Sénard, and Leven. The actual authors of the manual, however, were lesser-known personalities making a first foray into politics: Clamageran, Dréo, Ferry, Floquet, Hérold.[54] The youngsters were at it again in May. They gathered chez Dréo and, in collaboration with the usual crew of well-wishing oldtimers—Crémieux, Garnier-Pagès, Marie—constituted an ad hoc committee to organize the opposition's electoral campaign. Funds were solicited. Clamageran, recruiting among Latin Quarter students, assembled bands of pollwatchers. In the first round of balloting in December 1863, the opposition made a clean sweep of the elections, prompting an exultant Clamageran to pronounce "a veritable awakening of opinion."[55]

But two of the elected candidates opted for seats outside Paris, requiring a set of complementary elections scheduled for March 1864. The Dréo committee geared up for a second campaign. This time, however, the regime took preemptive action. Two weeks before election time, the police broke up a meeting at the Garnier-Pagès house. Dréo's home was subjected to search and seizure. And thirteen committee members (including Clamageran, Dréo, Ferry, and Hérold) were brought up on charges of membership in an unauthorized association.[56] Given the nature of the indictment, the case did not require a jury trial but was sent before a judge of the tribunal correctionnel.

The Paris bar was outraged and took a series of extraordinary actions to defend its own. Bâtonnier Dufaure paid a visit to the imperial prosecutor to express his disquiet at the authorities' conduct. The council of the order urged bar members, as a gesture of sympathy, to attend the upcoming trial in robes, and a sizable number did turn out. Last and most remarkable of all for an institution that prized discretion, the council delivered a letter to the press clarifying its position on what was coming to be known as *l'affaire des treize*.[57] The trial had become a public event. Defense lawyers, Favre in the lead, exploited the occasion to take potshots at the empire and its "destruction of universal suffrage." In the end, the presiding judge imposed a fine of 500 francs on each defendant, a sentence upheld on appeal.[58]

The affair demonstrated how the courts might be used to embarrass the regime and prick the curiosity of a no longer dormant public. The young bar profited twice over in the process. As individuals, they acquired a notoriety that enhanced prospects for a career in politics. As a group, they laid claim to a special status in public life: they were the public's most articulate spokesmen, champions of civil liberties at a time when both public and liberty had few defenders.

There is no doubt that the new generation relished this status, seizing every occasion to assert it. The tsar visited Paris in 1867 for the World's Fair. A trip to the Palais was scheduled but cut short when a band of young lawyers, including Floquet, greeted the visiting potentate with cries of "Vive la Pologne!"[59] In December of the same year, Floquet was in court, defending Acollas, Naquet, and ten suspected Blanquists against accusations of membership in a subversive secret society. But for Gambetta's generation of rising lawyers, it was the Baudin affair that marked the moment of real breakthrough, when words uttered in court rang out loud and clear beyond those narrow confines.

In May 1868 the empire relaxed press censorship, prompting a rash of new journals. The Paris reading public was serviced by 74 papers in October 1867; two years later the figure was 88. Of the new papers, more than one had an oppositional flavor: Ernest and Alfred Picard's *L'Electeur libre,* Eugène Pelletan's *La Tribune* (later *La Tribune française*), Charles Delescluze's *Le Réveil.* The regime responded not with a mailed fist but with a barrage of court cases. In 1868–69 some 447 journalists were charged with violations of the press code. In the event, 337 were convicted and 92 sentenced to prison terms of a year or more. Such trials afforded bar members, young and old, repeated occasions to demonstrate their credentials as the tribunes of an embattled opinion.[60]

It was in this climate that the Baudin affair erupted. In August 1868 Eugène Ténot, a journalist at *Le Siècle,* published *Paris en décem-*

3. Edouard Manet, *Portrait of Théodore Duret*, 1868

bre 1851, a blow-by-blow recounting of Louis-Napoleon's seizure of power. The book made pointed reference to the unhappy fate of Dr. Alphonse Baudin, a republican loyalist who died on the barricades resisting the coup. Ténot's book caused an immediate stir, and republicans maneuvered to profit from the occasion. On the *jour des morts,* a demonstration was organized at Baudin's tomb in the Montmartre cemetery. The small crowd was struck by the dilapidated condition of the gravesite. Editors from *L'Avenir national* and *Le Réveil* agreed to mount a subscription campaign to erect a proper monument in Baudin's memory. The papers published notices to that effect and were soon joined in the enterprise by Challemel-Lacour's *Revue politique et parlementaire* and *La Tribune,* now under Théodore Duret's direction (fig. 3). Plans were also laid for a second gathering at Baudin's tomb, scheduled for 3 December, the anniversary of the good doctor's death.[61]

Authorities acted with dispatch to bring all this to a halt. The police broke up the 3 December demonstration with little trouble, arresting twenty in the process. As for the subscription campaign, an issue of *L'Avenir national,* listing contributors, was seized, and a half-dozen journalists were dragged into court on charges of disturbing the peace. A round of convictions was handed down: a six-month prison term for Delescluze and fines for Challemel, Duret, Alphonse Peyrat (of *L'Avenir national*), Charles Quentin (of *Le Réveil*), and three others.

The interest of the case, however, lies not in the trial's predictable outcome but in how the defense was conducted. The composition of the defense team was not that remarkable, the standard mix of old and new faces: Crémieux for Quentin, Favre for Duret (who was in the end tried separately), Emmanuel Arago for Peyrat, Gambetta for Delescluze, Laurier for Challemel. But the defense set to its work with an unusually aggressive zeal. Crémieux and Arago, as the senior men, addressed the court first. They turned the tables on the regime, recalling its origins in the coup of 2 December 1851, accusing *it* of violating the law. Then Gambetta spoke, electrifying the audience with a tirade against the empire, attacking Bonapartism at its very core:

> There are but two anniversaries, the eighteenth Brumaire and the second of December, which have never attained the status of founding holidays *(solennités d'origine),* for you know all too well that, were you to celebrate them as such, universal conscience would spew them out.[62]

The speech, for its eloquence and daring, made Gambetta's reputation overnight. Once a young man on the make, he had now become a public man who spoke truth to power.

An alliance between the press and the bar began to crystallize in the waning days of the empire. They made common cause, calling a public into being: a public that over time became a real presence, crowding to funerals, to courtrooms, and not least of all to the polls. To graduates of the young bar, it was not the public's capacity for spectatorship that appealed so much as its potential as a source of votes. In the elections of 1863, the opposition in Paris fielded a list of candidates dominated by 48ers and veterans of the old bar. In the fall elections of 1869, for the first time the new generation made its strength felt. Gambetta, still basking in the afterglow of the Baudin affair, was swept into office on the first round by working-class Belleville.[63] Ferry, made famous by the *Comptes fantastiques* that *Le Temps* had serialized the preceding year, won in the second round in a more bourgeois constituency.

The newcomers came armed as well with a program that expressed the particular concerns of a generation come of age under a Bonaparte. Gambetta and Ferry both spoke of dismantling the imperial state, of decentralizing institutions and abolishing standing armies. Both proclaimed themselves friends of civil liberty (a free press and freedom of association) and of secularism. Gambetta's Belleville program was explicit in its call for a universal system of secular primary education. On Ferry's electoral committee were to be found, in the words of one biographer, the entire "general staff of positivism": Littré, Robinet, and so on. Last of all, Gambetta and Ferry pledged themselves to a new relationship between constituent and representative. Ferry castigated Bonaparte's system of official candidates, singling out for special abuse the "caesarist" candidacy of Palais de Justice colleague Chaix d'Est-Ange in the Gironde. As for Gambetta, he dreamed of remaking a waffling republican left into what he called "a government of public opinion." A deputy was meant to be at once a shaper of opinion and a servant of the public. In Belleville, Gambetta went to an open meeting of constituents, embraced the program the assembly presented to him, and promised to return to answer for his conduct in office. Yet even as he adopted a pose of submission, he made himself master of the situation, the people's pedagogue no less than its spokesman.[64]

The *jeune barreau*, as it made its electoral mark, translated its particular concerns and practices into a new kind of politics. Experience, at the bar as at the polls, had taught them what the central drama of public life was: the people and its liberties standing in need of protection against the predatory state and an obscurantist church. Experience had taught how that defense was to be conducted: through voter manuals and pollwatching, committeework and oratory, the press and the *profession de foi*. The electoral victories of 1869, if limited in scope, gave the new generation reason to hope that experience had taught them well, that the public they imagined and the public who voted were one and the same.

Servants of the Republic

L'année terrible delivered a serious but temporary setback to such pretensions. When the empire collapsed in 1870, the *jeune barreau* was well positioned to lay claim to a share of the spoils, and, as we have seen, it was rewarded: with ministerial posts (Gambetta was made minister of the interior), a score of prefectoral appointments,[65] the mayoralty of Paris (Ferry), and on and on. But this was power by appointment, and it didn't last. The elections of February 1871 finished off the Government of National Defense. The voters of France returned a landowning, conservative majority, "the rurals." Republicans styled themselves the people's tribune, but the elections revealed how far they had to go. The proletarian left delivered a second and, for the moment, no less decisive blow to republican prospects in March, seizing Paris through insurrection and making itself into the revolutionary Commune.

In 1871 the status so coveted by republicans, to be the people's one and true representative, was contested by a multiplicity of parties. The communard left, however, did not long remain in the running, succumbing in only two months to the assaults of the armies of Versailles. Members of the republican bar had played a range of roles in the unfolding of the drama. Picard served as the Versaillais minister of the interior; Gambetta left for Spain where he kept a calculated silence; Floquet and Le Chevalier joined the conciliationist Ligue d'Union Républicaine. But whether republicans adopted a posture of hostility or conciliation, they reaped enormous advantage from the Commune's demise. A critical rival for the public's favor had been reduced to a silence that would last a full decade. The field did not lay altogether open, but the remaining contestants, Orleanists and rurals, proved a poor match for a republican movement that came to the competition equipped with a program and a method perfected in the anti-imperial battles of the 1860s. In the decade and a half that followed, republicans busied themselves in assembling a national majority and, once in office, deploying their new power to embed in law the principles that got them there in the first place.

In the 1870s the *parti républicain* fanned out from its urban strong-holds, winning a series of electoral victories that demonstrated a swelling presence in the countryside. Republicanism's success at the polls can be explained in part by the character of its electoral pitch: a promise of small property for all, a reasoned progress, a secular (but not areligious) and self-governing future. To rural and smallowning constituencies, initiated by two decades of economic growth into the wonders of the marketplace, such appeals made eminent good sense. But just as critical as the content of the republican message was its form. Campaigns were organized by electoral committees, which collected funds and canvassed voters; aspirants to office stumped constituencies, declaiming at banquets, lodge meetings, and public assemblies; and what was not conveyed by word or gesture was communicated in print by local newspapers, often founded for the express purpose of puffing a candidate's moral and political virtues. By such means, republicans turned out the vote, giving substance to a national public hitherto more invoked than real.

Now, the style of politics pioneered at the republic's origins became, over time, standard practice. Committeework and editorializing, public oratory and glad-handing, this remained the stuff of public life well into the present century, despite efforts by mass-based parties, trade unions, and right-wing leagues to steer politics in a different direction. The new style, moreover, proved congenial to lawyers who had, after all, done so much to shape it. It is unsurprising that the republic's greatest champion in the 1870s was a lawyer, Gambetta, who demonstrated just how effective the new politics could be, as he criss-crossed the nation on speaking tours that earned him the nickname "traveling salesman of the republic." Gambetta defined by personal example how public life was to be conducted in a democratic order. As political resistance gave way before the republican assault, lawyers stepped forward to take possession of the commanding heights of the state. The ultimate failure of the 16 May coup in December 1877 forced the resignation of Prime Minister Gaëtan de Rochebouët; he was succeeded by Dufaure. MacMahon himself resigned the presidency in January 1879, to be replaced by Grévy. The very same month, Gambetta acceded to the presidency of the Chamber of Deputies.

Once in office, the young bar moved with dispatch to legislate, even to impose by administrative fiat, an agenda that had been in gestation for almost two decades. In late 1878 the Paris municipal council, egged on by council members Abel Hovelacque (who did not leave the council to join the Chamber of Deputies until 1889) and Aristide Rey, had begun to agitate for the laicization of local primary schools. The prefect of the Seine blocked such efforts, but he was replaced in early 1879 by the more sympathetic Hérold, a "raging priest-hater" in the words of one contemporary.[66] The anticlerical coalition was lent a critical helping hand by central authorities. In March, Minister of Public Instruction Ferry (appointed to the office a month before) submitted a bill to the Chamber, empowering local administrations to purge unauthorized clerical personnel from public schools. Hérold embarked on a program of thoroughgoing secularization. By the opening of the new schoolyear in October, 32 Paris schools had been secularized. In December of the following year, school authorities began the removal of classroom crucifixes. Hérold's contribution to the cause of laicity extended beyond his life. He died in January 1882 and was accorded a public burial, without aid of clergy. The top brass of the army of Paris marched in the cortege, an unprecedented event much remarked on at the time. Thus was buried a veteran of the young bar, remembered by friends as a champion of *l'idée moderne.*[67]

This campaign indirectly fueled demands for a purge of the state's legal apparatus. Clamor for a judicial housecleaning began in 1878, spearheaded, as might be expected, by members of the republican bar—Sénard and Floquet. Prime Minister Dufaure responded halfheartedly to the pressures. Not so his successor, Waddington, who had all the more incentive to act as the school issue heated up. Clerical teachers, discharged under the 1879 Ferry law, brought suit to contest the legality of the measure, and it was feared the Conseil d'Etat might decide for the plaintiffs. To forestall that, the council was subjected to a legislative overhaul in July 1879. Ten new posts were created; ten sitting councillors were retired or fired outright; only a dozen members from the old council were kept on, now far outnumbered by new appointees. The result of the reshuffling was a council dominated by a republican and anticlerical majority that included men like Castagnary and Clamageran.[68]

This was only the opening shot of an even more wide-ranging assault on the judiciary. In addition to the purge of the Conseil d'Etat, Waddington dismissed or reassigned eighteen of twenty-six state prosecutors. In 1880, 500 magistrates resigned rather than enforce the state's secularization decrees. In 1883, under the guise of streamlining the court system, the republic abolished over 600 judgeships. The occasion was used, needless to say, to discard magistrates deemed unreliable in political matters. In all, it has been estimated, well over a thousand justices quit or were obliged to leave public service in the years 1879–1883, a turnover of personnel that amounted to a "judicial revolution."[69] And it was not only personnel who were at issue, but the extent and nature of judicial authority. The laws governing freedom of association and freedom of the press were rewritten in the summer of 1881. Prior authorization was no longer required either for the convocation of a public meeting or for the starting of a newspaper. Legislators shortened the list of libel offenses. Henceforth, violations of the press code were to be heard in jury trial. Indeed, in 1883, the practice of jury trials was extended to all misdemeanor cases.[70] Magistrates in the new civil order were to play a reduced role in the regulation of public liberties, and where the law sanctioned judicial intervention, it also obligated judges to share power with an empaneled citizenry.

The lawyer republicans who came to power in the late 1870s were by no means radical libertarians. They used the law to purge undesirables. They harassed the church. Religious organizations, unlike public meetings or even, after 1884, trade unions, were still required to seek state authorization. But compared to preceding regimes, the Third Republic was indeed a friend of liberty, prepared to extend the exercise of civil rights insofar as it was consistent with the promotion of a secular and democratic public realm. In practice, this entailed both a liberalization and a simultaneous, at times illiberal, attack on the prerogatives of entrenched hierarchies, whether religious or judicial. But such a project, whatever its ambiguities on civil liberties, reflected faithfully the complex experience of a generation of republican lawyers, positivist-realist in orientation, who had spent years in court defending newspapermen and demonstrators against an intolerant officialdom.

The *jeune barreau* conceived the lawyer as the quintessential public man, a pedagogue and exemplar, the maker and giver of opinion. He was a practical man, attuned to the needs of business and businesslike himself. And he was a political man: a committee organizer, an editorialist, a votegetter who addressed his fellow citizens in language they understood. Implicit in such a conception was a particular understanding of what public life was all about. The limitations of that vision are, looking back, all too evident. If public life is about men and manliness, how do women fit in? If it is about business and property, what is to become of labor? If it is about committees and newspapers, what room is there for the mass party or trade union?

Yet, looking at the young bar in terms of its own aspirations and experiences, the record of achievement appears more nuanced. The new generation battled for its autonomy vis-à-vis its elders; with greater fervor still, it battled to push back the limits on public life imposed by an authoritarian regime. In the process, it fashioned for itself a particular identity—realistic in contrast to the grandiloquent ways of old; and it honed new forms of democratic practice, which brought into being and empowered new publics. What is curious is how little effort was made to inject the new style into the bar's own affairs. Lawyers may have become a mainstay of the new republic, but not the bar, which remained wedded to its old corporate ways. No such reticence was shown when it came to the reconstruction of national institutions.

As political power accrued to veterans of the young bar, they used it to give legal sanction to the new politics: to liberalize press and association laws, to restrict the public role of judicial and religious authorities. Under the empire and the regime of Moral Order, republicans struggled to widen the sphere of public activity. In the decade that followed, they consolidated those advances by legislation and decree. The republican bar had redrawn the boundaries of public life. They made, to be sure, some gross exclusions, and the excluded would eventually return to demand redress. But for a brief moment in the 1880s, before the coming of Boulangism and the socialist revival, before the onset of a revitalized feminism, lawyer republicans had reason to congratulate themselves on a job well done.

[7]

The New Painting

THE STIRRINGS OF dissent that so agitated the institutional land-scape of midcentury France did not spare the world of the arts. Until 1863 the Académie des Beaux-Arts had exercised a de jure monopoly on appointments to the Ecole des Beaux-Arts, the principal training ground for aspiring painters. A state commission assumed control of appointments, but continued to nominate academicians to all senior teaching posts. The state and the academy collaborated in much the same way in running the annual salon, the primary locus for the public exhibition of paintings in nineteenth-century France. A jury determined which canvases merited display at the salon, but jury selection was far from democratic. In the 1860s and 1870s, the state reserved to itself the right to appoint a variable portion of jury members. The rest were elected, but the suffrage was restricted to winners of the Prix de Rome and medalwinners at previous exhibits. The voting population constituted a select body that cast ballots with a right-thinking regularity for academy members. It is true that in 1868–1870 the rules regulating salon selection were relaxed, but, in the aftermath of the Commune, the restrictive system was restored.

Artists of many persuasions bridled against a system that invested state appointees and academicians with such extensive authority to monitor access to education and the marketplace. None made a greater ruckus than the partisans of the so-called *nouvelle peinture,* a heterogeneous band that worked in a mixture of styles from Barbi-zon-influenced landscape painting to impressionism to realism.

The new painting's advocates, no less than its antagonists, characterized the artists involved as independents, intransigents, revolutionaries, words with a potent political charge any time, but all the more so in the turbulent decades of midcentury. Nor were such epithets mere rhetoric. The artistic dissidence of midcentury did have a political dimension. To the painters, of course, it was art that counted first and foremost. Yet, in pursuit of aesthetic innovation, they found themselves drawn, above all by friendly critics, into a wider political struggle. The new painters did not bristle at the temptation but threw themselves into it, often with gusto. Almost without exception, they were themselves men and women of republican conviction, which helps to explain why the campaign they conducted against the salon bore such a strong family resemblance in both method and motive to the institutional battles republicans were waging elsewhere—in France's lodges, schools and consistories. My argument, then, is twofold: the new painters as individuals moved in republican circles, painted pictures with republican content, and even on occasion militated in the republican cause; but more than that, the institutional and artistic agenda they pursued was congruent with a more encompassing republican project.

Constituting the Group

But who are we talking about here? A narrow aesthetic definition of the group in question—focused on the technique of painting out of doors, a brighter palette, and the rendering via rapid brushstrokes of immediate visual experience—will exclude artists, such as Degas and perhaps Manet, who in the judgment of contemporaries and historians were pioneers of the new school. One possible criterion of membership is participation in one of the eight independent exhibitions that the new painters organized in 1874–1886. The object of the enterprise was simple: to offer artists frustrated by salon juries or opposed to them in principle an alternative avenue of access to the public. But certain artists associated in the public mind with the new painting never took part: Frédéric Bazille, who died too young, and Edouard Manet, who opted to combat the salon on other terrains. Well over fifty artists, though, did join in at one time or another in the endeavor; about half only exhibited once. Such passing connections would not seem to merit inclusion in the group.

Recourse to a single test generates a collectivity either too narrow or too inclusive. A more balanced outcome might result from applying a mix of criteria. The new painters, first of all, saw themselves as an institutional-aesthetic opposition. They harbored grievances against a salon system that thwarted them. And they repudiated as outdated and mediocre the aesthetic practices of William Bouguereau or Alexandre Cabanel or Jean-Louis Gérôme. Those men were the accredited masters of the day, members all of the academy, the latter two professors at the École des Beaux-Arts. They turned out detailed and finely finished canvases depicting classical nudes or historical landscapes. The new school by contrast was "modern." This might mean contemporaneity of subject: the depiction, without narrative flourish, of the world of midcentury France, its interiors and pastimes, its cityscapes and country scenes. Or it might mean a willingness to experiment in technique, a willingness to lay bare on canvas, without the concealing or consoling conventions of academic practice, the very processes by which visual experience was transformed into representational form.

The new painters, moreover, were youthful. Born between 1830 and 1850, they liked to think of themselves as a *jeune école.* A distinct generational identity marked them off from artists of an earlier cohort, even those they admired. Adolphe Cals showed five times with the independents, but no one mistook him, a Barbizon painter well past sixty, for a member of the new school.[1] The young painters in turn stood in a similar relation to the generation of avant-garde artists who succeeded them. In the 1880s Camille Pissarro (b. 1830) began to work with a band of younger artists, including Georges Seurat (b. 1859) and Paul Signac (b. 1863), who were experimenting in pointillist technique. This pair, thanks to Pissarro's efforts, was recruited to take part in the last independent exhibition in 1886. But the idiom in which they worked and their extreme youth distinguished them unmistakably from "veteran" new painters who were at least in their mid-thirties, if not a ripened fifty like Pissarro himself.

But commonality of aspiration and age does not in itself suffice to constitute a group. The members must also feel some affinity to one another, born of comradeship and mutual endeavor. Reconstructing the networks of sociability and cooperative action that bound the new painters is a delicate and to some extent arbitrary exercise. The best we can expect is a rough sense of the group's contours, in full awareness that the lines might be redrawn to include or exclude particular individuals.

The artists and critics who constituted the core of the new painting movement first began to congregate in the late 1850s and early 1860s. The Académie Suisse was an independent studio without formal instruction. Students paid a small fee and came to practice drawing from live models. It was at the academy that Pissarro met Claude Monet in 1858 and then Paul Cézanne and Armand Guillaumin not long afterward. The grand gallery at the Louvre represented a second *lieu de rencontre*. Henri Fantin-Latour was a regular visitor, meeting Manet there in 1857, Berthe Morisot in 1859, and Bazille and Auguste Renoir in 1863.[2] Then there was the teaching atelier of Charles Gleyre. Monet enrolled in 1862 and soon became fast friends with fellow students Bazille, Renoir, and Alfred Sisley. But the group chafed under Gleyre's tutelage. When the master advised Monet to study "from the antique," he proposed to his comrades that they quit the studio. "Let's get out of here," he is reported to have said. "The place is unhealthy: they lack sincerity."[3] The little band struck out on its own, but autonomy did not translate into success. Monet exhibited at the official salons of 1865 and 1866 but was rejected the next year. So was Bazille, who resolved never again to submit himself to the "administrative caprice" of a salon jury. But how could they reach the public? Bazille and Monet mulled over the idea of forming an independent association that would mount exhibitions outside regular channels.[4]

The notion of an independent association of artists was by no means a novel one.[5] In 1862 the printer Auguste Delâtre and the publisher Alfred Cadart organized the Société des Aquafortistes. The society's primary impetus was commercial: to popularize the medium (etching with nitric acid) and drum up sales for the artists who worked in it. But the organization was more than a mere business venture. By its very existence it represented a slap at the academy's pretensions to sovereignty in the arts. In an 1863 review, the critic Philippe Burty made the point explicit, hailing the society as an "independent group, very much outside academic tradition."[6]

The "work of emancipation and progress" on which Cadart and his associates had embarked (the phrase is from Jules Castagnary, who was himself involved in the enterprise) collapsed in bankruptcy in 1867, but not without leaving a trace of the more enduring ties it had nourished. Fantin, one of the first acolytes, felt keenly that a new school was in the making, and he sought to represent it in painting. The result was *Hommage à Delacroix,* a canvas completed in 1864 depicting ten artists and critics—among them Edmond Duranty,

Fantin himself, Félix Bracquemond, and Manet—gathered about a portrait of the eponymous master (fig. 4). What bound the sitters, and they were to remain on close terms for years to come, was a common connection to etching: a long-standing link to Cadart in Duranty's case, actual membership in the Société des Aquafortistes in the case of the other three.[7]

Japonisme, like etching, enjoyed a certain vogue among independent-minded artists in the 1860s, and it was a passion that prompted two former aquafortists, Bracquemond and Fantin, to attempt a second plunge into the realm of autonomous organization. Not long after the international exposition of 1867, the Société du Jing-Lar was formed, composed of eight men: the two just named, who were joined by the poet and critic Zacharie Astruc, Burty, Alphonse Hirsch (a painter), Jules Jacquemart (an engraver), and Marc-Louis Solon (an employee at the Manufacture de Sèvres). All were amateurs of japonaiserie; Hirsch and Jacquemart were collectors. The wider public owed much of what it knew about things Japanese to Astruc, who published a series of boosterish articles in 1866 under the title "The Empire of the Rising Sun." That same year Bracquemond, a skilled ceramicist, completed the design of a dinner service, so orientalist in conception and detail that it became known as the *service japonais.*[8]

The Jing-Lar was in part a drinking society, but there was a more serious side to the enterprise.[9] Burty was among the first to vaunt the sober beauties of Asian ceramics and understood full well that such a view ran counter to current artistic convention. But the buying public's evident appetite for eastern objets d'art, its taste for "sincerely original works," he wrote in 1866, had shaken the "sensibilities of classicizers."[10] Aficionados of japonaiserie saw themselves as partisans of a new aesthetic, of a sober originality that represented a step up from classical traditionalism.

Overlapping currents of autonomous action—among painters, aquafortists, japonists—began to form in the later 1860s. They converged at decade's end, coursing into Paris' Batignolles quarter. Since 1861 Manet had maintained a studio on the quarter's fringes; Bazille installed himself some years later in an atelier not far away. Comrades and colleagues frequented the artists' studios to socialize and exchange shoptalk. Two records of these conclaves have been preserved: a canvas by Fantin, *A Studio in the Batignolles Quarter,* completed in 1870, and a second by Bazille, *Studio in the rue La*

4. Henri Fantin-Latour, *Hommage à Delacroix*, 1864

5. Henri Fantin-Latour, *A Studio in the Batignolles Quarter*, 1870

6. Frédéric Bazille, *Studio in the rue La Condamine*, 1870

7. Edgar Degas, *Portrait of Emile Edmond Duranty*, 1879

8. Edouard Manet, *Portrait of Emile Zola,* 1868

9. Frédéric Bazille, *The Artist's Family on a Terrace near Montpellier*, 1868

10. Auguste Renoir, *Madame Charpentier and Her Children,* 1878

11. Claude Monet, *Rue Saint-Denis, Celebration of 30 June 1878*, 1878

12. Claude Monet, *Rue Montorgueil, Celebration of 30 June 1878*, 1878

13. Edouard Manet, *Lady with Fans: Nina de Callias*, 1873-74

14. Edouard Manet, *Vive l'amnistie,* 1880

15. Paul Cézanne, *The Artist's Father,* 1866

16. Jean-François Raffaëlli, *Clemenceau Addressing
His Montmartre Constituents*, 1883–84

17. Mary Cassatt, *Moïse Dreyfus,* 1879

Condamine, painted in the same year (figs. 5 and 6). The first shows Manet seated at an easel surrounded by friends frozen in a variety of formal postures: Astruc, Bazille, Monet, Renoir, and Emile Zola.[11] The second has a more casual construction: on the right, the musician Edmond Maître sits at a piano; center canvas, Bazille and Manet talk over a painting in progress; three more figures appear on the left, variously identified as Astruc, Monet, Renoir, Sisley, or Zola. Such studio assemblies were complemented by gatherings at the nearby Café Guerbois. Here friendly conversation often spilled into raucous debate. Manet, by all accounts, was the dominant figure in a mixed crowd that included writers as well as artists. Letters and criticism were represented by Burty, Théodore Duret (a friend of Manet's), Duranty, Armand Silvestre, and Zola, all stalwart backers of the new painting. Among the artists, the most assiduous habitués were Astruc, Bazille, and Bracquemond. Degas, Fantin, Pissarro, and Renoir came often, Cézanne and Monet sometimes.[12] To the public mind, this heterogeneous group had the look of a school, which in honor of the quarter they made their artistic home, became known as the Ecole des Batignolles.

The "school" was soon dispersed, a victim of war and civil war. Bazille was killed in the Franco-Prussian war. Monet and Pissarro, at the outbreak of hostilities, left for London. After returning, Monet ensconced himself at Argenteuil, Pissarro at Pontoise. Degas spent a portion of the post-Commune years in New Orleans. Manet remained in Paris, but events had left him in a state of severe depression.

A combination of circumstances brought the group back to life. The exhibition franchise was tightened in the early 1870s, making the salon even less accessible than it had been under the late empire. The painters at the same time found themselves less strapped for money than before. In England, Monet and Pissarro made the acquaintance of the art dealer Paul Durand-Ruel, who bought paintings from the pair and later from Sisley and Degas. When Durand-Ruel was flush, which was more often than not, he proved himself a firm and paying patron.

The painters had the incentive and now the wherewithal to strike out on an independent course. In late 1873 an agreement was drawn up to form a cooperative association[13] with the express purpose of sponsoring an exposition of independent art.[14] Sixteen names can be identified among the founders. Of these, only eleven exhibited with the independents after the first show: Edouard Béliard, Degas, Guillaumin, Degas' friend Ludovic-Napoléon Lepic, Léopold Levert (by age and inclination, more of a Barbizon landscapist), Monet, Morisot, Henri Rouart (another friend of Degas'), Pissarro, Renoir, and Sisley. A difference of opinion flared among the organizers as to who would be invited to participate in the projected show. Monet wanted the new painters to exhibit "among themselves," but Degas insisted on a more inclusive policy and he prevailed.[15] When in April 1874 the first independent exposition opened at the vacated studio of the photographer Félix Nadar, a full thirty artists were represented.

The 1874 exposition was not the only sign of renewed collective activity. New centers of friendship and collaboration had begun to form, first at Pontoise, Pissarro's base of operations in the western suburbs of Paris. The experiments Pissarro was undertaking in landscape painting attracted a widening circle of collaborators. In 1872 Béliard, Cézanne, and Guillaumin moved out to join him. The little colony expanded in the following year with the addition of the more conventional *paysagiste* Victor Vignon. Ludovic Piette, an old friend of Pissarro's, paid regular visits and, after the late 1870s, so did Paul Gauguin.[16]

In town too there were signs of a regrouping of forces. The 1874 exposition was not a success. Monet, Renoir, and Sisley, in need of money, cast about for a way to approach the public again, settling on the idea of selling their work at auction. The sale, held at the Hôtel Drouot in 1875, caused a near riot, but there were a few buyers nonetheless, among them Gustave Caillebotte. Caillebotte, a well-to-do bourgeois, was a sometime painter, but his encounters with Monet and Renoir (Gennevilliers, Caillebotte's future residence, was located across the Seine from Monet's Argenteuil) transformed an avocation into a serious commitment. Caillebotte's 1875 purchase represented a first step toward his formal involvement in the new painting group. He exhibited with the independents the next year, and four more times after that. Rich and energetic, Caillebotte exercised a role of increasing importance in the group's affairs as a sponsor and organizer of its exhibits.

Caillebotte was not the only one whose influence was growing. In the aftermath of *l'année terrible,* the gatherings at the Café Guerbois had lost their sparkle. But in the mid-1870s, a successor café materialized, the Nouvelle-Athènes. Many from the old crowd resurfaced: Burty, Degas, Duranty, Manet. But Degas also introduced a host of new talents, not all of them welcome, into the group. To the Nouvelle-Athènes he brought two refugees from Gérôme's academic atelier, Jean-Louis Forain and Jean-François Raffaëlli, and a transplanted Italian, Federico Zandomeneghi. The trio, known as Degas' disciples, were more inclined to the realist mode than to the impressionist. Raffaëlli in particular favored dark scenes of urban down-and-outs. At the café it was not so difficult to tolerate the newcomers, but when Degas insisted that they be allowed to exhibit with the independents, there was loud complaint, which required all of Pissarro's diplomacy to placate. In the end Forain and Zandomeneghi showed with the group four times, the more-contested Raffaëlli twice.

By the late 1870s, the old Ecole des Batignolles had been recast. It was less centered on Manet, more diverse in character. Each subgroup had a certain internal coherence, clustered about a particular personality: Manet, Degas, or Pissarro. And each cluster was marked, up to a point, by stylistic affinities, whether realist or impressionist. The loose contours of the group did not change much over the next decade. Individuals withdrew, as did Fantin. Others were added: Mary Cassatt, for example, who came out of the Degas camp, or Marie Bracquemond, Félix's wife. Both women exhibited with the independents for the first time in 1879 and returned to show again.

But for all the comings and goings, there were threads that held the group together: ties of generation, friendship, and collaborative effort. On this basis, a rough approximation of the group's membership may be ventured. Among the nonartists, the name of Durand-Ruel, who did more than any dealer or collector to keep the enterprise of independent painting afloat, comes first to mind. Then there are the critics—Astruc, Burty, Duranty, Duret, Silvestre, Zola, and at a pinch Castagnary—who shared conversation with the new painters and spoke up for them in print.

Among the artists, Bazille, Fantin, and Manet have more than a fair claim to be counted in. Bazille, one of the Gleyre breakaways, died too young to exhibit with the independents in the 1870s and 1880s, but no doubt he would have. Fantin, it is true, abandoned the group in later years, but in the beginning he was among the more devoted partisans of the Batignolles school, a painter of its ateliers and a regular at the Guerbois. In Manet's case, there was no break after 1870, only a taking of distance. He still came to the Nouvelle-Athènes to keep up with old friends and retained much of the prestige earned the preceding decade as the *jeune école*'s undisputed champion.

Yet there can be little argument about the membership credentials of that band of artists who, despite harsh reviews and disappointing sales, displayed with the group over and over again. Fifteen painters in the 1830–1850 cohort showed three or more times with the independents: Félix and Marie Bracquemond, Caillebotte, Cassatt, Degas, Gauguin, Guillaumin, Monet, Morisot, Pissarro, Renoir, Rouart, Sisley, Vignon, and Zandomeneghi. Forain, though a little young (b. 1852), also has a claim to membership. He participated in four of the independent salons, frequented the Nouvelle-Athènes, and was esteemed by core members like Pissarro. Three additional names might be mentioned as candidates: Béliard, Cézanne, and Raffaëlli, all of whom took part in only two of the group's showings. But Béliard had frequented the Guerbois, worked side by side with Pissarro at Pontoise, and was a charter member of the independents' 1874 cooperative. Cézanne's connection to the group went back farther still, to the Académie Suisse. Like Béliard, he was a hanger-on at the Guerbois and a sometime member of Pissarro's colony at Pontoise. Raffaëlli is a borderline case. Though not well respected by many, he did have advocates in the group, and he certainly wanted to be included, showing with the independents when the opportunity presented itself and keeping company with them at the Nouvelle-Athènes.

Artists and Republicans

Of the thirty-odd dealers, critics, and artists just listed, it might be expected that at least a few took an active interest in public affairs. What is surprising is that most of them did and that, with varying degrees of intensity, they inclined to the republican point of view. An immediate and glaring exception is Durand-Ruel, a self-styled legitimist who in 1873 made a public declaration urging the exiled Comte de Chambord's return to France.[17]

The critics fitted the republican mold especially well. Edmond Duranty (fig. 7) spent a lifetime writing for the republican press. In 1867 he had collaborated with Jules Vallès on *La Rue* and in 1868–69 with Quinet's freethinking amanuensis, Charles-Louis Chassin, on *La Démocratie*.[18] In the early 1870s Duranty moved over to *L'Avenir national,* a journal of the opposition, so militant in tone that it was closed down in mid-1873 by the Broglie administration (the first of the Moral Order governments).[19] Armand Silvestre's journalistic career followed a similar trajectory. In the seventies he wrote salon criticism for *L'Opinion nationale* which, on Guéroult's death in 1872, passed into the hands of moderate republicans. In the 1880s he shifted to *La Vie moderne,* owned and edited by the publisher Georges Charpentier. The magazine made no pretense of partisanship, but Gambetta's death in 1882 prompted an elegiac obituary from Antonin Proust (Gambetta's former minister of fine arts) and then a cover story on the funeral. Silvestre knew and corresponded with Gambetta and was well enough situated in the republican establishment to land himself a plum appointment in 1893 as state inspector of fine arts.[20] As for Zola (fig. 8), in the late 1860s he wrote for a string of republican newspapers, including Duret's *La Tribune* and Hugo's *Le Rappel,* and was prosecuted for a pacifist article published on the eve of the Franco-Prussian war. During the war itself he served a brief stint as secretary to Alexandre Glais-Bizoin, an old 48er who was then a minister in the Government of National Defense.[21]

But without doubt it was Burty, Castagnary, and Duret who, among the critics, were the most *engagés.* Philippe Burty described himself in an 1879 letter to Auguste Scheurer-Kestner as, since the days of the empire, a friend of liberty and a devoted republican. In fact, Burty's bookplates (designed for him in the late 1860s by Bracquemond) bore the motto "free and faithful" inscribed on a banner floating atop a phrygian cap. During the Commune, Burty as a writer at *Le Rappel* had hewn to the line of republican conciliation.[22] And in the Commune's aftermath, he accepted a full-time post as art critic on Gambetta's *La République française.* Gambetta, as prime minister, had occasion to repay the years of steadfast collaboration, appointing Burty to the inspectorate of fine arts in 1881.

Jules Castagnary, like Burty, had a long and varied career as a servant of the republic. He was a lawyer before taking up journalism. He worked first at *Le Nain jaune* in the 1860s and then at the staunchly republican *Le Siècle* in the ensuing decade, but throughout he remained active in politics, campaigning for Carnot in 1863[23] and winning election to the Paris municipal council in 1874. It was from there, in 1879, that Castagnary moved up to the Conseil d'Etat. In the midst of all these activities, he still found time to write salon criticism. But, to Castagnary, art and politics were not separate spheres. The publication in 1892 of his collected art criticism gives some indication of the ways in which the two realms could intersect.

The multivolume project was brought to fruition in the first place through the joint efforts of Gustave Isambert and Roger Marx—the former an activist in the 1860s Latin Quarter, the latter a newly minted inspector of fine arts. Gambetta's old crony Spuller wrote the preface, while the aquaforte portrait used as a frontispiece was supplied by Bracquemond.[24]

Théodore Duret was also a man of many faces. In the early sixties, he worked in his family's cognac business. It was in Spain, en route from a sales trip to Portugal in 1865, that he first met Manet. By decade's end, Duret had moved into journalism. For a while he served as director of *La Tribune* and was prosecuted for the paper's involvement in the Baudin affair. Duret's famous review of the 1870 salon, in which he took Manet's part with such eloquence, first appeared in *L'Electeur libre,* a journal of the republican opposition published by the Picard brothers. During the Commune, Duret was employed at *Le Siècle,* a paper of strong conciliationist views, whose principal shareholder was Henri Cernuschi, a well-to-do Italian expatriate and Garibaldino. It was in Cernuschi's company that Duret was arrested by Versaillais troops during "bloody week," and the two escaped summary execution by the narrowest of margins. Chastened by the experience, they left France, spending 1871–72 on an art-acquisition tour in the Orient.[25]

Of all the critics, it is Zacharie Astruc who seems least connected to the republican milieu. Still he did belong to the Jing-Lar, which some have argued was merely a republican coven in *japonisant* disguise.[26] The case is a strong one. Burty had clear republican connections, and so did Bracquemond. In 1868, while a member of the Jing-Lar, Bracquemond designed a plate for the delectation of friends, the so-called *assiette républicaine,* which depicted an imperial eagle screeching at a Phrygian cap set against a radiant sun. Astruc, it appears, swam in republican waters, even though he may not have been of them.

The mid-nineteenth-century critic was not obliged to specialize. He might straddle worlds, tacking back and forth between art reviewing and politics. Such liberties were not available to painters, who had to devote themselves more single-mindedly to their craft. In such circumstances, evidence of political involvement is bound to be in short supply. And so it is, but not as much as might be expected.

Take the case of the four Gleyre graduates: Sisley, Bazille, Renoir, and Monet. Little is known of Sisley beyond the work itself. Bazille's politics, on the other hand, are not difficult to pin down. He came from a well-to-do Protestant family in Montpellier (fig. 9). Bazille père was a republican, a senator who sat with Ferry's party. Bazille's aunt and uncle, the Lejosnes, were also republicans. They lived in Paris, hosting a salon in the 1860s that was frequented by many artists and politicians: Fantin, Gambetta, Manet, Nadar, and the young Bazille himself. Given such company, the conversation was often peppered with anti-imperial invective, and there is reason to believe that Bazille shared such opinions. Coming to Paris originally to study medicine, he was present at the Ecole de Médecine riots that greeted Dean Rayer's inauguration in 1862. In early 1870 he planned to attend Victor Noir's funeral but did not; instead he posed for Fantin's *Studio in the Batignolles Quarter.* But Bazille kept a memento from the day, obtaining a copy of Rochefort's *La Marseillaise* before police closed the paper down.[27] That September, when the detested empire was swept away, Bazille found himself in the army. He wrote home on the occasion, giving a clear indication of how he felt about the unfolding of events: "I am still stunned by the most recent news, but, my God, well pleased with the Republic, provided that it lasts."[28]

Republican politics was not Renoir's birthright as it was Bazille's. He was a tailor's son who grew up in Paris' third arrondissement. There was an incendiary air about the neighborhood. Aunt Lisa, an adept of Auguste Blanqui and Louise Michel, frequented the local "revolutionary group." Renoir himself had a brush or two with the politics of insurrection. He was painting at Fontainebleau one day in 1870 when he was approached in the forest by a radical journalist in flight from imperial authorities. It turned out to be the Blanquist Raoul Rigault, then a staffer on *La Marseillaise* and soon to become prefect of police under the Commune. Renoir agreed to take him in for a spell while Pissarro contacted the fugitive's friends in the capital. The connection proved propitious. Renoir remained in Paris during the Commune and, so that he might travel in and out of the city at will, paid a visit to Rigault to obtain safe-conduct papers. Rigault did not only comply but had a band on the spot strike up "La Marseillaise" for citizen Renoir. The comic dimensions of the episode should not obscure Renoir's genuine feelings of sympathy for the insurrectionaries, whom in later years he described as "brave fellows, full of good intentions."[29] Nor did those sympathies disappear in old age. In the 1890s, living in Montmartre, Renoir struck up a friendship with his neighbor Clovis Hugues, a veteran communard turned socialist deputy who had shown a certain susceptibility to the attractions of Boulangism and antisemitism.[30] However ambitious he was for success, Renoir always had a dislike for rules and regulations. In younger years, his fractious independence of mind expressed itself in an understanding generosity toward communard revolt. With the passage of time, it curdled into a cranky "populist" chauvinism that drove him to abandon old friends like Pissarro, who was Jewish, and at the turn of the century to side with the anti-Dreyfus camp.

In the 1870s and 1880s, however, the will to succeed modulated Renoir's *frondeur* impulses and his political connections as well. He became a regular at the celebrated Charpentier salon. Georges Charpentier was the leading publisher of naturalist novels; he cultivated good relations in republican circles; and he fancied himself a patron of the arts. All three interests were represented at the salon. Daudet and Zola attended, as did Clemenceau, Gambetta, and Spuller. Duret, Manet, and Monet came too, but among the painters it was Renoir who became the household favorite, an attachment he reciprocated by painting the Charpentier family time and again in the most flattering light (fig. 10).[31]

Renoir knew how to take advantage of contacts made at the salon. It was at the Charpentiers' that he first met the wealthy Protestant businessman Paul Bérard, who soon became one of the artist's staunchest patrons. Renoir was just as adept at exploiting political contacts. At the independents' salon of 1877, on the eve of the *seize mai* crisis, he exhibited a portrait of Spuller. Not long before, in an effort to arrange favorable publicity for the exhibition, he had paid a visit to the offices of *La République française.* Challemel-Lacour, with whom Renoir spoke at first, was not well disposed to the request, but Gambetta arrived and the matter was straightened out. Renoir, in fact, felt a particular affinity for Gambetta, calling him "the simplest and most courteous man I ever met," and did not hesitate to solicit (without result) the tribune's patronage for a curatorial appointment.[32]

In the 1870s Renoir carved out a comfortable niche for himself in republican society. It was a position he edged away from as the century drew to a close. Not so, however, Monet, who remained a steadfast republican patriot his whole life. When Monet came to Paris in the late 1850s, he made straight for the precincts of radical bohemia, spending time at the Brasserie des Martyrs where he rubbed shoulders with the likes of Castagnary and Courbet. He haunted the cafés of the Latin Quarter as well, meeting and befriending Paul Dubois and Antonin Lafont, both militant freethinkers and, at the time of the Commune, members of the Ligue d'Union Républicaine. Monet gave them paintings; they introduced him to Clemenceau, who became one of the artist's best friends.[33] Monet's decision in 1870 to decamp to England rather than fight in the emperor's war has been imputed to radical conviction. The point may be debated, but beyond doubt is Monet's execration of Versaillais conduct toward the Commune. In 1871, on hearing false rumors of Courbet's execution at the hands of Thiers' troops, he wrote to Pissarro: "What shameful conduct, that of Versailles, it is frightful and makes me ill. I don't have heart for anything."[34]

After *l'année terrible* and his return to France, Monet again started moving in republican circles. When in Paris he frequented the Charpentier salon. In 1889–90 Monet and some friends solicited funds to purchase the *Olympia* from Manet's cash-strapped widow (the artist had died in 1883). The range of contributors is a veritable who's who of art-world republicans. The ultimate aim of the project was to donate the canvas to the state. When the time came to approach officialdom, Monet enlisted the help of Camille Pelletan, who was a Mason, a senior editor on Clemenceau's *La Justice,* and in 1901 a charter member of the Radical Party.[35]

Evidence of republican conviction crops up even in Monet's work. The defeat of MacMahon's 16 May coup in December 1877 marked the republic's definitive triumph. A clamor arose for an official celebration of the event. Hard-core republicans agitated for the 14 July, but the moderate Dufaure administration demurred. The date settled on in the end was 30 June, two months into the World's Fair of 1878. Depending on political persuasion, the holiday lent itself to differing interpretations: as a celebration of the republic's consolidation or, more neutrally, as a rousing accompaniment to the exposition. At the fourth independents' salon in the following spring, Monet exhibited two paintings of the 30 June fête, both representing jammed Paris streets festooned with blazing tricolors (figs. 11 and 12). In the *Rue Saint-Denis* canvas, Monet made quite explicit his understanding of the occasion, inscribing in gold letters on a flag in the foreground: "Vive la République."

Such consistency of belief illumines Monet's conduct in later years. Monet was, as is well known, a firm Dreyfusard, but not merely because he signed a petition avowing the captain's innocence. In 1898 Clemenceau's newspaper *L'Aurore* published Zola's "J'accuse," that famous inflammatory exposé of the army's complicity in concocting the case against Dreyfus. Soon afterward, Clemenceau was the recipient of a gift. Monet sent him a canvas painted ten years before, less interesting in the present context for its subject matter, a seaside cliff, than for its title, *Le Bloc.* Clemenceau was renowned for having proclaimed the French revolution "a bloc," an event that had to be swallowed whole, 1793 and the Terror included. Monet's gift, in light of the associations it conjured up, was a gesture of both political and moral solidarity. The Great War prompted Monet to another round of gift giving. Just after armistice day in 1918, he wrote to Prime Minister Clemenceau, offering to donate to the state two panels of water lilies. "It's not much," the painter explained, "but it's the only way I have of taking part in the Victory."[36]

SISLEY MAY have been indifferent to politics, but not Bazille, Renoir, or Monet, republicans all. A similar tempered claim can be made of the group of artists gathered about Manet: the Bracquemonds, Fantin, and Morisot.

Nothing is known of Marie Bracquemond's political preferences. It would be convenient to claim that she shared her husband Félix's views. But the two differed in important respects on aesthetic matters—she was drawn to the impressionist mode, he was not—so there is no reason to presume harmony on political matters either.

More certain are Félix Bracquemond's republican loyalties. In the late 1860s he paid regular visits to the salon maintained by Paul Meurice. Burty, Fantin, and Manet were also regulars. In light of the host's affiliations—he was a member of Victor Hugo's coterie and a journalist at *Le Rappel*—it is little wonder that discussion often turned to political matters, to democracy and its relationship to art in particular. It was at this time that Bracquemond designed the *assiette républicaine* and the Burty bookplate mentioned above. In later years the Burty connection opened many doors to Bracquemond. He was invited to take part in the independents' first salon, thanks to Burty's intercession. In the early sevenites, he was hired as director of the Haviland ceramics studio in Auteuil, co-owned by Charles Haviland, an amateur collector of Japanese porcelains and Burty's son-in-law. Bracquemond managed as well to attach himself to the Charpentier circle. It is not clear that he frequented the Charpentier salon, but he did contribute with some regularity to Charpentier's *La Vie moderne*. Such assiduous cultivation of republican ties was not without reward. The Gambetta administration gave Bracquemond the Légion d'Honneur in 1881.[37]

Fantin's republicanism was of a more lukewarm variety. A witness to the art-and-democracy debates at the Meurice household, he did not join in. As he wrote to a friend, genuine "art has nothing to do with such matters." Still Fantin socialized with the Jing-Lar crowd. At a Société des Aquafortistes function in 1864, he left the table in protest when an after-dinner speaker paid compliments to the empire. He grew less and less reticent about political matters as the years went by. In the Paris byelections of 1889, he was moved to vote for the first time, casting his ballot for the regime and against the obstreperous General Boulanger; and in 1898 he "naturally"—the word is his—rallied to the side of a beleaguered Zola, who had put himself at such risk on behalf of the Dreyfus cause.[38]

It was through Fantin that Berthe Morisot was first introduced to the Manet circle. For a period in the late 1860s, she worked in close collaboration with Edouard and then in 1874 married the painter's brother Eugène. All three Manet brothers were devoted to the republican cause. Gustave Manet was an LUR member at the time of the Commune and in the seventies took to frequenting the Café Frontin, a radical rendezvous well known to police.[39] As for Eugène, he was the author in later years of an anticlerical novel set in the late empire and dedicated, in the words of a recent biographer, to those "persecuted by Napoleon III."[40] But a woman cannot be held responsible for the politics of her husband, let alone her inlaws.

Still there are hints that Morisot shared the Manets' republican views. During the siege of Paris in 1871, the entire Morisot household (parents Tiburce and Cornélie, Berthe, sister Edma, brother Tiburce) remained staunch in their determination to continue the fight. Armistice terms, however, were negotiated by Foreign Minister Jules Favre, providing for the election of a National Assembly, which sat first at Bordeaux before moving to Versailles. The elections returned a number of red republicans, among them Garibaldi, but the majority was conservative, even monarchist, and voted in Thiers as chief executive. M. and Mme. Morisot approved the new administration, but Berthe and Edma were of a different mind. In late February, Edma wrote a letter from the provinces to Berthe in Paris. The letter made disparaging remarks about that "reactionary Chamber" (the Bordeaux assembly) and waxed indignant about mounting attacks on Gambetta.[41] Berthe replied in kind less than a week later:

> It appears from what you tell me that Garibaldi is as much detested in the provinces as Favre . . . and the others are detested here; it seems to me that the Parisians have more justification than the provincials. If I happen timidly to voice this opinion at home, father throws up his hands and says that I am a madwoman.[42]

In earlier correspondence Berthe had made reference to political differences with papa, and it is clear now what was probably at stake. He favored Thiers, she preferred Gambetta and Garibaldi.[43]

In Morisot's case, the paucity of evidence leaves room for doubt; in Manet's, however, the evidence of republican commitment is abundant.[44] A seventeen-year-old Edouard spent the winter of 1848–49 in Rio de Janeiro. In March 1849 he wrote to his father: "try to preserve our good republic until my return, for I well and truly fear that L. Napoléon is not himself much of a republican."[45] Such clarity of conviction is not that surprising, even in one so young, given the republican bias of the milieu he grew up in. His father was a judge. Brother Gustave was a member of the *jeune barreau* who brought home to dinner like-minded colleagues such as Gambetta. Gambetta was in fact employed for a period in the law offices of Manet's older cousin, Jules de Jouy, also a republican. And when Edouard traveled to Italy in 1853, it was in the company of yet another lawyer, Emile Ollivier, soon to become a leading light of the young bar.[46]

The mature Manet took to frequenting fashionable boulevard cafés like Tortoni's, but he was equally at home in republican society. In the late 1860s, as we have seen, he was a regular at the Meurice salon. He was, in the same period, a sometime visitor to the Café de Londres, a favorite haunt of Gambetta's. It was there that the two men, artist and politician, got to know one another well, striking up a friendship that lasted until Gambetta's untimely death in 1882. After the war, Manet took to paying occasional visits to the Café Frontin to see his brother Gustave, Ranc, and Spuller.[47] And in the mid-seventies, through the poet Charles Cros, Manet was introduced to the salon of Nina de Callias (fig. 13). The salon attracted a heterogeneous crowd of poets (Mallarmé was a regular), musicians, and painters, but Callias' interests were as much political as artistic.

"It is she," claimed a police report of 1872, "who is most generous in aid and succor to [former] communards."[48]

In view of Manet's background and the company he kept, the position he staked out during *l'année terrible* will come as no surprise. During the siege, Manet served as an artilleryman. He was a great patriot and, it seems, not in full sympathy with the Government of National Defense's lackluster prosecution of the war. In September, accompanied by his brother Eugène and by Degas, he attended a rally at the Folies-Bergère. The principal speaker was Gustave Cluseret, a former Union officer in the American civil war and a well-known partisan of *la guerre à l'outrance*. Manet wrote of the event to his wife: "The present provisional government is not at all popular and the real Republicans seem to intend overthrowing it after the war."[49]

But is Manet himself to be counted among the real republicans? He execrated "that little Thiers" and expressed in March 1871 the fond wish that the chief executive "crap out *(crever)* one day at the speaker's podium." After the Commune, Manet continued to rant against Thiers as a "demented old man" and against Thiers' savage repression of the insurrection.[50] But Manet was no firebrand, sympathizing less with the Commune than with the conciliationist camp that included so many of his friends: his brother Gustave, Burty, Duret, and Paul Meurice. And the public figure Manet admired most was neither Versaillais nor revolutionary, but Gambetta, "the only capable man we have," as he is reported to have said to Mme. Morisot. Indeed, in July 1871, Manet made several trips to Versailles to sketch Gambetta at the speaker's tribune and even cajoled him into several studio sittings.[51]

Manet's commitments, then, spanned the die-hard patriotism of Gambetta and the conciliationist radicalism espoused by the LUR and newspapers like *Le Rappel*. It was a range of commitments that the artist maintained into the next decade. Certainly the bond to Gambettism never weakened. In 1877, in the heat of the parliamentary campaign pursuant to the *seize mai* coup, Manet opened his atelier to a republican electoral meeting, chaired by a long-time acquaintance and Gambetta's right-hand man, Spuller. In 1879, as president of the Chamber, Gambetta hosted an unofficial celebration of the *quatorze juillet* at the Palais-Bourbon. Manet was invited and came in the company of Antonin Proust, who two years later became Gambetta's minister of fine arts. In that capacity, it was Proust who arranged Manet's award of the Légion d'Honneur in 1882.[52]

But for all that Manet cultivated the Gambettist connection, he retained a radical edge throughout, the best evidence for which is to be found in the artist's own work. Manet first got in trouble with the authorities in the late sixties. He made a lithograph representing the execution of Emperor Maximilian of Mexico. The censor read the work as a slam at Louis-Napoleon's foreign policy and forbade its reproduction. Manet was in trouble with officialdom again in 1874. At issue this time was a color lithograph titled *Polichinelle*. Manet had struck a bargain with *Le Temps* to set aside 8,000 copies of the lithograph for circulation to the paper's subscribers. The police confiscated and destroyed the prints as well as the stones from which they were made, discerning in Manet's figure a mocking image of President MacMahon. Even in the late seventies, as official opinion softened, Manet continued to strike dissonant chords. He, like Monet, painted a street scene, emblazoned with tricolor flags, in commemoration of the *fête de la paix* of 1878. In the lower right quadrant of Manet's canvas there hobbles a one-legged man on crutches, a "reminder," in the words of one art historian, "of the horrors of war and of the civil war that followed it."[53] Then in 1879–1881 Manet painted a series of portraits, not of solid citizens like Gambetta or Spuller but of the two most notorious radicals of the day: Clemenceau and Rochefort.

That Rochefort, exiled after the Commune, had been able to return to France at all was because of a general amnesty voted in July 1880, just days before the first official observance of Bastille Day. It was radical republicans who had championed the cause of amnesty throughout the seventies, and so the first *quatorze juillet* afforded double cause for rejoicing. A pair of watercolors Manet executed in commemoration of the day shows that he shared such sentiments in full. The first depicts a single tricolor transversed with the inscription "Vive la République." The second takes the form of a handwritten note to the model Isabelle Lemonnier, decorated with two crossed flags and next to them the exhortation "Vive l'amnistie" (fig. 14).

MANET AND HIS CIRCLE espoused a republicanism more or less conventional in character. The same cannot be said of Pissarro's Pontoise group. They were far less correct in manner and breeding than Manet or Morisot, and they tended to a less well-bred politics, republican at least until the 1880s but a republicanism shot through with eccentricity and plebeian contentiousness. Pissarro himself may be taken as an example. He ended as an anarchist, but in younger days it was different. At the outbreak of war in 1870, Pissarro left for England. Once the empire collapsed, he experienced, although a Danish citizen, a powerful impulse to return and enlist in the French army. It required the death of his child, the sickness of the child's mother (whom Pissarro married some months later), and his own mother's pleas to persuade him to abandon the enterprise.[54] As for the Commune, Pissarro did not take the part of the revolutionaries whom he referred to as "those socialist assassins." But neither, it seems, did he back the Versaillais. His friend Piette wrote to Pissarro in early 1872 describing the Versaillais repression, the ferocity of which, he claimed, made the Saint Bartholomew's Day massacre pale in comparison. Pissarro may well have shared such views. He gave up on Commune baiting in short order and took to preserving souvenirs from the event, in later years growing ever more exasperated with colleagues like Millet, who continued to rant about communard excesses.[55]

In general outline, Pissarro's response to events—the wish to enlist in 1870, the initial antagonism to the Commune, the subsequent shift to ambivalence as news of Versaillais savagery sunk in—do not distinguish him from the garden-variety conciliationist. But he did not fit the standard republican mold in all respects. For one thing, he had pronounced social concerns. The artist's Pontoise paintings bespoke his commitment to representing productive manual labor, the peasant working in harmony with nature. In 1874, as the new painters reconnoitered possible forms of independent association, Pissarro, that "vieille barbe de '48" as one colleague called him, proposed the Pontoise bakers' union as a model. He also nurtured a quirky interest in alternative sciences, such as magnetism and homeopathic medicine. Such idiosyncrasies, while not without resonance in the republican milieu, did situate Pissarro on the movement's more radical fringes.[56]

Over time, though, the appeal of republicanism faded. Pissarro's correspondence from the early 1880s on is studded with laudatory asides to Kropotkin, Michel, and Proudhon; as for the electoral process and all the paraphernalia of republican democracy, it more and more struck him as a bourgeois sham. Pissarro admitted that he had changed, that what he had once taken as "pure gold" now seemed to him "vile metal." All the same, he never broke with the regime completely. On hearing rumors of a royalist coup in 1883, Pissarro hoped for the republic's survival, still preferring bourgeois democracy to base reaction.[57] It was a preference he acted on once again at the turn of the century, when he joined the Dreyfusards.

To all appearances, Pissarro's colleagues at Pontoise thought much as he did. Little is known of Vignon, but Béliard once worked as a secretary to the historian and republican socialist Alphonse Esquiros, and he was known in earlier years to have been a friend of Proudhon's.[58] Guillaumin had a reputation as a socialist. Renoir at least thought him one. When invited to take part in the independents' salon of 1882, Renoir at first balked, explaining himself to Durand-Ruel in these terms:

> To exhibit with Pissarro, Gauguin and Guillaumin, it's as though I were exhibiting with the first socialist who came along *(comme si j'exposais avec une sociale quelconque)*. It won't be long, and Pissarro will be inviting the Russian Lavrof or some other revolutionary to join in. The public does not like what smells of politics, and, for my part, I don't want at my age to be a revolutionary.[59]

But it has also been claimed that Guillaumin was a republican,[60] and Renoir may have exaggerated in Gauguin's case as well. No doubt there was a socialist twist to Gauguin's otherwise pure republican pedigree. He was the grandson of the utopian socialist Flora Tristan. Aline—Tristan's daughter, Gauguin's mother—was raised in a republican pension and counted Saint-Simonian Elisa Lemonnier a lifelong friend. In 1846 Aline married Gauguin's father, Clovis, an editor at the moderate republican *Le National,* in a ceremony witnessed by a future 1848 minister, Armand Marrast. What little is known of Gauguin's own political preferences, however, gives us no reason to believe he embraced the radical heritage passed down to him through the maternal line. Quite the contrary. Pissarro, a real firebrand, found Gauguin's political views exasperating, especially his apparent enthusiasm for the imperial policies of the Ferry ministry of 1883–1885.[61] The most that might be claimed of Gauguin is that, by breeding and reflex, he was a republican well disposed to politicians of Ferry's ilk; but that he was a true socialist, no.

What of the last major figure in the group, Paul Cézanne? He came, like so many of the new painters, from good republican stock. His father, a banker, was a mover in Aixois republican circles in the late imperial period (fig. 15), and there is every reason to think that

Paul, at least in his younger days, held similar opinions. The painter, reclusive by nature, did not like coming to Paris, but when he did it was to radical bohemia, to the Callias salon, that he was drawn. Even when back home in Aix, Cézanne kept abreast of political happenings in the capital city. He corresponded with his childhood friend Zola, read *Le Siècle,* and followed as best he could Rochefort's oppositional antics.[62] In the 1870s Cézanne took to frequenting the local democratic library in Aix and kept up as before with political developments in the radical press. An anticlerical note began to creep into Cézanne's correspondence as well. In an 1876 letter to Pissarro, he voiced an intent to "delve into" *La Religion laïque,* a newspaper of extreme secularist views. He wrote to Zola not half a year after the *seize mai* crisis to recount with unconcealed glee a political fracas in Marseille, where one "Coste junior, municipal councillor, distinguished himself by cracking a few clerical pates."[63] A Callias habitué, an avid reader of newspapers of advanced views, and an anticlerical: this evokes a Cézanne with a political edginess that may have made him an awkward guest at cultured soirées, but most suitable company for the fractious crowd out at Pontoise.

THE PONTOISE colony gives evidence of a clear tilt to the left. Degas' circle, though it included a bohemian or two, was more cultivated and not half so radical. Degas himself, as we know, ended up an anti-Dreyfusard. But considering the artist's reactionary old age, it is remarkable just how freethinking were the painters he made his companions at midcentury. Federico Zandomeneghi, an ardent Italian nationalist, had taken part in Garibaldi's 1860 Sicilian expedition and some years later was thrown into a Venetian jail by the Austrian police.[64] Jean-François Raffaëlli was a confirmed clémenciste. He may best be remembered in fact for an 1885 canvas, *Clemenceau Addressing His Montmartre Constituents,* which represents a vigorous Clemenceau declaiming at center stage, surrounded by all the stalwarts of contemporary radical republicanism: Gustave Geffroy, Charles Longuet, Camille Pelletan—and the painter himself (fig. 16).[65]

Cassatt, Forain and Rouart are less easy to place. Mary Cassatt, as an American, may be expected to have regarded sympathetically republican strivings to found a sister regime in France. Her father Robert was certainly moved by such sentiments. In a letter from Paris to his son, he recounted goings-on at the 1878 exhibition. The fair's success, he reported with satisfaction, "has helped to establish the Republic—The Monarchists cannot conceal their spite at this."[66] But what of Cassatt herself? In May 1871, in the midst of bloody week, she forwarded a "plea for the Commune" to a close friend. "I wish you would read [this]," Cassatt urged. "I think it does them more justice than most of the newspaper correspondents." In the seventies, Cassatt befriended the art collector Moïse Dreyfus, a member since imperial days of the Alliance Israélite. Cassatt exhibited a pastel of Dreyfus at the independents' salon of 1879, one of the few male portraits she ever did (fig. 17). And she never departed from the unconventional course she had charted for herself, in later years making common cause with the women's suffrage movement in the United States and dabbling in spiritualism.[67] Such evidence, while spotty, does suggest a conclusion. Communards and liberal Jews, the bogies of the day, held no terrors for Cassatt, who proved herself over the years a consistent friend to progressive causes.

Jean-Louis Forain, it is certain, did not end as a freethinker. By the turn of the century, he had experienced a rekindling of his Roman Catholic faith, which fueled an anti-Dreyfusism of the most virulent sort. But Forain's return was that of a prodigal son. In the early 1870s, he shared quarters with Arthur Rimbaud and witnessed first hand the violent unfolding of Rimbaud's relationship with fellow poet (and former communard) Paul Verlaine. It was in the same period that Forain struck up a friendship with Charles Cros and began to frequent the Callias salon, where he met Manet. In the eighties, though, Forain shed the guise of bohemian irregular in favor of a more *mondain* persona. He enjoyed a measure of professional success, less as a painter than as a cartoonist, and began to keep better company, lunching on occasion at Camondo's and frequenting the Charpentier salon. The mature Forain was a reactionary, but in the heyday of the new painting he was a young man on the rise, a bohemian en route to a comfortable life in republican society.[68]

Henri Rouart turns out to be the most elusive of the Degas coterie. There is a Saint-Simonian aura to his career. Rouart graduated from the Ecole Polytechnique in the 1850s and in subsequent decades went on to make a fortune as an inventor-entrepreneur. In 1875 Degas painted a portrait of a dark, commanding Rouart, posed in front of a smoke-belching factory, which communicated a notion of the industrialist as Prometheus. But there was an authoritarian streak to such strength. Rouart had friends high in France's military hierarchy, among them General Auguste Mercier who, as minister of war in 1894, did so much to orchestrate Dreyfus' conviction and then to hush up the affair. Rouart, like Mercier himself, was a ferocious anti-Dreyfusard.[69]

Degas' circle was a motley crew. But whether Garibaldino, suffragette, or captain of industry, they all counted themselves friends of progress, confident that history was pushing in the right direction. They exhibited a strong-willed, often prickly individuality that colored the kind of politics they were drawn to. Most were republicans (with perhaps a Saint-Simonian or two) but not of the well-fed lawyerly sort, a breed they in fact disliked. Anti-establishment sentiment ran so strong among them that it led more than one at century's end to turn on the republican establishment as well.

What has been said of Degas' artist friends may well be said of Degas himself. Degas as an old man railed against the upstart pretensions of Jews and would-be intellectuals,[70] but in younger days he was the very antithesis of close-minded. The commercial dynamism of New York City, which he visited in the early 1870s, prompted him to marvel at the wonders of Yankee ingenuity. He distanced himself from the aristocratic affectations of the banking family from which he came. They spelled the family name de Gas; he dropped the particule in favor of the less high-flown Degas.[71] And the company he kept was not of the most exclusive sort. Degas paid an extended visit to Florence in 1858–59. He stayed with an uncle, Baron Gennaro Bellelli, a veteran of the Neapolitan revolution of 1848; at a café he fell in with a band of artists known as the macchiaioli, the spot painters, who were Italian nationalists all, if not outright Garibaldini. Degas made friends as well in the local French colony, among them Georges Lafenestre, a future inspector of fine arts under the republic, and a young Koenigswarter, scion of the Jewish banking family that counted in its ranks a liberal Bonapartist deputy and several charter members of the Alliance Israélite.[72] The Bonapartist connection evoked by the Koenigswarter name is intriguing. Since 1861 Degas had been a friend of the artist Lepic, a vicomte and confirmed Bonapartist. Through Lepic, Degas made the acquaintance of Princess Pauline von Metternich (whom he painted in oil) a member of the liberal-minded circle that gathered at the salon of Louis-Napoleon's cousin Mathilde.

In the 1860s Degas was not active in democratic politics, but the more progressive currents of the day eddied about him: repub-

licanism, Italian nationalism, liberal Bonapartism. In the decade
that followed, he gravitated toward the republican camp, an evolution partly driven by the events of *l'année terrible.* Degas' position
in these months approximates Manet's. Both saw military service
during the siege of Paris. They went together to the Folies-Bergère
to hear Cluseret's denunciations of the provisional government's
half-hearted defense policies. Zealous patriots in 1870, Degas and
Manet were just as ardent anti-Versaillais in 1871. In June, Mme.
Morisot reported on an encounter between the two painters and
her son: "Tiburce has met two Communards, at this moment when
they are all being shot . . . Manet and Degas! Even at this stage
they are condemning the drastic measures used to repress them. I
think they are insane."[73] Neither artist, of course, was ever a communard, but both were disgusted by Thiers' conduct of the civil
war, a sentiment that found expression in work they did at the
time. Manet did several prints of Versaillais firing squads executing
captured revolutionaries. Degas painted in oil a double portrait of
Grand Rabbi Astruc and one-time masonic Grand Master Mellinet
(fig. 2), both of whom did so much to lend humanitarian aid to
wounded combatants during the terrible year.

In the 1870s, Degas' schedule of activities brought him still
further into the republican milieu. Like Renoir, he visited the Charpentier household.[74] Degas also attended the lesser-known Hayem
salon. Charles Hayem was heir to a prosperous shirtmaking business,
which he helped to run with his father Simon. The family, Jewish
and practicing, had consistorial connections, and both father and son
were AIU members. They were republicans in the bargain, though of
the tepid variety that was more at home with Opportunist lawyers
like Gambetta and Méline than with radical hotheads.[75]

In such a milieu Degas socialized, and its inhabitants crop up in
the work he did from the period. It is curious how often Degas did
portraits of Jewish subjects. He made a sketch of Mme. Hayem
(depicted in conversation with Adolphe Franck), an oil of Henri
Michel-Lévy (a fellow painter and scion of the Calmann-Lévy publishing house), and a grand canvas of the banker and art collector
Ernest May, dealing at the stock exchange. Nor were representatives
of France's liberal Protestant elite absent from Degas' portrait gallery. In 1879 he began work on a painting of Mme. Dietz-Monnin,
in all likelihood the wife of UPL member Charles Dietz-Monnin,
who not two years before played a prominent role in organizing

opposition to MacMahon's *seize mai* coup. Degas' republicanism, however, did not come untainted. He wrote in slighting tones of May's Jewishness, and the portrait he painted of the banker bordered on caricature.[76] Signs of the prejudice and irritability that were to overtake the artist in old age were there in muted form in the seventies, but still only straws in the wind. Degas at midcentury was a man of progress: an Italian no less than a French patriot, a conciliationist, a beneficiary of Jewish and Protestant patronage who moved on the borders of a republican establishment in the making. Inclined as he was to self-mockery and irony, he may not have welcomed such a position in all its particulars, but whatever rancor he may have felt did not explode until his later years.

This leaves one last artist to consider, Gustave Caillebotte. He appears in the secondary literature in two guises: as a grand bourgeois, a yachtsman and patron of the arts who bailed out the impressionist movement at various critical junctures; and as an artist in his own right, more realist than impressionist in style, but who understood better than most what the new painting was about. One last detail may be added to the portrait. Caillebotte was elected municipal councillor of Gennevilliers in 1888, placing four slots behind Manet's cousin Jouy in the balloting. In a legislative byelection the preceding year, the town had made a clear showing of its mainstream republican convictions, voting decisively against General Boulanger in favor of the Freemason and future radical Gustave Mesureur. It is reasonable to suppose that Caillebotte shared the political sentiments of his constituents and of his friends and colleagues on the town council. The particular interests he pursued as a public servant were most certainly of the classic republican sort: public celebrations and education.[77]

What conclusions can be drawn from all this? With a few exceptions, mostly among the critics, the men and women associated with the new painting were not *intellectuels engagés*. But from time to time they did feel called upon to enter the public forum. They signed petitions and voted; they volunteered or refused to do so; they painted pictures by turns critical and civic-minded in inspiration. But more than that, the new painters inhabited a particular milieu—a network of salons and cafés, newspapers and clubs—that was deeply implicated in the political struggles of the era. A dazzling record of that world is to be found in their artwork. My claim here is that the new painters, while not activists, took a lively interest in politics and approached politics from a definite perspective, as friends and sympathizers of a reawakening republican movement.

Institutions and Rhetorics

Such a claim helps to explain why contemporaries, especially in the mid-1870s as the regime of Moral Order saw its authority slipping away, so often conflated experimentalism in painting with radical politics. It was easy to collapse the two phenomena into one, given the republican-style campaign that the *jeune école* mounted against the official salon, and given the democratizing rhetoric its friends employed to further the new painting's cause.

An important current in recent scholarship has taken a somewhat different tack, emphasizing not so much the political as the commercial stakes in the painters' attack on academic institutions. The *jeune école,* it has been pointed out, was intent on attracting new buyers: "the professional, the merchant, the civil servant, the intellectual, other artists."[78] They worked in smaller formats than did conventional *grande peinture,* the better to suit the needs of a prosperous but not very rich clientele more interested in apartment decoration than in the production of imposing effects. Similar concerns shaped the subject matter of their work. Classical, religious, or historical themes, which presupposed audiences educated in the canons of western tradition, were eschewed in favor of scenes more accessible to all, drawn from everyday life. The new painters had a market in mind and a product to sell but, so the argument goes, were blocked from tapping into it by the hidebound salon system; academicians and state administrators regulated what passed before the public. The *jeune école* wanted to reduce, if not eliminate altogether, the authority of intermediaries so that viewers and buyers might be approached directly. Though correct in outline, such an analysis misses the political dimension of the situation, as even a summary review of impressionist marketing strategies will show.

The academics and administrators who dominated midcentury salon juries did not much cotton to the new painting and sometimes were more than obdurate. The year 1863 was one such occasion, when over half of all submissions were turned away. The agitation that followed was strident enough to persuade the emperor to agree to an alternative salon, the Salon des Refusés, where the rejected artists could exhibit. Manet, for one, took part, showing his *Déjeuner sur l'herbe.* The occasion and defiant radicalism of the canvas estab-lished him as the "leader of the young independents."[79]

The refusés set a precedent that came back to haunt administra-tors. In 1866 Cézanne's submission to the salon was turned down flat. He fired off two letters to the superintendant of fine arts, insisting on a second Salon des Refusés.[80] Zola, in a review of the exhibit, backed Cézanne's entreaties, arguing for salons unburdened by state or aca-demic tutelage, a kind of *bazar du beau* in which all might partici-pate. The choice, as he presented it in a later formulation, was stark: either "the dogma of the Institute" or "complete liberty, an entrepôt open to all producers."[81]

Demands for an alternative salon emerged again the following year. The jury had come down hard on salon applicants, rejecting two of every three canvases submitted. A petition for a repeat of the 1863 experiment circulated among artists, signed, according to Bazille, "by all the painters in Paris of any value," but to no avail.[82] For a third time, in 1871–72, the gambit was tried and with the same negative results. In December 1871 Thiers' minister of fine arts, the moderate republican Charles Blanc, promulgated the terms governing jury selection for the next salon. They were quite restrictive, disenfran-chising all artists save Prix de Rome recipients or medalwinners from previous salons. A protest was at once forwarded to Thiers, bearing the signatures of almost a hundred artists, Manet's among them. Blanc proceeded with the jury elections as planned. The jury in the event proved itself severe, prompting artists once more to step into the breach. Cézanne, Fantin, Manet, Pissarro, Renoir, and thirty colleagues appealed to the authorities to convoke a new Salon des Refusés.[83]

But the protest petition was not the only strategy pursued by painters unhappy with obstructive salon practices. In 1870 the em-pire made a gesture toward liberalizing the salon, lifting restrictions on who might run for office in jury elections. Dissident artists took advantage of the opening to mount a campaign. An electoral com-mittee was formed and a slate of candidates drawn up, which featured well-known independents like Manet but not a single member of the academy. At Manet's suggestion, the list was preceded by a brief manifesto, proclaiming the right of all artists to take part in the jury-selection process. The document made the rounds of the cafés, and Manet prevailed on Zola to have it published in *Le Rappel* and *La Cloche.*[84]

Such petitions and campaigns came to very little in the end. But dissident artists had more success when they attempted, as individuals, as a collectivity, or with the aid of dealers, to bypass the salon system altogether. Manet felt most comfortable in the maverick's role, acting alone. The tough-mindedness of the 1867 jury prompted him to organize a one-man show, paid for by himself, at a temporary structure on the Place de l'Alma. Determined to cause as much stir as possible, he planned to exhibit a version of the death of the Emperor Maximilian, but was prohibited from doing so by state authorities. Manet contented himself with issuing a brochure, explaining why he had decided to strike out on his own rather than waiting for a more favorable verdict from the next salon jury: "In these circumstances the artist has been advised to wait. To wait for what? Until there is no longer a jury? He has preferred to settle the question with the public."[85]

The exclusionary turn taken by juries in the early 1870s provoked a new bout of protest. Duranty in an 1872 review was moved to denounce the salon system's monopolistic practices. "If you want ardor in the struggle," he wrote, "artists with élan, then laissez-faire, laissez-passer."[86] To slip the stranglehold of the official salon, independents this time around took action as a collective body. The notion of concerted action had first been floated by the critic Paul Alexis in a May 1873 article in L'Avenir national. Alexis, invoking "this powerful idea, the idea of association," proposed that the painters act like the "artistic corporation" they were and organize a chambre syndicale. Such associationist rhetoric might well have made the authorities nervous in the post-Commune era, all the more so given the paper in which Alexis' article appeared, but the painters were not put off. Monet in fact drafted a public letter of thanks to L'Avenir national and pursued the project with interested colleagues.[87] Before the year was out, an association had indeed been formed, not the chambre syndicale of Alexis' imagining but a cooperative.

The independent salons staged by the cooperative did not solve the painters' financial problems, and they continued to pursue, in tandem with group efforts, various personal strategies. Renoir went so far as to return to the official salon. He exhibited there in 1879, 1880, and 1881 and was joined in the enterprise, at least in 1880, by Monet. The two artists were not altogether happy with the results, in particular with how their paintings had been hung, and planned to publish a letter of protest in the radical Le Voltaire.[88] Over time, the new painters tended to drift away from official channels of market access in favor of patron- or dealer-sponsored shows. Charpentier mounted a series of such exhibits at the offices of *La Vie moderne*: in 1879 for Renoir, in 1880 for Monet, and so on. Durand-Ruel was also active in this domain, organizing in 1883 alone one-man shows for Monet, Renoir, and Pissarro.

It is fair to understand the new painting as an attempt to restructure modes of market access, but in the mid-nineteenth-century context this cannot be seen as a nonpartisan issue. The *jeune école* understood itself as appealing to an unspecified public; it invoked the principles of liberty, free trade, and cooperative association; it made its pitch through petition campaigns, electoral drives, and the republican press. The new painters' commercial agenda was not without a political dimension.

But it was not only that the antisalon campaign had a republican look to it. The very language in which the project was framed, both its institutional and to a lesser extent its aesthetic aspects, was steeped in republican phraseology and metaphor. On the whole this was the work of the new painting's critic friends, and it may be ventured that sometimes they didn't get it altogether right. The *jeune école* problematized the means and conventions of pictorial representation, fashioning a world of painted images that was accessible to the untutored eye, but at the same time they set out in plain view just how difficult it was to assemble that world, to communicate the sensations they had experienced in confronting it.[89] Castagnary, to take one example, grasped the thematic innovations of the new painting well enough, but not always its technical experiments. What he celebrated in the new painting was not work done by artists locked in agonistic embrace with resistant materials or problems of representation but work that was in many ways untroubled, the product of a way of seeing now undimmed by the heavy veils of a classical or Christian past. But too much should not be made of such disjunctions between critical discourse and artistic practice. The new painters were happy to have friends in the critical fraternity, even those who were only half right. They cheered the critics on and sometimes joined in. The critics imposed a political reading on the new painting and often did so with the painters' explicit consent.

The case is easiest to make on the institutional front. Duranty reviled the salon system as "a bureaucracy of spirit" that weighed on artists as much as feudalism had weighed on the serfs of prerevolu-

tionary times. Burty took aim at the salon's authoritarian constitution, which placed too many obstacles in the path of artists with
strong character and temperament.[90] Who was it that profited from
such a system? Burty and Castagnary had no trouble identifying the
winners. They were a new nobility: an intolerant aristocracy of the
"semiofficial and rich," a caste of "privileged electors."[91] As for the
mass of artists, they had been reduced to "riotous plebs," to a disenfranchised "gent taillable et corvéable."[92] When Cassatt cast about for
metaphors to convey the oppressed status of the contemporary artist,
she borrowed not from Roman or feudal models but from the American experience. "Liberty," she wrote, "is the first good in the world
and to escape the tyranny of a jury is worth fighting for, for surely no
profession is as enslaved as ours."[93]

There were certainly political stakes involved in salon organization. Despotism stood on the one side, liberty on the other. No one
was more explicit on the point than Castagnary. Public opinion, he
said in 1869, favored a separation of church and state. No less urgent
was a separation of art and state. With the coming of the republic in
1870, he and like-minded critics anticipated a decrease in official
controls, but they were bitterly disappointed. The ministry of fine
arts, under Blanc's stewardship from 1871 to 1873, tightened state
regulation of the jury-selection process. Duranty exploded: Blanc,
"although a republican," had revealed himself as "very authoritarian,
very papist, very infallibilist." Blanc was ousted in 1873, but the
situation did not improve under his successor, the Marquis de Chennevières. A legitimist, Chennevières carried forward Blanc's statist
policies, prompting an exasperated Castagnary to lament: "for four
years and more, we have lived in a republic, [but] not a single
republican principle has penetrated the administration of fine arts."
With Chennevières in office, "the monarchical regime perpetuates
itself."[94]

To the regime in place, which reeked of privilege, popery, and
despotism, the jeune école counterposed an imagined new order, the
polar opposite of the status quo. The present system was monarchical,
while the new painters dreamed of a "republic of the arts."[95] No one
doubted how such a republic was to be organized. In lieu of the salon
franchise of old, the new painters advocated the enfranchisement of
the entire artistic community. Jury selection would be determined
by a democracy of artists, by universal suffrage. Thus the state and
the academy might be subtracted from the equation of power, allow-

ing artists to address face to face the one accredited arbiter of taste, *monsieur tout le monde.*[96] The new school, like so many of the institutional insurgencies of the era, placed its faith and its fate in the hands of "the public."[97]

Partisans of the *jeune école* transposed an institutional battle between the salon establishment on the one hand and artistic dissidents on the other into a political confrontation between the republic and its enemies. Political language was so pervasive that it even infiltrated the presentation of the painters' aesthetic ambitions. The markings here are fainter but present nonetheless, and most visible in the *jeune école*'s critique of academic aesthetics.

Dissidents dismissed academic aesthetics as a derivative of Victor Cousin's eclecticism, which understood the good, the true, and the beautiful as timeless, spiritual categories. The academic artist accordingly, to the dismay of critics like Duret, was trained to believe "that there exists an abstract standard, and only one, of the beautiful-in-itself." To the academic painter, absolute beauty hovered "beyond history and geography, beyond time and space." And how were artists taught to attain to such perfection? Academic pedagogy, it was claimed, slighted the individualizing detail that rooted the artist in the here-and-now. Aspiring painters were instead encouraged to copy from the past, to model themselves on the pioneers of the ideal: the Greeks, the Romans, and the Italians of the Renaissance.[98]

Partisans of the new school objected to the academic aesthetic first on philosophical grounds. To Castagnary, talk about revelations of ideal beauty smacked of theology, and he had no use for the smoke and mirrors of the divine. In opposition to the "divine Eden" beloved of theologians, Castagnary imagined a secularist garden, and he wrote: "I will place at the entrance Progress, invisible sentinel; I will put a flaming sword in his hand and I will say to God: 'You will not enter!'" In a secular universe transformed by unceasing and progressive change, notions of eternal beauty made no sense.[99]

Then why was the ideal pursued? For Zola, the answer was simple: "The encroachments of science and industry have prompted artists, in reaction, to throw themselves into dreams, into a cut-and-paste heaven made of tinsel and silk paper."[100] Painters fled a hard, challenging reality, taking refuge in the safe haven of the studio. This meant that academic art lacked the vibrancy born of contact with the real. Its colors—bitumen, chocolate, chrome yellow—rang false. Its poses were stilted, untrue to life. The practitioners of official art were, as one critic remarked of Alexandre Cabanel, little better than costumers who dressed up models in the rhetoric of the ideal.[101]

To its enemies, academic painting was a mix of false philosophy and bad technique. At best, such a combination produced an art "honestly mediocre," but very little separated honest mediocrity from a deceitful slickness. Pelletan was appalled by what he saw at the 1872 salon. He jeered at "the pomaded *orientales*" and ridiculed the nudes as "great helpings of female flesh." Nor was he any more generous to the salon audience, "fine, beribboned gentlemen, dandies and élégants afloat in a sea of satins and laces."[102] Academic art paid lip service to the ideal, but far too often it pandered to the aesthetic pretensions of the sleek and well-heeled.

Wedded in principle to an authoritarian set of aesthetic rules but dishonest in its practices, idealistic in its presentation but servile to the rich and famous, in all these respects, critics felt, academic art betrayed its kinship to Bonapartism. When Félix Nadar, an admirer of Manet's, wanted to characterize historical landscapists resistant to the freer renderings of the *jeune école,* he referred to them as the "bemedaled" denizens of an artistic Saint Helena. Georges Rivière, a critic friend of Renoir's, contrasted the emancipatory impulses that animated the new painters with the constraining aesthetic code, "contemporaneous with all the other Napoleonic codes," under which artists of the old school still labored.[103] The time had come to break the codes of yesteryear, whether Cousinist or imperial. A new society was in the making, "egalitarian and democratic,"[104] and to represent it, artists were called on to paint new subjects in new ways.

Radical critics gave a distinct political twist to the *jeune école*'s attempts at iconographic renewal. History painting had contented itself with the representation of "operetta kings tricked out in blue or yellow robes." Themes borrowed from an outworn ancien régime, however, had no place in an art of this century. Artists who wanted to paint history were advised to paint "the history of their own times," "the spectacle of everyday life."[105] In Castagnary's estimation, that was the truth the new painters had seized upon, and in pursuing it they were dedicated to carrying forward "the general spirit of the French revolution."[106]

The new painters, in tune with a secularist and revolutionary present, had cast aside the thematic conventions of yesteryear, devoting themselves to modernity: to the Haussmannized metropolis, its streets and interiors, its railroad stations and places of entertainment. But it was not only new locales that attracted these painters, but the men and women who were found there. The picturesque peasant was always a staple in the repertory of academic art; the well-born and powerful always had an easy time finding artists to fix them on canvas—but what of all the rest? It was the expanding social territory in between the lowest and the highest that the new painters laid claim to. They chose to paint, in Mallarmé's words, the "beauties of the people," the "graces which exist in the bourgeoisie."[107] They populated their work with laundry girls, wharf porters, floor scrapers, but above all with denizens of the middle class: businessmen and *femmes de foyer,* decked out in the latest department-store finery.[108] In 1872 Gambetta commented on a sea change in public life: a *nouvelle couche sociale* was beginning to take an active part in the nation's political affairs. Into art as well, remarked Castagnary only a year later, the "new social strata" had "erupted."[109]

Critics detected a democratizing impulse behind this commitment to the painting of everyday life. But what about the new painters' artistic practices? Little, it seems, could be said to bestow a political gloss on the *jeune école*'s technical innovations. And yet, in describing how the painters worked, partisans time and again had recourse to a critical idiom shot through with political formulas. They wrapped the new painting in the legitimating mantles of science and nature; they attributed to it the virtues of simplicity and sincerity. In so doing, they defined the new art not just as formalist experiment (indeed, they were often insensitive to technical innovation), but as an aesthetic counterpart to republican politics.

Critics of a realist bent extolled the new painters' matter-of-factness and supposed devotion to clear-eyed observation. Manet painted his *Dead Christ with Angels* in 1864. The Jesus he represented, however, was not the son of God, but a cadaver laid out as in a morgue or medical amphitheater. Critics did not hesitate to draw a parallel between Manet's all-too-human Jesus and the secular Christ portrayed in Renan's *Vie de Jésus,* published the year before.[110] And when the new painters turned to living subjects, they sought to capture individual human beings, not abstract types. They cultivated a keen eye for the particularizing detail: for the "professional stigmata," attitudes and gestures, the tic that betrayed a sitter's social position or personality.[111] Such detached devotion to the facts prompted more than one critic to draw parallels between the new painting and experimental science. Zola pushed the analogy relentlessly, writing of Manet:

> [The artist] is a child of our times. To me he is an analytical painter. Since science required a solid foundation and returned to the exact observation of facts, everything has been called in question. This movement has occurred not only in the scientific world. All fields of knowledge, all human undertakings, look for constant and definite principles in reality. Our modern landscape painters have far surpassed our painters of history and genre because they have studied our countryside, content to set down the first edge of a wood they come to. Manet applied the same method in each of his works.[112]

The new painting's commitment to a candid recording of the world, it was said, prompted a rethinking of how nature was to be approached. Many artists were moved to abandon the atelier and its habits of mind to work in the open air. They encountered outdoor spaces bathed in luminous colors, whose rendering required a bright, clear palette. Castagnary celebrated the new school's shunning of bitumen as a "return to simplicity."[113] In certain instances, though, the painters' zeal for the simple and direct produced unconventional, even disturbing results. In a summer's sun, thick foliage imparts a violet tint to the skin and clothing of subjects posed in a shaded setting. The light filtering through atmosphere and trees produces marked visual palpitations. The new painters, "true to nature," represented such effects, painting what they saw and felt and, for such pains, were denounced by hostile critics as "communards" and "scoundrels." What was the artist's stock response to such accusations? In vain, Duret claimed, the new school protested "its perfect sincerity." The catalogue published for Manet's one-man show of 1867 opened with the disarming declaration: "The artist does not say today, 'Come and see faultless work,' but 'Come and see sincere work.'"[114]

When the *jeune école* cast about for ways to finesse the salon system, they addressed themselves to allies in the republican movement. They made use of the movement's resources and borrowed from its stock of mobilizing techniques. Friendly critics conceptualized the new art as a democratic assault on oligarchical and authoritarian institutions and represented its aesthetic ambitions as secularizing and antimetaphysical in thrust. They recognized democratic and egalitarian impulses at work in the choice of subject matter and, on questions of technique, advanced the more disputable claim that the *jeune école,* in casting aside the conventions of the past, had plumped for a sincere rendering of reality. Here was an art, practiced by men and women of democratic convictions, which was conceived of and even conceived of itself in the language of republicanism.

THE REPUBLIC, when it came into its own in the 1880s, repaid the *jeune école* with a measure of public acknowledgment. The new painting's institutional agenda was in effect enacted into law in 1880. Jules Ferry, minister of public instruction and fine arts, decreed the abolition of the old jury system. Oversight of salon organization was vested in a ninety-member Société des artistes. The society was an elective body, all former *exposants* having the right to vote. In so doing, Ferry did not see himself as buckling to the artistic avant-garde, but neither can it be said that he was ignorant of the *jeune école* or its ambitions. He may not have liked much of the new art, but he knew the artists (Morisot quite well) and, as a republican, was in sympathy with the democratized exhibition system they advocated.

The new school benefitted as well from state patronage. Manet and Bracquemond received the Légion d'Honneur. Various critic friends—Burty, Castagnary, Silvestre—got state appointments. Republican officialdom's tastes, especially in the regime's first years, ran to the realist, a predilection reflected in its buying habits. The state made its first purchase of a canvas executed by a new painter in 1886, Raffaëlli's *Chez le fondeur.*[115] Over time, the regime became more even-handed in its largesse, and the impressionist wing of the new movement profited from the change. At the state-mounted exhibition of 1889, organized in connection with that year's World's Fair, nineteen works by the *jeune école* were shown. At the 1900 fair, the number had risen to fifty-four.[116]

No doubt the now not-so-young school hoped for more and better from the regime. Manet's *Olympia* was offered to the state in 1890 on condition that it be hung in the Louvre; the state accepted the gift but, after much debate, placed it in the Luxembourg instead. Caillebotte died in 1894, bequeathing his substantial art collection to the state. Officials did not act with dispatch; opposition to the bequest, emanating in particular from academicians like Gérôme, had a chance to mobilize; and in the end only 38 of the 65 paintings offered were taken. Still, the great *Olympia* did come to the Louvre in 1907, thanks to Prime Minister Clemenceau's intercession. As for the Caillebotte bequest, once accepted it was housed in a special annex built onto the Luxembourg just for that purpose.

The *jeune école* emerged from pariah status in the years of the republic's consolidation, a coincidence that was no chance occurrence. The new painting and the republican movement were conjoined by bonds of friendship and conviction, by common institutional aspirations, by a shared democratizing rhetoric. The fit was not perfect: not all new painters were republicans and, certainly, not all republicans understood the new painting. But a fit there was, even if rough: the new painters found a niche for themselves in republican society. Indeed, their work offers a quick route of visual access into that milieu. Here, on canvas, are to be encountered its heroes and habits, representations of its political rituals and domestic interiors. It is to a discussion of these—the public and private faces of republicanism—that I now turn.

[8]

Political Culture

THE CONSTITUTION of the Third Republic was set aside in 1940, and few mourned its passing. In the domain of public ritual and symbol, however, the regime left a more enduring mark. The "Marseillaise" was proclaimed France's national anthem in 1879, the *quatorze juillet* its national holiday the following year. From 1880 on, the motto "Liberty, Equality, Fraternity" was inscribed by law on all public buildings. And a half decade later, the republic reclaimed the Pantheon as its own. A church under the Second Empire and the regime of Moral Order, under the Republic of the republicans it became a "lay temple," the official resting place of a thankful nation's great men. The first to be accorded such an honor was the national poet Victor Hugo, buried in 1885 in a state ceremony of monumental proportions. In song and ceremony, in inscriptions and holidays, the republic anchored itself in the daily lives of its citizens. Long after the regime's constitutional structure had been swept away, its symbolic structure remained intact, still capable of stirring loyalties and mobilizing consent.

A number of points need to be kept in mind about the new republican political culture. It did draw on the repertory of practices and symbols elaborated at the time of the Great Revolution, but it updated that heritage. The cult of great men was still celebrated, but a panoply of nineteenth-century figures—scientists, historians, littérateurs, politicians—were added to the list of recognized heroes. The political culture of the Third Republic, far more than its revolutionary forebear, was aimed at the young. The late-nineteenth-century city with its monuments and statues was transformed into a great outdoor classroom, bristling with moral lessons for youth. Indeed, it is important to conceive of the monuments of the republic in the broadest terms possible, to encompass not just structures carved in stone or marble but the great literary edifices of the day as well: Littré's dictionary of the French language, Larousse's encyclopedia of the nineteenth century, and so on. For republican political culture, however critical its ceremonial aspect, was at the same time a culture centered on the printed word and its means of dissemination. That republican print culture nursed pedagogical ambitions of a scientistic, encyclopedic cast is beyond doubt, but to sum it up as "positivist" in orientation is to submerge its utopian aspect, its imagining of a universal order in which human beings might live in harmony with nature and themselves.

Such a rich cultural melange did not, of course, come into being at the stroke of a legislator's pen. It was worked out over a period of decades. In the aftermath of Louis-Napoleon's coup, what remained of the republican movement was driven underground or abroad. The problem for exiles, as for the rising generation of militants at home, was how to talk politics to an awakening public without exciting the censor's ire. All sorts of strategies were devised to insinuate or dramatize the republican message, to conduct politics by indirection. But to score points, it was not enough merely to finesse the authorities. A resonant chord in the public imagination had to be struck, and the public could be an exigent taskmaster. Militants, even as they played cat-and-mouse games with the police, had to woo opinion.

A stock of symbolic and textual practices was used to arouse and orient public opinion. That orientation was political in character, but not in any simple, electoral sense. Republicans invited the nation to participate in a range of activities that encouraged beliefs and habits supportive of a democratic public life. The idea was to shape a particular kind of citizen: a conscientious human being who revered the *philosophes* and the revolutionaries of 1789, who valued liberty, laicity, and the riches afforded by literacy and a vital associational life. With such citizens, elections might be won and democratic institutions made to work, but the citizens had to come first.

My argument is this: the republican movement, well before its accession to national office in 1879–80, had articulated a culture of its own. Once in power, republicans deployed state authority to make

cult. of Repub, existed in to before 1879

that culture official. The new order of things took hold, not just because it had the weight of law behind it but because it already had the sanction of public opinion, a sanction earned over two decades of political combat.

Bringing Politics Home

Louis-Napoleon's coup scattered the *parti républicain,* driving scores of asylum seekers across France's borders. But the refugee communities that sprang up abroad—in Belgium, Switzerland, and around the Hugo family on the Channel Islands—found ways soon enough to make themselves heard. Emile Deschanel, a Brussels-based exile, organized a series of public lectures. He rented a hall, opened it to a paying public, and spoke, as fancy moved him, on the literary and artistic topics of the day, all the while spicing the proceedings with well-placed political allusions.[1] The written word afforded exiles another avenue of expression. The editor-in-chief at *L'Indépendance belge,* a good friend of publisher-in-exile Pierre-Jules Hetzel, opened the paper's columns to a raft of *proscrits:* Deschanel, Edgar Quinet, and the art critic Théophile Thoré (one of Manet's earliest admirers).[2] To exiles, the northern border states were places of more or less permanent refuge; to dissidents remaining on French soil, they afforded havens of temporary escape as well. The decades of midcentury witnessed a proliferation of international conferences, and Belgium and Switzerland were the preferred locales. Radical students gathered at Liège in 1865. Pacifists organized a series of congresses in Switzerland, which convened on an annual basis from 1867 to the outbreak of the Franco-Prussian war. The meetings gave birth to a permanent organization, the Ligue de la Paix, and to a periodical, *Les Etats-Unis d'Europe,* edited by Charles Lemonnier, a former Saint-Simonian. It may have been easy enough to find ways abroad to express opposition, but the problem remained: how to bring politics back to France.

The Second Empire simplified the task somewhat. In 1859 it declared an amnesty that allowed a number of exiles to return. In 1868 it liberalized the press and association laws. As the regime withdrew its forces, republicans poured into the spaces opened, driving hard to widen the range of public activity, inventing strategies to circumvent and confound authorities, confronting them with an array of borderline cases that tested the limits of the permissible.

Nowhere was this more apparent than in the domain of the spoken word. Courtrooms, as we have seen, were transformed time and again into platforms for a legal oratory that oftentimes erupted into out-and-out political denunciation. The public conference was used to a similar end.

Deschanel profited from the 1859 amnesty, returned home, and set about organizing the same kind of lecture series he had pioneered in Brussels. A room was rented on the Rue de la Paix (the venue changed several times in subsequent years), and an array of speakers were invited to discuss scientific or literary subjects of potential interest to the well-informed amateur. All harmless enough at first glance, except that the speakers—Bancel, Brisson, Castagnary, Floquet—were recruited almost without exception from republican ranks. What did such men talk about? Camille Flammarion regaled audiences with projections demonstrating the marvels of scientific invention; Eugène Pelletan discoursed on the history of progress; Pierre-Oscar Lissagaray, in the name of "liberal youth," chastised Alfred de Musset as a retrograde "religious [man] without beliefs, a royalist without convictions." Science, progress, liberty, such were the watchwords of Deschanel's effort. No one addressed political issues in an overt manner, and the law in fact forbade political speech, but it was a prohibition respected more in the letter than in the spirit.[3]

Deschanel's example caught on. From 1866 on, the Grand Orient hosted a series of public "philosophic conferences" (women admitted free). Here it was, thanks to an invitation arranged by Léon Richer, that Maria Deraismes' career as a feminist militant got its start. Before the decade was out, she had made the move from oratory to journalism, joining the staff of Richer's new *Droit des femmes* in 1869.[4] Masonic conferences proved no less instrumental in launching or, better, relaunching the fortunes of that old 48er and former exile, Désiré Bancel. In December 1868 the lodge Mars et les Arts invited Bancel to speak on "Civilization and Freemasonry." He was invited back the next March, this time to a public or so-called white session. Pelletan opened the evening's proceedings with a tribute to two celebrated masonic brothers: Abraham Lincoln, "who abolished slavery in America," and Joseph [sic] Garibaldi, "who liberated Italy." As for Bancel's own talk, the subject has not been recorded, but it went over so well that lodge members debated arranging its publication; they balked in the end because of the speech's "compromising" content.[5] Bancel was at it again in May, this time under the auspices of the Association Philotechnique. He delivered an address at the Châtelet theater on a topic that must have seemed neutral enough, "the genius of Corneille," but he contrived to give the event a political twist. He fired up the crowd with a paean to Hugo, and the audience responded with shouts of "Vive Hugo! Vive la liberté!" prompting police to shut the meeting down.[6]

The public seminar had since its inception been a kind of masquerade, speakers discoursing in high-minded tones as they pursued hidden agendas. In the supercharged climate of the late empire, it took little indeed—an allusion, a shout—to bring the politics foaming to the surface. The public-reunion campaign of 1868–1870 revealed just how politicized the form had become.

In the summer of 1868 the empire liberalized legislation governing public meetings of more than twenty persons. Prior authorization was no longer required, provided that political issues were not discussed. It sufficed to notify the police in advance (who as a rule sent an agent along to maintain order). The opposition organized thousands of such events in the empire's waning years. But the first to take advantage of the relaxed order was Edouard Horn, a liberal economist of impeccable republican credentials: an editor at *L'Avenir national,* a Mason, and a member of the Alliance Israélite.[7] Horn inaugurated a series of public debates at the Pré-aux-Clercs meeting hall in June 1868. Illegitimate children, women's work, divorce, such were the themes taken up by the assembly. These might pass as neutral concerns, but debaters as a matter of course spoke in political, often demagogic accents, blaming bastardy on the existence of standing armies or the stigma attached to illegitimacy on religious prejudice. Indeed, to Horn's associates, André Rousselle and Charles Limousin, politics was what the entire enterprise was about: to afford a widening public a "civic education" in "democratic principles."[8]

The enterprise that Horn and his friends had launched may have begun as an exercise in political pedagogy, but it soon overflowed into politicking pure and simple. Internationalists and Proudhonists opened debating halls of their own, treating crowds to lessons not in civics but in revolution.[9] But the republican cause profited just as much from the explosion of public meetings. Republican speakers, who had honed their skills on the conference circuit, abandoned the lecture hall for the hustings during the elections of 1869. The meetings they organized resembled *conférences publiques* in every particular, except that the politics were no longer concealed. The results were gratifying: 1869 afforded the Third Republic's founding generation its first taste of political victory.

The public meeting, shedding its parapolitical chrysalis, matured into a new form, the electoral meeting or *réunion électorale*. Under the Third Republic, the *réunion électorale* acquired almost institutional status, but its origins were far from humdrum, anchored as they were in years of shadow boxing with a hostile imperial officialdom.

The Cult of Voltaire

Verbal legerdemain, of course, was not the sole technique by which dissidents might score political points. Symbolic means—statuary, ceremonials, and the ritual organization of public memory—served the purpose just as well. In this arena, too, militants improvised habits and forms that, although tactical in origin, entered over time into the permanent repertory of republican political practice.

The burgeoning Voltaire cult of the 1860s and 1870s may be cited as an example. *Le Siècle* in January 1867 financed publication of an inexpensive edition of Voltaire's works. At the same time it started a public subscription to pay for a statue in the philosopher's memory. The gesture elicited a remarkable surge of support: by year's end, over 200,000 people had made a contribution.[10] This would be a monument that would speak for the demos—speak for and to, since the sponsors of the subscription intended the Voltaire monument as a lesson to the public, a form of "moral education."[11] But what was the public to learn?

To Frédéric Morin, the message conveyed was anti-Cousinist, and it does seem to have been Victor Cousin's passing that triggered the subscription campaign in the first place. Cousin died on 14 January; *Le Siècle* made its announcement eleven days later. The choice of Voltaire as a counterweight to Cousin was to Morin's mind a fitting one. For a younger generation laboring to emancipate itself from the "incurable mysticism" of the doctrinaire school and its eclectic offspring, it was hard to imagine a more apposite standard bearer than the antimetaphysical skeptic Voltaire.[12]

Anti-Cousinism may account for the timing of the campaign, but it was Voltaire's capacity to catalyze antigovernment and, of course, anticlerical sentiment that lent him so much symbolic appeal. In 1863 the regime replaced the statue of Napoleon as little corporal atop the Vendôme column with a statue of Napoleon as emperor, toga-clad and crowned with laurel wreath. What better way to answer such tributes to despotism than with a memorial to Voltaire, the friend of liberty? And there was no better way to reply to Catholic reaction, to the Mortara affair and the Syllabus of Errors, than to honor Voltaire, coiner of that clarion call of anticlericalism, "Ecrasez l'infâme."[13]

Masons, as might be imagined, embraced the Voltaire cult with particular zeal. In December 1869 the lodge L'Ecole Mutuelle hosted a Voltaire celebration. An audience of 1,500, presided over by lodge venerable Amédée Dréo, was treated to a varied program of entertainment: a dramatic reading from Voltaire's "manly tragedy" *Brutus,* an appearance by the Comédie actress Mlle. Agar draped in masonic sash, and a rousing speech by Bancel.[14]

The first round of the Voltaire revival went to the republican side. The empire prosecuted the editor of *Le Siècle* for organizing an unauthorized public subscription. But plans for the statue—a bronze replica of Houdon's robed and seated philosopher—went ahead unchecked. And in 1870, not long after the imperial regime's collapse, the casting at last made its public debut on an outdoor pedestal.

Voltaire went into symbolic battle once again in 1878 and emerged triumphant. The spring of that year was a moment of unsettled political transition. The *seize mai* coup had failed, but President MacMahon remained in office. Broglie had been ousted as prime minister but was replaced by a one-time Orleanist and latecomer to the democratic fold, Armand Dufaure. True-blue democrats pressured the government to give a sign of its republican colors. The Gambettist deputy Emile Menier pressed Dufaure to set aside a room at the upcoming 1878 exposition to commemorate the centenary of Voltaire's and Rousseau's deaths. The radical Paris municipal council lobbied for an official commemoration of Bastille Day. On the first point, Dufaure refused; on the second, he budged a little designating 30 June a national festival of peace and no more.

Republicans were not discouraged by official foot dragging. In late January, Menier presided at a meeting in the Tivoli Vaux-Hall. A Voltaire centennial commission was nominated, composed of the usual republican luminaries, plus the architect and municipal councillor, Eugène-Emmanuel Viollet-le-Duc. The commission, seconded by the Société des Gens de Lettres, undertook three tasks: to publish an edited edition of Voltaire classics, to erect a second statue in the philosopher's honor, and to organize an elaborate celebration. Menier supplied the material backing for the first enterprise. Financing the statue proved more troublesome. The Grand Orient and eight individual lodges made donations, but in the end most of the funds came from a public body, the Paris municipal council.[15] The sculptor Joseph Caillé had a plaster model, a standing Voltaire with skeptical smile, ready in time for the centennial.[16] As for the celebration itself, it was a grand affair. A huge public assembly gathered at the Cirque Myers. Hugo addressed a smaller paying crowd at the Gaïté theater. The authorities tolerated the event, but only just. Minister of the Interior Emile de Marcère, reviling the celebration as "an outrage to Christian religion," prohibited outdoor demonstrations of any kind during the day's festivities.[17]

Civil Ceremonies

Republicans battered away at sullen authorities with monuments and centenaries. Private ceremonials, a marriage, a funeral, were made use of in much the same way: to make a statement, lodge a protest, or challenge officialdom outright.

A wedding at the mayor's office without benefit of clergy was a simple and direct means of affirming secular belief. The freethinking press recorded these events—such as Charles Floquet's civil marriage in 1869—with satisfaction. In the era of Moral Order, the police sent informants to jot down names of guests, as they did, for example, to Edouard Lockroy's wedding to Alice Hugo in 1877.[18]

In the seventies, it became possible to laicize not just the marriage ceremony but the very setting in which it took place. Republicans captured municipal offices in increasing number and set about giving symbolic form to the takeover by way of redecorating schemes of all sorts. The republic's initials "RF" were inscribed over the local mairie's entranceway or a bust of Marianne was installed in the mayor's office. The salle des mariages was also subject to overhaul, all the better to dramatize the serene and fecund joys of civil matrimony.

The Paris municipal council in the 1870s was all too happy to gather secularizing points by such means, but not until decade's end did it have the leeway to act with boldness. Beautification schemes for the city's various offices had to be approved by a prefect-appointed committee of fine arts, which reserved to itself as well the right to commission the artists and sculptors. Parisian councillors bridled at such constraints. In 1878, in the aftermath of the *seize mai* fiasco, the council at last managed to extract concessions. More committee seats were set aside for municipal officers, and artists' commissions were henceforth determined not by direct order but by public competition. In the area of town-hall decoration, the new arrangement bore immediate results. Plans were made to refurbish the marriage hall of the *mairie* of the nineteenth arrondissement. A competition organized the following year yielded two winners, Emile Blanchon and Henri Gervex. Gervex went on to paint a wall-sized panel, *Civil Marriage,* which was remarkable on several counts. It depicted an actual event: the wedding of the local mayor's son as performed by the mayor himself, Mathurin Moreau (in tricolor sash), before an assembly of invited guests. All the figures were painted in contemporary dress, and several were recognizable: Camille Pelletan, the Prince of Wales, Zola. The suave execution and the artist's choice of figures imparted a fashionable urbanity to the work. But the panel was at the same time a realistic treatment of a secular event and represented a distinct break with the idealizing, saccharine conventions of academic tradition.[19]

As a ritual of contestation, however, civil marriage never excited public passions to the same degree as civil burial. Whether freethinkers believed, as materialists did, that the body of the deceased, even as it decomposed, replenished the eternal stream of life or, as deists did, that the deceased's immortal soul lived on, communing with other souls in contemplation of God, all agreed in rejecting church dogma.[20] They were just as resolved to invent a counter-ritual that would "speak to the eyes as well as to the spirit," stirring enough to persuade the faithful to abandon the obscurantist ways of old in favor of "the liberty of the tomb."[21]

At a freethinking funeral, it was still accepted practice to march through the streets in cortege to the cemetery, but the church no longer figured on the itinerary. The coffin was most often draped in black. The drapery might be plain or embellished with a symbol of solidarity (clasped hands, for example), but it bore no markings of a religious significance. At the graveside, the priest and Latin prayers were replaced by the deceased's friends, who spoke in fond remembrance. Mourners as always dressed in black, but freethinking custom called as well for an immortelle pinned to the lapel (the coffin might also be decorated with wreaths or sprays of flowers). At ceremony's end, the assembled did not simply depart but, one by one, cast handfuls of dirt into the open grave.[22]

This model, simple and sober, exerted a particular attraction on working-class Parisians. By 1908, a full quarter of the burials in the nation's capital were civil in character, with the highest concentrations in the outer arrondissements. That the practice caught on owed more than a little to the propaganda efforts of freethinkers themselves. Students returning from Liège in 1865 founded one of the first civil burial societies, Agis comme Tu Penses (Act as You Think). In 1866 the masonic lodge L'Avenir formed a Comité des Enterrements Civils but was punished for its efforts with a six-month suspension. In the Moral Order years, police harassed civil burial proceedings. Informers attended funeral ceremonies (as they did Massol's in 1875), and a graveside eulogist who spoke with too much ardor risked prosecution.[23] But once 16 May had come and gone, the movement took off with redoubled vigor. In 1878 a journalist at *Le Rappel*, Victor Meunier, soon joined by former communard Edmond Lepelletier, launched L'Association pour la Propagation de la Foi Civile, which in a year's time attracted a membership of over 7,000.[24]

To political as to religious authorities, the moment of death was fraught with political menace. It was not simply that dissidents took advantage of such occasions to stage freethinking values in ritual form. Remembrance of the dead, though a somber business, might take an overt oppositional turn, a solemn march turning into an angry demonstration or a violent mob. And this is what happened over and over again.

Abraham Lincoln's assassination occasioned a first round of agitation. *L'Opinion nationale* floated a proposal to present the dead president's widow with a commemorative medallion and invited the public (an illegal move) to contribute to the fundraising effort. A committee of students, among them, it seems, Clemenceau, drafted a letter of condolence. The letter was meant to be hand-delivered to the American embassy, but when a crowd of 1,200 gathered for that purpose, police stepped in and broke up the march.[25]

The Lincoln demonstration was only a curtainraiser to an event of yet more explosive proportions: the Victor Noir funeral. Noir, a muckraking journalist at Rochefort's *La Marseillaise*, was gunned down in 1870 by an incensed relative of the emperor's, Pierre Bonaparte. This so enraged the Paris populace that Noir's burial services almost erupted into insurrection. A crowd of 100,000 advanced to the Noir family home in Neuilly the day of the funeral, in January 1870. Future communards Flourens and Vermorel were on the spot, hoping to exploit the occasion to incite a popular uprising. They were opposed by Delescluze and Rochefort (fig. 18), the quarrel and the *journée* coming to an abrupt end when police arrested the latter and closed down *La Marseillaise.*

Burials in the late empire had become vehicles for the expression of mass opposition, and so they remained in the era of Moral Order. In 1874 some 100,000 mourners turned out for Ledru-Rollin's funeral. The crowd at Quinet's burial the next year was estimated at the same size.[26] Then, at the very height of the *seize mai* crisis in the fall of 1877, Thiers died. He had never been popular, but late in life had rallied to the republican cause. In the heat of a confrontation that threatened the republic's life, this is what the huge crowds who attended Thiers' funeral chose to remember. Ferry, who was present, described the scene to his wife:

> From the rue Lepeletier to Pére Lachaise, a million men, drawn up in serried ranks along the route of the funeral cortege, standing, bare-headed, contemplative, an immortelle in the button-hole, salut[ed] the carriage—covered with mountains of flowers . . .—with one single cry . . . rolling, grave, resolute, formidable: Vive la République![27]

As republicans assumed positions of national authority in the 1880s, they made official the practices of homage and commemoration elaborated in preceding decades. The grand state funerals of the 1880s, culminating in the Hugo apotheosis of 1885, codified rites that had served as forms of political opposition in more censorious times. Funerals, affecting in any circumstances, acquired a particular power in republican France, wrapped as they were in the shrouds of past struggles. The republic made good use of that power, transforming funerals into dramatic devices to illustrate, through the commemoration of exemplary citizens, the regime's basic values.

The Revolutionary Tradition

It was not only the cult of great men that the republic made official. After the 16 May crisis, the *parti républicain* put together a string of electoral victories that propelled the movement into office. A battle

18. Edouard Manet, *Portrait of Henri Rochefort*, 1881

over symbols, no less intense, unfolded in parallel. At stake was the status, legal and emotive, of the nation's revolutionary inheritance. Thiers, as chief executive, had made any display of the Phrygian cap a punishable offense.[28] Singing the "Marseillaise" had been outlawed under the empire. The ban was lifted in 1870. During the war and siege, public performances of the anthem at the Comédie Française and Opéra had raised the spirits of audiences in need of patriotic uplift, but in the Moral Order seventies the song once again fell into official disfavor.[29] Officialdom's attitude toward the *quatorze juillet* was no warmer. In 1872 and again in 1873, Paris authorities prohibited Bastille Day banquets in a city still operating under martial law. As the political climate cooled, formal prohibition gave way to simple disapproval, but disapproval all the same.[30] Yet by 1880 the situation had been reversed. In the space of a few years, taboo revolutionary symbols—the cap, the holiday, the anthem—had become constituent parts of a national heritage consecrated by the state and embraced by the public.

It was the failure of *seize mai* that triggered all these spasms of symbolic confrontation. As we have seen, the Dufaure administration that took office in the wake of MacMahon's miscarried coup came under pressure to acknowledge the change in political climate. It responded, but took care not to impart too militant a character to such gestures as it made. The government decided to unveil a statue to the republic at the opening ceremonies of the 1878 exposition. The commission was awarded to Jean-Baptiste Clésinger, who sculpted a most reassuring Republic: a seated woman, helmeted (or so it appears) and armed with a sword and the tables of the Constitution (fig. 19). At the same time, in celebration of France's recovery from the calamities of *l'année terrible,* Dufaure decreed 30 June, midway through the fair, a national holiday. MacMahon, still president of the republic, arranged an anthem to be written for the occasion, "Vive la France."

The half-heartedness of such measures was not to the liking of the Paris municipal council, which objected to the Clésinger commission. Clésinger did not compete in *concours public.* On the matter of the statue's design, council members Viollet-le-Duc and Hovelacque proposed a dramatic alternative: a standing Republic coiffed in Phrygian cap. Lest anyone doubt this was meant to be a people's republic, they proposed to situate the monument on what is now the Place de la République in the midst of one of Paris' more working-class

19. Jean-Baptiste Clésinger, *The Republic*, 1878

neighborhoods. The prefect of the Seine, who had final word in such matters, replied to the council's scheme with a flat veto.[31]

Come inauguration day of the exposition, however, and it was the public's turn to have its say. At the unveiling of the Clésinger Republic, the crowd responded with calls for the band to strike up the "Marseillaise." Marcère gave a reluctant assent (for which he was later reprimanded by MacMahon). The song was played, and the crowd marched off to pay its respects to another monument in the making on display at the fair: the gigantic head of Bartholdi's unfinished Statue of Liberty.[32] From the republican point of view, Bartholdi's oeuvre represented a distinct improvement on Clésinger's. Liberty, it is true, was crowned with rays of light, not the Phrygian cap. But in the final design she was at least represented standing, a torch in one hand, a table of laws imprinted with the centennial date of the American revolution in the other. The imagery of light dispelling darkness had masonic overtones (Bartholdi himself was a Mason), but whatever its exact connotation, the lamp of Enlightenment, as a symbol, was far more in tune with republican sensibilities than the unsheathed sword of Clésinger's statue.[33]

Opening day at the fair then did not come off quite as authorities planned. The *fête de la paix,* by contrast, was a great success, with two exceptions. When MacMahon's band played "Vive la France" at the Tuileries, the tune met with an icy reception.[34] Second, while republicans were willing to observe 30 June, this did not deter them from organizing an unofficial Bastille Day all the same. On 14 July, gala dinners were held all over the city, more than ever before. Banqueteers plunged into song, and, as police reported, it was the "Marseillaise" that was the order of the day. A central event was planned as well, a music festival at the Tuileries presided over by Menier. A crowd of 200,000 turned out to hear bands and choral societies from all over France. Authorities kept a close watch on the day's proceedings, and Marcère made it clear that no street demonstrations or parades would be condoned.[35]

MacMahon's resignation in January 1879 caused an abrupt aboutface in official attitudes. The "Marseillaise" was an instant beneficiary of the new climate. Not two weeks into February, the minister of war, replying to queries in the Chamber of Deputies, allowed that a 1795 decree proclaiming the "Marseillaise" as France's national anthem had never been abrogated. The minister's gesture, however back-handed, amounted to official recognition of the song's anthem status.[36]

The Phrygian cap's elevation to official symbol was accomplished with greater fanfare. MacMahon's departure led to a change in prefectoral personnel. The new prefect of the Seine, Ferdinand Hérold, gave immediate approval to the Paris municipal council's year-old project for a monument to the republic. A public competition was held, and the commission went to a design by the Morice brothers, which satisfied in every particular the council's aesthetic and political agenda. The Morice statue (inaugurated on Bastille Day, 1883) represented the Republic as a woman standing. To one observer, she appeared "an energetic *faubourienne,* calm and strong, virile and terrible, as in somber days of revolt." Calm and strong, she raised an olive branch in her right hand; virile and terrible, she wore the Phrygian cap (fig. 20).[37]

Bastille Day's moment of consecration came not long afterward. The *quatorze juillet* of 1879 was, as in the year before, a great triumph and for much the same reason. Local grassroots festivities were organized, with neighborhood celebrants hanging out flags or holding banquets. At the same time, a more formal reception was hosted by Gambetta, now president of the Chamber of Deputies, at the Palais Bourbon. A dinner for a select crowd of republican dignitaries gathered at the Pré Catalan, and Floquet took the occasion to call on the government to legislate the fourteenth a national holiday. That is what happened the following year, with Benjamin Raspail initiating the legislation in the Chamber and Henri Martin shepherding it through the Senate.[38]

With the passage of time, republican culture—with its myriad public rituals, rich iconography, and statue mania—may have acquired the patina of a cherished and consensual national patrimony. But at its origins that culture was improvised, the outgrowth of skirmishes between republicans and the party of order. Much of the fighting occurred on the terrain of symbol and ritual but, after all, on what better terrain to challenge authority and address the public without at every turn winding up in jail?

The Print Culture

For all the importance attached to symbol and ritual in republican culture, it remained in large measure a culture of the printed word.

20. Léopold and Charles Morice, *The Republic*, 1883

In this domain, the business of publishing and distributing texts, republicans outpaced all rivals. The alliance of press and republic was first sealed in the liberalized climate of the empire's final years. In the post-Commune era, authorities mounted a counteroffensive, exercising the exceptional powers conferred by martial law to harass or shut down papers deemed seditious. Louis Ulbach, editor of *La Cloche,* was jailed in 1872. *Le Radical* was closed in the same year, *Le Corsaire* and *L'Avenir national* in the next. But the assault failed. The circulation of the political press in Paris expanded from 470,000 to 640,000 in the 1870–1880 period, and republican newspapers, it is estimated, outsold the conservative competition by a ratio of three to one. Even the city's largest-selling daily, the *Petit Journal,* which purported to be nonpolitical, tilted to the republican side in the Moral Order years. Edmond About credited the paper with winning "over a million voters to the republican cause."[39]

The book market was also expanding, and the annual number of published titles soared from 7–8,000 at the empire's inception to 12,000 at its end. The publishers who navigated the expansion, brokering between writers and an avid public, became figures of note, and more than one was a republican. Charles-Antoine Pagnerre, Louis Blanc's publisher, and Alexandre Paulin, one-time administrator at *Le National,* were the veterans of the republican publishing establishment. They were joined by a new generation, which included Charpentier, Hetzel, Lacroix, Le Chevalier, and Reinwald. Charpentier's and Hetzel's republican credentials have been discussed earlier. Albert Lacroix, based in Belgium, made a specialty of émigré literature by Hugo, Michelet, and Quinet. It was Armand Le Chevalier, said to have published the bulk of the opposition's pamphlets, who took the risk of printing Ténot's book on Louis-Napoleon's coup. The Maison Reinwald handled cutting-edge scientific work, in particular the speculations of Broca's freethinking and materialist acolytes.[40]

These men, to be sure, were entrepreneurs first and foremost, who championed new forms and sought out new markets with an eye to profit. But for many, business and politics were not antithetical and made for a lucrative, if explosive, mix. Take the case of Georges Charpentier. He assumed control of the family publishing house in 1871, making an instant name for himself when he signed on Zola a few years later. Charpentier's decision to publish the author of scandalous realist novels in an era of Moral Order was a daring one, all the more so in light of the political dangers he was running. Zola was a well-known republican; the novels he turned over to Charpentier, such as *Nana* and *L'Assommoir*, had first appeared in feuilleton form in the republican press. The former was serialized in *Le Voltaire*, parts of the latter in *Le Bien public*. But Charpentier, who himself hosted a celebrated republican salon, was not a man to shrink from such perils. Zola's bestsellers helped to make Charpentier rich, but it was still a risky venture to publish novels that were so controversial on political no less than on moral and aesthetic grounds.

As for scientific publishing, in an age of religious controversy it lent itself easily to the communication of hidden messages, whether secularizing or antiauthoritarian in character. Reinwald's authors—Hovelacque, Lefèvre, Letourneau—took few pains to conceal the freethinking credo they shared. Hetzel's authors were more circumspect. Pierre-Jules Hetzel returned to France after the amnesty of 1859 and reopened his old firm. Two writers in particular helped to relaunch the firm's fortunes: Jules Verne, who will be discussed in the next chapter, and that old democratic socialist Jean Macé. Macé sent Hetzel, a friend since high-school days, a popularizing scientific treatise, *Histoire d'une bouchée de pain* (History of a Bit of Bread), which Hetzel published to great acclaim in 1861. The book, intended for young readers, has no obvious politics. Yet the text, with its description of the digestive system as a republic of self-regulating parts, its warm asides to the revolution, its invocations of a benign deity, progress, and the harmony of all creation, does manage to convey in tones of childlike simplicity that current of humanitarian idealism which Macé as a 48er and Freemason cherished.[41]

Publishers who traded in realist novels or popular science sold not only entertainment but a mode of thought. In a midcentury context, that mode situated readers in a particular way in the field of philosophical and religious debate. To this extent, such literature had a political meaning. And it was not just certain forms that were charged in character, but certain marketing strategies as well.

Republicans cast about for ways to tap into a working-class audience. The cheap-edition series proved a simple means to that end. The so-called *Bibliothèque utile*, founded in 1859, set the pattern. Edited by Henri Leneveux (of *Le Siècle*) and published by Pagnerre, the series offered readers at 50 centimes each edifying texts on historical and contemporary subjects written by various republican notables. The *Bibliothèque démocratique,* specializing in reprints of Enlightenment and French Revolution classics, was launched in 1869. Similar efforts were attempted into the seventies. The repression of the Commune silenced the labor movement's revolutionary wing, but less militant voices continued to make themselves heard in the pages of the radical republican press. *Le Rappel, Le Radical,* and *Le Corsaire* ran regular columns by such labor-scene veterans as Joseph Barberet and Louis Pauliat, touting the virtues of cooperation and trade unionism. A book series was also published, the *Bibliothèque ouvrière,* which featured inexpensive texts by Barberet and Pauliat, alongside the more standard republican fare.[42]

As the example of Macé's *Bouchée de pain* suggests, the children's market was another principal target of the new promotional efforts. Publishers competed hard, but it was Hetzel who won out. An illustrated children's magazine *Le Magasin d'éducation et de récréaction* proved his trump card. He started the magazine, the first of its kind, in 1864 with Macé. To promote sales, Hetzel struck a deal with *Le Temps,* offering free delivery of the magazine to all the paper's new subscribers. And what was it that he had offer to the children of *Le Temps* readers? Features by Macé and the ex-communard Paschal Grousset, science fiction by Verne, architecture and science columns by the likes of Viollet-le-Duc, Flammarion, and the geographer and anarchist Elisée Reclus.[43] Hetzel purveyed a new genre of writing by authors who were almost all well-known partisans of progressive causes. In the business of children's literature, at least in this instance, creative marketing, innovative literary practice, and leftist politics went hand in hand.

The republican press network churned out reams of books and magazines for a growing audience. The problem of course was how to reach potential readers. Serialization in newspapers or periodicals, everyman editions, promotional schemes, all helped to boost sales, but the marketplace was not the sole avenue of access explored. For militants more worried about uplift than profits, it was the library that opened the most promising vistas.

It was a combination of local and central initiatives that got the library movement started in the 1860s. Saint-Simonians and republicans had, since July Monarchy days, organized evening courses for working-class Parisians. The unavailability of books proved a persistent problem. A partial solution was worked out by knowledge-hungry residents of the third arrondissement, who in 1861 banded together to form the Société des Amis de l'Instruction. The founders contributed a small sum (half price for women) for the purchase of books and rental of library premises. The library operated both as a lending institution and as a cooperative enterprise. All members had a say in the selection of books as well as the society's officers. The model proved very attractive, inspiring parallel efforts elsewhere in the Paris region. By 1882 a city-wide syndicate of popular libraries had been formed, grouping eighteen neighborhood associations with a combined membership of 8,000.[44]

Such a groundswell of activity was bound to attract the attention of the well-placed and powerful. The Second Empire in principle favored public instruction, and some of its more enterprising loyalists undertook to extend patronage to the library movement. In 1862 the commandant at the Ecole Polytechnique, Colonel Ildefousse Favé, organized the Société Franklin. Although the creation of enlightened officialdom, the society soon tapped into bordering constituencies, recruiting Saint-Simonians (Edouard Charton), liberal Protestants (Jean Dollfus, Fernand Schickler), and even the occasional republican. To the fledgling library movement, the Société Franklin offered a double service: free advice on how to set up and manage a *bibliothèque populaire* and, of greater significance, a series of titles that the society would obtain at cut-rate prices.[45]

The Franklin group, however, was not the most important organization in the business of funneling reading materials to local lenders. In 1866 *L'Opinion nationale* announced to great fanfare the formation of the Ligue de l'Enseignement. The new Ligue was federalist in its organization. It consisted, as of 1868, of twenty-four local societies or *cercles,* each enjoying a full measure of autonomy. Individual circles might engage in a variety of activities, but sponsorship of a *bibliothèque populaire* appears to have been the main one. At first, circles undertook themselves to obtain books directly from the publishers, but over time they funneled orders through the central Parisian branch, which threw itself into the intermediary's role with gusto. It helped to stock an estimated 600 local libraries, disbursing hundreds of thousands of francs of its own money in the process. The Paris circle's organizational initiatives and substantial membership (2,500 in 1883) placed it in the forefront of a national federation that, as it grew in size, grew as well in republican commitment.[46]

There were some circles, such as Rouen's, that cultivated good relations with imperial authorities. But the two most important

Ligue branches, the Parisian and the Alsatian, were republican in orientation from the start. The Paris circle was headed first by the astronomer Camille Flammarion, a self-described socialist, who was succeeded by that republican grandee, Henri Martin. Macé was the guiding spirit in Alsace, with support from liberal Protestant businessmen and publicists. The republican bias of the Ligue's principal branches helps to account for its early commitment to compulsory, free, and secular primary education. In February 1870 the Strasbourg circle of the Ligue established a petition in favor of compulsory primary schooling that garnered 350,000 signatures across the nation. The Franco-Prussian war brought the campaign to a halt, but in 1871–72 the Paris branch took up the cause again. It sent around petitions in a variety of drafts, insisting on some mix of compulsory, free, and laic public instruction. In all, an additional 900,000 signatures were gathered. The republican press—from *Le Rappel* to *Le Temps*—joined in the enterprise, and it was to the republican group in the National Assembly that the stack of petitions was eventually submitted.[47]

The Ligue's apparent republicanism earned it the enmity of the Moral Order governments of the mid-seventies. The organization, now the object of official harassment, was obliged to soften its political profile. But once MacMahon stepped down, prudence was jettisoned with a grand flourish. The Ligue convened its first national congress in 1881, a founding moment that turned out to be as much political as constitutional. Fifteen lodges were represented at the gathering, which met at Grand Orient headquarters in Paris. Gambetta himself presided, signaling by his presence the Ligue's transformation from a patron of library societies to an institutional pillar of the lay republic.[48]

The press, the publishing industry, the library movement: my claim is not that such institutions were inherently democratic, only that they could be, and were, made to serve democratic ends. Republicans proved themselves dextrous at the task, outbidding all rivals for mastery of the new media. In such endeavors the *parti républicain* reached out to an ever wider audience. What it had to offer the literate public was in part propagandistic. But it offered knowledge as well, a new way of thinking that, while not partisan in a bare-faced way, had a political bias nonetheless. The problem as always is how to characterize that new way of thinking. There is much to be said for understanding it as a scientized *réchauffé* of

Enlightenment rationalism, but, I will argue, such a characterization tells only half the story.

Science and Vision

The encyclopedic ambitions of the republican print culture are beyond doubt. The anti-imperial opposition, as we have seen, churned out encyclopedias of all shapes and sizes. The best remembered of the genre today is Pierre Larousse's *Grand dictionnaire universel du XIXe siècle,* the first volume appearing in 1864, the last in 1890. Hugo, on reading the first installment, dashed off a letter to Larousse, praising the encyclopedia as a worthy "pendant to Diderot's, more complete and more grandiose still."[49]

Both in substance and in design, the new Larousse bore the clear imprint of its author's republican and secularizing convictions. Entries were leavened with antimonarchical asides.[50] Republican personages of even minor stature were accorded biographical sketches. The work, indeed, remains a helpful source in this respect to the present day. On the matter of design, twentieth-century readers may find little in the encyclopedia format that is controversial, but such was not the case a century ago. To understand knowledge as a compendium of useful information about practical, everyday matters, to accumulate such knowledge fact by discrete fact and lay it all out in accessible form, and then to presume that such an assemblage is comprehensive or universal in compass, that in a mid-nineteenth-century context is a political statement. It is to claim that empirical observation is the sole source of real understanding and that knowledge through religious faith or philosophical speculation is, by contrast, simply not worthy of the name.

The positivist ring of such epistemological claims is unmistakable. Perhaps the era's most impressive monument to knowledge, the *Dictionnaire de la langue française* (1863–1872), was created by one of the great positivists, Emile Littré. It may be remembered that Littré was refused membership in the Académie Française in the 1860s. Monseigneur Dupanloup orchestrated the campaign against his candidacy and resigned when it was at last accepted in 1871. But academicians as well as clerics had reason to take issue with the man and his work, for Littré's oeuvre was a direct slap at the accredited dictionary of the day, the Académie's own. Their dictionary decreed the meanings of words. Littré adopted what he understood to be a more scientific approach, breaking down entries into a listing of current usages, a chronology of past ones, and etymology. Littré's epistemological point was clear enough: meaning emerged from history and common practice. The Littré, as the dictionary has come to be known, was hailed at the time and even now as an application of the experimental method to language. It represented a triumph, as *La Pensée nouvelle* exulted, of "individual initiative" over that of "patented, instituted and protected collectivities [such as the Académie]."[51]

Armed with positivist encyclopedias and dictionaries, republicans assaulted the ramparts of knowledge. But some care needs to be shown in summing up the new way of thinking under the rubric of positivism. The midcentury pursuit of a rational, secular under-standing of the world bred some strange hybrids, scientific-looking plants that at the same time plunged roots deep into a visionary soil. In the catalogues of both the Société Franklin and the Ligue de l'Enseignement, novels accounted for the bulk of books on offer. But add together the next three genres in importance—science, history, and geography—and they outnumber the novels.[52] In those fields it is positivism that ought to reign supreme, and yet, among the great popularizers in each area, spiritualist or quasi-religious influences were still making themselves felt.

The case is easiest to make for Flammarion, the best-known sci-ence writer of the day. A would-be seminarian, Flammarion aban-doned that vocation to work first in Nadar's photography studio and then at the Paris observatory. Here he discovered the joys of astron-omy and at the same time made the acquaintance of Jean Chacornac, a fellow employee who initiated him in the ways of spiritism. Flam-marion became an adept of the master spiritist Allan Kardec, remain-ing all his life a firm believer in parapsychological phenomena. As for Flammarion's political convictions, he moved in republican and so-cialist circles: writing for *Le Siècle,* presiding for a period over the Paris branch of the Ligue de l'Enseignement, attending the 1869 conference of the Ligue de la Paix.[53]

Such a mix of commitments—astronomical, spiritist, pacifist—found its way into Flammarion's work. He published his first major book in 1862, *La Pluralité des mondes habités,* and it made him an instant celebrity. The text laid out in readable form the latest astronomical findings of modern science. But along the way, Flammarion sketched a grand portrait of the universe, a divine creation pulsing with life. It was not just Earth that providence had stocked with living things but a multitude of worlds unknown to us. Yet, however separated by infinite space, all creatures great and small were bound by nature's beneficent laws, by the material principles of gravity and magnetism, and by the spiritual principles of universal solidarity and conscience. Drawn by an inner impulse toward the light, all creation went spinning its way in stellar majesty to a distant but radiant terminus ad quem of peace and brotherhood. Warmongers and militarists might interrupt nature's progress, but they could not stop it.[54] In Flammarion's hands, astronomy for the people turned out to be as much poetry as science, but a poetry that for all its stratospheric flights resonated with the moral and spiritual preoccupations of midcentury life.

Flammarion's good friend, Henri Martin, wrote history in a similar vein. In terms of reputation if not quality of work, Martin has a fair claim to be counted, alongside Quinet, among the elite of republican historians. The multivolume history of France that he published during the July Monarchy earned him the sobriquet of "national historian,"[55] and when he died in 1883, the republic accorded him a full state funeral. It was not just the limelight that Martin shared with Quinet, but spiritual concerns as well. Quinet, as we know, was drawn to Unitarian Protestantism; Martin set up camp not far away among spiritualist freethinkers. As a young man, he flirted with Saint-Simonianism. In the late 1860s, he became involved in the affairs of the Alliance Religieuse Universelle and, in fact, presided at its great philosophical conference of 1870.[56]

There was a quirkiness to Martin's patriotic and religious temperament that left a distinct trace on his historical work. In 1855–1860 a revised edition of the *Histoire de France* was printed. Martin had reworked the first volume in particular, touching on the nation's origins.[57] France's true ancestors, he wrote, were the Gauls, a "federative democracy" of tribes and peoples, bound under the moral dominion of the druidic cult. Whether civil or religious, all authority derived from the exercise of the "elective principle . . . a natural emanation of the Gallic genius." Ancient Gaul ("our mother" as Martin called it) represented a special moment of democratic and religious communion. It had but one failing, an excess of individualism, and that left it vulnerable to Caesar's predations. Yet the French soul remained anchored in its Gallic past, and what had been achieved then might be recovered, all the more so, Martin implied, if the friends of liberty curbed individualist impulses and consecrated themselves to the democratic cause.[58] There is much that is worrisome in Martin's mythic vision of French identity, with its insistence on Gallic rootedness and an integralist patriotism. It is not surprising that he was one of the charter members of Paul Déroulède's Ligue des Patriotes in 1882. Yet in the 1860s and 1870s, the Martin revered by the public was not Martin the revanchiste but Martin the druid,[59] the seeker of democratic revelation.

Elisée Reclus was another scientific visionary, but of an altogether different sort. The son of a Protestant pastor, he had studied for the ministry. Reclus abandoned the enterprise in 1849 and then, in the aftermath of Louis-Napoleon's coup, abandoned France as well for an extended sojourn in the New World. He returned home in 1857 and took up travel writing, from which it was but a short step into serious geographical research. Reclus published his first major work in the field, *La Terre,* in 1868–69. It went through ten editions, made Reclus' professional name and earned him, in the words of one biographer, "the largest readership of any modern geographer."[60]

Like Flammarion and Martin, Reclus led more than one life. He was a master scientific popularizer as well as a man of intense political passion. In the 1860s, Reclus straddled the frontier between the radical republican camp and a more militant anarchism. On the republican side, he dabbled in Freemasonry and militated in the freethinking burial society Agis comme Tu Penses. At the same time, he kept company with firebrands like Mikhail Bakunin, with whom he attended the 1868 congress of the Ligue de la Paix. The Commune, for Reclus as for so many of his generation, proved a moment of radicalizing clarification. He joined the communard cause, was driven into exile, and returned to France in the 1880s, a straddler no more but an out-and-out anarchist.[61]

Once again, as with Flammarion and Martin, the multiple strands of Reclus' life intersected in his work. The science he practiced was steeped in a quasi-religious freethinking creed. In *La Terre* Reclus anthropomorphized the earth as a living, breathing body with a skin of crust, atmospheric lungs, and a physiognomy of harmonic parts. It even had a soul, and that soul was humankind: risen by spontaneous generation from inorganic matter, fused by the progress of civilization into a single humanity. But man (the gendered term in this instance is deliberate) was more than the soul of the earth—he was at the same time its keeper and conscience. Armed with science, he might for good or ill reshape the globe, embellishing it with invention or destroying it with war. Earth herself taught the ways of solidarity; her children had only to bend an ear to her loving counsel. But there were also the bellicose voices of despots and priests. Humankind had a choice:

> so long as the nurturing soil is reddened with the blood of unhappy madmen who fight for a scrap of ground, for a question of so-called honor, out of pure rage, as did the barbarians of ancient times, the earth will never become that paradise whose contours the researcher's gaze can even now make out in the mists of a distant future . . . To become truly beautiful, our "beneficent mother" awaits the moment when her sons will embrace one another as brothers and conclude at long last that great federation of free peoples.[62]

The new print culture of mid-nineteenth-century France housed its fair share of straight-thinking positivists, but the visitor does not have to turn into dark alleys or by-ways to encounter residents of a different cast of thought: tableturners, druids, proto-greens. The character of midcentury republicanism suggests how deep the mythic currents can run in a democratic culture, leaving traces in every corner: in symbol and ritual, of course, but also in the writings of scientists and historians, rationalism's would-be high priests.

NOT EVERYONE participated in republican political culture, but many believers there were and still are. The republican state worked hard to obtain such results, using its authority to inculcate and, if need be, impose a particular notion of good citizenship. But that notion was not simply legislated from above. It was a living idea articulated across a quarter century (at least) of political contestation. Republicans made a cult of the public, summoning *réunions publiques,* opening public subscriptions, organizing *concours publics.* The crowds came, shaping by their presence and action the form that republican political culture was to take. That culture was in this degree a joint enterprise, a common tongue for militants and an awakening civil society. The idea and even the practice of democratic citizenship were in place before a republican Third Republic existed to give them sanction. That republican culture managed to catch on for so long owes less to laws enacted in the 1880s than to the rituals and myths elaborated over preceding decades.

Perhaps more than the electoral confrontations of the era, the midcentury battles over word and symbol defined what it meant to be a republican. What is striking is just how encompassing the claims of citizenship could be. Loyal citizens thrilled to the national anthem and mourned at the funerals of great men. They lived in cities and towns crammed with commemorative monuments swathed in lamps, rays, and liberty caps. They moved through a calendar year punctuated by centenaries and holidays and through a lifecycle structured by secular ceremonials. They read the newspapers, frequented the local library, belonged to a league or lodge, and kept up with the latest literature in science and history. All these activities had a formative impact on participants, exercising their reason, to be sure, but shaping their feelings as well. For republican political culture, even at its most didactic, still spoke in lyrical accents, appealing to the heart and eye with visions of a redeemed humanity living in harmony with God and Nature. Republican citizenship, then, entailed far more than voting and committeework, extending its hold deep into the sphere of daily life.

But this last observation raises a final and difficult issue. Women were excluded from voting and office in the new republic. To the extent that women were represented in the public sphere, it was generally in symbolic or allegorical form as the Republic, Liberty, Mother Gaul, or Mother Earth. Yet there was at the same time a clear intent to include women in the daily activities of republican culture. Indeed, women played an important part in the elaboration of that culture: speaking and militating, joining in the new civil ceremonials, enrolling in library associations, attending conferences and writing for the press. Women could not be citizens in the same sense as men, but neither were they simple, apolitical stay-at-homes.

It is tempting to understand the new republican order in dichotomous terms. Men ruled the public, political domain. Women were consigned to the peaceful backwaters of private life. If "public" is understood to include more than just voting and officeholding, then the first claim requires some nuancing. As for the second, the next chapter will suggest just how worried and politicized the contours of private life were in midcentury France.

Repub. cit. about lit. etc. ∅ (Just politics about art, marriages, funerals)

[9]

The Middle-Class Interior

THE MIDDLE CLASSES in France have become the subject of a burgeoning literature, and historical attention has concentrated in particular on the period 1851–1885, from the end of the Second Republic to the consolidation of the Third. These three decades, it is said, witnessed a recasting of bourgeois life, and the principal locus of that recasting was sited in the home. Placed at the center of the new middle-class interior is the *femme de foyer:* angel on the hearth, devoted wife and loving mother, for the middle-class home became child-centered as never before. Women, the argument goes, frozen out of public life, turned their energies with redoubled zeal to the nurture of their offspring. But it was not mothers alone who lavished attention on the young. A booming toy industry stocked the nursery with dolls and soldiers; a new children's literature—illustrated magazines, stories, and novels—made its way onto nursery book-shelves. Men, as husbands or fathers, played only a walk-on role in this domestic drama, even though it was for them—to display what they achieve and what they own—that family life was reframed.[1]

What kind of accommodations might be suitable to such a household, populated by gentle mothers, distant fathers, and cossetted children? Perhaps, it is suggested, they will find lodgings in one of the new apartment houses of Haussmann's Paris or in a suburban villa development. Wherever, the principles guiding the layout of rooms will be the same. Staff (what bourgeois household does not employ at least a maid?) will have special quarters, serviced by a separate staircase and connected to the rest of the house by unobtru-sive passageways. The family living space will be divided into func-tionally specific rooms: some private—the boudoir, study, bedrooms, nursery—and some public—the hall, dining room, salon. Special care will be devoted to the decoration of the salon, for here it is that the family shows its face to the world and makes its claim to distinc-tion. Well-stuffed furniture, a piano, a mantel clock, and, through-out, an assortment of bibelots constitute the minimal accoutrements of a well-appointed sitting room.[2]

It is not that this account of bourgeois self-fashioning is untrue. The prosperous decades of midcentury did indeed generate new forms of middle-class employment and poured money into the pock-ets of these new social strata. Technological advance and the reor-ganization of work trimmed consumer prices and placed a widening range of merchandise within the reach of new buyers. The people and the goods existed from which a new mode of life might be and was constructed. But the remaking of the bourgeoisie was by no means a consensual process, nor was the outcome predetermined. Few ques-tioned that the place of the bourgeoise lay in the home, but the extent and nature of women's domestic responsibilities became a matter of contention. Men of course were meant to work, but did that mean they had no role in the new middle-class home? There was wide agreement that children constituted one axis on which bour-geois private life turned, that a decent middle-class home came equipped with certain identifiable goods. Moralists and pedagogues fought all the same over what constituted proper childrearing, and art critics fought over the definition of good taste in home design and furnishing.

All such arguments, moreover, were tinctured by deep-seated political differences. The debate on family life heated up partly because of the particular political conjuncture in midcentury. France was governed from 1852 to 1870 by Louis-Napoleon's Second Em-pire. The empire gave way to a republic in 1870, but on the whole it was men of conservative, often royalist convictions who com-manded the new regime. Not until 1877 did genuine republicans begin to accede to positions of executive authority. In the uncertain and authoritarian climate of the 1860s and 1870s, the subject of private life provided men and women of the left a forum of debate, a relatively safe haven where the censor exercised less vigilance. But more than that: the failure of the Second Republic prompted many republicans to self-criticism. The regime had faltered, Michelet for one argued, because the French lacked the moral underpinnings necessary to sustain republican institutions. For a future republic to survive, it was imperative first that private life be revamped, that the French learn the domestic virtues conducive to a democratic public life.[3]

The political climate of midcentury fastened republican attentions on the private sphere, and indeed it was in large part republicans who opened the debate on the proper organization of the family interior. It should be remembered at the same time that "republican" was a capacious label encompassing men and women of a wide range of views—from former utopian socialists on the left to moderates on the right who were in certain respects indistinguishable from nonrepublican conservatives. The debate on family life was politicized in a double sense: pitting republicans against partisans of order, but also pitting republicans against themselves.

Marriage

In 1866 the republican jurist Emile Acollas issued a call for an overturn of the marital status quo, for a *révolution du foyer*.[4] Republicans indicted the marital regime in place on two counts. First, it smacked of Bonapartism. The civil code that governed marriage relations was after all the brainchild of "the man of the Eighteenth Brumaire, the future Caesar," Napoleon Bonaparte.[5] The code made husbands into petty dictators, investing them with absolute authority in all family matters. It enshrined, in Louis Blanc's words, a "domestic despotism" that functioned as a prop to despotism in public life.[6] Prevailing marital practice bred authoritarian attitudes, and it incited spouses, at least among the upper classes, to immorality. The well-born male suitor looked less for a love match than for the hefty dowry. Unions were arranged not so much by the consent of the couple as between families seeking advantageous dynastic alliances. The spouses so chosen rarely knew one another well. No wonder that there was little tenderness or intimacy among aristocratic couples, that they cheated on one another with such abandon.[7] "Wherever the aristocracy reigns," intoned Eugène Pelletan, "*la galanterie* is sure to dance in attendance."[8]

To the authoritarianism of the code, to the depravity of the aristocracy, republicans like Pelletan offered an alternative vision. Marriage was conceived as a constitutional union, a free association of individuals joined by affection and tenderness, by a conformity of principles, and by shared tastes and sentiments. It was not a strict egalitarianism that republicans promised. They endorsed a division of labor: men were destined to work, women to manage the household and raise the children. The husband, as Pelletan put it, held down the ministry of foreign affairs and the wife the ministry of the interior. But when problems arose, both spouses were supposed to deliberate together as peers "in a council of ministers."[9]

The principle of "equality in difference," the idea of matrimony as a partnership binding complementary personalities, guided the thinking of republicans in the matter of marriage reform.[10] The problem was to close the spiritual gap that separated husbands and wives. Michelet was a vociferous advocate of early marriage for women. The less formed a young wife, the more malleable would she be in the hands of her husband. Republican feminists like Jenny d'Héricourt and Clarisse Coignet, on the other hand, insisted on a compatibility of age between spouses so that women might be treated not as minors but as equals.[11] It was in the name of marriage as a union of souls that Jules Ferry championed the cause of high-school education for women. (The republic legislated into existence the first state-run lycées for girls in 1880.) An educated wife made an intelligent companion and helpmate, not to mention a good mother. Not least of all, republicans expected to reap political dividends from equality of education. Secular schooling would wean women from the reactionary influence of clergy and foster a spirit of rational mutuality among spouses. It encouraged in these ways the democratization of the home, which would in turn contribute to the triumph of democracy in the public realm.[12] There were bound to be men, of course, who would cling to the high-handed and philandering ways of old. In those cases republicans were prepared to countenance recourse to the courts. One republican woman characterized marriage without divorce as a kind of "New Caledonia in perpetuity." Wives so imprisoned had but two avenues of escape—adultery and religion. Divorce in such circumstances was an unmitigated good both for the nation's morals and for the republic. The possibility of divorce would have a sobering impact on men too. The threat of judicial proceedings would keep wayward husbands in line in much the same way that the threat of revolution checked the authoritarian pretensions of government.[13] These concerns motivated the republic's legalization of divorce in 1884, for the first time since the Bourbon restoration.

The consolidation of democratic institutions, republicans were persuaded, presupposed a reformation of morals. A redefinition of the marriage bond was part and parcel of such a reformation. No less critical was a redefinition of proper conduct for women and men, whether married or not.

The Place of Women

Midcentury republicans liked to bemoan the sorry state of French womanhood. The fault was laid squarely at the door of Louis-Napoleon's wife Eugénie, a "clothes-mad coquette" with a taste for luxury.[14] The empress made a cult of Marie-Antoinette but lacked delicacy or proportion. The graceful *paniers* worn by the women of Louis XVI's court were resuscitated but in the monumental and extravagant form of the crinoline. To Charles Blanc, who served the Second Republic as minister of fine arts and the Thiers administration in a similar capacity, the fashionable woman of the Second Empire, all trussed up, appeared in profile like a creature in flight, the very antithesis of the sedentary *femme de foyer*.[15] Juliette Adam, the pioneering publicist and host of a celebrated republican salon, also had unkind words for the crinoline. Her first published essay was in fact a send-up of crinoline fashions, of the absurdity of what she called "the circle of steel."[16]

Eugénie's extravagance opened the door to an even more depraved class of woman, the courtesan. To republican moralists and littérateurs, the courtesan embodied the governing creed of the empire: "the reign of the false, the triumph of hypocrisy, the success of scandal."[17] She was a false-faced creature, "her lips enflamed with carmine, her cheeks daubed with rice powder."[18] Republicans conceived of the painted woman, like the red-pantalooned Zouave, as a vestige of barbarian times, as "the final manifestation of a savage aesthetic."[19] Pelletan's description of the courtesan—seated on a red divan, dressed in a black velour gown layered over a substructure of metal cages and hoops—was intended to conjure up shocking images of a modern-day Babylon. And this new Babylon took a political form as well. When republicans made up an address for the prostitutes of their imagining, they inevitably chose one freighted with political meaning. Pelletan's prototypical prostitute lived on the Avenue de l'Impératrice and Zola's Nana on the Boulevard Haussmann.[20]

Republicans placed enormous stock in the moralizing potential of womanhood, but first women had to be moralized themselves. In the 1870s a coalition of feminists, Protestant moral reformers, and civil libertarians mounted a fierce campaign to secure the abolition of France's system of state-regulated prostitution. The system operated outside the law, overseen by a special morals police and a network of administrative courts. The abolitionist cause was a moral crusade, but it carried a clear political message. Militants referred to whorehouses as "shameful bastilles." To Maria Deraismes, who was active in the campaign, state-sanctioned prostitution reeked of the old regime with its extralegal arrangements and system of privilege.[21]

The redemption of womanhood entailed the disciplining or rescue of "public women," as prostitutes were called. Did that mean there was no place at all in the public domain for women? When it came to men, no republican doubted that the surest path to a virtuous life lay in gainful employment. A minority of republicans believed that women too might profit from the "secret moralizing power" of work.[22] There were many tasks at which women excelled by nature: shopkeeping, sewing, flowermaking, anything that required a dextrous hand. Middle-class women might find suitable employment in teaching or in the professions. Adam pointed to Elizabeth Blackwell as an exemplary woman doctor. But even republicans like Coignet, who recognized a woman's right to work, still insisted that her true vocation lay in homemaking, and for a greater number still, *ouvrière* remained what it had been for Jules Simon in the 1860s, an "impious word."[23]

For bourgeois women, the domestic interior constituted the principal theater of moral life. How then were women to comport themselves in the home? The question raised two further issues that divided republicans: the place of fashion in women's lives and the proper character of female pastimes.

On the matter of fashion, opinion ranged across a wide spectrum. Charles Blanc waxed nostalgic for the styles of the July Monarchy, when women wore mutton sleeves and skirts puffed at the hips. Attired in clothing that spread out sideways, sitting did not pose the problem that it did for the crinoline-encumbered women of the Second Empire. "So accoutered," Blanc wrote of the women of the July Monarchy, they seemed "foredestined to family life."[24] Simplicity and modesty were indeed favored words in the fashion lexicon of most republicans. "Be simple therefore," admonished d'Héricourt: "this does not exclude elegance, but only those piles of silks and laces which trail in the dust of the streets."[25]

A glimpse of what d'Héricourt might have had in mind can be found in the paintings of Mary Cassatt and Berthe Morisot. Both women were of bourgeois background. The pursuit of a career in painting, however, strained their ties to more conventional family members, strains exacerbated, at least in Morisot's case, by the espousal of progressive politics. Yet, for all the distance such women placed between themselves and their class, they returned over and over to the portrayal of bourgeois family life. And they represented the women of that world with an unsentimental matter-of-factness, posed without mannerism, dressed in stylish but not pretentious clothing. Fashion had a part to play in such a milieu, but it was a fact of life and not, to the eye of the female painter, a source of tactile or erotic gratification. In much of Morisot's work, the clothing of the models, who were recruited for the most part from the painter's immediate family, is so underemphasized as to constitute little more than background, a frame to the personalities and activities of the sitters.[26]

The same cannot be said, however, of Renoir and Monet, both men of more or less conventional republican views. In the interiors they painted, there is little of the self-absorbed domesticity to be found in the work of Cassatt or Morisot, little of the simplicity so esteemed by republican moralists.[27] Renoir's *Madame Charpentier and Her Children* may be taken as an example. He painted the sitter presiding comfortably over her salon; the room, it seems, was painted as it was without moving the furniture for stage effect. Yet there is no doubt that the salon is fashionably appointed with the latest Japanese imports or that Mme. Charpentier herself is a woman who relishes modish clothing. Monet's early portrait of *Madame Gaudibert* (1868) places a stronger accent still on fashion (fig. 21). Her dress, its cut and garniture, seems more the subject of the painting than the actual sitter. It has been argued in fact that Monet made use of fashion-magazine plates for compositional suggestions.[28] The weight of republican discourse on *la mode* tilted toward a virtuous sobriety, but a strong appetite for the moment, for the charms of modern women regarded as objects of visual pleasure, led a few artists to delight in the kaleidoscopic effects of female fashion.

21. Claude Monet, *Madame Gaudibert*, 1868

Opinion was divided on almost the same lines when it came to the treatment in debate and imagery of women's domestic pastimes. On certain points, to be sure, there was agreement. The domestic activities of women—embroidering, piano playing, and the like—were a matter of the utmost seriousness, a worthy subject of high art. Jules Dalou, who served on the arts committee of the Commune in 1871 and in later years achieved the status of semiofficial sculptor to the Third Republic, submitted a life-size statue called *La Brodeuse* to the salon of 1870 (fig. 22). The piece caused a stir for its monumental handling of a "minor" subject, a woman embroidering, and for its stress on the subject's contemporaneity (she is posed casually in modern dress).[29] Impressionist artists, of course, returned time and again to similar subjects with an almost obsessive zeal. They depicted women absorbed in serving tea or playing music to friends. Again, it is the handling and not solely the subject matter of the paintings that invites comment: the picturing of private life on large canvases (conventionally reserved for more heroic themes); and the representation without didactics or storytelling of women's domestic pastimes as subjects deserving of interest.

The esteem extended to such activities was enforced when it came to one activity in particular: reading. Painted and sculpted representations of *la liseuse* multiplied from midcentury on.[30] The theme was a special favorite of avant-garde artists (Fantin-Latour, Monet, Manet, Morisot), all of whom aligned themselves with the republican left. The proliferation of such renderings attests of course to a new cultural reality—middle-class women were reading as never before—but not only that. The *liseuses* were usually related to the painter by marriage, blood, or friendship (fig. 23). The middle-class woman with book in hand was more than a social fact; she was also a gentle, beloved presence. Republicans reverenced literacy, for women as well as men. A wife who read made a companionable spouse and was more likely to be immune to priestly influence. As Pelletan put it, "every woman who opens a book exorcises a demon."[31]

What books were women supposed to read? On this question, unanimity dissolved. The more straitlaced, such as Pelletan, prescribed history books and moral tracts, spurning the novel as an instigation to frivolity.[32] On a moral plane with the novel was *Le Figaro.* How better to illustrate the corruption of taste under Louis-Napoleon than to cite the newspaper's success with female readers?

22. Jules Dalou, *La Brodeuse*, 1870

23. Berthe Morisot, *The Mother and Sister of the Artist:*
Cornélie Morisot and Edma Pontillon, 1869–70

In the days of the empire, exclaimed an outraged republican feminist, "people preferred [Offenbach's] *Belle-Hélène* to the verse of Corneille and Victor Hugo . . . *Le Figaro* had become the standard reading of the boudoir."[33] Yet in 1883 Cassatt painted an admiring portrait of her mother reading the very same *Figaro*.[34] Stéphane Mallarmé, a republican fellow traveler, recommended Zola and Daudet to the female readership of *La Dernière Mode,* the short-lived fashion journal he edited in 1874.[35]

There was a consistency to the republican critique of midcentury mores. The empress-courtesan reigned, and she set a corrupting example that incited French womanhood to a deceitful and excessive luxury. To the wiles of the imperial coquette, republicans counterposed the virtues of the *femme de foyer.* She might be a person of modest habits or affect a modish but not extravagant stylishness; she might read Victor Hugo or naturalist fiction. Whatever her tastes, she was sober-minded and literate. Such a woman might work but was more likely to find fulfillment in the absorbing and serious business of domestic life.

The Role of Men

Men also had a part to play in the reconstruction of the *foyer.* The bourgeois male was duty-bound to work, to produce—and to marry. Republicans had unflattering words for the single life. After all, who was the classic male bachelor? The priest who preached obscurantism or the soldier who consorted with prostitutes.[36] And once married, men were expected to be thoughtful husbands. D'Héricourt counseled gentleness for young men to mitigate what she called "the brutality of the wedding night."[37] The question was discussed from a male point of view by Gustave Droz in *Monsieur, madame et bébé,* a semiclassic book first published in 1866 by Hetzel. Droz's hero also worries about the potential for brutality in the first conjugal encounter. The considerate husband's part, he muses, is a delicate one. He must be "at one and the same time diplomat, lawyer, man of action, and all this without making himself ridiculous."[38] Droz pursued the issue beyond the nuptial night, urging husbands and wives alike to tend to one another's sexual needs. "Where's the harm," he wrote Hetzel, "in adding a dash of salt to that old ragout we call marriage?"[39]

Men were called upon to exert a similar tact and delicacy of feeling in relations beyond the family. The run of humankind had a right to polite treatment, and republicans were at some pains to define what they meant. They did not mean "that *politesse* of yesteryear," that old-regime etiquette which enabled the grand seigneur in a single gesture to greet an interlocutor with grace and at the same time to insult him.[40] "The handshake of a hearty soul," a frankness expressing respect for the dignity of others, that was genuine courtesy.[41] Republicans had a favorite word to describe upright conduct toward others: *sincérité,* a notion that carried a powerful political charge. A free people, Coignet wrote, was a people practiced in the ways of sincerity.[42] Ernest Legouvé, a veteran of 1848, was more explicit: "If the charm of the old regime was to be polite, the duty of a democracy is to be sincere."[43]

But was it possible to give expression to sincerity not just in forms of politeness but in one's physical carriage? Old-regime gentlemen were given to striking poses. Such affected behavior impressed mid-century Frenchmen as pretentious and comical.[44] But more than one republican still prized a certain formality of bearing. Blanc liked short hair for men because it communicated "an air of austerity, of *tenue,* of respect for the rules," in a word, virility. It was, he wrote, impossible to conceive of Brutus, the manliest of men, otherwise than with a close-cropped head.[45] In the 1860s Pelletan reproached republican youth, up-and-coming luminaries like Gambetta, for a lack of *tenue.*[46] As such criticism implies, the cult of correctness was not observed universally in republican ranks, least of all among the painters and photographers who inhabited the movement's bohemian fringes. Degas painted Manet sprawled on a couch, one hand to his chin and the other tucked in his pocket; Bazille painted Renoir (fig. 24), in Linda Nochlin's words, "with both feet drawn up on a chair, like an illustration of bad manners in a current book on deportment."[47] The casual poses so favored by Manet, Degas, and the impressionists were intended in part to communicate the unmannered freeness of the milieu in which they lived, but not only that. Félix Nadar, a 48er and pioneer of modern photography, sat subjects in characteristic postures, without props or costumes. The guiding principle of his photographic technique was straightforward: the truth of an individual's personality was to be sought not in poses or accessories that defined a social type, but in the particularizing details of physiognomy and dress.[48] Implicit in such thinking was an alternative model of conduct to the correctness esteemed by Blanc and Pelletan. A candid manner in dress or expression bespoke a sincerity

24. Frédéric Bazille, *Portrait of Renior*, 1867

of being, a willingness to make the self transparent without the cloaking of affectation. Republicans were prepared to strike more than one attitude: the austere virility of the ancient Roman, along with the open naturalness of the modern democrat.

The building of a republican order required a new kind of man, one who eschewed pose in favor of sincerity. Just as there had been disagreement about the place of fashion and fiction in women's lives, so was there disagreement about the importance of *tenue* in men's. But one assumption remained throughout: private and public virtue were linked and mutually reinforcing. The force of this assumption was nowhere more visible than in republican debates on childrearing.

Raising Children

A prime object of domestic reform was the moralization of the home, the fashioning of a fit environment in which to raise future citizens and mothers of citizens. Authoritarian childrearing methods bred authoritarian attitudes. To raise a generation insistent on its claims to citizenship, capable of self-government, that was the task of the moment, and its execution was inconceivable without a new emphasis on tenderness and nurturance in family life.[49]

"Affection," Legouvé asserted, "is to the family what liberty is to the state." Happily for the future of liberty, it was more and more the heart that reigned in the modern household. In days gone by and still among the well-born, parents addressed children as *vous*, but now the familiar *tu* was the rule, and the *vous* was reserved as a form of punishment for the naughty child. In times past, the death of a child was scarcely marked in formal fashion, but now it was cause for an extended period of ritualized mourning.[50] A relaxation of authority, however, did not mean the collapse of moral vigilance. Quite the contrary. Republicans rebuked both rich and poor for abandoning children, whether out of vanity or necessity, to the care of governesses, chambermaids, and wet nurses. It was different, they claimed, in the middle classes.[51] Here involvement in childrearing was intense, and that involvement, at least for women, began right at birth.

Republicans made a secular cult of the breast-feeding mother. Dalou sculpted a suckling infant titled *Jeune Mère* (1872); Renoir depicted a variation on the theme, *La Maternité* (1886); and Cassatt, though herself childless, painted many representations of the subject.[52] In 1874 Théophile Roussel, a doctor and militant republican, sponsored legislation subjecting the wet-nursing business to strict and what was meant to be deterrent state supervision.[53] Progressive opinion feared for the health of children farmed out to wet nurses. The mother's breast, by contrast, was venerated as a font of good health, but breast feeding was more than a matter of hygiene. Adolphe-Charles Clavel, a republican doctor of staunch positivist views, drew a simple equation between *allaitement* and *tendresse.* "With mother's milk," Eugénie Pierre told a republican feminist audience, flows "morality, wisdom, science, joy."[54] From the tenderness expressed first at the breast, mothers derived an extraordinary moral authority, and fathers did well to take a lesson from the maternal example.

Republican educators repeatedly exhorted men to be gentle with their children. Legouvé entreated fathers to shun the birch rod, branding corporal punishment "a leftover from more brutish times when soldiers were led by blows from the flat end of a saber."[55] Mastery of the child lay not through domination of the body but through governance of the soul. Droz urged fathers to "learn the art of entertaining your child, imitate the cock's crow and roll around on the carpet."[56] A playful intimacy, of course, cost some loss of paternal authority, but it was more than compensated by a gain in emotional influence, and the home was transformed in the process. The absolute monarch of yesteryear gave way to the "constitutional father."[57] To grow up in such a household was to learn lessons in citizenship, in the limits and leverage of consensual authority. As Droz put it, "It is with fathers that one makes citizens."[58]

Such paeans to intimacy, however, conceal a deeper anxiety about paternal absenteeism. The child in search of a father was a stock figure in republican literature. Jules Verne's *Les Enfants du Capitaine Grant,* first serialized in 1864 in Hetzel and Macé's children's magazine, recounted at length the exertions of a girl and boy to track down a father who had been lost at sea. With the assistance of a freedom-loving Scots lord, they succeed in the enterprise, in the process learning world geography and their own capacity for love and independent action. Verne himself may have been a Mason; it has been suggested that he was a utopian socialist; he was most certainly a republican, a friend of Hetzel's, and from 1888 a radical-socialist municipal councillor.[59] In Mme. Alfred Fouillée's *La Tour de France par deux enfants* (1877), the republican text par excellence for children, the *recherche de la paternité* is undertaken at the level of metaphor. The father of two Alsatian boys has just died in an accident related to wounds received in the Franco-Prussian war. The fatherless children leave Alsace on the trail of an uncle said to be in Marseille. The tour of France they conduct en route introduces them to a surrogate parent, *la grande patrie,* and teaches them an abiding love for the land that has nurtured them. In both the Verne and Fouillée stories, the father is found, either in the flesh or in spirit, and the odyssey matures and educates the participants. In real life, not all children had such good fortune. Under the Napoleonic code, natural children were forbidden to seek out the identity of their biological fathers. Such a prohibition, in the eyes of progressive and moralizing republicans, amounted to protection for libertines.[60] A campaign was launched to legalize the *recherche de la paternité,* which finally achieved partial victory in 1912.

For republican educators, however, a loving home constituted only the starting point of a genuine parental pedagogy. A "sentiment of liberty" resided in every child.[61] To coax it out required not only loving involvement but also technique, a careful balance of guidance and discipline. Two particular problems absorbed republican educators: the shaping of learning environments and the uses of literacy in the service of moral instruction.

On the first matter, republicans looked to a variety of sources for inspiration, but above all to the work of Friedrich Froebel.[62] Whether in the nursery or at the *Ecole maternelle,* children should learn through play. In a well-constituted learning environment, toys—blocks, dolls, a sandbox—were plentiful. The astute educator, mother or teacher, allowed children free play: freedom of movement and choice in the matter of toys and playmates. But such freedom did not preclude guidance. As children amused themselves, in groups or alone, sharing toys or hoarding them, they might be taught lessons of sociability and respect for the property of others. It required little more than a well-placed phrase or gesture on the part of a teacher to bring out the moral implications of play situations. Things also had lessons to teach. Ask little ones, parents were told, the names and purposes of the objects encountered in daily life. By such questions, "object lessons," were children made to feel at home in the world.[63] But all learning was not to be spontaneous, especially in matters of hygiene and decorum. To Pauline Kergomard, a Protestant, a republican, and one of France's first woman inspectors of schools, there was a moral dimension to cleanliness. She prescribed regular hair washings, daily scrubbings, and weekly baths for children. "Self-respect," she claimed, began with a concern for personal hygiene.[64]

At its worst, the pedagogical regimen elaborated by Kergomard was manipulative and class-biased.[65] The practices of the progressive middle-class household set the standard of correct behavior. Kergomard herself admitted as much. Working-class children, in the home if the mother did not work, at the maternal school if she did, were to be molded according to that standard. But at its best, the program would turn out preschoolers well on the way to free citizenship: self-respecting youngsters with a capacity for camaraderie, prepared to engage the world, and endowed with a spontaneous curiosity unsquelched by birch-toting authorities.

As an instrument of home-based character building, the book came a close second to the nursery. The *Magasin d'éducation et de récréation* was the most successful children's periodical of the day. As we have seen, its editors were men of republican conviction. Hetzel and Macé understood their magazine as serving a double purpose. They intended it to be read "in the bosom of the family," transforming the home into a "center of affection." But Hetzel and Macé were not mere sentimentalists. Parents were to exercise "vigilant reason" in the selection of common reading matter, and reason dictated that the books chosen be not only amusing but didactic: "The instructional must be presented in a form which stimulates interest: otherwise, it will repel and disgust; the amusing must conceal within itself a reality which is moral, that is to say, useful: otherwise, it will encourage frivolity."[66] But what moral lessons were children to glean from this parent-approved literature?

The renaissance in children's literature, dating from midcentury, has often been noted. Less well known is the extent to which the new literature, in France at least, carried a political charge. Take the case of the two towering figures of children's literature in midcentury France: the Comtesse de Ségur and Jules Verne. Ségur, a Russian noblewoman by origin (Sophie Rostopchine), married into one of France's great titled families. She was at home in clerical no less than aristocratic circles. From the 1850s on, Ségur maintained close relations with the ultramontane journalist Louis Veuillot.[67] The bourgeois Verne, by contrast (he trained as a lawyer), was peddling mediocre boulevard dramas in the 1850s. It was Hetzel who gave him a break, agreeing to publish in 1862 *Cinq semaines en ballon,* Verne's first great success. Hetzel launched the *Magasin d'éducation et de récréation* two years later, assuring Verne a reliable forum for the serialization of subsequent novels. The connection to Hetzel, and to Macé, brought Verne into the republican orbit. It is possible to overdraw the contrasts between Ségur and Verne, but they are real nonetheless and colored the work of both.

Ségur's most successful book, *Les Malheurs de Sophie,* appeared in 1859 and sold in subsequent years an estimated 1.7 million copies.[68] The heroine of the volume is Sophie de Réan, a little girl of about four years whose willfulness and high spirits land her in repeated trouble. Sophie inhabits an aristocratic and rustic world. The characters all bear particuled names, and the setting turns out to be an aristocratic country home. It is also a rough-and-tumble world where animals die in large numbers and punishments for bad behavior can be harsh. Correction is plentiful, but not always physical in nature. In one episode, Sophie gobbles up quantities of candied fruit. Punishment takes the form of an unsettling dream in which she must choose between the fruits of good and bad gardens. Mama interprets the dream, explaining that it was sent by God to teach Sophie to be obedient, sweet, and good.[69]

It is quite a contrast with Verne's universe. God does merit mention in *Voyage au centre de la terre,* but described according to masonic usage as the "grand architect of the universe."[70] It is not so much religion or the providential dream that governs as it is science, but Verne's science was of a visionary, sometimes cranky cast. He did anticipate scientific inventions of all kinds but was also an adept of phrenology and a stickler for hygiene. Verne thought to equip the *Nautilus* in *Vingt mille lieues sous les mers* (1869) with full bathing facilities. In *Les 500 millions de la Bégum* (1879), the phrase "to clean, to clean without ceasing" is used to sum up the hygienic philosophy of Franceville, a utopian city situated in the western United States. Verne's passion for physiognomies and sanitation, for engineered environments like the *Nautilus* or Franceville, calls to mind the utopian social science of Fourier or Saint-Simon.[71] Verne's heroes are also men of science: geographers, engineers, a far cry from the titled folk so dear to Ségur. Her characters are suited to a pastoral setting, but the adventurers of Verne's novels take the world at large (and other worlds) as their field of action. At moments, it seems, Sophie and her aristocratic friends might just as well have lived in the ancien régime. But Verne's protagonists conjure up thoughts of the republic, especially Captain Nemo. In the captain's study there hang portraits of a pantheon of republican heroes: Manin, Washington, Lincoln, John Brown. Riou, who illustrated the 1871 edition of *Vingt mille lieues,* modeled the figure of Nemo on Jean-Baptiste Charras, an austere republican colonel who urged armed resistance to Louis-Napoleon's coup.[72]

Although gender set Ségur and Verne apart—she wrote for girls, he for boys—it was also politics. The divergent worlds they created were as ideologically opposed as Veuillot and Charras, but each fictional universe had its moral lessons to teach. How to be an obedient, sweet, and good young woman in Ségur's case. In Verne's, how to be a man of action, liberty-loving and determined, ready to engage the wider world equipped with the technological wonders of science. A youth steeped in Vernian ways made fit material for republican citizenship.

The education of children in citizenship began in the home. Loving parents were essential to the enterprise, mothers who breast-fed, fathers who played on all fours, but love in itself was not enough. There was a science to childrearing, and the informed parent came to the task armed, Froebel tucked under one arm and Hetzel's *Magasin* under the other. Drawn by cords of affection, children were to be guided through constructed environments, through nurseries and books that taught lessons in self-mastery and, ultimately, in democratic self-government.

Home Furnishings

Republicans cherished the notion that moral being was formed by physical setting, and they applied the idea as much to grown-ups as to children. Mold the home, its look and decor, and the adult character might be molded in the process. So argued Charles Blanc in *Grammaire des arts décoratifs* (1882), a compendious guide to the aesthetics of home furnishings. "It is through the private virtues," he wrote in the book's opening pages, "that man initiate[s] himself to the public virtues."[73]

Midcentury debate on home design was not politicized in the outspoken way that the debate was, say, on family constitution or clothing. But if the politics was not explicit, it was there at one remove. Several of the principals in the furnishing debate were as much aesthetic politicians as critics of the arts *tout court.* Blanc is a case in point. So too is Philippe Burty. Burty got his start in the

1860s writing criticism for the *Gazette des beaux-arts* (founded by Blanc). At the same time, we have seen, he maintained close ties in republican circles, a connection that paid rich dividends later. In recompense for a lifetime of service to art and the republic, Burty was appointed, with Gambetta's patronage, inspector of fine arts in 1881.[74] Henry Havard offers a third example of the art critic turned political appointee. Havard came of good republican stock. His father Joseph-Louis, a paper wholesaler, made a minor reputation in the 1860s and 1870s agitating for the republican cause in the Paris business world. Havard fils applied himself to art criticism, publishing in 1884 *L'Art dans la maison (grammaire de l'ameublement)*, intended as a rejoinder to Blanc's *Grammaire*. The republic in fact adopted Havard's text as its "official decorative handbook" and rewarded the well-connected young critic with a position as Burty's colleague in the inspectorate of fine arts.[75]

It is not just that Burty and Havard were republicans; they also made use of a critical vocabulary that hummed with politically charged codewords and formulas. Both writers decried the degeneration of public taste. An uncontrolled appetite for luxury, they claimed, had seized consumers. And consumers got the luxury they craved, either the shameless, ostentatious luxury of a nouveau riche salon or the false luxury of its middle-class equivalent.[76] The anarchy of contemporary taste—the "anomalous hodgepodge" of styles, the "profusion of fake Boule furniture," the mania for bric-à-brac heaped on mantel pieces,[77]—tokened a profound moral confusion. What better way to dramatize that confusion than to associate bad taste with the errancy of modern woman? To intimate the dubious morals of *la femme à la mode,* Pelletan set her in a salon "decorated in garish taste with red and black velvet."[78] When Burty wanted to evoke the chaos of the modern home, buried under piles of garish junk, he likened it to the "permanent carnival" of women's fashions.[79]

Critics like Pelletan and Burty proposed a series of equations, linking bad taste to false luxury to moral degeneracy to the corruption of womanhood. These were not novel moves but standard rhetorical devices in the republican debate on private life. There were to be sure many issues on which republican critics disagreed, but even here the quarrels were cast in familiar form. They were argued in a vocabulary heavy with political meaning (sincerity, once again, was a favorite word); or they were couched in binary oppositions (*tenue* versus personality) encountered in other phases of republican polemic.

Blanc considered himself a classicizer, but what did that amount to in matters of home furnishing? It meant first a powerful appetite for symmetry. Nature "seen in the large," according to Blanc, fell short of the beautiful because it lacked regularity. "Above all things," he advised, "a certain order is required, a perceptible order, particularly in the rooms one opens to one's friends and all the more so in the rooms where visitors are received. An absence of all symmetry would constitute an act of impoliteness toward the visitor." In practice, good order meant well-proportioned furniture (Blanc was partial to Louis XVI designs), ensembles of identical chairs arranged in harmonious patterns. The propriety of the salon was to match the bearing of the black-suited gentlemen who inhabited it.[80] No less important to Blanc than *tenue* was what he called "domestic peace." The home should be an oasis of tranquillity, insulated against the world. Doors should be weighty and armored with solid bolts, lighting should be gentle, with rooms cocooned in carpeting, wall hangings, and thick drapes. Modern man, Blanc wrote, craved "a sentiment of intimacy"; he felt a "desire to close himself in," to seal himself off. If heavy padding gave the appearance of luxury, so much the better, provided the luxury was not excessive. Blanc believed in the democratization of luxury. Was it so wrong that "the advent of democracy" had sharpened and diffused the appetite for well-being? Modern industry had found inexpensive ways to satisfy this deepening hunger through a variety of simulative materials and techniques: trompe l'oeil wallpaper, electroplated metals, metalized plaster. Blanc, for one, approved all such methods. "Luxury in the household," he claimed, "far from being contrary to good mores favors them, inspiring in each a love for his home, which is the first of the private virtues."[81]

But for every classical opinion expressed by Blanc, there was an opposing voice that spoke in the accents of modernity. Blanc's obsession with symmetry so irritated Renoir that he proposed the creation of a Société des Irrégularistes. Renoir rejected the grammarian's "mania for a false perfection," insisting instead that nature, in all its unevenness, be taken as the home decorator's model.[82] Burty also spoke up for irregularity. He associated the classical ideal of the Beaux-Arts school, the checkerboard layout of French gardens, the perfection of Sèvres porcelains, with the "solemn wig of Louis XIV," with the aesthetics of absolutism. To such a stifling, authoritarian correctness, Burty proposed a series of life-giving alternatives: the landscape painting of the Barbizon school, English gardens, and oriental pottery, which was all the more "vital" for its flaws and imperfections.[83]

Critics of symmetry were no less antagonistic to the classical school's preoccupation with *tenue*. The proprieties were to be respected, of course, but Havard placed more stress on the potential of home furnishings to express personality. "So!" he exclaimed, "are we then, we of the nineteenth century, so in thrall to an official art, to fixed precepts, to an inflexible style, that we are forbidden to intermix a parcel of ourselves?"[84] Blanc worried about the grouping of furniture; Havard talked of comfort and temperament, of furniture arrangements that would express "the imprint of our preferences, the stamp of our dominant preoccupations, the unmistakable reflection of our taste."[85] Blanc extolled the nobility of the Greco-Roman ideal. His critics—Burty or painters of the *jeune école* like Manet and Monet—were more enamored of the expressive simplicities of japonaiserie.

Burty shared another liking with the painters of the modern school: windows. Urban vistas as seen from a window, apartment dwellers gazing out at the street, window-lighted scenes of readers and meditators, these were themes to which Manet and the impressionists returned again and again (fig. 25). The city revealed in such paintings was not a messy locale to be sealed out, but an engaging and vital spectacle pleasing to the city dweller, and perhaps necessary as well. As flats grew smaller and more claustrophobic, Burty pointed out, the need for large windows, which gave "an illusion of liberty" and let in soothing light, became all the more pressing.[86] Havard added a hygienic twist to the argument. Windows were conduits of sunshine and fresh air, essential to dispelling the unhealthful "miasmas" that collected in stuffy apartments.[87] Blanc saw interior and exterior as mutually hostile environments. Whether for reasons of visual pleasure, mental well-being, or physical health, partisans of the modern aesthetic understood the relationship as one of fluid exchange.

On one last issue, Blanc and the modernists found themselves at odds: the place of imitation and ornament in furniture. Apartments, Burty complained, were glutted with "inferior and lying products," with objects made of pseudo-bronze, pseudo-leather, pseudo-wood. He longed for furniture "in pure wood," unpainted, unvarnished tables and chairs that required simple wax and polish for their

25. Edouard Manet, *Reading*, 1873–1875

upkeep. Better still if the ornamentation on furniture were kept to a minimum. "The essence of the beautiful," Burty wrote, "is sobriety." On this point he was seconded by Havard, who implored in almost identical language that embellishments "be more sober than prolix, more contained than overflowing." To the vulgar excess of much French furniture, Burty contrasted the lightness and elegant simplicity of Japanese design.[88]

The debate between classicizers and modernists reverberated with political overtones: first, the principal participants were themselves republicans; second, they criticized the aesthetic status quo, its false luxury, its moral and sexual corruption, in accents characteristic of republican polemic; third, they advanced politically charged alternatives. In the case of the modernists, this charge was republican. Their critical vocabulary was veined with words—simplicity, sincerity, personality which were the stock-in-trade of republican discourse. The politics of classicism were more complicated. Blanc defended canons of taste widely subscribed to, not only in republican but in official circles. With invocations of Brutus and denunciations of imperial taste, he gave a republican bias to what was at base a conservative position. Little wonder that he felt at home as Thiers' minister of fine arts in the 1870s and that, while in office, he was roundly denounced by more intransigent republicans as lacking in political conviction.

The notion of bourgeois domesticity, in much of the literature on the subject, is filled with unhappy connotations. The middle classes know what private life is about and are determined, through the domestic and hygienic sciences, to impose their standards on the weak: women, the working classes, the so-called deviant. Such an image of the smug bourgeois imposing a disciplinary rationality on the powerless requires qualification.

At midcentury, the proper constitution of bourgeois private life was contested terrain. There were important givens in the debate: the preeminence of the nuclear family, the general division of labor between working husbands and homemaking wives, the centrality of the household's childrearing functions. But the areas of dispute were numerous: marital relations, manners, parental behavior, children's education, home furnishings. The debate was pursued not just in words but in legislation touching on divorce, schooling, wet nursing, and so on. The economic boom of the period made possible a reconstruction of bourgeois private life. The actual outcome of that remaking, however, was the result of many forces—market pressures, public argument, the law. Bourgeois men and women did not have a unitary conception of what they expected domestic life to be for themselves, let alone for others.

The debate on private life was also shaped in fundamental ways by political convictions. Republicans who weighed into the argument—and many of the principals were republicans—made it abundantly plain that they understood the regeneration of private life as a stepping stone to a larger political end. The same rhetorical strategy was employed repeatedly by republican polemicists. They constructed a loaded stereotype of prevailing domestic practice. The civil code, the Roman Catholic religion, and the persistence of aristocratic habits had poisoned family life, breeding authoritarian and violent attitudes in men, inciting women to coquetry and superstition. The situation had gone from bad to worse under the empire. The unbridled extravagance of the regime was matched by a collapse of morals, the empress' appetite for false luxury finding its fullest expression in the sexual corruption of the courtesan. The republican antidote to France's moral decline was straightforward: the democratization of public life, which was in turn premised on the regeneration of private morals.

Republicans debated among themselves the most suitable means to purify private life. Classical advocates like Pelletan, Adam, or Blanc wanted wives to dress with a certain austerity and confine their reading to uplifting literature; husbands were called on to respect the rules of *tenue;* and it was urged that homes be decorated with attention to correct appearance and classical principle. By contrast, modernists like Cassatt or Burty took an interest in fashions and were not embarrassed to depict women immersed in the pages of *Le Figaro;* they favored a more casual appearance in men, expressive of individual personality; and they liked less formal home furnishings in tune with the temperament and personal taste of the inhabitants. But such differences should not obscure a single core of concern. Make marriage "constitutional," teach wives sober domestic habits and the virtues of literacy, teach husbands gentleness and sincerity, raise children to self-mastery, regenerate public taste: such were the common prescriptions of republican family reformers. Fill these prescriptions and the home would become a nursery of citizens, a school for democracy.

Finally, the republican project, for all its disciplinary tendencies, was not without liberating potentiality. The causes of feminism, progressive education, and aesthetic experimentation all found a home in republican ranks. The contours of bourgeois private life cannot be taken as given; it was shaped not only by unconscious processes but by debate and legislation, in a word, by politics. Despite the bourgeoisie's deserved reputation for repressive Grundyism, in midcentury France middle-class life contained within itself an emancipatory moment, however limited then and however unrealized now.

CONCLUSION

In Defense of
the Republic

THE SPECTER OF 1940, of failure, hovers over the Third Republic, which helps to explain why assessments of the regime have generally been cast in negative terms. Vichy and the right dismissed the republic as a cabal of Protestants, Freemasons, and Jews. Its institutions did not represent the *pays réel* so much as the interests of an alien coterie. Such criticisms from the sworn enemies of democracy come as no surprise. But the friends of democratic institutions have not been much more generous toward the regime, accusing it of an immobilism that stifled associational life and entrepreneurial dynamism. The regime's aperitif-sipping, parish-pump politicians may have represented a certain France, so the argument goes, but it was a backward nation of bourgs and bourgades populated by *petits commerçants* and *petits propriétaires*. The republic and its blocked society could not accommodate the economic, social, and political demands of a fast-paced, industrial modernity. On the one account, the republic is said to have lacked roots; on the other, it is conceded roots, but roots that could draw little sustenance from the poor soil of a stalemated status quo. Either way, with the hard winds of 1940, it is no wonder that the regime was blown away with so little resistance.

There is much in this book to sustain these stereotypes, although in the end, I hope, far less than is usually supposed. The republic had its share of weaknesses, many of them built in from the start. Republican culture itself created ideological strains that in critical instances evolved into antidemocratic hybrids. Jules Soury's freethinking materialism hardened into racism, Henri Martin's nationalist mythmaking into ultrapatriotism. Nor did it require much tinkering to translate the regime's hygienic and moralistic commitments into a punitive welfare-statism aimed at sorting out deviants. As for the republic's missionary zeal, it led many into dangerous overreaching. The regime's unbending faith in a civilizing pedagogy tempted it down the imperialist path. It is one thing to educate a nation's young in the responsibilities of citizenship; it is another to impose "civilization" on subject peoples in preparation for a citizenship that may not come for generations, if at all. A home-grown nationalist right, a disciplinary statism, and the rot of imperialism did not help to extend the regime's life. On the other hand, it is easy to think of at least one democratic culture, riven with globalist, moralizing, and racist impulses, that has survived and even prospered.

Yet it was not just that French republican culture concealed a hidden, authoritarian self. From its earliest days, the republic operated with certain exclusions—of women and of labor. But what after all was to be expected of a regime that made such a virtue of manliness, that understood itself as the special handiwork of a new middle class of businessmen and professionals? The republic's record, however, is not altogether negative.

The republican project centered above all on forming citizens and reconstructing the state. Within the limits imposed by such an agenda, the regime was prepared to accommodate the interests of workers and women. On the labor front, the republic legalized the workers' right to organize in 1884; in 1901 it created a network of labor councils with a portion of seats set aside for elected union representatives. Association and conciliation, these were principles that republicans had little trouble understanding. But for a regime that committed itself to reducing state intrusion into the public domain, welfare reform—insurance against accidents, ill health, and old age—proved much more difficult to enact. These measures came in the end, but in watered-down form and with reluctance. As for women, the regime acted with some dispatch in family and educational reform. Republicans fussed over women's special role in raising and training a democratic citizenry. As wives and mothers, as committee members, teachers, and nurses, they had a special contribution to make to public life. Still that did not entitle them to vote or hold office. It was the republic's pedagogical commitments, more than any generous egalitarianism, that account for such feminist reforms as it undertook.

In dealing with labor and women, the regime traveled some distance. But on the whole it abandoned those constituencies to fate, relegating them to the status of junior partners in what purported to be an inclusive democratic state. Neither feminists nor, until the 1930s, labor militants were able to muster sufficient organizational strength to prod the republic into a serious rethinking of its priorities.

For all that, feminists and militant labor were not implacable enemies of the regime. The republic did all too often respond to the demands of workers and women with repression, but it came through with doses of reform as well. And there were some in the republican establishment who promised more, who talked of welfare improvements and women's suffrage. Further, since the 1860s the women's and labor movements grew up in close proximity to republicanism, sharing personnel and a measure of democratic conviction. What is most disappointing about the actual republic was its failure to be true to itself, to live up to its promise of equal citizenship. But the regime had opened some avenues of access, and hopes lingered that it could yet be made to deliver. If the feminist and labor movements did not in the end stir up more trouble, it was in part because of those lingering loyalties and hopes. Within the feminist camp, a deep republican strain endured, which hesitated to push too hard lest the republic suffer. In certain corners of the labor camp as well, a guarded faith in the regime persisted. During the Dreyfus affair, during the Great War, and once more in the Popular Front era, workers rallied to the republic, defending it against enemies at home and abroad, looking to it for a recognition that often did not come. The republican project did have certain exclusions built into it, but such exclusions did not in the end pose that serious a danger to its existence.

Of the Third Republic's genetic flaws, far more serious in the long run was its compromising attitude toward old elites. To be sure, in its first years the regime took measures to drive out of public service notables discredited by ties to earlier regimes. Efforts were made at the same time, through imposition of a state examination system, to make bureaucratic service a more meritocratic affair. But in other areas, the regime hesitated to act. The republic, despite the pacifist professions of so many of its founding fathers, backed away from dismantling the army. Gambetta above all, shaken by the reverses of

1870–71, became a firm believer in military preparedness. Something of the old pacifist faith lingered, on the republican left in particular. Radicals advocated reduction in the term of military service, the resolution of international conflicts through arbitration, the formation of a League of Nations. But the army as an institution survived the coming of the new regime in good order, and not just the army.

In the end, the republic recoiled from full-scale purges, conceding old elites more or less uncontested a huge swath of institutional terrain. The diplomatic corps (and the army as well) remained quite aristocratic in recruitment, although less so than elsewhere in Europe. The Académie Française continued in its hidebound ways, settling into a stodginess that bordered on reaction. As for the Roman Catholic hierarchy, which retained an institutional connection to the republic through 1905, it never brought itself to a wholehearted reconciliation with the new democratic order.

Important fractions of the private sector as well maintained a wary distance from the new regime: the Lille textile patriciate, the ironmasters of the Nord, the great landlords of the Parisian basin. And over time they made their influence felt in the corridors of power through a web of interest groups that included the Comité des Forges and the Société des Agriculteurs.

Of equal importance, there were critical sections of the republican establishment itself that were prepared to listen to the entreaties of yesterday's powerful. The Ecole Libre des Sciences Politiques was founded to train a new elite with the requisite moral vigor and administrative skill to restore the nation after the defeat of 1870–71. The project was launched by liberal Protestants, such as the Siegfried brothers, but over time it attracted the patronage of social Catholics as well, partisans of a conservative, religiously inspired reform. The school's project was both liberal and conservative in orientation, a mix of new and old in terms of both curriculum and clientele. Its graduates went on to employment in the senior civil service, which they came to dominate. The men who staffed the upper echelons of the republic's bureaucracy were not so much pure democrats as an amalgamated elite, willing to serve the present regime but not of necessity married to it. In the business world, too, there were pressures for amalgamation. The onset of the depression in the 1880s and the rekindling of socialist militancy in the ensuing decade fueled a *ralliement* of business opinion in the interests of protectionism and social defense. The enterprise attracted the backing of iron magnates, gentlemen farmers, and portions of the Paris commercial community as well, who had in former years been so staunch in their republican loyalties. A new conservative coalition was in the making which involved old elites but operated under the political aegis of men like Jules Méline, republican veterans who were moving away from their youthful democratic militancy.

The Third Republic, as aggressive as it was in the pursuit of institutional democratization, left the old elites ample room for maneuver. The notables accommodated themselves to the new order, turned it to advantage as circumstances permitted, and courted alliance with more conservative segments of the governing class. This did not mean that they had become true republicans, and the point is an important one. With the defeat of 1940, *Vernunftrepublikaner* such as these—senior civil servants, military men, *agriculteurs,* corporate executives—abandoned democracy without a backward glance, proving themselves all too willing to enlist in Maréchal Pétain's National Revolution. A deal was struck with France's old notability in the 1870s, which expedited the consolidation of the new republic. It seemed a good bargain at the time, but not from the perspective of *l'étrange défaite* and the first years of Vichy.

There is no denying the regime's evident limitations. Its political culture was streaked with authoritarian impulses; it relegated particular categories of citizen to minority status; important sections of the republic's governing elite remained doubtful about the value or effectiveness of democratic institutions. It was the accumulation of such weaknesses, aggravated by the high costs of world war and depression, that in the end left the republic vulnerable to its enemies, internal as well as external.

All this may be so, but two caveats are in order, which taken together point to a more positive appreciation of the republic's achievement. It is worth remembering that the litany of weaknesses just recited were in no way the peculiar possession of France, then or now. They are endemic to the democratic form itself. Sister republics exist that have their own paranoid style, their own marginalized populations, their own elites none too respectful of democratic procedure. And if such republics have survived the hard blows of twentieth-century history, it may be—happily for them—that their democratic mettle has not been put to the ultimate test, the heavy bludgeoning of total defeat in war. Second and of greater importance, a too narrow focus on the republic's shortcomings makes it impossible to answer the question posed at the outset of this book. If the regime was so rotten, why did its institutions survive a full seventy years and its political myths and rituals even longer?

The question gains in urgency when placed in comparative perspective. The *parti républicain* in France was not one of a kind. Gambetta and Ferry, as we have seen, rubbed shoulders in a kind of democratic internationale with the likes of Garibaldi and Virchow. But democratic movements had a hard time of it in mid-nineteenth-century Europe. There was one exception to that rule, and it was France, which became the first of the great powers to adopt a democratic constitution. Just over half a century later, even through the dismal decade of the 1930s, France stuck by that constitution, however much confidence in it had eroded. That is a good deal more than can be claimed for the vast majority of continental states.

In the final analysis, then, what is impressive is not the regime's brittleness or immobility but its capacity to command loyalty over time. It is the republic's comparative success that I have focused on in the preceding pages, drawing attention to the peculiar circumstances of the regime's birth, to its origins in a cycle of institutional confrontations that gathered momentum from midcentury on.

In each of these battles, the demands and methods were the same. Dissidents staked out a claim to institutional autonomy. Masons, university people, and artists insisted on the right to self-government. Self-government in turn was conceived as the rule of informed opinion, constituted in public debate and expressed through the exercise of universal suffrage. Such demands in every instance met with opposition, whether from an unbudging imperial state or from entrenched elites. But militants pressed on, petitioning constituted authority, mounting press campaigns or wooing institutional electorates.

These battles gradually took on an oppositional character. In every case, republican minorities were involved, which maneuvered to turn the conflict to political advantage. Given the structure and terms of the contest, the task was fairly easy. On the one side stood the state or constituted elites, accused of dogmatism, exclusivity, or high-handedness; on the other side was an aroused public that embraced the principles of openness, universal suffrage, and self-government. What might have begun as a localized dispute over the office of Grand Master or a university appointment ended as a political confrontation between self-styled democrats and defenders of an elitist or authoritarian status quo. These divers institutional struggles were by no means isolated phenomena. They intersected and overlapped, recruiting from a common pool of militants. They were bound by a shared democratic rhetoric, the ensemble constituting the infrastructure of an awakening republican movement.

That movement derived critical strength from the institutional struggles that fired its rebirth and expansion. Decades of institutional combat trained a republican counter-elite practiced in the arts of democratic politicking; that elite in turn fashioned for itself a thick institutional mail, a mesh of semi-independent bodies (the university and minority consistories) and voluntary associations (from the UNCI to the AIU, from the lodges of Freemasonry to the circles of the Ligue de l'Enseignement). So armed, republican militants launched themselves on the conquest of opinion out of doors. In every venue and by all means, whether in the courts or in the press, by word or by symbol, they pushed the republican message.

As for message itself, it operated on several levels, visionary and rational, invoking solidarity and science in a single breath. But the republican creed in all its variants, whether positivist or freethinking, materialist or spiritist, reverted time and again to the same themes: the emancipation of conscience from the strictures of philosophical or clerical orthodoxy, the emancipation of civil society from the intrusions of state or corporate authority. In both respects, republican thinking bore the clear impress of the institutional struggle in which it had been forged, battles against imperial appointees and academic elites, against idealist metaphysics and evangelical religion.

But that thinking was as much pedagogical as emancipatory in thrust, and on this score it may well have been the Second Republic's failure, more than institutional infighting, that was the decisive shaping influence. The experience of defeat and exile spurred sober reflection: the last republic had faltered for want of citizens; it was a mistake the next dared not repeat. The sooner republicans set themselves to the task of teaching good citizenship, the better. Any and all means, it was judged, might prove suitable to that purpose—books and libraries, of course, but statues, centennials, and even city-hall design as well. It was just such a comprehensive pedagogical ambition that inspired, at least in part, the republican advocacy of family reform. What better way to nurture republican mores—the simple and sincere manner of the true democrat—than to make the home itself into a model of constitutional government?

Even the market, tempered by free association and liberated from the coils of monopoly and privilege, might be made to teach lessons of right conduct, of probity and reciprocity, independent-mindedness and cooperation.

The *parti républicain,* then, represented far more than an assemblage of ambitious politicians. No competitor could match the electoral, oratorical, and journalistic skills of the professionals and businessmen who made up its general staff. As for the party itself, it was a huge and labyrinthine conglomerate, a patchwork of committees, institutions, and associations, animated by a vision in turn emancipatory and pedagogical in orientation, infused with a peculiar secular mystique all its own.

The republican awakening of midcentury France coincided with a general stirring of civic activism, which republicans both fed upon and incited. The authoritarian and statist political conjuncture simplified the politicization of civic discontents, and with considerable political skill republicans capitalized on the moment. The result—a resurrection of civil society under republican auspices—swept aside the dynastic parties of old, which never again occupied center-stage in French political life.

As the *parti républicain* acceded to office, it acted with dispatch to institutionalize the civic awakening of which it was both symptom and prophet. The school, the family, and the arts were bent to the task of making citizens. At the same time, the state made a measured retreat from the public domain, conceding the common run of French men and women a wider latitude to speak, to write, to organize, than they had ever known before, more indeed than was known in most of contemporary Europe and North America. It is important, of course, not to make exaggerated claims. Late nineteenth-century France, with its anticlerical persecutions and scoundrel laws, was no civil libertarian's paradise. But in a world of Jim Crow and Irish coercion, of antisocialist legislation in Germany and martial law in the Mezzogiorno, the French achievement does not look that bad.

The important point is not only that the French state pulled back from civil society, but that citizens at the same time pushed into the new spaces. If a bureaucratized trade-union movement or powerful employers' organizations are taken as the indicators of a vital civic life, then France in the late nineteenth century merits its reputation as an associational wasteland. But once the focus is widened to

include *cercles* and *amicales,* lodges and leagues, the myriad committees and congresses that proliferated under the federalist umbrella of
the republican movement, then the picture no longer looks so bleak.
France's associational landscape had a fraternalist, not a corporatist,
topography, and it invites comparison in this respect with the American republic. No doubt, given the extent and complexity of the
fraternal phenomenon in the United States, French associational life
will still look somewhat wan. But the comparison illuminates those
associational strengths that France did have, and it is a parallel that
French republicans themselves would have welcomed, looking as
they did on America as a sister regime.

In light of all this, the *parti républicain*'s success at generating
consent over time becomes easier to understand. At the same time, it
becomes more difficult to grasp all of the negative images associated
with the regime. Since Tocqueville's *Democracy in America,* France's
purported lack of a vibrant associational life has become a common-
place of critical commentary, especially in reference to the Third
Republic. The regime is all too often portrayed as a species of
Rousseauan experiment gone wrong, an atomized and stiff-necked
citizenry squaring off against an oppressive state with little in between to dampen the shock of contending forces. I have argued, to
the contrary, that the republic did not lack for intermediary bodies.
Its politicians were no more out of touch and its citizens no more
atomized than in the common run of democracies. To state the case
in more positive terms, the Third Republic was a democratic regime
that sprang from and then nurtured a resurrected civil society. It
rested on solid institutional and associational foundations, sustained
by a citizenry that in the main embraced its myths and promises.
How else could it have fought off the virus of anti-Dreyfusism; or
survived the catastrophic bloodletting of World War I; or dragged
itself through the plague years of 1918–1939, which all but extin-
guished democracy elsewhere in Europe?

Looking back from 1940 across a political landscape ravaged by
war, depression, and defeat, the Third Republic may well appear a
failure. Looking at the regime from its origins, however, the perspective is altogether more invigorating. July Monarchy liberals, now so
much in vogue in current historical work, had great difficulty in
coming to terms with a democratizing nineteenth century. In our
own time, when democratic constitution making and the ends of
democratic government are once again major subjects of debate, to

whom does it make sense to turn for guidance, let alone inspiration? Surely not to democrats *à contre-coeur,* but to republicans for whom democracy, both as a set of procedures and a code of civic behavior, was not so much an obstacle to be overcome as an end in itself, and a point of departure.

Notes
Acknowledgments
Index

Abbreviations

AIU   Alliance Israélite Universelle
AN   Archives Nationales
APP   Archives de la Préfecture de Police
BA   Bibliothèque des Avocats, Palais de Justice
BCC   Bibliothèque de la Chambre de Commerce
BHVP   Bibliothèque Historique de la Ville de Paris
BN   Bibliothèque Nationale
CCF   Consistoire Central de France
LUR   Ligue d'Union Républicaine
UNCI   Union Nationale du Commerce et de l'Industrie
UPL   Union Protestante Libérale

Notes

Introduction

1. François Furet, *La Gauche et la révolution au milieu du XIXe siècle: Edgar Quinet et la question du Jacobinisme, 1865–1870* (Paris, 1986), 7–97, and *La Révolution, de Turgot à Ferry, 1770–1880* (Paris, 1988), 499–507; John Eros, "The Positivist Generation of French Republicanism," *Sociological Review,* 3 (1955), 255–273.

2. Stanley Hoffmann, "Paradoxes of the French Political Community," in Hoffmann et al., *In Search of France* (New York, 1965), 1–117. See also David Landes, "French Entrepreneurship and Industrial Growth in the Nineteenth Century," *Journal of Economic History,* 9 (1949), 45–61; Michel Crozier, *La Société bloquée* (Paris, 1970).

3. Sanford Elwitt, *The Making of the Third Republic. Class and Politics in France, 1868–1884* (Baton Rouge, 1975); Eugen Weber, *Peasants into Frenchmen: The Modernization of Rural France, 1870–1914* (Stanford, 1976).

4. Christophe Charle, *Les Elites de la République, 1880–1900* (Paris, 1987).

5. Robert Dahl, *Polyarchy: Participation and Opposition* (New Haven, 1971); Samuel Huntington, "Will More Countries Become Democratic?" *Political Science Quarterly,* 99 (Summer 1984), 193–218; Dankwart A. Rustow, "Transitions to Democracy: Toward a Dynamic Model," *Comparative Politics,* 2 (April 1970), 337–363.

6. Nancy Bermeo, "Democracy and the Lessons of Dictatorship," *Comparative Politics,* 24 (April 1992), 273–291.

7. Gabriel Almond and Sidney Verba, *The Civic Culture: Political Attitudes and Democracy in Five European Nations* (Princeton, 1963); Jürgen

Habermas, *Strukturwandel der Öffentlichkeit. Untersuchungen zu einer Kategorie der bürgerlichen Gesellschaft* (1962; Darmstadt, 1986).

8. Larry Diamond, "Persistence, Erosion, Breakdown, and Renewal," in Diamond, Juan Linz and Seymour Martin Lipset, *Democracy in Developing Countries* (Boulder, 1989), 3.1–52; Diamond and Linz, "Politics, Society, and Democracy in Latin America," ibid., 4.1–58; Alfred Stepan, "State Power and the Strength of Civil Society in the Southern Cone of Latin America," in Peter Evans, Dietrich Rueschemeyer, and Theda Skocpol, eds., *Bringing the State Back In* (New York, 1985), 317–343. For a flavor of how such processes worked themselves out in the eastern bloc, see Vaclav Havel, *Disturbing the Peace* (New York, 1990); Boris Kagarlitsky, *The Thinking Reed: Intellectuals and the Soviet State from 1917 to the Present* (London, 1988).

9. Bermeo, "Democracy and the Lessons of Dictatorship."

10. Guillermo O'Donnell and Philippe C. Schmitter, "Tentative Conclusions about Uncertain Democracies," in O'Donnell, Schmitter, and Laurence Whitehead, eds., *Transitions from Authoritarian Rule* (Baltimore, 1986), 16–56.

11. See Huntington, "Will More Countries Become Democratic?" 212; O'Donnell and Schmitter, "Tentative Conclusions," 61–64.

12. The issue of how states may act to determine the content of political culture is addressed in Skocpol, "Bringing the State Back In: Strategies of Analysis in Current Research," in *Bringing the State Back In*, 3–37.

13. The classic texts here are by Maurice Agulhon: *La République au village* (Paris, 1970); *1848 ou l'apprentissage de la République, 1848–1852* (Paris, 1973); *Le Cercle dans la France bourgeoise, 1810–1848* (Paris, 1977).

14. On the general usefulness of an institutional focus to historical research, see Patrick Fridenson's programmatic statement, "Les Organisations, un nouvel objet," *Annales ESC,* 44 (November–December 1989), 1461–77. It may be, in the French context, that such an approach biases discussion in favor of the Paris scene. In a centralized state such as France, institutional life is bound to be concentrated in the nation's capital. My own book no doubt suffers from Paris-centeredness. For a provincial take on these processes, see Raymond Huard, *Le Mouvement républicain en Bas-Languedoc, 1841–1881* (Paris, 1982).

15. Georges Weisz, "Le Corps professoral de l'enseignement supérieur et l'idéologie de la réforme universitaire en France, 1860–1885," *Revue française de sociologie,* 18 (1977), 203.

16. The majority of French Protestants belonged to the Reformed Church. The Protestant community also included an important Lutheran minority and a number of smaller sects, which are not discussed here.

17. In 1869, the empire embarked on a short-lived experiment in liberalization, which led to a warming of relations between the academy and the regime.

18. Between Bonaparte's fall and Thiers' installation, France was ruled by the republican-dominated Government of National Defense, but this republican interlude lasted only six months, from September 1870 to February 1871.

19. Once again, pioneering work has been done in this area by Agulhon: *Marianne into Battle: Republican Imagery and Symbolism in France, 1789–1880,* tr. Janet Lloyd (Cambridge, Eng., 1981); *Marianne au pouvoir, l'imagerie et la symbolique républicaines de 1880 à 1914* (Paris, 1989).

1. Freemasonry

1. Jean Estèbe, *Les Ministres de la République, 1871–1914* (Paris, 1982), 210.

2. Mildred J. Headings, *French Freemasonry under the Third Republic* (Baltimore, 1949), 39.

3. For variations on this line of argument, see Serge Berstein, "La franc-maçonnerie et la République (1870–1940)," *Histoire,* 49 (1982), 30; John Eros, "The Positivist Generation of French Republicanism," *Sociological Review,* 3 (1955), 255–273; François Furet, *La Révolution, de Turgot à Ferry, 1770–1880* (Paris, 1988), 499–507.

4. Pierre Chevallier, *Histoire de la franc-maçonnerie française* (Paris, 1974), 2.298–299; John Merriman, *The Agony of the Republic: The Repression of the Left in Revolutionary France, 1848–1851* (New Haven, 1978), 59.

5. Chevallier, *Histoire de la franc-maçonnerie,* 2.328, 379.

6. It is not that provincial Masonry was prostrate in the aftermath of the 1851 coup. Lodges outside Paris, as in the capital itself, often provided safe haven to republicans who continued, even in the repressive climate of the 1850s, to agitate against the regime. But provincial Masons, however much engaged in wider political struggles, played a modest role in the constitutional battles of Freemasonry itself. See Jean-André Faucher and Achille Ricker, *Histoire de la franc-maçonnerie en France* (Paris, 1967), 304, 307; Raymond Huard, *Le Mouvement républicain en Bas-Languedoc, 1848–1881* (Paris, 1982), 117, 132, 323.

7. On the crisis of 1861–62, see Jean-Marie Caubet, *Souvenirs, 1860–1889* (Paris, 1893),48–68; BN FM1 206, Registre du Conseil du Grand-Maître, 1860–1863, 50–100; BN FM1 211, Faisceau de 41 documents pour servir à l'histoire du Grand Orient de France en 1861–1862, 50–127.

8. On the public utility debate, see BN FM1 206, session of 23 February 1863, 244–249, and sessions of 4 and 18 May 1863, 278, 282; "Assemblée annuelle du Grand Orient," *Le Monde maçonnique* (July 1863).

9. "Assemblée législative du Grand Orient de France," *Le Monde maçonnique* (July 1862), 130; "Chronique," ibid. (May 1870), 5; Isis-Mon-

tyon, proposal for revision of the constitution, BN FM1 92bis, "Révision de la constitution, 1864," 776, 780; La Renaissance par les Emules d'Hiram, proposal for revision of the constitution, ibid., 569–570, 572; also Chevallier, *Histoire de la franc-maçonnerie,* 2.461.

10. L. Redon, "Convent maç de 1865," *Le Monde maçonnique* (June 1865), 65–87.

11. "Assemblée du Grand Orient de France," *Le Monde maçonnique* (July 1869), 160; "Assemblée," ibid. (June 1870), 86–107; "Chronique," ibid. (July 1870), 134; "Chronique," ibid. (November 1871), 388; BN FM1 202, 1870–1872, session of 4 September 1871, 151.

12. BN FM1 201, Procès-verbaux du Conseil de l'Ordre, 1868–1870, session of 11 April 1870, report of F Ratier, 502–506; "Assemblée générale du Grand Orient de France," *Le Monde maçonnique* (August–September 1872), 210, and (October 1873), 292.

13. Desmons as cited in Chevallier, *Histoire de la franc-maçonnerie,* 2.543.

14. Faucher and Ricker, *Histoire de la franc-maçonnerie,* 361; Nadine Lubelski-Bernard, "Freemasonry and Peace in Europe, 1867–1914," in Charles Chatfield and Peter van den Dungen, eds., *Peace Movements and Political Cultures* (Knoxville, 1988), 82, 89.

15. A trove of biographical information on masonic activists in the 1850s and 1860s can be found in André Combes, "Jean-Charles Fauvety (1813–1894), fondateur de la 'religion laïque'," *Annales historiques de la Francmaçonnerie,* 19 (1977), 26–41, and "Une Loge sous le Second Empire, La Renaissance par les Emules d'Hiram," *Humanisme,* 111 (June 1976), 13–17.

16. BN FM1 211, "Sédition au sein de la maçonnerie," 104. The author of this document is unknown, but he was most certainly a supporter of Murat.

17. Ibid., 101–102.

18. Ibid., 102.

19. Lemonnier and Caubet were also regulars. See Caubet, *Souvenirs,* 2–11.

20. Montanier, a veteran of 1848, was appointed prefect by Gambetta in 1870 and, during the Commune, advocated conciliation. See "Docteur Montanier," *Le Monde maçonnique* (March–April 1872), 616–625. On Richer, see Caubet, "Bibliographie," *La Morale indépendante* (26 July 1868), 412–413; D.G. Charlton, *Secular Religions in France, 1815–1870* (London, 1963), 216; Richer, *Lettres d'un libre-penseur à un curé de campagne* (Paris, 1868–69).

21. Combes, "Une Loge sous le Second Empire," 13.

22. Massol, "Bulletin," *La Morale indépendante* (6 August 1865); Brisson, "Contre une équivoque," ibid. (6 August 1865); Morin, "Le Principe

moral," ibid. (20 January 1867), 195–96; Massol, "Bulletin," ibid. (24 March 1867), 264. For views on liberal Protestantism, see Massol, "Bulletin," ibid. (7 July 1867), 386; Caubet, "Le Protestant libéral et la morale indépendante," ibid. (7 October 1866), 78–79; and BN FM1 211, Riche-Gardon as cited in the *Journal des initiés* (December 1861), 341–342.

23. "Chronique," *Le Monde maçonnique* (May 1867), 26.

24. BN FM1 211, clipping from *Journal des initiés* (September–October 1861), 227; Guépin, "Lettres phrénologiques," *La Morale indépendante* (17 July 1870), 403–404, and "Esquisse d'une philosophie maçonnique," *Le Monde maçonnique* (August 1868), 237.

25. Guépin cited in Jean Chesneaux, *Jules Verne* (Paris, 1982), 73; J. Gourdon, "De la transformation et de l'origine des espèces," *Le Monde maçonnique* (October 1868), 385–387. For examples of the veneration of Lincoln, see BN FM1 200, Procès-verbaux du Conseil de l'Ordre, 1862–1865, sessions of 1 and 8 May 1865, 536, 542; remarks by Caubet and Massol in "Le F Abraham Lincoln," *Le Monde maçonnique* (May 1865), 44–46.

26. Caubet, "De l'oeuvre de l'enseignement," *Le Monde maçonnique* (February 1867), 640; "Chronique," ibid. (February 1869), 586; Jean Macé, *Les Origines de la Ligue de l'enseignement, 1861–1870* (Paris, 1891), 221, 478; Bernard Nöel, *Dictionnaire de la Commune* (Paris, 1978), 2.275; Paul Lachapelle, "Le Cercle parisien de la Ligue française de l'enseignement," *Cahiers laïques,* 47–48 (September–December 1958), 86–87.

27. "Chronique de la Ligue," *Ligue de l'enseignement* (15 February 1869); "Nécrologie," *La Morale indépendante* (10 June 1866); François Favre, "Enseignement professionnel des femmes," *Le Monde maçonnique* (November 1862), 385; Charles Lemonnier, *Elisa Lemonnier, fondatrice de la Société pour l'enseignement professionnel des femmes* (Paris, 1974), 34–37.

28. BN FM1 201, session of 11 April 1870, report of Dr. Guépin, 496; Caubet, "Du rôle de la francmaçonnerie dans l'avenir," *Le Monde maçonnique* (April 1876), 523; Juliette Adam, *Mes Premières Armes littéraires et artistiques,* 8th ed. (Paris, 1904), 367–368. Article 1 of the old constitution affirmed Masonry's commitment not only to the existence of God and immortality of the soul, but also to "human solidarity." The first two principles were hotly contested, of course, but never the last.

29. Caubet, *Souvenirs,* 7; BN FM1 202, Procès-verbaux du Conseil de l'Ordre, 1870–1872, sessions of 25 July, 1 and 8 August 1870, 43ff; Nord, "The Party of Conciliation and the Paris Commune," *French Historical Studies,* 15 (Spring 1987), 21; BN FM1 203, Procès-verbaux du Conseil de l'Ordre, 1872–1874, session of 25 January 1873, 71–72.

30. On the pacifism of the 1860s and 1870s, see Katherine Auspitz, *The Radical Bourgeoisie, The Ligue de l'Enseignement and the Origins of the Third Republic, 1866–1885* (Cambridge, Eng., 1982), 87; I. Tchernoff, *Le Parti républicain au coup d'état et sous le Second Empire* (Paris, 1906), 467–468, 483;

also APP B/a 1151, Lemonnier, report of 8 August 1875 and a Ligue de la Paix flier of uncertain date (1870s).

31. For the preceding, see Claire Goldberg Moses, *French Feminism in the Nineteenth Century* (Albany, 1984), 180–188; Maïté Albistur and Daniel Armogathe, *Histoire du féminisme français* (Paris, 1977), 2.493.

32. BN FM1 201, session of 11 May 1868, 59–61.

33. Rousselle as cited in "Chronique," *Le Monde maçonnique* (March 1868), 662–663. See also Moses, *French Feminism,* 201–202.

34. Adolphe-Charles Clavel, *La Morale positive* (Paris, 1873), 127; "Chronique," *Le Monde maçonnique* (June 1866), 120–121; Massol, "Bulletin," *La Morale indépendante* (16 December 1866), 153; Léon Richer, *Le Code des femmes* (Paris, 1883), 92–97.

35. "Nouvelles des ateliers," *Le Monde maçonnique* (October 1862), 343. See also BN FM1 201, session of 11 April 1870, report of Guépin, 496.

36. "Chronique," *Le Monde maçonnique* (July 1866), 156; Jean Gaumont, *Histoire générale de la Coopération en France* (Paris, 1924), 1.464–475; APP B/a 1151, Lemonnier, report of 28 January 1873.

37. Charles Sowerwine, *Sisters or Citizens? Women and Socialism in France since 1876* (Cambridge, Eng., 1982), 72–75; Steven Hause and Anne Kenney, *Women's Suffrage and Social Politics in the French Third Republic* (Princeton, 1984), 34–35.

38. Serge Berstein, *Histoire du Parti Radical, la recherche de l'âge d'or, 1919–1926* (Paris, 1980), 1.37–40

39. APP B/a 898, Clamageran, "Appel à l'opinion," 15 July 1898.

40. Henri Sée, *Histoire de la Ligue des droits de l'homme, 1898–1926* (Paris, 1927), 11–12; Headings, *French Freemasonry,* 98–99.

2. The Latin Quarter

1. Christophe Charle, *Naissance des "intellectuels"* (Paris, 1990), 83.

2. The phrase is used by George Weisz in "Le Corps professoral de l'enseignement supérieur et l'idéologie de la réforme universitaire en France, 1860–1885," *Revue française de sociologie,* 18 (1977), 203.

3. Paul Gerbod, *La Condition universitaire au XIXe siècle* (Paris, 1965), 316.

4. Jan Goldstein, *Console and Classify: The French Psychiatric Profession in the Nineteenth Century* (New York, 1987), 358.

5. Henri Dabot, *Souvenirs et impressions d'un bourgeois du quartier latin* (Péronne, 1899), 14.

6. Francis Schiller, *Paul Broca, Founder of French Anthropology, Explorer of the Brain* (Berkeley, 1979), 123.

7. Gerbod, *La Condition universitaire,* 351–352; Auguste Dide, *Jules Barni, sa vie et ses oeuvres,* 2nd ed. (Paris, 1892), 42ff.

8. See Vermorel's untitled article in *La Jeune France*, 3 February 1861; also Georges Clemenceau, "Causerie," *Le Travail*, 12 January 1862.

9. Auguste Scheurer-Kestner, *Souvenirs de jeunesse* (Paris, 1905), 66; Jacques Léonard, *La Médecine entre les pouvoirs et les savoirs* (Paris, 1981), 225.

10. André Lefèvre, *La Renaissance du matérialisme* (Paris, 1881), 133.

11. Isambert, "Qu'allons-nous faire?" *Le Mouvement*, 11 February 1862.

12. Longuet, "La Tradition des écoles," *Les Ecoles de France*, 31 January 1864; Clemenceau, "Causerie," *Le Travail*, 12 January 1862.

13. Isambert, "Un Cours d'hébreu," *Le Mouvement*, 1 March 1862; Dabot, *Souvenirs*, 98.

14. Longuet, "La Tradition des écoles"; Paul Lafargue, "La Méthode idéaliste et la méthode positive," *La Rive gauche*, 22 April 1866; A. Blatin, "Science et philosophie," *Les Ecoles de France*, 28 February 1864; "Nouvelles," *La Rive gauche*, 20 May 1866; Lefèvre, *La Renaissance*, 73, 124–125.

15. "Meeting républicain," *La Rive gauche*, 5 November 1865. On the Liège congress, see Patrick Hutton, *The Cult of the Revolutionary Tradition: The Blanquists in French Politics, 1864–1893* (Berkeley, 1981), 39–41; Angelo, "Le Congrès de Liège," *La Rive gauche*, 12 November 1865.

16. "Conseil académique de Paris," *La Rive gauche*, 24 December 1865; "L'Affaire des étudiants," ibid., 31 December 1865; Dabot, *Souvenirs*, 188–189.

17. Angelo, "Choses et autres," *La Rive gauche*, 24 December 1865; Dabot, *Souvenirs*, 190–191.

18. "Choses et autres," *La Rive gauche*, 31 December 1865.

19. Maurice Dommanget, *Blanqui et l'opposition révolutionnaire à la fin du Second Empire* (Paris, 1960), 122; Lefèvre, *La Renaissance*, 127–129.

20. APP B/a 982, Paul Broca, report of 26 January 1877.

21. Coudereau, "Programme," *La Libre Pensée*, 21 October 1866. See also Abel Hovelacque, *La Linguistique* (Paris, 1876), ix.

22. *Encyclopédie générale* (Paris, 1869), vol. 1, frontispiece and insert signed Jules Mottu et Cie. The encyclopedia's chief editor was Jules Mottu, a businessman well connected in freethinking circles. He recruited contributors from the editorial boards of *La Libre Pensée* and *La Pensée nouvelle*.

23. Georges Renard, "L'Ecole normale de 1867 à 1870," *La Revue bleue* (18 February 1922), 97–98; Victor Glachant, "Pasteur disciplinaire, un incident à l'Ecole normale supérieure," *Revue universitaire*, 47 (July 1938), 100, 102–104.

24. Nisard, *Souvenirs et notes biographiques* (Paris, 1888), 2.61–65; Roger Bellet, "Une Bataille culturelle, provinciale et nationale, à propos des bons auteurs pour bibliothèques populaires (janvier–juin 1867)," *Revue des sciences humaines*, 135 (July–September 1969), 462–468; Renard, "L'Ecole normale de 1867 à 1870," *La Revue bleue* (5 April 1919), 198–199; Roger Fayolle,

"Sainte-Beuve et l'Ecole normale, l'affaire de 1867," *Revue d'histoire littéraire de la France,* 67 (July–September 1967), 562–569.

25. Fayolle, "Sainte-Beuve et l'Ecole normale," 571–573; R. D. Anderson, *Education in France, 1848–1870* (Oxford, 1975), 230.

26. Renard, "L'Ecole normale de 1867 à 1870," *La Revue bleue* (10 January 1920), 8, and "L'Ecole normale de 1867 à 1870" (18 February 1922), 98–100. See also James Friguglietti, "Alphonse Aulard: Radical Historian of the Radical Republic," *Proceedings of the Annual Meeting of the Western Society for French History,* 14 (1987), 243–244.

27. Dabot, *Souvenirs,* 109–113, 138; Léonard, *La Médecine,* 194, 225.

28. See Longuet's articles: "L'Association des écoles," *Les Ecoles de France,* 20 April 1864; "La Liste indépendante," 1 May 1864; "Elections de la commission," 8 May 1864.

29. APP B/a 1300, Charles Wurtz, clipping from *Les Ecoles,* 20 May 1877, and reports dated 4 October 1872 and 22 June 1875.

30. Robert Fox, "Science, the University and the State in Nineteenth-Century France," in Gerald Geison, ed., *Professions and the French State, 1700–1900* (Philadelphia, 1984), 98–99; D. R. Watson, *Georges Clemenceau, a Political Biography* (London, 1974), 29; Jean Hamburger, *Monsieur Littré* (Paris, 1988), 134–135.

31. David Cohen, *La Promotion des juifs en France à l'époque du Second Empire, 1852–1870* (Aix-en-Provence, 1980), 1.172–174; Dabot, *Souvenirs,* 249–251.

32. Goldstein, *Console and Classify,* 355–358.

33. Alfred Vulpian was a neurologist, freethinker, and Wurtz's successor as dean of the medical faculty.

34. Cited in Schiller, *Broca,* 273.

35. E. Littré, "Des opinions administratives sur le libre arbitre," *La Philosophie positive* (May–June 1868), 457.

36. Fox, "Science, the University and the State," 101, 137n. APP B/a 24, Etudiants, clippings from *La Marseillaise,* 31 March and 1 April 1870, and *Le Rappel,* 4 May 1870.

37. APP B/a 24, Etudiants, reports of 10, 11, 12, and 17 November 1874; reports of 1, 7, 8, and 9 December 1874; clipping from *Le Rappel,* 11 November 1874.

38. Robert J. Smith, *The Ecole Normale Supérieure and the Third Republic* (Albany, 1982), 63–64.

39. A. Blatin, "Les Origines de la vie," *La Rive gauche,* 4 December 1864.

40. Broca, *Mémoires d'anthropologie de Paul Broca, 1871–1888* (Paris, 1871), 1.36, 262. See also Michael Hammond, "Anthropology as a Weapon of Social Combat in Late-Nineteenth-Century France," *Journal of the History of the Behavioral Sciences,* 16 (1980), 118–132; Jacqueline Lalouette, "Science

et foi dans l'idéologie libre penseuse (1866–1914)," in *Christianisme et science, Etudes réunies par l'Association française d'histoire religieuse contemporaine* (Paris-Lyon, 1989), 36–37.

41. Peter Bowler, *The Invention of Progress: The Victorians and the Past* (Oxford, 1989), 83–84; Hovelacque, *La Linguistique,* 26.

42. Schiller, *Broca,* chaps. 9–10; Anne Harrington, *Medicine, Mind, and the Double Brain: A Study in Nineteenth-Century Thought* (Princeton, 1987), 35–36, 40–45, 65–66.

43. Bowler, *Invention of Progress,* 83–84. It was Mortillet who first schematized the sequence of ages in which human prehistory is still conceived.

44. Hovelacque, *La Linguistique,* 350ff.

45. Lefèvre, "L'Ecriture," *La Pensée nouvelle,* 10 January 1869.

46. Letourneau, *La Sociologie d'après l'ethnographie,* 3rd ed. (Paris, 1892 [orig. 1880]).

47. Lalouette, "Science et foi," 32–33.

48. Jacques and Michel Dupâquier, *Histoire de la démographie, la statistique de la population des origines à 1914* (Paris, 1985), 402–404; Michel Dupâquier, "La Famille Bertillon et la naissance d'une nouvelle science sociale: la démographie," *Annales de démographie historique* (1983), 293–311; Jules Béclard and Alexandre Axenfeld, *Rapport sur les progrès de la médecine en France* (Paris, 1867), 67–68; Léonard, *La Médecine,* 159, 311.

49. Letourneau, *La Sociologie,* 439.

50. Cited in Schiller, *Broca,* 268.

51. Broca, *Mémoires,* 1.29, 32–33.

52. Lefèvre, *La Renaissance,* 130; Stephen J. Gould, *The Mismeasure of Man* (New York, 1981), 74, 83, 104–105; Harrington, *Medicine, Mind,* 100–101.

53. Edward Berenson, *Populist Religion and Left-Wing Politics in France, 1830–1852* (Princeton, 1984), 79–81; Hammond, "Anthropology as a Weapon of Social Combat," 119, 123.

54. Albert Rogeard, "L'Emploi de la force," *La Rive gauche,* 26 November 1865.

55. Dommanget, *Blanqui,* 120–121; I. Tchernoff, *Le Parti républicain au coup d'état et sous le Second Empire* (Paris, 1906), 579; R. Luzarche, "La Semaine politique," *La Rive gauche,* 2 July 1865; L. Fontaine, "Un Mot d'explication," *La Rive gauche,* 24 June 1866.

56. Letter from Jean-Jules Clamageran to Félix Clamageran, 15 December 1863, in Clamageran, *Correspondance, 1849–1902* (Paris, 1906), 266–267; Dabot, *Souvenirs,* 124–125; Maurice Reclus, *Jules Ferry, 1832–1893* (Paris, 1947), 26, 52; Renard, "L'Ecole normale de 1867 à 1870," *La Revue bleue* (4 September 1920), 516–517.

57. C. Talès, *La Commune de 1871* (1921; Paris, 1971), 60; Edmond Lepelletier, *Histoire de la Commune de 1871* (Paris, 1911–1913), 2.271; Gaston da Costa, *La Commune vécue* (Paris, 1903–1905), 1.245.

58. Benoît Malon, *La Troisième Défaite du prolétariat français* (Neuchâtel, 1871), 238–240; P. Lanjalley and P. Corriez, *Histoire de la révolution du 18 mars* (Paris, 1871), 236–237; Louis Fiaux, *Histoire de la guerre civile de 1871* (Paris, 1879), 267.

59. On the Ligue and its membership, see Nord, "The Party of Conciliation and the Paris Commune," *French Historical Studies,* 15 (Spring 1987), 6–14; AN 49 AP 1, Floquet papers, minutes of the Ligue d'Union Républicaine.

60. Smith, *Ecole normale,* 86; APP B/a 25, Etudiants, 31 December 1876.

61. Henri Bourrelier, *La Vie du quartier latin* (Paris, 1936), 189–190, 197.

62. APP B/a 25, Etudiants, 2 February 1876; B/a 982, Broca, clippings from *La France,* 10 July 1880, and *Le Moniteur,* 9 July 1880; Goldstein, *Console and Classify,* 361–363.

63. William Keylor, *Academy and Community: The Foundation of the French Historical Profession* (Cambridge, Mass., 1975), 61; Schiller, *Broca,* 278; Joy Harvey, "Evolutionism Transformed: Positivists and Materialists in the *Société d'anthropologie de Paris* from Second Empire to Third Republic," in D. Oldroyd and I. Langham, eds., *The Wider Domain of Evolutionary Thought* (Dordrecht, 1983), 301; George Weisz, *The Emergence of Modern Universities in France, 1863–1914* (Princeton, 1983), 280; Reclus, *Jules Ferry,* 185; Smith, *Ecole Normale,* 136; Steven Lukes, *Emile Durkheim, His Life and Work: A Historical and Critical Study* (Stanford, 1985), 95.

64. On university reform, see Louis Capéran, *Histoire contemporaine de la laïcité française* (Paris, 1957), 1.153–54, 160; and the detailed account in Weisz, *Emergence of Modern Universities,* chap. 4.

3. Commercial Politics

1. *Discours et plaidoyers politiques de M. Gambetta* (Paris, 1881), 3.101.
2. Ibid. (1882), 7.224.
3. Gaston de Saint-Valry, *Souvenirs et réflexions politiques* (Paris, 1886), 2.116–117.
4. APP B/a 1420, Syndicat général, 8 April 1875.
5. Ibid., 22 May 1872.
6. Joseph-Louis Havard, *Les Syndicats professionnels* (Paris, n.d. [1870s]), 53.
7. APP B/a 1274, Eugène Spuller, 17 January 1879.

8. APP B/a 1420, Syndicat général, 26 March 1881; clipping from *L'Union nationale,* 2 April 1881.

9. J. Techener and Emile Cottenet, eds., *Annuaire des notables commerçants de la ville de Paris* (Paris, 1861), viii–x.

10. Havard, *Syndicats,* 74–77, 122–123.

11. BCC, Chambre de Commerce de Paris, *Procès-verbaux,* 1866–1871, meeting of 27 May 1868, 155; letter of 29 May 1868, cited in Chambre de Commerce de Paris, *Avis émis sur les principales questions soumises à son examen pendant les années 1868 et 1869* (Paris, 1870), 28.

12. More conservative UNCI members wanted eligibility restricted only to taxpayers who had paid the patente regularly over a five-year period. The assembly, in fact, voted to enfranchise anyone who had paid the tax for a single year. J. Allain, "Pétition sur la notabilité commerciale," *L'Union nationale,* 5 March and 12 March 1870.

13. See the discussion in BCC, Chambre de Commerce de Paris, *Procès-verbaux,* 1866–1871, meeting of 2 March 1870, 332ff; and letter from Chamber of Commerce to Minister of Commerce, 9 March 1870, in *Avis émis sur les principales questions soumises à son examen en 1870, 1871 et 1872* (Paris, 1873), 3.

14. "Des traités de commerce," *L'Union nationale,* 26 January 1870; Havard, *Syndicats,* 118–119. On Levallois, see APP B/a 1155, Ernest Levallois, 24 November 1888 and 22 September 1906.

15. BCC, Chambre de Commerce de Paris, *Procès-verbaux,* 1866–1871, meetings of 1 December 1869, 282–283, and 8 December 1869, 288–293.

16. Havard, *Syndicats,* 70.

17. APP B/a 1420, Syndicat général, clipping from *Le Réveil,* 7 July 1870; see also clipping from *La Cloche,* 6 July 1870.

18. Allain published a rash of articles in *L'Union nationale* under the title "Des grèves et des moyens proposés pour les prévenir," 21 May, 15 June, 18 June, 25 June 1870.

19. "Chambre syndicale des articles de Paris et des Industries diverses." *L'Union nationale,* 15 June 1870.

20. Andrew Lincoln, "L'Union nationale du commerce et de l'industrie, 1858–1871: A Study in Employers' Trade-Unionism," manuscript (1979). Lincoln was the first to undertake a study of the UNCI, and I owe him a special debt of gratitude for allowing me to cite from his work.

21. Jean Gaumont, *Histoire générale de la coopération en France* (Paris, 1924), 1.558. APP B/a 1420, Syndicat général, clipping from *L'Union des travailleurs,* 15 January 1874; reports of 15 and 17 January, 11 February, 9 April 1874. See also Georges Weill, *Histoire du mouvement social, 1852–1924,* 3rd ed. (Paris, 1924), 190.

22. BCC, Chambre de Commerce de Paris, *Procès-verbaux,* 1871–1874, meeting of 13 March 1872, 51–55. See also Lincoln, "L'Union nationale du commerce et de l'industrie," 26.

23. J.-L. Havard, "Note relative au mode d'élection à adopter pour les Tribunaux et Chambres de Commerce," *L'Union nationale,* 11 November 1871. On Havard's political views, see AN 45 AP 1, Floquet papers, "Dossier action électorale," document titled "Pièce. Discussion."

24. APP B/a 1420, Syndicat général, 5 May 1874.

25. *L'Union nationale,* 12 March 1870.

26. Notelle, "Réponse au discours de M. Thiers sur la question économique," *L'Union nationale,* 2 February 1870. See also "Chambre syndicale des Industries diverses (12 juillet 1871)," ibid., 15 July 1871.

27. Notelle, "Premier article," *L'Union nationale,* 12 January 1870.

28. Ibid. See also Notelle, "Réponse au discours de M. Thiers sur la question économique," ibid., 2 February 1870.

29. On the representation of protectionist interests in the Corps Législatif, see Enna Jeloubovskaia, *La Chute du Second Empire et la naissance de la Troisième République en France* (Moscow, 1959), 141; and Michael Smith, *Tariff Reform in France, 1860–1900* (Ithaca, 1980), 36.

30. Havard, *Syndicats,* 101; remarks by Hiélard in "Syndicat général, 20 juillet 1870," *L'Union nationale,* 13 August 1870.

31. *Discours et plaidoyers politiques de M. Gambetta* (Paris, 1883), 9.175.

32. The word "moralization" is used by Notelle in "Réponse," *L'Union nationale,* 9 March 1870.

33. "Syndicat général, 20 juillet 1870," ibid., 13 August 1870.

34. Ibid.

35. The address was delivered by Levallois. The text can found in *Journal officiel de la Commune* (ed. V. Bunel), 5 April 1871, 163–164.

36. G. Henriot and G. Bourgin, eds., *Procès-verbaux de la Commune* (Paris, 1924), session of 11 April 1871, annex, 1.174–178. For details on UNCI policy during the Commune, see Nord, "The Party of Conciliation and the Paris Commune," *French Historical Studies,* 15 (Spring 1987), 14–20.

37. "Syndicat général (14 juin 1871)," *L'Union nationale,* 17 June 1871.

38. "Syndicat général (21 juin 1871)," ibid., 24 June 1871.

39. "Commission des élections (16 juin 1871)," ibid., 21 June 1871.

40. AN 49 AP 1, Floquet papers, "Dossier action électorale," document marked "Comité électoral de la Ligue, séance du 23 juin."

41. "Elections du 2 juillet," *L'Union nationale,* 1 July 1871; Pascal Bonnin, "Les élections," ibid., 1 July 1871; Lincoln, "L'Union nationale du commerce et de l'industrie," 30.

42. O. Ranc, *De Bordeaux à Versailles, l'Assemblée de 1871 et la République* (Paris, n.d.), 37–38.

43. On the November petition and police reaction, see APP B/a 485, Pétitions addressées à Monsieur le Maréchal Président, par les commerçants

de Paris et de la France, undated clipping from *Le Temps* (establishing that the petition was dated November 24); and two police reports of 30 November 1877.

44. APP B/a 485, Pétitions, report of 4 December 1877.

45. On the delegation and the Salle Frascati meeting in general, see Fresnette Pisani-Ferry, *Le Coup d'état manqué du 16 mai 1877* (Paris, 1965), 303–304; APP B/a 485, Pétitions, clipping from *Le Siècle,* 3 December 1877.

46. APP B/a 485, Pétitions, reports of 3 and 4 December 1871.

47. Ibid., 3 and 4 December 1877.

48. APP B/a 1420, Syndicat général, report of 6 December 1877. See also APP B/a 485, Pétitions, 6 December 1877.

49. APP B/a 485, Pétitions, reports of 6 and 9 December 1877 and a ream of newspaper clippings from *Le Siècle, Le Rappel, XIXe Siècle,* etc.

50. Alfred Cobban, *A History of Modern France* (Harmondsworth, 1970), 3.20.

51. *Discours et plaidoyers politiques de M. Gambetta,* 9.182. Gambetta delivered the speech on 27 March 1881, two days after his better-known UNCI speech.

52. Daniel Halévy, *The End of the Notables,* tr. Alain Silvera (Middletown, 1974); Saint-Valry, *Souvenirs* (Paris, 1886), 1.218.

53. APP B/a 485, Pétitions, reports of 4 and 5 December 1871.

54. APP B/a 1420, Syndicat général, 8 April 1875; "Assemblée générale des adhérents. Dimanche 21 mars 1880," *L'Union nationale,* 10 April 1880; Etienne Villey, *L'Organisation professionnelle des employeurs dans l'industrie française* (Paris, 1923), 225.

4. Jewish Republicanism

1. Phyllis Cohen Albert, *The Modernization of French Jewry: Consistory and Community in the Nineteenth Century* (Hanover, 1977), vii.; François Delpech, "De 1815 à 1894," in Bernhard Blumenkranz, ed., *Histoire des juifs en France* (Toulouse, 1972), 313.

2. Simon Schwarzfuchs, *Du juif à l'israélite: histoire d'une mutation, 1770–1870* (Paris, 1989), 304; David Cohen, *La Promotion des juifs en France à l'époque du Second Empire, 1852–1870* (Aix-en-Provence, 1980), 2.381, 783.

3. Albert, *Modernization of French Jewry;* Michael Marrus, *The Politics of Assimilation: A Study of the French Jewish Community at the Time of the Dreyfus Affair* (New York, 1971), tr. *Les Juifs de France à l'époque de l'affaire Dreyfus: l'assimilation à l'épreuve* (Paris, 1972).

4. Aron Rodrigue, "L'Exportation du paradigme révolutionnaire, son

influence sur le judaïsme sépharade et oriental," in Pierre Birnbaum, ed., *Histoire politique des juifs de France* (Paris, 1990), 186.

5. On consistory elections, see Albert, *Modernization of French Jewry,* 104–106, 112, 118; Michael Graetz, *Les Juifs en France au XIXe siècle* (Paris, 1989), 69–71; CCF, ICC 53, Elections consistoriales, letter from Consistoire de Paris to Consistoire central, 21 December 1857.

6. Graetz, *Les Juifs en France,* 291, 406; Jonathan Helfand, "French Jewry during the Second Republic and Second Empire 1848–1870" (Ph.D. diss., Yeshiva University, 1979), 118; Cohen, *La Promotion des juifs,* 2.399.

7. Schwarzfuchs, *Du juif à l'israélite,* 244.

8. Albert is especially insistent on this point, in *Modernization of French Jewry,* 117, 311.

9. Graetz, *Les Juifs en France,* 96.

10. Ibid., 96, 98; Cohen, *La Promotion des juifs,* 1.125–126, 128; Helfand, *French Jewry,* 122–126, 183, 185, 192; Schwarzfuchs, *Du juif à l'israélite,* 299.

11. Isidore Cahen, "Chronique du mois," *Archives israélites* (September 1861), 526; see also Schwarzfuchs, *Du juif à l'israélite,* 262.

12. Albert, *Modernization of French Jewry,* 162–163.

13. The group later changed its name to Société des Jeunes Garçons Israélites de Paris. Léon Kahn, *Les Professions manuelles et les institutions de patronage* (Paris, 1885), 132–133; Lee Shai Weissbach, "The Jewish Elite and the Children of the Poor: Jewish Apprenticeship Programs in Nineteenth Century France," *Association for Jewish Studies Review,* 12 (Spring 1987), 123–142.

14. Graetz, *Les Juifs en France,* 74, 76, 291. Anspach was a veteran of the July days. See "Philippe Anspach," *Archives israélites* (1 December 1875), 247–248.

15. Mortara was never returned to his parents. He grew up as a Catholic and later became a priest.

16. I. Cahen, "L'Alliance israélite universelle," *Archives israélites* (December 1858), 697, and "Le Droit légitime de défense," ibid. (March 1859), 142; and S. Cahen, "Culte," ibid. (December 1859), 685.

17. Aron Rodrigue, *French Jews, Turkish Jews: The Alliance Israélite Universelle and the Politics of Jewish Schooling in Turkey, 1860–1925* (Bloomington, 1990), 21–22.

18. I. Cahen, "L'Affaire Mortara de Bologne," *Archives israélites* (October 1858), 548, and "L'Alliance israélite universelle," *Archives israélites* (December 1858), 700.

19. "Exposé," *Bulletin de l'AIU* (1860), 14–15.

20. Ibid., 10, 12.

21. R., "Un Regard en avant," *Archives israélites* (January 1862), 3; "Appel aux israélites," *Bulletin de l'AIU* (1860), 18–19.

22. "Appel aux israélites," *Bulletin de l'AIU* (1860), 19.

23. Graetz, *Les Juifs en France,* citing from AIU manifesto, 397.

24. For the six, see "Appel aux israélites," *Bulletin de l'AIU* (1860), 19; for the seventeen, Narcisse Leven, *Cinquante ans d'histoire: l'Alliance israélite universelle, 1860–1910* (Paris, 1911), 1.67.

25. Leven, *Cinquante ans d'histoire,* 1.63, and "Un souvenir de la vie d'Eugène Manuel," *Bulletin de l'AIU* (1901), 19.

26. André Kaspi, "La Fondation de l'Alliance israélite universelle" (DES, University of Paris, 1959), 82, 86–87; Graetz, *Les Juifs en France,* 297.

27. André Chouraqui, *Cent ans d'histoire: L'Alliance israélite universelle et la renaissance juive contemporaine, 1860–1960* (Paris, 1965), 146.

28. Albert, *Modernization of French Jewry,* 163; CCF, AA5 Procès-verbaux du Consistoire de Paris, 10 April 1861, 235, and 14 June 1861, 242; I. Cahen, "Chroniques israélites de la quinzaine," *Archives israélites* (1 November 1866), 927–928.

29. *L'Opinion nationale,* 16 December 1865, letter to editor signed Jules Carvallo; "Chronique du mois," *Archives israélites* (July 1862), 407; Kaspi, "La Fondation de l'Alliance," 113–114. Kaspi judges Carvallo to have been a Bonapartist. A Saint-Simonian past and employment with Guéroult, however, do not of necessity signify a Bonapartist affiliation.

30. Alexandre Weill, "Mort de Charles Netter," *L'Univers israélite* (16 October 1882), 77–78; Georges Weill, "Charles Netter ou les Oranges de Jaffa," *Les Nouveaux Cahiers,* 21 (June 1970), 2–36.

31. Graetz, *Les Juifs en France,* 297; Kaspi, "Note sur Isidore Cahen," *Revue des études juives,* 121 (July–December 1962), 417–419; "Nos adieux au public," *Archives israélites* (December 1860), 669–670.

32. "Nouvelles diverses," *Archives israélites* (August 1862), 481.

33. On Horn, see "Edouard Horn," ibid. (November 1875), 693; on Lévy-Alvarès, see A. H. Navon, *Les 70 ans de l'Ecole normale israélite orientale, 1865–1935* (Paris, 1935), 19.

34. Letter from Ulmann to Netter, 23 July 1860, cited in Kaspi, "La Fondation de l'Alliance," 162.

35. CCF, 1B5 Procès-verbaux, 18 October 1860, 219.

36. Ibid., 22 November 1860, 223.

37. Ibid., 21 March 1861, 231; Kaspi, "La Fondation de l'Alliance" 165.

38. CCF, 1B5, 10 October 1861, 236–237; 21 July 1862, 251; 20 July and 16 September 1863, 273, 288; 11 February 1864, 298.

39. On the 1860 elections, see Isidore Cahen, "Nouvelles," *Archives israélites* (October 1860), 589; "Elections consistoriales de Paris," ibid. (December 1860), 687; letter from Carvallo to I. Cahen, 20 November 1860, ibid. (December 1860), 689; "Chronique du mois," ibid. (December 1860), 701–703; Simon Bloch, "Les Consistoires," *L'Univers israélite* (De-

cember 1860), 153; I. Cahen, "Une nouvelle direction," *Archives israélites* (December 1860), 674.

40. Kaspi, "La Fondation de l'Alliance," 194n28.; CCF, AA5, 27 May 1863, 299–300.

41. On the 1863 elections, see I. Cahen, "Chronique israélite de la quinzaine," *Archives israélites* (15 January 1863), 45–47, and (1 February 1863), 92; Prosper Lunel, "Elections consistoriales de Paris," *L'Univers israélite* (February 1863), 263–264; "Elections consistoriales à Paris," *Archives israélites* (1 February 1863), 128.

42. "Elections consistoriales," *Archives israélites* (15 December 1865), 1088–90.

43. "Elections consistoriales à Paris," ibid. (1 December 1865), 1047–48, and "Elections consistoriales," 1087; Prosper Lunel, "Elections consistoriales de Paris du 17 décembre," *L'Univers israélite* (January 1866), 217.

44. "Elections consistoriales," *Archives israélites* (15 December 1865), 1095; Carvallo circular cited in "Incidents électoraux," *L'Univers israélite* (February 1866), 164–165; Benoît Lévy, "Causerie," *Archives israélites* (15 February 1866), 157; S. Bloch, "Incidents électoraux," *L'Univers israélite* (January 1866), 213–214.

45. For Carvallo's campaign and the consistory's counterefforts, see "Elections consistoriales du 17 mars," *Archives israélites* (15 March 1867), 270–271.

46. "Elections consistoriales," ibid. (1 March 1867), 215. The noisy quarrels agitating the Jewish community piqued the interest of the non-Jewish press. *La Presse* for one was moved to comment, interpreting the high abstention rate in the 1867 elections as a gesture of protest against consistorial rule. See "Nouvelles diverses," *Archives israélites* (1 March 1867), 237.

47. S. Bloch, "Elections consistoriales de Paris," *L'Univers israélite* (April 1867), 352; CCF, 1B5, 12 November 1867, 377–379; S. Bloch, "Bulletin," ibid. (March 1868), 290; R., "Elections consistoriales à Paris," *Archives israélites* (1 February 1868), 137; Prosper Lunel, "Elections consistoriales de Paris," *L'Univers israélite* (December 1867), 172–173; Benoît Lévy, "Causerie parisienne," *Archives israélites* (15 February 1868), 164.

48. Léon Kahn, *Histoire des écoles communales et consistoriales israélites de Paris, 1809–1884* (Paris, 1884), 98–101; "Réunion à Paris," *Archives israélites* (1 February 1873), 76–77. Since no representative of the Sephardic community was elected to the new board, the consistory dissolved itself and called for another round of balloting. Edmond Delvaille of the Portuguese rite was elected, taking Lévy-Bing's position. See "Culte," *Archives israélites* (15 May 1873), 298.

49. Leven, *Cinquante ans d'histoire,* 1.72.

50. Cahen, "Chronique israélite de la quinzaine," *Archives israélites* (1 July 1863), 542; "Alliance israélite universelle, Assemblée générale du 31 mai," ibid. (15 June 1864), 510; "Liste générale des membres de l'Alliance israélite universelle," *Bulletin de l'AIU* (January 1865), vi.; "Elections du 3 mai," ibid. (1st semester 1868), 12. For the expression "official Judaism," see Cahen, "Chronique israélite de la quinzaine," *Archives israélites* (15 June 1864), 500.

51. Graetz, *Les Juifs en France*, 411.

52. Aron Rodrigue, *De l'Instruction à l'émancipation. Les enseignants de l'Alliance israélite universelle et les juifs d'orient, 1860–1939* (Paris, 1989), 51.

53. Kahn, *Histoire des écoles communales*, 79–80, 81n. For evidence of Hendlé's membership, see "Liste générale des membres de l'Alliance israélite universelle," *Bulletin de l'AIU* (January 1865), ix.

54. On the Alliance's school system and finances, the work of Aron Rodrigue is indispensable: *De l'Instruction à l'émancipation* and *French Jews, Turkish Jews*. See also Navon, *Les 70 ans*, 73; "Nécrologie. Louis-Raphaël Bischoffsheim," *Archives israélites* (1 December 1873), 730–731; I. Cahen, "Chronique israélite de la quinzaine," ibid. (1 January 1874), 5–6; "Séance générale de l'Alliance israélite universelle" and "Nouvelles diverses," ibid. (1 June 1865), 470; Chouraqui, *Cent ans d'histoire*, 149.

55. I. Cahen, "Les intérêts moraux et le communisme," *Archives israélites* (15 April–15 June 1871), 78; "Le panthéisme et la démocratie," ibid. (15 October 1872), 623; "Les élections législatives et les israélites," ibid. (1 May 1869), 259–261; Astruc as cited in Cahen, "Le livre récent de M. le Grand-Rabbin Astruc," ibid. (1 March 1870), 145.

56. For Grand Rabbi Isidor's and Cahen's observations, see Cahen, "La Crise israélite," ibid. (15 May 1870), 297–298.

57. L. Holloenderski, "L'Initiation religieuse," ibid. (1 April 1864), 285–286; I. Cahen, "Chronique israélite de la quinzaine," ibid. (1 July 1864), 545–546.

58. Cahen in *L'Avenir national*, 22 November 1866, as cited in Cohen, *La Promotion des juifs*, 2.711; I. Cahen, "Quelques idées sur le sermon israélite," *Archives israélites* (November 1857), 619–620; S. Rosenthal, "Nécessité d'un synode français," ibid. (15 August 1871), 205; Victor Blum, "Culte," ibid. (1 September 1875), 523.

59. Hippolyte Rodrigues, *Les Trois Filles de la Bible*, 3rd ed. (Paris, 1867), 130; I. Cahen, "Chronique israélite de la quinzaine," *Archives israélites* (1 October 1873), 580–581.

60. Cahen, "Chronique israélite de la quinzaine," *Archives israélites* (15 October 1873), 611.

61. Weill, "Quelques observations sur le culte du Kippour à Paris," ibid. (15 October 1876), 634.

62. Cahen, "Manifeste," ibid. (1 January 1869), 9.

63. "Culte," ibid. (15 February 1875), 111. A similar sentiment was expressed at the same ceremony by Grand Rabbi Isidor, who urged the assembled faithful to combine devotion to Judaism, which "was the first to make heard the words of justice and liberty," and devotion to *la patrie,* which "was the first to put them into practice and bring them to the world." "Culte," ibid. (15 January 1875), 43.

64. I. Cahen, "L'Autorité dans la synagogue," ibid. (1 July 1870), 397.

65. Auguste Dide, *Jules Barni, sa vie et ses oeuvres,* 2nd ed. (Paris, 1892), 157.

66. Derenbourg, the third member of the committee, became director of the Ecole des Hautes Etudes in 1877. Navon, *Les 70 ans,* 17–19.

67. For what follows, see Rodrigue, *French Jews, Turkish Jews,* chaps. 4–5; Leven, *Cinquante ans d'histoire* (Paris, 1920), 2.10–41.

68. Leven, *Cinquante ans d'histoire,* 2.10.

69. Astruc, *Histoire abrégée des juifs et de leurs croyances* (Paris, 1869), 8, 101; Cahen, "Judaïsme et prosélytisme," *Archives israélites* (July 1862), 368; Rodrigues, *Les Trois Filles,* 40–46.

70. On the connection between Jewish and French messianism, see Rodrigue, *French Jews, Turkish Jews,* 20–21.

71. "Culte," *Archives israélites* (15 January 1875), 45.

72. From an address to the general assembly of the AIU, cited in "La France et le Judaïsme," ibid. (15 July 1872), 432.

73. An English Jew, Moses Montefiore, made this comment, but the sentiment was fully shared by Cahen, who professed a positive if low-key unionism. Cahen, "Chronique israélite de la quinzaine," ibid. (1 June 1865), 468–469.

74. Isidore Loeb, *Biographie d'Albert Cohn* (Paris, 1878), 170.

75. Cahen, in *Archives israélites* (October 1861), 543.

76. On Cahen's commitment to laicity, see "La quinzaine politique et religieuse," ibid. (1 January 1869), 14.

77. Rodrigues, *Les Trois Filles,* 53.

78. Astruc, *Histoire abrégée des juifs,* 40; Rodrigues, *Les Trois Filles,* 76.

79. Cited in Cahen, "Le livre récent de M. le Grand-Rabbin Astruc," *Archives israélites* (1 March 1870), 143.

80. Rodrigues, *Les Trois Filles,* 48–49; I. Cahen in *Archives israélites* (15 April 1870), 227, (1 March 1870), 142, (15 September 1873), 550.

81. On Weill, see BHVP, Fonds Bouglé-Léon Richer I, letters from Weill to Léon Richer, 8 December 1864 and 12 March 1882; Jean-Marie Caubet, *Souvenirs, 1860–1889* (Paris, 1893), 5; Joë Friedemann, *Alexandre Weill, écrivain contestataire et historien engagé, 1811–1899* (Strasbourg, 1980).

82. Rodrigues, *Les Trois Filles,* 78–79.

83. Cahen, "Chronique israélite de la quinzaine," *Archives israélites* (1 May 1865), 379, and (15 August 1863), 680; L. Lévy-Bing, "Le Livre de

M. Renan," ibid. (15 August 1863), 693, 695; S. Lévy, "Etude israélite sur le livre de M. Renan," ibid. (15 September 1863), 778.

84. Henri Carle, "Mouvement religieux libéral parmi les israélites," *La Libre Conscience* (11 January 1868), 98; "Collaborateurs," ibid. (19 October 1867), 1; Rabbinowicz, "Tendance du mouvement religieux de notre époque," *Archives israélites* (15 September 1865), 799; Graetz, *Les Juifs en France*, 309.

85. A. Carénou, "Paris, 25 décembre 1867," *Le Protestant libéral*, 26 December 1867. See also Etienne Coquerel, "Paris, 26 juin," *Le Lien* (27 June 1863), 201–202, and "Paris, 7 août" (8 August 1863), 250; "Alliance israélite universelle," *Archives israélites* (15 December 1866), 1069.

86. Cited in Cahen, "La quinzaine politique et religieuse," *Archives israélites* (1 April 1869), 198–199. See also "Installation rabbinique à Paris," ibid. (1 February 1869), 73.

87. "Les Idées religieuses et la Franc-maçonnerie," ibid. (15 August 1867), 736; S. Posener, *Adolphe Crémieux, a Biography* (Philadelphia, 1940), 177; Christiane Buisset, *Eliphas Lévi: sa vie, son oeuvre, ses pensées* (Paris, 1984), 73; Graetz, *Les Juifs en France*, 308.

88. "Les Idées religieuses et la Franc-maçonnerie," *Archives israélites* (15 August 1867), 737; "Variétés," ibid. (1 June 1868), 513–515; Cahen, "La quinzaine politique et religieuse," ibid. (1 November 1869), 648–649.

89. Cahen, ibid., and "Chronique du mois," ibid. (November 1860), 656. Cahen described the B'nai Brith as in itself constituting "a whole masonic order, an ensemble of lodges." See his "Par monts et par vaux," ibid. (15 August 1875), 488.

90. "Nouvelles des ateliers," *Le Monde maçonnique* (October 1862), 342–343; Linda Nochlin, "Degas and the Dreyfus Affair: A Portrait of the Artist as an Anti-Semite," in Norman Kleeblatt, ed., *The Dreyfus Affair: Art, Truth, and Justice* (Berkeley, 1987), 102.

91. See the exchange of letters between Carvallo and Jean Macé in "Les Bibliothèques communales et israélites," *Archives israélites* (1 January 1864), 39–40.

92. Dide, *Jules Barni*, 157; I. Cahen, "Chronique israélite de la quinzaine," *Archives israélites* (15 February 1867), 151; Jean Gaumont, *Histoire générale de la coopération en France* (Paris, 1924), 1.549; "Situation générale de l'oeuvre de la Ligue," *Ligue de l'enseignement*, 15 May 1868; "Chronique de la Ligue," ibid., 15 February 1869.

93. I. Tchernoff, *Le Parti républicain au coup d'état et sous le Second Empire* (Paris, 1906), 546.

94. Cahen, "La quinzaine politique et religieuse," *Archives israélites* (1 December 1869), 708; Cohen, *La Promotion des juifs*, 2.603. In the provinces as in Paris, Jews were active in supporting roles: Gaston Crémieux and

Naquet at Marseille, Jassuda Bédarride at Aix, and David Raynal at Bordeaux.

95. Kaspi, "La Fondation de l'Alliance," 82; Hendlé's dossier, APP B/a 1114, clipping from *Paris,* 20 January 1892. For a portrait of Hendlé and his descendants, see Birnbaum, "De génération en génération: une famille de juifs d'état, les Hendlé," in *Histoire politique des juifs de France,* 58–73. Eugène Lisbonne, a Jewish lawyer, was also named to the prefectoral corps in 1870.

96. See three articles in *Archives israélites:* "Post-scriptum" (1 November 1873), 671; "Manifestation du commerce parisien" (15 November 1873), 683–684; "Politique et religion" (1 December 1873), 719.

97. "Culte," ibid. (15 September 1874), 557.

98. The document in fact carried 97 signatures. Schornstein, "Chronique israélite de la quinzaine," *Archives israélites* (15 October 1877), 611; Victor Blum, "Toujours la même insinuation," ibid. (15 December 1877), 748.

99. Birnbaum, "L'Entrée en République, le personnel politique juif sous la Troisième République," in Yves Mény, ed., *Idéologies, partis politiques et groupes sociaux* (Paris, 1989), 94. Birnbaum's essay contains much fascinating material on elected and appointed Jewish officials across the entire history of the Third Republic. For an even fuller treatment of the same subject, see his *Les Fous de la République, histoire politique des juifs d'état de Gambetta à Vichy* (Paris, 1992).

100. "Nouvelles diverses," *Archives israélites* (1 January 1878), 27; Levaillant's dossier, APP B/a 1155, clippings from *Le Temps,* 24 October 1911, and *Le Monde,* 18 April 1885.

101. George Weisz, *The Emergence of Modern Universities in France, 1863–1914* (Princeton, 1983), 64, 68, 145; Cohen, *La Promotion des juifs,* 2.492.

5. Liberal Protestantism

1. André Encrevé, *Protestants français au milieu du XIXe siècle: les réformés de 1848 à 1870* (Paris, 1986), 520, 713, 728, 768, 804–805.

2. D. Robert, A. Encrevé, J. Baubérot, and P. Bolle, "L'Etat, l'opinion et les protestants, depuis le début du XIXe siècle," *Histoire des protestants en France* (Toulouse, 1977), 360–361.

3. Encrevé, *Protestants français,* 808–809; Theodore Zeldin, *France, 1848–1945* (Oxford, 1973), 1.628.

4. For the phrase *protestantisme dilué,* see Jean Baubérot, *Le Retour des Huguenots, la vitalité protestante, XIXe-XXe siècle* (Paris, 1985), 82. For arguments similar to the position outlined here, see Stephen Englehart, "Social and Political Strains in the Reformed Church During the Second Empire

and Early Third Republic," *Proceedings of the Annual Meeting of the Western Society for French History,* 6 (1978), 275–284; Vincent Wright, "Allocution de clôture," in A. Encrevé and M. Richard, eds., *Les Protestants dans les débuts de la Troisième République* (Paris, 1979), 731–732; Phyllis Stock-Morton, *Moral Education for a Secular Society: The Development of Morale Laïque in Nineteenth Century France* (Albany, 1988), 87–92.

5. My discussion will focus exclusively on developments within the Reformed Church. France also had a small Lutheran population, endowed with its own consistorial apparatus. See also André Encrevé, *Les Protestants en France, de 1800 à nos jours* (Paris, 1985), 53–54.

6. Clarisse Coignet, *L'Evolution du protestantisme français au XIXe siècle* (Paris, 1908), 102–103; Encrevé, *Les Protestants en France,* 59–60, and *Protestants français,* 297.

7. Encrevé, *Protestants français,* 502, 518ff. See also Jean Pédézert, *Cinquante ans de souvenirs religieux et ecclésiastiques* (Paris, 1896), 208, 210.

8. Englehart, "Social and Political Strains in the Reformed Church," 278, 280; Union Protestante Libérale, *Cinquième rapport, 1865–1866* (Paris, 1866), 14; E. Paris, "Sept années de lutte," *Le Protestant libéral,* 28 November 1867.

9. "Paris, 20 février," *La Renaissance,* 21 February 1874.

10. "Conseil presbytéral de Paris, Séance du 19 février 1864," *Le Lien* (12 March 1864), 89. See also Samuel Mours and Daniel Robert, *Le Protestantisme en France du XVIIIe siècle à nos jours* (Paris, 1972), 304; Georges Weill, *Histoire de l'idée laïque en France au XIXe siècle* (Paris, 1925), 149.

11. René Martin, *La Vie d'un grand journaliste, Auguste Nefftzer* (Paris, 1953), 2.21, 61–62, 68.

12. Encrevé, *Protestants français,* 706–707; A. Coquerel fils, "L'Union protestante libérale," *Le Lien* (1 June 1861), 89; "Union protestante libérale" (14 December 1861), 205; "Paris, 10 janvier" (11 January 1862), 9; Etienne Coquerel, "Paris, 17 janvier" (18 January 1862) 17.

13. E. Coquerel, "1864," ibid. (2 January 1864), 2; B. Fabre, pasteur, "La Version de Genève et les conférences de Paris," ibid. (30 May 1863), 173; "Correspondance française," ibid. (31 January 1863), 35; E. Coquerel, "Union protestante libérale," ibid. (15 August 1863), 261.

14. Pédézert, *Cinquante ans,* 316–317; Martin, *La Vie d'un grand journaliste,* 2.116, 137n.

15. See E. Coquerel, "Destitution de M. le Pasteur A. Coquerel fils," *Le Lien* (27 February 1864), 65–68.

16. Coquerel fils, "Lettres à M. Renan," ibid. (1 August 1863), 241; Pédézert, *Cinquante ans,* 298–299, 307.

17. Pédézert, *Cinquante ans,* 312–313; E. Coquerel, "Destitution de M. le Pasteur A. Coquerel fils," *Le Lien* (5 March 1864), 75.

18. The 1868 reshuffling was quite complicated. Paumier was not

posted to Coquerel's old parish but to the neighboring one of Penthemont. The presbyteral council then had two posts to fill at the Oratoire, Coquerel's vacant pulpit and the new position it had just created. Both went to evangelical ministers.

19. Carénou, "Paris, 26 février 1868," *Le Protestant libéral*, 27 February 1868. Paumier's fate also hung in the balance. His appointment was not confirmed by the state until the advent of the Ollivier ministry in 1870. Ollivier undertook at the same time to resolve the Martin-Paschoud affair, rejecting the presbyteral council's decision to fire the ageing minister. The council's maneuvering against the liberal pastorate is recounted in Encrevé, *Protestants français,* 753–758, 767–768, 771.

20. Encrevé, *Protestants français,* 766n; Carénou, "Paris, 8 avril 1868," *Le Protestant libéral*, 9 April 1868; Mours and Robert, *Le Protestantisme,* 301; Ernest Stroehlin, *Athanase Coquerel fils* (Paris, 1886), 330–331.

21. Encrevé, *Protestants français,* 749n.

22. Francis Schiller, *Paul Broca* (Berkeley, 1979), 125; "Affaire du registre paroissial," *Le Lien* (27 August 1864), 324–330. It is not clear whether Broca was married by Coquerel père or Coquerel fils.

23. Pédézert, *Cinquante ans,* 352; "Répertoire des journaux et revues," *Le Lien* (17 December 1864), 478; "Répertoire des journaux et revues," ibid. (11 March 1865), 86.

24. A.M., "Paris, 8 mars 1865," *Le Protestant libéral*, 9 March 1865; Pédézert, *Cinquante ans,* 355.

25. Pédézert, *Cinquante ans,* 403; Encrevé, *Protestants français,* 766n; "Circulaire," *Le Protestant libéral,* 23 January 1868; "Elections de Paris de 1868," ibid., 21 April 1870.

26. "Bulletin électoral," *La Renaissance,* 30 January 1872 supplement; "Elections de Paris," ibid., 10 February 1872; "Paris, 14 février," ibid., 15 February 1872; "Paris, 23 février," ibid., 24 February 1872.

27. Pédézert, *Cinquante ans,* 442. See also Encrevé, *Les Protestants en France,* 112–113.

28. When in the late sixties the prospects for convocation of a national synod improved, liberals urged that representatives be elected on the basis of universal and direct suffrage; they were defeated on the point. See Carénou, "Paris, 6 novembre 1867," *Le Protestant libéral,* 7 November 1867.

29. For two opposing assessments of the electoral regulations, the one critical and the second apologetic, see Mours and Robert, *Le Protestantisme en France,* 314; D. Robert, A. Encrevé, J. Baubérot, and P. Bolle, "Les Réveils et la vie interne du monde protestant (depuis environ 1800)," in *Histoire des Protestants,* 296.

30. "Le registre paroissial," *La Renaissance,* 4 April 1874.

31. "Paris, 21 juin," ibid., 22 June 1872; "Le Synode, 21 novembre," 29 November 1873.

32. Mours and Robert, *Le Protestantisme en France,* 316–317; "Paris, 12 mars," *La Renaissance,* 13 March 1875.

33. "Paris, 29 juillet," *La Renaissance,* 30 July 1880; "Paris, 9 décembre," 10 December 1880; "Décret," 31 March 1882; "Paris, 22 juin," 23 June 1882; "Paris, 6 juillet," 7 July 1882.

34. Robert et al., "Les Réveils et la vie interne du monde protestant," 298; "Paris, 17 novembre," *La Renaissance,* 18 November 1881, and "L'Assemblée de Nîmes," 3 November 1882.

35. Union Protestante Libérale, *Réponse à la communication du conseil presbytéral de l'Eglise Réformée de Paris sur le non-renouvellement de la suffragance de M. le pasteur Athanase Coquerel fils* (Paris, 1864), 7.

36. Carénou, "Paris, 18 janvier 1865," *Le Protestant libéral,* 19 January 1865.

37. "Union protestante libérale," *Le Lien* (14 December 1861), 205; Carénou, "Paris, 18 janvier 1865," *Le Protestant libéral,* 19 January 1865.

38. "Paris, 9 décembre," *La Renaissance,* 10 December 1880; Carénou, "Paris, 22 janvier 1868," *Le Protestant libéral,* 23 January 1868.

39. Pédézert, *Cinquante ans,* 405. It was not only evangelicals who arrived at this conclusion. The election returns were analyzed in almost identical language by the radical journalist A. Desonnaz in *L'Avenir national* (27 January 1868). Cited in "L'Election du 19 janvier et la presse politique," *Le Protestant libéral,* 30 January 1868. See also Englehart, "Social and Political Strains in the Reformed Church," 277–278.

40. "Circulaire," *Le Lien* (14 January 1865), 24; Dide, "Les Deux Issues," *Le Protestant libéral,* 8 February 1866; Clamageran on Delessert as cited in Encrevé, *Protestants français,* 706n; Coquerel fils, "Paris, 13 janvier," *La Renaissance,* 14 January 1871; letter from J.-J. Clamageran to his cousin Félix Clamageran, 18 February 1861, in J.-J. Clamageran, *Correspondance, 1849–1902* (Paris, 1906), 199.

41. *L'Espérance,* as cited by E. Coquerel in "1865," *Le Lien* (31 December 1864), 499.

42. E. Coquerel, "Paris, 15 avril," *Le Lien* (23 April 1864), 169. Liberal discourse was saturated with rhetorical invocations of liberty. For instance: a Protestantism true to itself, claimed one UPL report, marched "in the paths of liberty"; an 1865 circular urged liberal voters to cast ballots for "the living liberty of faith." Union Protestante Libérale, *Troisième rapport, 1863–1864* (Paris, 1864), 22; "Circulaire," *Le Lien* (14 January 1865), 24.

43. Dide, "La Statue de Voltaire," *Le Protestant libéral,* 1 August 1867; "Un Ministre protestant du parti orthodoxe," 5 December 1867.

44. Adolphe Michel, "Paris, 22 février 1865," ibid., 23 February 1865; P. Lecoq de Boisbaudran, "Le Droit des électeurs," 16 November 1865; Michel, "Revue de quinzaine," 9 March 1865; "Paris, 9 février," *La Renaissance,* 10 February 1872; UPL, *Réponse,* 6.

45. Léon Vèzes, "L'Urgence des publications populaires," *Le Protestant libéral,* 13 August 1868; Dide, "La Société des publications populaires protestantes," 11 July 1867; Carénou, "Paris, 30 décembre 1868," 31 December 1868; Vèzes, "L'Urgence des publications populaires," 26 August 1868.

46. See the press citations in "Répertoire des journaux et revues," *Le Lien* (11 March 1865), 86.

47. Coquerel fils as cited in Stroehlin, *Athanase Coquerel fils,* 445–446.

48. Cited in ibid., 460.

49. "Nouvelles religieuses," *La Renaissance,* 18 November 1871.

50. "Paris, 12 septembre," ibid., 13 September 1873.

51. "Paris, 12 septembre," ibid., 13 September 1873; "Paris, 2 janvier," 2 January 1874; "Paris, 24 février," ibid., 25 February 1876; "Paris, le 24 mai," 25 May 1877.

52. Réville, "De l'Eglise protestante et de ses conditions d'existence," *Le Protestant libéral,* 10 October 1867.

53. Cited in Stroehlin, *Athanase Coquerel fils,* 136.

54. Réville, "De l'Eglise protestante et de ses conditions d'existence," *Le Protestant libéral,* 10 October 1867.

55. Carénou, "Paris, 2 octobre 1867," ibid., 3 October 1867.

56. Dide, "Le Demi-catholicisme," ibid., 8 March 1866.

57. UPL, *Réponse,* 7.

58. "Union protestante libérale," *Le Lien* (14 December 1861), 205; E. Paris, "Sept années de lutte," *Le Protestant libéral,* 28 November 1867.

59. Coquerel fils, "Paris, 6 janvier," *La Renaissance,* 7 January 1871.

60. I. Tchernoff, *Le Parti républicain au coup d'état et sous le Second Empire* (Paris, 1906), 468; Dide, *Jules Barni, sa vie et ses oeuvres,* 2nd ed. (Paris, 1892), 163ff.

61. "Paris, 14 avril," *La Renaissance,* 15 April 1871; "Paris, 28 avril," 29 April 1871; "Paris, 29 mai," 30 May 1871. There were also evangelicals revolted by Versaillais repression, such as pastors Edmond de Pressensé and Eugène Bersier of the independent Taitbout chapel. See Baubérot, *Le Retour des Huguenots,* 114.

62. André Combes, "Une Loge sous le Second Empire, La Renaissance par les Emules d'Hiram," *Humanisme,* 111 (June 1976), 17. The Reclus brothers, Elie and Elisée, were also sometime members; both were of Protestant origin but had fallen away from the faith.

63. Union Protestante Libérale, *Sixième rapport, 1866–67* (Paris, 1867), 27; "Synode général," *La Renaissance,* 15 June 1872. The examples can be multiplied. Dide and Michel Nicolas were Masons and so too, it appears, was the lawyer and UPL member P. Lecoq de Boisbaudran. In 1868 Boisbaudran attended a cooperative-movement meeting; almost all the participants, among them Ernest Hendlé, Antide Martin, and André

Rousselle, were Masons. See Daniel Ligou, "Les Protestants et la franc-maçonnerie aux débuts de la Troisième République," in *Les Protestants dans les débuts,* 232, 238; "Chronique de la Ligue," *Ligue de l'enseignement,* 15 July 1868.

64. Cercle Parisien circular in Chassin papers, BHVP, Ms. 1419, 136.

65. Pierre Albert, *Histoire de la presse politique nationale au début de la Troisième République, 1871–1879* (Paris, 1980), 2.1067; Martyn Lyons, *Le Triomphe du livre: une histoire sociologique de la lecture dans la France du XIXe siècle* (Paris, 1987), 179; *Bulletin Franklin,* 15 (August 1870), 818.

66. Coquerel fils, "Aux électeurs de Paris," *La Renaissance,* 4 February 1871, and "Paris, 13 janvier," 14 January 1871; Albert, *Histoire de la presse politique,* 2.1071–72; Tchernoff, *Le Parti républicain,* 318.

67. APP B/a 906, E. Coquerel, clipping from *Le Temps,* 18 July 1901; "Paris, 30 juin," *La Renaissance,* 1 July 1871.

68. It is tempting to cite as well the example of Paul Reclus, a Broca student. He was a Ligue founder and a Protestant but not, so far as I know, active in church affairs.

69. "Paris, 18 octobre," *La Renaissance,* 19 October 1872.

70. Jean-Marie Mayeur, *Les Débuts de la IIIe République, 1871–1898* (Paris, 1973), 50; Daniel Halévy, *La République des ducs* (Paris, 1937), 316–317.

71. APP B/a 485, Pétitions, clipping from *Le Siècle,* 3 December 1877; reports of 3 and 4 December 1877.

72. Henri Cordey, *Edmond de Pressensé et son temps, 1824–1891* (Lausanne, 1916), 158n.

73. Ligou, "Les Protestants et la franc-maçonnerie," 238.

74. Jacqueline Lalouette, "Science et foi dans l'idéologie libre penseuse (1866–1914)," in *Christianisme et science. Etudes réunies par l'Association française d'histoire religieuse contemporaine* (Paris, 1989), 38–39.

75. E. Coquerel, "Paris, 1er février," *Le Lien* (2 February 1861), 12.

76. Cited in Jean-Marie Mayeur's introduction to Encrevé, *Protestants français,* 10.

77. Quinet, *La Révolution* (Paris, 1987 ed.), 152–153, 158, 165, 226–227, 320, 362, 410–411, 473, 476–477, 505. See also Mme. Edgar Quinet, *Mémoires d'exil* (Paris, 1869), 21–23.

78. Stock-Morton, *Moral Education,* 87.

79. Baubérot, *Le Retour des Huguenots,* 78.

80. See Françoise Mayeur, *L'Enseignement secondaire des jeunes filles sous la Troisième République* (Paris, 1977), 91–93, 116–121, 365; a pair of fine articles in *Les Protestants dans les débuts*—one by Françoise Mayeur, "Les Protestants dans l'Instruction publique au début de la Troisième République," 37–48, and the other by Alice Gérard, "Le Rôle des pédagogues protestants: l'exemple du `Dictionnaire pédagogique'," 49–57; Linda Clark,

Schooling the Daughters of Marianne, Textbooks and the Socialization of Girls in Modern French Primary Schools (Albany, 1984), 30.

81. Program in *la morale,* Section permanente of the Conseil supérieur de l'instruction, as summarized by Stock-Morton, *Moral Education,* 102.

82. Jean-Marie Mayeur, "La Foi laïque de Ferdinand Buisson," *Libre Pensée et religion laïque de la fin du Second Empire à la fin de la Troisiéme République* (Strasbourg, 1980), 257; Baubérot, *Le Retour des Huguenots,* 81–82.

83. Carénou, "Paris, 6 septembre 1865," *Le Protestant libéral,* 7 September 1865; Bost, "L'Orthodoxie," *Le Lien* (20 July 1861), 118.

84. Pécaut, "L'Ordre constant et divin," *Le Protestant libéral,* 25 February 1869; Dide, "Le Congrès de Liège," 16 November 1865; Michel, "La Descente de Jésus aux enfers," 3 January 1867; "Aux membres des consistoires et des conseils presbytéraux," 9 June 1870.

85. Weill, *Histoire de l'idée laïque,* 151.

86. Carénou, "La Confession de foi de la Rochelle," *Le Protestant libéral,* 9 March 1865; Michel, "Paris, 5 avril 1865," 6 April 1865.

87. Encrevé, *Protestants français,* 634, 668–69; "Conseil presbytéral de Paris. Séance du 19 février 1864," *Le Lien* (12 March 1864), 88–91; Marie Dutoit, *Madame Edmond de Pressensé: sa vie, d'après sa correspondance et son oeuvre* (Paris, 1904), 51, 56–58, 68, 87.

88. Pécaut, "L'Ordre constant et divin," *Le Protestant libéral,* 25 February 1869.

89. Coignet, *L'Evolution du protestantisme,* 106, 136; Mme. Quinet, *Mémoires,* 22; Fontanès, "Etudes," *Le Lien* (16 March 1861), 42, and (30 March 1861), 54; remarks by Pellissier to third general assembly of the UPL, *Sixième rapport,* 26–27.

90. Carénou, "La Confession de foi de la Rochelle," *Le Protestant libéral,* 13 April 1865; Fontanès, "Etudes," *Le Lien* (30 March 1861), 54; Dide, "Les Oeuvres du libéralisme," *Le Protestant libéral,* 6 April 1865.

91. Pellissier to third annual assembly of the UPL, *Sixième rapport,* 27; E. Albaric, "Le Christ de la théologie libérale," *Le Lien* (1 July 1865), 222; Carénou, "La Morale indépendante," *Le Protestant libéral,* 24 August 1865.

92. Dide, "Qu'est-ce qu'un protestant libéral?" *Le Protestant libéral,* 23 March 1865.

93. Clarisse Gautier-Coignet, "De l'enseignement des femmes," *La Revue philosophique et religieuse* (November 1855), 421; Clamageran's speech to third annual assembly of the UPL, *Sixième rapport,* 12. See also Bost, "L'Orthodoxie," *Le Lien* (20 July 1861), 118; Coquerel fils as quoted in "Rapport du 5 février 1864," *Le Lien* (5 March 1864), 78.

94. Coquerel fils, "Bulletin littéraire," *Le Lien* (30 August 1862), 278; Clamageran to Abel Jay, 2 February 1869, in Clamageran, *Correspondance,*

311; Carénou, "Paris, 20 décembre," *Le Protestant libéral*, 21 December 1865.

95. Stroehlin, "Channing et Parker," *Le Protestant libéral*, 10 October 1867, and *Athanase Coquerel fils*, 168; Pelletan as cited in "Répertoire des journaux et revues," *Le Lien* (17 December 1864), 478; "Paris, 8 octobre," *La Renaissance*, 9 October 1875.

96. E. Coquerel, "Paris, 18 janvier," *Le Lien* (19 January 1861), 9; Stroehlin, *Athanase Coquerel fils*, 169; Coignet, "Association des dames françaises en faveur des esclaves affranchis," *Le Protestant libéral*, 29 June 1865; Cordey, *Edmond de Pressensé*, 231. Antislavery sentiment was widespread in French Protestant circles, among evangelicals no less than among liberals.

6. The Republic of Lawyers

1. Jean-Pierre Rioux, "Le Palais-Bourbon de Gambetta à de Gaulle," in Pierre Nora, ed., *Les Lieux de mémoire: la nation* (Paris, 1986), 3.505; Mattei Dogan, "Political Ascent in Class Society: French Deputies, 1870–1958," in Dwaine Marvick, ed., *Political Decision-Makers* (Glencoe, 1961), 69–70, 78; Jean Estèbe, *Les Ministres de la République, 1871–1914* (Paris, 1982), 107, 114; Yves-Henri Gaudemet, *Les Juristes et la vie politique de la IIIe République* (Paris, 1970), 15–16.

2. André Damien, *Les Avocats du temps passé* (Versailles, 1973), 467.

3. Ernest Cresson, *Usages et règles de la profession d'avocat* (Paris, 1888), 2.213; Jules Fabre, *Histoire du Barreau de Paris, 1810–1870* (Paris, 1895), 374–375.

4. Maurice Joly, *Le Barreau de Paris* (Paris, 1863), xix.

5. See Lucien Karpik, "Lawyers and Politics in France, 1814–1950: The State, the Market and the Public," *Law and Social Inquiry*, 13 (Fall 1988), 707–736; Charles Limet, *Un Vétéran du barreau parisien: quatre-vingts ans de souvenirs, 1827–1907* (Paris, 1908), 95–96; Léon Lyon-Caen, *Souvenirs du jeune âge* (Paris, 1912), 300; Cresson, *Usages et règles*, 1.210, 295–296, 305, 309–310, 325 and 2.271; François-Etienne Mollot, *Règles de la profession d'avocat*, 2nd ed. (Paris, 1866), 1.xvi–xvii, 113–116.

6. Mollot, *Règles de la profession*, 1.70–71; Cresson, *Usages et règles*, 1.301.

7. Albert Decourteix, *Quelques avocats jugés par leurs oeuvres: études d'éloquence judiciaire* (Paris, 1874), 23, 25, 29, 103.

8. Cited in Oscar Pinard, *Le Barreau au XIXe siècle* (Paris, 1864–65), 2.329. See also Decourteix, *Quelques avocats*, 120.

9. Pierre Jacomet, *Avocats républicains du Second Empire* (Paris, 1933), 56; Pierre Antoine Perrod, *Jules Favre: avocat de la liberté* (Lyon, 1988), 264, 269.

10. Damien, *Les Avocats,* 434, 440; Decourteix, *Quelques avocats,* 2–3, 29, 75, 120, 139; Rioux, "Le Palais-Bourbon," 497.

11. Joly, *Le Barreau de Paris,* 127.

12. Mollot, *Règles de la profession,* 1.xv; Jules Le Berquier, *Le Barreau moderne,* 2nd ed. (Paris, 1882), 41, 70–71; Joly, *Le Barreau de Paris,* xx, xxiv, 131.

13. Joly, *Le Barreau de Paris,* xx.

14. Mollot, *Règles de la profession,* 1.134.

15. Joly, *Le Barreau de Paris,* xvii. See also Le Berquier, *Le Barreau moderne,* 147.

16. Mollot, *Règles de la profession,* 1.134. Gambetta expressed feelings of filial admiration for the bâtonnier Liouville in a letter to his father, 17 February 1858, in P.-B. Gheusi, ed., *Gambetta par Gambetta* (Paris, 1909), 115.

17. Fabre, *Histoire du barreau,* 382.

18. Ibid., 352; Jean-Louis Debré, *Les Républiques des avocats* (Paris, 1984), 294.

19. Liouville had himself stood for election but lost. See René Martin, *La Vie d'un grande journaliste Auguste Nefftzer* (Paris, 1948/1953), 1.172.

20. Maurice Choury, *La Commune au quartier latin* (Geneva, 1971), 33–34; Damien, *Les Avocats,* 286. On the problem of facial hair, see also Henri Dabot, *Souvenirs et impressions d'un bourgeois du quartier latin de mai 1854 à mai 1869* (Péronne, 1899), 255.

21. The Proudhonist connection is not that surprising given Méline's later interest in peasantism and "the return to the earth." Emile Acollas, *Nécessité de refondre l'ensemble de nos codes et notamment le code Napoléon au point de vue de l'idée démocratique* (Paris, 1866); Auguste Dide, *Jules Barni, sa vie et ses oeuvres,* 2nd ed. (Paris, 1892), 163; Louis Fiaux, *Histoire de la guerre civile de 1871* (Paris, 1879), 174; Lyon-Caen, *Souvenirs,* 110–111; Méline, "Reflexions d'un spiritualiste," *Le Travail,* 16 February 1862.

22. APP B/a 1020, Georges Coulon, 11 November 1886; Lyon-Caen, *Souvenirs,* 187, 228, 231, 245, 247–251; Pierre Sorlin, *Waldeck-Rousseau* (Paris, 1966), 92; Aurélien Scholl's introduction to *Plaidoyers et oeuvres choisies de Clément Laurier* (Paris, 1885), 5–6; Gaudement, *Les Juristes,* 36.

23. Cresson, *Règles et usages,* 1.146ff.

24. BA, dossier Conférences des avocats, "La Conférence vue par la presse judiciaire," 192. See also Estèbe, *Les Ministres,* 109–110.

25. *Association amicale des secrétaires et anciens secrétaires de la conférence des avocats à Paris* (Paris, 1939) gives a full listing of *secrétaires de stage.* The roster for the period 1840–1870 is studded with the names of future luminaries of the republic, not only elected officials like Ferry and Gambetta but also prefects (Delattre, Hendlé, Ferdinand Hérold, Le Chevalier), councillors of state (Clamageran), inspectors of fine arts (Albert Kaempfen), and so on.

26. Ibid., 131; Maurice Reclus, *Jules Ferry, 1832–1893* (Paris, 1947), 19.

27. BA, dossier Conférences des avocats, "Sur les conférences particulières," Bournat (1858), 42.

28. Ibid., 40, 43.

29. Letter to Gambetta père, 2 December 1861, in *Gambetta par Gambetta,* 191.

30. Lyon-Caen, *Souvenirs,* 109; Reclus, *Jules Ferry,* 18.

31. BA, dossier Conférences des avocats, "Sur les conférences particulières," Deroy (1882), 12, 38–39; Bournat (1858), 1–2, 9, 15, 51; Corne, Lacoin, Martin (1863), 10–11, 38.

32. Reclus, *Jules Ferry,* 25; Juliette Adam, *Mes Premières Armes littéraires et artistiques,* 8th ed. (Paris, 1904), 416, and *Mes Sentiments et nos idées avant 1870,* 6th ed. (Paris, 1905), 307; Mme. Alphonse Daudet, *Souvenirs autour d'un groupe littéraire* (Paris, 1910), 77–78.

33. Denis Rouart, ed., *The Correspondence of Berthe Morisot* (New York, 1957), 17–18; Pierre Barral, *Jules Ferry: une volonté pour la République* (Nancy, 1985), 24.

34. Berthelot, *Science et philosophie* (Paris, 1886), 371–372, 374–375.

35. "Petits Olliviers" was the nickname Juliette Adam conferred on the group; *Mes Premières Armes,* 71. See also Reclus, *Jules Ferry,* 22–23; Limet, *Un Vétéran,* 253. The Ferry circle expanded in the 1860s to include Allain-Targé, Spuller, and Adrien Hébrard, a future editor of *Le Temps.* See Debré, *Les Républiques,* 365n26.

36. Allain-Targé, "Souvenirs d'avant 1870," *La Revue de Paris,* 5 (1 September 1903), 6–10.

37. Joly, *Le Barreau de Paris,* 141, 224; Le Berquier, *Le Barreau moderne,* 81, 95; Pinard, *Le Barreau au XIXe siècle,* 1.26; Joseph Reinach, *L'Eloquence française depuis la Révolution jusqu'à nos jours,* 2nd ed. (Paris, 1894), iii, ix, xxxi. See also Damien, *Les Avocats,* 361, 440; Reclus, *Jules Ferry,* 24.

38. Joly, *Le Barreau de Paris,* 224; Pinard, *Le Barreau du XIXe siècle,* 1.26; Reinach, *L'Eloquence française,* xxii. See also Sorlin, *Waldeck-Rousseau,* 95.

39. Joly, *Le Barreau de Paris,* 224, 238, 287.

40. Le Berquier, *Le Barreau moderne,* 90.

41. For Gambetta's elevated conception of trade, see the letter he wrote to his father, 17 February 1857, in *Gambetta par Gambetta,* 65.

42. Ernest Daudet said that Gambetta quoted Horace to trash collectors and Virgil to stevedores. Daudet, *Panorama de la IIIe République,* 23rd ed. (Paris, 1936), 13.

43. Paschal Grousset, "Les Evénements," in Castagnary et al., *Le Bilan de l'année 1868* (Paris, 1869), 120.

44. "Chronique," *La Gazette des tribunaux,* 2 August 1860, 2 August 1861.

45. Norbert Billiart, *Le Monde judiciaire* (August 1862), 518–519; Lyon-Caen, *Souvenirs*, 214. More generally, see Mollot, *Règles de la profession*, 2.14–16; Cresson, *Usages et règles*, 2.196, 198–199.

46. Thomas, "Les Quinzaines du palais," *Le Siècle*, 15 August 1865.

47. Debré, *Les Républiques*, 331.

48. Norbert Billiart, *Le Monde judiciaire* (August 1862), 515–523; Fabre, *Histoire du barreau*, 428. For the election results, see *La Gazette des tribunaux*, 2, 6, 8, and 10 August 1862.

49. Mollot, *Règles de la profession*, 2.8.

50. *La Gazette des tribunaux*, 2, 5, 7, and 9 August 1863; Norbert Billiart, *Le Monde judiciaire* (August 1863), 466–469.

51. Cresson, *Usages et règles*, 2.194.

52. *La Gazette des tribunaux*, 3, 5, and 7 August 1864; Billiart, *Le Monde judiciaire* (August 1865), 433–441; Thomas, "Les Quinzaines du palais," *Le Siècle*, 15 August 1865.

53. Mollot, *Règles de la profession*, 1.147.

54. *Manuel électoral, guide pratique pour les élections au corps législatif, aux conseils généraux, aux conseils d'arrondissement et aux conseils municipaux* (Paris, 1861), 2, 70; the historian Ernest Hamel also had a hand in the project. See I. Tchernoff, *Le Parti républicain au coup d'état et sous le Second Empire* (Paris, 1906), 397.

55. Letter from J.-J. Clamageran to his cousin Félix Clamageran, 15 December 1863, in Clamageran, *Correspondance, 1849–1902* (Paris, 1906), 266. See also "Justice criminelle," *La Gazette des tribunaux*, 6 and 7 August 1864.

56. Of the thirteen, three were not lawyers (Carnot, Corbon, Garnier-Pagès). Debré, *Les Républiques*, 274–275.

57. Cresson, *Usages et règles*, 2.4; "Justice criminelle," *La Gazette des tribunaux*, 6 August 1864.

58. Debré, *Les Républiques*, 281, 284. Favre used the phrase cited during the appeals trial.

59. Floquet got credit for the gesture, but there is doubt as to whether he deserved it. Dabot, *Souvenirs et impressions*, 226–227; Adam, *Mes sentiments*, 138.

60. Irene Collins, *The Government and the Newspaper Press in France, 1814–1881* (Oxford, 1959), 148, 154; Charles Seignobos, *Le Déclin de l'empire et l'établissement de la IIIe République, 1859–1875* (Paris, 1921), 69; Pierre Albert, *Histoire de la presse politique nationale au début de la Troisième République, 1871–1879* (Paris, 1980), 1.85.

61. Seignobos, *Le Déclin*, 71–72; Jean Maurain, *Un Bourgeois français au XIXe siècle. Baroche, ministre de Napoléon III d'après ses papiers inédits* (Paris, 1936), 425; AN 45 AP 5, Papiers Rouher, "Rapports de police," 10 November 1868.

62. Cited in Debré, *Les Républiques,* 315–316; see also Grousset, "Les Evénements," 119–120.

63. He was also elected in Marseille and opted to sit for that constituency.

64. On Ferry, see Reclus, *Jules Ferry,* 52, 54–55, 63, 129; Louis Girard, "Jules Ferry et la génération des républicains du Second Empire," in François Furet, ed., *Jules Ferry, fondateur de la Troisième République* (Paris, 1985), 54–55. On Gambetta, see J.P.T. Bury, *Gambetta and the Making of the Third Republic* (London, 1973), 4–6; letter from Gambetta to Clément Laurier, 12 October 1869, in *Gambetta par Gambetta,* 306.

65. Debré, *Les Républiques,* 330–35.

66. Louis Capéran, *Histoire contemporaine de la laïcité française* (Paris, 1957, 1960), 1.124.

67. Letter from Ranc to Castagnary on Hérold's death, as cited in Capéran, *Histoire contemporaine de la laïcité,* 2.250–251. See also idem., 1.132, 134, 141 and 2.15; and Berthelot, *Science,* 414.

68. Vincent Wright, "L'Epuration du Conseil d'état en juillet 1879," *Revue d'histoire moderne et contemporaine,* 19 (October–December 1972), 621–656. See also Jean-Pierre Machelon, *La République contre les libertés?* (Paris, 1976), 284–285. Machelon sees the purges as an assault on civil liberties.

69. Jean-Pierre Royer et al., *Juges et notables au XIXe siècle* (Paris, 1982), 359–370, 376.

70. Jean-Marie Mayeur, *Les Débuts de la IIIe République, 1871–1898* (Paris, 1973), 108; Seignobos, *L'Evolution de la IIIe République, 1875–1914* (Paris, 1921), 101; Collins, *Government and the Newspaper Press,* 181–182.

7. The New Painting

1. A similar observation may be made of Léopold Levert and Charles Tillot. Both were regulars at the independents' salons, Levert showing with the group four times, Tillot six. Both were landscapists, born in the 1820s, and painted under the influence of the Barbizon school.

2. Roy McMullen, *Degas: His Life, Times, and Work* (London, 1985), 151.

3. Gustave Geffroy, *Sisley* (Paris, 1923), 10.

4. See two letters from Bazille, the first to his mother (April 1867), the second to both parents (May 1867), as cited in Didier Vatuone, ed., *Frédéric Bazille, Correspondance* (Montpellier, 1992), 137, 140. See also François Daulte, *Frédéric Bazille et son temps* (Geneva, 1952), 58.

5. For an excellent discussion of independent organization, see Jean-Paul Bouillon, "Sociétés d'artistes et institutions officielles dans la seconde moitié du XIXe siècle," *Romantisme,* 54 (1986), 89–113.

6. Burty in *La Gazette des beaux-arts,* February 1863, cited in Janine Bailly-Herzberg, *L'Eau-forte de peintre au XIXe siècle: la société des aquafortistes, 1862–1867* (Paris, 1972), 1.84.

7. Douglas Druick and Michel Hoog, *Fantin-Latour,* exhibition catalogue, National Gallery of Canada (Ottawa, 1983), 175, 177.

8. Ernest Chesneau, "Le Japon à Paris," *La Gazette des beaux-arts,* 2nd ser., 18 (September 1878), 387–388.

9. See Bouillon, "'A Gauche': note sur la société du Jing-Lar et sa signification," *La Gazette des beaux-arts,* 6th ser., 91 (March 1978), 107–118.

10. Burty, *Chefs d'oeuvre des arts industriels* (Paris, 1866), 8, 255.

11. Edmond Maître and Otto Scholderer are also represented.

12. Adolphe Tabarant, *Pissarro,* tr. J. Lewis May (New York, 1925), 18: Duret, *Renoir,* tr. Madeleine Boyd (New York, 1937), 88–89; John Rewald, *Histoire de l'Impressionnisme* (Paris, 1955), 1.246.

13. "Société anonyme à capital variable" was the legal formula used to describe a cooperative body. See Ellen Furlough, *Consumer Cooperation in France: The Politics of Consumption, 1834–1930* (Ithaca, 1991), 45–46.

14. McMullen, *Degas,* 243.

15. Georges Rivière, *Renoir et ses amis* (Paris, 1921), 43–44.

16. Kathleen Adler, *Unknown Impressionists* (Oxford, 1988), 53ff; Ralph E. Shikes and Paula Harper, *Pissarro, His Life and Work* (New York, 1980), 149–154.

17. Durand-Ruel was involved as well in the Union générale bank scheme. Catholic interests had launched the enterprise as a pious counterweight to what they judged to be the overweening influence of Jewish high finance. But Durand-Ruel was a man of paradox: for all that he flirted with antisemitism, he counted the Bischoffsheims, the Cahen d'Anvers, the Camondos, and the Goldschmidts as valued clients. Lionello Venturi, *Les Archives de l'impressionnisme* (Paris, 1939), 2.176, 185, 188, 210; Pierre Vaisse, *La Troisième République et les peintres: recherches sur les rapports des pouvoirs publics et de la peinture en France de 1870 à 1914* (Doctorat d'Etat, University of Paris IV, 1980), 4.883n77.

18. Louis Edouard Tabary, *Duranty: étude biographique et critique* (Paris, 1954), 61–62, 201–202.

19. Paul Tucker, "The First Impressionist Exhibition in Context," in Charles Moffett et al., *The New Painting: Impressionism, 1874–1886,* exhibition catalogue, National Gallery of Art (Geneva, 1986), 104; Pierre Albert, *Histoire de la presse politique nationale au début de la Troisième République, 1871–1879* (Paris, 1980), 2.1472–73.

20. Albert, *Histoire de la presse,* 2.1260–63; Proust, "Gambetta," *La Vie moderne,* 13 January 1883; "Les Obsèques de Gambetta," *La Vie moderne,* 20 January 1883; Gambetta to Silvestre, 14 August 1882, in Daniel Halévy

and Emile Pillias, eds., *Lettres de Gambetta, 1868–1882* (Paris, 1938), no. 557.

21. F. W. J. Hemmings, *Emile Zola* (Oxford, 1953), 63–66.

22. Letter from Burty to Scheurer-Kestner, 9 February 1879, AN 276 AP 1, Scheurer-Kestner papers; Bouillon, "A Gauche," 113; Louis Fiaux, *Histoire de la guerre civile de 1871* (Paris, 1879), 421.

23. BHVP, Chassin papers, Ms. 1396, Second Empire, 245–246.

24. Geffroy, *Claude Monet: sa vie, son temps, son oeuvre* (Paris, 1922), 34.

25. The artworks collected are now on display at the Musée Cernuschi in Paris. For details of Cernuschi's political activities, see the obituary in *Le Figaro*, 12 May 1896; a clipping can be found in APP B/a 1268, "Sernuschi."

26. Bouillon, "A Gauche."

27. Daulte, *Frédéric Bazille*, 38; McMullen, *Degas*, 163; Vatuone, ed., *Frédéric Bazille*—letters from Bazille to his mother, November 1862, 30, and January 1870, 184–185.

28. Letter from Bazille to his parents, 6 September 1870, ibid., 196.

29. But he went on: "You can't start Robespierre all over again." Jean Renoir, *Renoir* (Ottawa, 1963), 127; Ambroise Vollard, *Renoir: An Intimate Record*, tr. H. Van Doren and Randolph T. Weaver (New York, 1990; orig. 1925), 24. The details are not quite the same in Jean Renoir's recounting of the Commune stories.

30. J. Renoir, *Renoir*, 262.

31. Anne Distel, *Impressionism: The First Collectors* (New York, 1990), 142–143; J. Renoir, *Renoir*, 127–128.

32. Distel, *Impressionism*, 144, 162, 165; Vollard, *Renoir*, 43; Rivière, *Renoir*, 89–90, 197.

33. Clemenceau, *Claude Monet: The Water Lilies* (New York, 1930), 15, 82.

34. Shikes and Harper, *Pissarro*, 96.

35. André Wormser, "Claude Monet et Georges Clemenceau: une singulière amitié," in John Rewald and Frances Weitzenhoffer, eds., *Aspects of Monet: A Symposium on the Artist's Life and Times* (New York, 1984), 196.

36. Wormser, "Claude Monet et Georges Clemenceau," 194, 206.

37. Druick and Hoog, *Fantin-Latour*, 99; Bouillon, "Félix Bracquemond," in Joel Isaacson, *The Crisis of Impressionism, 1878–1882*, exhibition catalogue, University of Michigan Museum of Art (Ann Arbor, 1980), 50, 56; Bouillon, "Les Lettres de Manet à Bracquemond," *La Gazette des beaux-arts*, 6th ser., 101 (April 1983), 153; Gabriel Weisberg, "Félix Bracquemond and Japanese Influence in Ceramic Decoration," *Art Bulletin*, 51 (September 1969), 278.

38. Bailly-Herzberg, *L'Eau-forte*, 1.47; Druick and Hoog, *Fantin-Latour*, 17, 99, 336.

39. Nord, "Manet and Radical Politics," *Journal of Interdisciplinary His-*

tory, 19 (Winter 1989), 451. Gustave Manet was elected municipal councillor of the Clignancourt quarter in 1876, thanks, as a police report put it, to the patronage of the local "chef du parti radical . . . M. Clemenceau."

40. Anne Higonnet, *Berthe Morisot* (New York, 1990), 43.

41. Letter from Edma to Berthe Morisot, 23 February 1871, in Denis Rouart, ed., *Berthe Morisot: The Correspondence,* tr. Betty Hubbard (London, 1987), 60–61.

42. Letter from Berthe to Edma Morisot, 27 February 1871, ibid., 61.

43. Letter from Berthe to Edma Morisot, 9 February 1871, ibid., 60. For a good discussion of the Morisot family during the war and the Commune, see Higonnet, *Berthe Morisot,* 67–73.

44. Nord, "Manet and Radical Politics"; for a similar line of interpretation, see Juliet Wilson-Bareau, John House, and Douglas Johnson, *Manet: The Execution of Maximilian. Painting, Politics and Censorship* (London, 1992).

45. Manet to his father, 22 March 1849, in Manet, *Lettres de jeunesse, 1848–1849. Voyage à Rio* (Paris, 1928), 67.

46. Charles Limet, *Un Vétéran du barreau parisien: quatre-vingts ans de souvenirs, 1827–1907* (Paris, 1908), 205, 249–250.

47. Antonin Proust, *Edouard Manet, souvenirs* (Paris, 1913), 56; Tabarant, *Manet et ses oeuvres,* 3rd ed. (Paris, 1947), 117.

48. APP B/a 988, Nina de Callias, 13 August 1872. See also *Manet, 1832–1883,* exhibition catalogue, Metropolitan Museum of Art (New York, 1983), 347.

49. Letter from Manet to Suzanne Leenhoff, 15 September 1871, in Mina Curtiss, ed., "Letters of Edouard Manet to His Wife during the Siege of Paris, 1870–71," *Apollo,* 113 (June 1981), 380.

50. Letter of 18 March 1871, in Bouillon, "Lettres de Manet à Bracquemond," 151; letter from Mme. Morisot to Edma, 29 June 1871, in *Correspondence,* 79.

51. Letter from Mme. Morisot to Edma, 29 June 1871, in *Correspondence,* 79; Proust, *Edouard Manet,* 65–66.

52. APP B/a 1274, Spuller, reports of 9 and 11(?) October 1877; Proust, *Edouard Manet,* 93, 114; Etienne Moreau-Nélaton, *Manet raconté par lui-même* (Paris, 1926), 2.89.

53. Theodore Reff, *Manet and Modern Paris* (Chicago, 1982), 240.

54. Letter from Pissarro's mother, 6 November 1870, *Correspondance de Pissarro,* 1.17; also 30–31.

55. Letter from Pissarro to Piette, undated (1871), *Correspondance de Pissarro,* 1.67; letter from Piette to Pissarro, postmarked 30 January 1872, in Bailly-Herzberg, ed., *Mon cher Pissarro: lettres de Ludovic Piette à Camille Pissarro* (Paris, 1985), 71; Shikes and Harper, *Pissarro,* 96.

56. Shikes, "Pissarro's Political Philosophy and His Art," in Christopher Lloyd, ed., *Studies on Camille Pissarro* (London and New York, 1986),

39–41; Rivière, *Renoir,* 43–44; letter from Pissarro to Georges de Bellio, 26 March 1882, in *Correspondance de Pissarro,* 1.161–163.

57. Letters from Pissarro to his son Lucien, 5, 8, and 25 July 1883; from Pissarro to his niece Esther Isaacson, 12 and 22 December 1885, *Correspondance de Pissarro,* 1.225, 227, 229, 362, 368–369.

58. Ibid., 1.76n2.

59. Sketch of letter from Renoir to Durand-Ruel, 26 February 1882, in Venturi, *Archives,* 1.122.

60. Christopher Gray, *Armand Guillaumin* (Chester, Conn., 1972), 31.

61. Pierre Daix, *Paul Gauguin* (Paris, 1989), 20; Georges Wildenstein, ed., *Gauguin, sa vie, son oeuvre* (Paris, 1958), 26; letters from Pissarro to Lucien, 20 November 1883 and 7 February 1884, *Correspondance de Pissarro,* 1.254.

62. I. Tchernoff, *Le Parti républicain au coup d'état et sous le Second Empire* (Paris, 1906), 412; McMullen, *Degas,* 322; letter from Cézanne to Zola, 2 November 1866, and from Cézanne to Numa Coste, July 1868, in Rewald ed., *Paul Cézanne: Letters* (New York, 1984), 121, 126–127.

63. Letters from Cézanne to Pissarro, 2 July 1876, and to Zola, 1 June 1878 and July 1878, ibid., 155, 166–167. By the 1890s, however, Cézanne had given over anticlericalism and returned to the church.

64. Edith Tonelli and Katherine Hart, eds., *The Macchiaioli: Painters of Italian Life, 1850–1900,* exhibition catalogue, Frederick S. Wight Art Gallery (Los Angeles, 1986), 77.

65. Geffroy, "Jean-François Raffaëlli, 1850–1924," *La Gazette des beaux-arts,* 5th ser. 10 (September–October 1924), 170–171.

66. Robert Cassatt to Alexander Cassatt, 4 October 1878, in Nancy Mowll Mathews, ed., *Cassatt and Her Circle: Selected Letters* (New York, 1984), 140.

67. Letter from Cassatt to Emily Sartain, 22 May 1871, ibid., 72. On Dreyfus, see ibid., 170n; "Adhésions," *Bulletin de l'AIU* (2nd semester 1868), 120. Cassatt's conversion to suffragism and interest in spiritualism are discussed in Mathews, *Cassatt,* 271–272.

68. Léandre Vaillat, *En Ecoutant Forain* (Paris, 1931), 104, 137, 144–45; Alicia Faxon, *Jean-Louis Forain: Artist, Realist, Humanist* (Washington, 1982), 13–14, 26; Mme. Alphonse Daudet, *Souvenirs autour d'un groupe littéraire* (Paris, 1910), 85.

69. Distel, *Impressionism,* 177–178; Marc S. Gerstein, *Impressionism: Selections from Five American Museums* (New York, 1989), 56; McMullen, *Degas,* 440.

70. Daniel Halévy, *Degas parle* (Paris, 1960), 15.

71. Ian Dunlop, *Degas* (London, 1979), 12.

72. Letters from Degas to Gustave Moreau, 27 November 1858 and 26 April 1859, in Reff, "More Unpublished Letters of Degas," *Art Bulletin,*

51 (September 1969), 283, 283n27, 285; "Alliance israélite universelle," *Archives israélites* (May 1862), 259; McMullen, *Degas,* 68, 74–77, 246.

73. Mme. Morisot to Berthe, 5 June 1871, in Rouart, *Morisot, Correspondence,* 73.

74. Distel, *Impressionism,* 143.

75. On the Hayems, see McMullen, *Degas,* 310; "Liste générale des membres de l'Alliance israélite universelle," *Bulletin de l'AIU* (January 1865), ix; Léon Lyon-Caen, *Souvenirs du jeune âge* (Paris, 1912), 199–202.

76. Distel, *Impressionism,* 225.

77. A. D., "Gennevilliers," *L'Echo, organe du canton de Courbevoie,* 20 May 1888; "Nouvelles locales," *Gennevilliers,* 29 May 1887; Marie-Josèphe de Balanda, *Gustave Caillebotte: la vie, la technique, l'oeuvre peinte* (Lausanne, 1988), 34.

78. Isaacson, *Crisis of Impressionism,* 11.

79. Albert Boime, "The Salon des Refusés and the Evolution of Modern Art," *Art Quarterly,* 32 (1969), 415.

80. Rivière, *Cézanne* (Paris, 1936), 64, 71.

81. Cited by Antoinette Ehrard in introduction to Zola, *L'Oeuvre* (Paris, 1974; orig. 1886), 44–45; Zola reviews cited in Venturi, *Archives,* 2.276, 277.

82. Letter from Bazille to his mother, April 1867, in Vatuone, *Frédéric Bazille,* 137.

83. AN F21 535, 1872 salon, letter to Minister of Public Instruction, Cults and Fine Arts, undated; Vaisse, *La Troisième République,* 2.267, 269–270; Boime, "Salon des refusés," 421.

84. Moreau-Nélaton, *Manet,* 1.119–120; Marilyn Brown, "Art, the Commune and Modernism: The Example of Manet," *Arts Magazine,* 58 (December 1983), 102; *Manet, 1832–1883,* 522–523.

85. Cited in George Heard Hamilton, *Manet and His Critics* (New Haven, 1986), 106. See also Edmond Bazire, *Manet* (Paris, 1884), 57.

86. Duranty, "Le Salon de 1872," *Paris-Journal,* 15 June 1872.

87. Daniel Wildenstein, *Claude Monet, biographie et catalogue raisonné* (Lausanne, 1974), 1.66; Tucker, "The First Impressionist Exhibition," in Moffett et al., *New Painting,* 104.

88. Letter from Cézanne to Zola, 10 May 1880, in *Cézanne, Letters,* 189–190. *Le Voltaire* was edited by Manet's old friend Aurélien Scholl and counted on its staff many veteran republicans—the freethinking Yves Guyot, the ex-communard Pierre Denis, and the less militant but no less republican Zola.

89. T. J. Clark, *The Painting of Modern Life: Paris in the Art of Manet and His Followers* (New York, 1984), 10–12.

90. Duranty, "The New Painting" (1876), in Moffett et al., *New Painting,* 40, 46; Burty, "Le Salon de 1873," *La République française,* 15 May 1873.

91. Castagnary, "Salon de 1875," *Le Siècle,* 4 May 1875; Burty, "Le Salon de 1873," *La République française,* 6 and 25 May 1873.

92. Castagnary, "Salon de 1875," *Le Siècle,* 4 May 1875.

93. Cited in Griselda Pollock, *Mary Cassatt* (New York, 1980), 22.

94. Castagnary et al., *Le Bilan de l'année 1868* (Paris, 1869), 297; Duranty, "Le Salon de 1872," *Paris-Journal,* 11 May 1872; Castagnary, "Salon de 1875," *Le Siècle,* 4 May 1875.

95. Duranty, "Le Salon de 1872," *Paris-Journal,* 11 May 1872.

96. Laurent-Pichat, "Salon de 1870," *Le Réveil,* 13 May 1870; see also Zola, "Mon salon" (1866), as reproduced in Gaëtan Picon and Jean-Paul Bouillon, eds., *Emile Zola, le bon combat* (Paris, 1974), 59–60.

97. See Silvestre's preface to Durand-Ruel's 1873 gallery catalogue, reproduced in Venturi, *Archives,* 1.19; or Burty's review of the first independent salon, "Chronique du jour," *La République française,* 16 April 1874, as reproduced in *Centenaire de l'impressionnisme* exhibition catalogue, Grand Palais (Paris, 1974), 256.

98. Duret, "Le Salon," *L'Electeur libre,* 2 June 1870; Zola, "Une Nouvelle Manière en peinture: Edouard Manet" (1867), reprinted in Picon and Bouillon, *Zola,* 78; Castagnary, "Académie des beaux-arts," *Encyclopédie générale* (Paris, 1869), 1.83; Duret, cited in Joseph Sloane, *French Painting between the Past and the Present: Artists, Critics, and Traditions from 1848 to 1870* (Princeton, 1973), 179.

99. Castagnary, cited in Sloane, *French Painting,* 69. See also Castagnary et al., *Le Bilan de l'année 1868,* 292; Proust, cited in Pierre Courthion and Pierre Cailler, eds., *Manet raconté par lui-même et par ses amis* (Paris, 1945), 1.25.

100. Zola, "Mon salon," 63.

101. On colors, see Rivière, "L'Exposition des impressionnistes," *L'Impressionniste,* 14 April 1877, reproduced in Venturi, *Archives,* 2.321; Duret, *Histoire des peintres impressionnistes,* 3rd ed. (Paris, 1922), 175; Rivière, *Renoir,* 55. On poses and costuming, see Laurent-Pichat, "Salon de 1870," *Le Réveil,* 18 May 1870; Camille Pelletan, "Le Salon," *Le Rappel,* 18 May 1872.

102. Silvestre, "Les Deux Tableaux de M. Manet," *L'Opinion nationale,* 23 April 1876; Pelletan, "Le Salon," *Le Rappel,* 16, 18, 20 May 1872.

103. Nadar, *Quand j'étais photographe* (1899; New York, 1979), 196; Rivière, *Renoir,* 58.

104. These are Raffaëlli's views. See Geffroy, "Jean-François Raffaëlli," 181.

105. Geffroy, "Jean-François Raffaëlli," 181; Rivière, "L'Exposition des impressionnistes," *L'Impressionniste,* 6 April 1877, reprinted in Venturi, *Archives,* 2.309. "The spectacle of daily life" is Bazille's formulation, as reported in J. Renoir, *Renoir,* 97.

106. Castagnary, "Salon de 1873," *Le Siècle,* 10 May 1873.

107. Mallarmé, "The Impressionists and Edouard Manet" (1876), in Moffett et al., *New Painting,* 30.

108. The cotton merchant's business shown in Degas' *Portraits in an Office, New Orleans* reminded one reviewer of a "wholesaler's shop on the rue du Sentier." Huysmans took delight in Cassatt's domestic portraits of her sister Lydia, which he praised as "quiet bourgeois scenes painted with a delicate and charming tenderness." The critic at *Le Radical,* ex-communard Edmond Lepelletier, was moved to comment on the modern dress and contemporary physiognomies of the fashionable couple depicted in Caillebotte's *Paris Street, A Rainy Day.* The umbrella they sheltered under, he observed, seemed "freshly taken from the racks of the Louvre and the Bon Marché." Marius Chaumelin in *La Gazette {des étrangers},* 8 April 1876, cited in Moffett et al., *New Painting,* 171; Huysmans, cited in Tamar Garb, *Women Impressionists* (Oxford, 1986), 32; Lepelletier, cited in Adler, *Unknown Impressionists,* 70.

109. Castagnary, "Salon de 1873," *Le Siècle,* 17 May 1873; *Le Bilan de l'année 1868,* 327. For a similar line of interpretation, see Mallarmé, "The Impressionists and Edouard Manet," 33; and Venturi, *Archives,* 1.11.

110. Nord, "Manet and Radical Politics," 456–458.

111. Rivière, M. *Degas, bourgeois de Paris* (Paris, 1935), 141; Dunlop, *Degas,* 63; Gustave Goetschy, "Edouard Manet," *La Vie moderne,* 12 May 1883.

112. Zola, cited in Hamilton, *Manet and His Critics,* 95–96.

113. Castagnary, cited in Geffroy, *Monet,* 73.

114. Duret, "Les Peintres impressionnistes" (1878), reprinted in his *Histoire des peintre impressionnistes,* 178; preface to Manet catalogue, cited in Hamilton, *Manet and His Critics,* 106.

115. The canvas depicted the founder Gonon casting a Jules Dalou bas-relief of a dramatic moment in France's revolutionary history. On 23 June 1789 the king's agent, the Marquis de Dreux-Brézé, paid a visit to the National Assembly and told it to disperse. Mirabeau, speaking for the nation, responded with a defiant gesture of refusal. This is the moment Dalou captured in bronze, which Raffaëlli committed to canvas. It is little wonder that the new republic snapped up the painting, and the bas-relief as well, with such alacrity. Philippe Durey, "Le Réalisme," in *La Sculpture française au XIXe siècle,* exhibition catalogue, Grand Palais (Paris, 1986), 376, 424n84; Vaisse, *La Troisième République,* 2.472.

116. Ibid., 2.390, 392; 3.724, 727–728.

8. Political Culture

1. Amédée Saint-Ferréol, *Les Proscrits français en Belgique* (Paris, 1870), 1.193; I. Tchernoff, *Le Parti républicain au coup d'état et sous le Second Empire* (Paris, 1906), 118–119.

2. A. Parménie and C. Bonnier de la Chapelle, *Histoire d'un éditeur et*

des ses auteurs, P.-J. Hetzel (Stahl) (Paris, 1953), 287; Saint-Ferréol, *Proscrits,* 1.195.

3. Robert Fox, "Les Conférences mondaines sous le Second Empire," *Romantisme,* 65 (1989), 51–52; Tchernoff, *Parti républicain,* 326–327; Flammarion, *Mémoires biographiques et philosophiques d'un astronome* (Paris, 1911), 345–346; Deschanel, *Les Conférences à Paris et en France* (Paris, 1870), 52; Robert Luzarche, "Entretiens de la rue de la Paix," *Les Ecoles de France,* 2 March 1864.

4. Eliane Brault, *La Franc-Maçonnerie et l'émancipation des femmes* (Paris, 1967), 50–54; Patrick Kay Bidelman, *Pariahs Stand Up! The Founding of the Liberal Feminist Movement in France, 1858–1889* (Westport, Conn., 1982), 76.

5. "Chronique," *Le Monde maçonnique* (November-December 1868), 537, and (April 1869), 722–724; AN 417 AP 7, Coulon papers, letter from Montanier to Coulon, 27 March 1869.

6. J. Caubet, *Souvenirs, 1860–1889* (Paris, 1893), 30–31, 39; APP B/a 1520, Réunions, Bancel meeting of 1 May 1869.

7. On Horn, see Alain Dalotel, Alain Faure, and Jean-Claude Freiermuth, *Aux Origines de la Commune, le mouvement des réunions publiques à Paris, 1868–1870* (Paris, 1980), 81; AN 417 AP 7, Coulon papers, letter from Horn to Georges Coulon, addressed "Très ch. fr." (Very dear brother), 15 December 1868; also Chapter 4 above.

8. AN 45 AP 6, Rouher papers, dossier "Questions sociales en général à Paris," meetings of 14 July, 4 and 11 August 1868. See also Limousin and Rousselle's brochure with the disingenuous title, *Manuel des réunions publiques non politiques* (Paris 1869), 6–7.

9. See Dalotel, Faure, and Freiermuth, *Aux Origines.*

10. Pierre Guiral, "Quelques notes sur le retour de faveur de Voltaire sous le Second Empire," in *Hommage au Doyen Etienne Gros* (Gap, 1959), 198.

11. Auguste Dide, "La Statue de Voltaire," *Le Protestant libéral,* 1 August 1867; C. d'Henriet, "La Statue de Voltaire," *La Philosophie positive* (May-June 1868), 368.

12. Morin, "La Statue de Voltaire," *Le Nain jaune,* 31 January 1867. See also, Eugène Spuller, "Victor Cousin," *Le Nain jaune,* 17 January 1867; Massol, "Bulletin," *La Morale indépendante* (10 February 1867), 217.

13. June Hargrove, *The Statues of Paris: An Open-Air Pantheon* (New York, 1989), 102.

14. "La Fête de Voltaire," *Le Monde maçonnique* (February 1870), 629, 633, 637.

15. "Le Centenaire de Voltaire," ibid. (March 1878), 483.

16. Hargrove, *Statues,* 114.

17. The Voltaire festival upset not just the authorities but many republicans as well, who believed that Rousseau was as much entitled to

centenary recognition as Voltaire. Rousseau partisans, among them Blanc, Hamel, and the historian Henri Martin, assembled a centennial committee of their own in June 1878. A celebration was projected, but the date settled on was not the actual centenary day, 2 July, but the *quatorze juillet*. At the event itself, a collection was taken up for political prisoners; the crowd, amid shouts of "Amnesty," broke into the "Marseillaise"; and at the dinner later, ex-communard Clovis Hugues entertained banqueteers with a poetic reading. Voltaire had been feted as a freethinking philosophe. The Rousseau festival, as the timing, personnel, and proceedings attest, conjured up a figure of another kind: the popular prophet of a century of democratic and social revolution. Bernard Marrey, "1878, le centenaire de la mort de Voltaire," *L'Histoire*, 1 (May 1978), 78-79; Jean-Marie Goulemot and Eric Walter, "Les Centenaires de Voltaire et de Rousseau," in Pierre Nora, ed., *Les Lieux de mémoire* (Paris, 1984), 1.388-389, 395, 409, 414.

18. "Cérémonies civiles," *Le Monde maçonnique* (May 1869), 55; APP B/a 1001, Castagnary, report of 3 April 1877.

19. Pierre Vaisse, *La Troisième République et les peintres: recherches sur les rapports des pouvoirs publics et de la peinture en France de 1870 à 1914* (Doctorat d'Etat, University of Paris IV, 1980), 3.611. See also *Le Triomphe des mairies: grands décors républicains à Paris 1870-1914,* exhibition catalogue, Musée du Petit Palais (Paris, 1986), 115, 117; and for the identity of the sitters, Gabriel Weisberg, *The Realist Tradition: French Painting and Drawing, 1830-1900,* exhibition catalogue, Cleveland Museum of Art (1980), 220.

20. Jacqueline Lalouette, "Funérailles civiles: d'un siècle l'autre," *Autrement,* 128 (March 1992), 209-212. Lalouette has just completed a dissertation on free thought in mid-nineteenth-century France. She has been exceptionally generous to me in sharing her thoughts and research on the subject.

21. Saint-Ferréol, *Les Proscrits,* 2.104, 106.

22. Lalouette, "Funérailles civiles," 196-202.

23. Tchernoff, *Parti républicain,* 316; "Chronique," *Le Monde maçonnique* (August 1866), 209-210; Lalouette, "Funérailles civiles," 198.

24. On the association, see Gérard Jacquemet, "Edmond Lepelletier et la libre pensée à Paris au début de la IIIe République," in *Libre Pensée et religion laïque en France de la fin du Second Empire à la fin de la Troisième République* (Strasbourg, 1980), 108-109, 119-121; APP B/a 1493, Libre pensée, undated report (1880) and clipping from *La Marseillaise,* 6 January 1879.

25. Taxil Delord, *Histoire du Second Empire* (Paris, 1873), 4.16-17; Juliette Adam, *Mes sentiments et nos idées avant 1870,* 6th ed. (Paris, 1905), 22-23; Tchernoff, *Parti républicain,* 358.

26. Avner Ben-Amos, "Molding the National Memory: State Funerals

of the French Third Republic" (Ph.D. diss., University of California, Berkeley, 1988), 187.

27. Letter from Ferry to Mme. Ferry, 8 September 1877, in *Lettres de Jules Ferry, 1846–1893* (Paris, 1914), 247–248.

28. Maurice Agulhon, *Marianne into Battle: Republican Imagery and Symbolism in France, 1789–1880,* tr. Janet Lloyd (New York, 1981), 174–175.

29. Louis Fiaux, *La Marseillaise, son histoire dans l'histoire des français depuis 1792* (Paris, 1918), 249–250; Michel Vovelle, "La Marseillaise," in Nora, *Lieux de mémoire,* 1.117.

30. APP B/a 470, Fête nationale du 14 juillet, press clippings from *La République,* 17 July 1872, and *Le Gaulois,* 15 July 1873; reports of 14 and 15 July 1876, 5 and 14 July 1877.

31. Agulhon, *Marianne into Battle,* 173–175, and 226n44; Daniel Imbert and Guénola Groud, *Quand Paris dansait avec Marianne, 1879–1889,* exhibition catalogue, Musée du Petit Palais (Paris, 1989), 2–5.

32. Fiaux, *La Marseillaise,* 263, 388–389; Louis Capéran, *Histoire contemporaine de la laïcité française* (Paris, 1957), 1.103.

33. Masons also played a role on the American side. The grand master of New York Masonry laid the cornerstone of the pedestal on which the statue now stands. There is a Protestant connection that also deserves mention: Bartholdi was of Protestant origins, and the organizer of the entire project, Edouard Laboulaye, was Channing's principal French translator and himself inclined to Unitarian views. Agulhon, *Marianne au pouvoir, l'imagerie et la symbolique républicaines de 1880 à 1914* (Paris, 1989), 96–106.

34. Fiaux, *La Marseillaise,* 389.

35. APP B/a 470, Fête nationale du 14 juillet, reports of 11 and 13 July 1878. The dossier contains, as might be expected, multiple reports for the fourteenth. See also Goulemot and Walter, "Les Centenaires," 410.

36. Vovelle, "La Marseillaise," 118.

37. Paul Marmottan, *Statues de Paris* (Paris, 1886), 252–253. Although the Morice submission won the competition, it was not the sentimental favorite. The crowds who turned out to inspect the mockups were drawn above all to Dalou's contribution. His Phrygian-capped Republic, like Morice's, called to mind a "simple and true woman of the people," but this was no working-class matron. She was young, svelte instead of robust, with one breast bared. More than that, she was striding atop a huge ball pulled by a lion-drawn chariot. Last, while Morice's Republic made an offering of peace, Dalou's promised justice, armed as she was with the Roman lictor's fasces. The movement and youthful vigor of the composition appealed to the public and also to a faction of municipal councillors, who arranged for the city to purchase the Dalou pro-

ject. The statue was cast in bronze and erected after much delay on the Place de la Nation in 1899. Henriette Caillaux, *Aimé-Jules Dalou* (Paris, 1935), 46; Gustave Geffroy, "Jules Dalou," *La Gazette des beaux-arts,* 3rd ser. 23 (1 March 1900), 222–223; John M. Hunisak, *The Sculptor Jules Dalou* (New York, 1977), 214–215.

38. Rosemonde Sanson, *Les 14 juillet, fête et conscience nationale* (Paris, 1976), 30–31; Imbert and Groud, *Quand Paris dansait,* 183, 185; APP B/a, Fête nationale du 14 juillet, reports of 15 July 1879.

39. Pierre Albert, *Histoire de la presse politique nationale au début de la Troisième République (1871–1879)* (Paris, 1980), 1.163, 330, 333, 597; 2.1566–72.

40. See Martyn Lyons, *Le Triomphe du livre: une histoire sociologique de la lecture dans la France du XIXe siècle* (Paris, 1987), 12; Henri-Jean Martin, "Librairie et politique de 1830 à 1852," in Roger Chartier and H.-J. Martin, eds., *Histoire de l'édition française* (Paris, 1990), 3.233–234, 240; Léon Lyon-Cahn, *Souvenirs du jeune âge* (Paris, 1912), 193; Anon., *L'Empire et les avocats* (Paris, 1872), 19; André Lefèvre, *La Renaissance du matérialisme* (Paris, 1881), 132–133.

41. Macé, *Histoire d'une bouchée de pain,* 46th ed. (Paris, n.d.); Katherine Auspitz, *The Radical Bourgeoisie: The Ligue de l'Enseignement and the Origins of the Third Republic, 1866–1885* (New York, 1982), 52–54.

42. Frédéric Morin, *Politique et philosophie* (Paris, 1876), 125; Tchernoff, *Parti républicain,* 318; Albert, *Histoire de la presse,* 2.1069–71; Jean Gaumont, *Histoire générale de la coopération en France* (Paris, 1923), 2.20–23; Georges Weill, *Histoire du mouvement social en France, 1852–1924,* 3rd ed. (Paris, 1924), 186–188; Michelle Perrot, *Les Ouvriers en grève: France, 1871–1890* (Paris, 1974), 1.40–41; the inside and back covers of Barberet's *Le Mouvement ouvrier à Paris de 1870 à 1874* (Paris, 1874).

43. Odile and H.-J. Martin, "Le Monde des éditeurs," in Chartier and Martin, eds., *Histoire de l'édition,* 3.212–213; Marc Soriano, *Guide de littérature pour la jeunesse* (Paris, 1975), 300.

44. Pascale Marie, "La Bibliothèque des amis de l'instruction du IIIe arrondissement," in Nora, *Lieux de mémoire,* 1.323–351.

45. Arlette Boulogne, "Les Bibliothèques populaires en France de 1860 à 1880: le rôle joué dans leur développement par la Ligue de l'Enseignement et la Société Franklin" (thèse de 3e cycle, University of Paris VII, 1984), 68–72; *Bulletin de la Société Franklin* (15 August 1870), 18; Pierre Emmanuel Raffi, "Le Cercle parisien de la Ligue de l'enseignement (1868–1881): de la société d'éducation populaire à l'institution républicaine" (mémoire de maîtrise, University of Paris IV, 1991), 56; Lyons, *Triomphe du livre,* 179.

46. Macé, *Les Origines de la Ligue de l'enseignement, 1861–1870* (Paris, 1891), 214–219; Raffi, "Cercle parisien," 17; Boulogne, "Les Bibliothèques

populaires," 85; Anne-Marie Chartier and Jean Hébrard, *Discours sur la lecture, 1880–1980* (Paris, 1989), 98.

47. Auspitz, *Radical Bourgeoisie,* 72–76; Raffi, "Cercle parisien," 119–125; Jean-Paul Martin, "La Ligue de l'enseignement et la République, des origines à 1914" (doctoral thesis, Institut d'Etudes Politiques, 1992), 1.29n12.

48. Boulogne, "Bibliothèques populaires," 160–162; Raffi, "Cercle parisien," 67, 108; Martin, "La Ligue de l'enseignement," 1.30; Chartier and Hébrard, *Discours sur la lecture,* 98.

49. André Retif, *Pierre Larousse et son oeuvre, 1817–1875* (Paris, 1975), 172. The 1880s did witness what amounted to a Diderot revival. In midcentury Paris, it was said, there were no more than 500 people who had first-hand knowledge of the philosopher's work. But in 1879–80 a new edition of Diderot's oeuvre, edited by André Lefèvre and Louis Assouline, was published. Diderot boosters also arranged for a memorial statue, which was unveiled in 1886 and now stands on the Boulevard Saint-Germain. Marmottan, *Statues,* 99.

50. Retif, *Larousse,* 223; Pascal Ory, "Le *Grand Dictionnaire* de Pierre Larousse," in Nora, *Lieux de mémoire,* 1.229–246.

51. Assouline, "Le Dictionnaire de la langue française de M. E. Littré," *La Pensée nouvelle,* 18 April 1869. See also Stanislas Aquarone, *The Life and Works of Emile Littré, 1801–1881* (Paris, 1958), 77, 81–82; Jean Hamburger, *Monsieur Littré* (Paris, 1988), 95–97, 152–153.

52. Raffi, "Cercle parisien"; Lyons, *Triomphe du livre,* 191–192.

53. Flammarion, *Mémoires,* 118, 142, 157, 223, 225, 325–326, 479, 498.

54. For the circumstances of the book's writing and reception, see Flammarion, *Mémoires,* 202, 222. For the book itself, see his *La Pluralité des mondes habités,* 4th ed. (Paris, 1865), 9, 133, 148, 187, 273–274, 284, 304, 316.

55. Gabriel Hanotaux, *Henri Martin, sa vie, ses oeuvres* (Paris, 1885), 264.

56. Georges Weill, *Histoire de l'idée laïque en France au XIXe siècle* (Paris, 1925), 191.

57. Hanotaux, *Henri Martin,* 262.

58. Henri Martin, *Histoire de France,* 4th ed. (Paris, 1865), 1.xvi, 1, 84–88. See also Hanotaux, *Henri Martin,* 223–229, 292.

59. Hanotaux, *Henri Martin,* 236.

60. Gary Dunbar, *Elisée Reclus: Historian of Nature* (Hamden, Conn., 1978), 11. See also *Les Frères Elie et Elisée Reclus* (Paris, 1964), 45–47; Marie Fleming, *The Anarchist Way to Socialism: Elisée Reclus and Nineteenth-Century European Anarchism* (London, 1979), 29–58.

61. For Reclus' evolution, see Fleming, *Anarchist Way,* 65–66; Dunbar, *Elisée Reclus,* 46–47, 57, 85, 93.

62. Reclus, *La Terre* (Paris, 1869), 2.757, 280, 505, 589, 622–624, 627–628, 746–748, 751; *La Terre,* 2nd ed. (Paris, 1870), 1.88, 757–758.

9. The Middle-Class Interior

1. On women's place in the new scheme of things, see Anne Martin-Fugier, *La Bourgeoise: femme au temps de Paul Bourget* (Paris, 1983); Linda Clark, *Schooling the Daughters of Marianne: Textbooks and the Socialization of Girls in Modern French Primary Schools* (Albany, 1984); Laura Strumingher, "*L'Ange de la Maison:* Mothers and Daughters in Nineteenth-Century France," *International Journal of Women's Studies,* 2 (January-February 1979), 51–61; Michelle Perrot and Anne Martin-Fugier, "Les Acteurs," in Michelle Perrot, ed., *Histoire de la vie privée,* (Paris, 1987), 4.89–303. On the place of the child, the essential work remains Philippe Ariès, *Centuries of Childhood: A Social History of Family Life,* tr. Robert Baldick (New York, 1962). Ariès dates the bourgeois discovery of childhood to the late eighteenth century, but recent research suggests the centrality of the mid-nineteenth century. See the splendid work by Maurice Crubellier, *L'Enfance et la jeunesse dans la société française, 1800–1950* (Paris, 1979), 68–69, 342–344; André Armengaud, "L'Attitude de la société à l'égard de l'enfant au XIXe siècle," *Annales de démographie historique* (1973), 303–312. The 1860s have long been recognized as the advent of a golden age in children's literature. See Marie-Thérèse Latzarus, *La Littérature enfantine en France dans la seconde moitié du XIXe siècle* (Paris, 1924); Marc Soriano, *Guide de littérature pour la jeunesse* (Paris, 1975). Historical work on men is much thinner, but see e.g. Philippe Perrot, *Les Dessus et les dessous de la bourgeoisie* (Paris, 1981).

2. On villa and apartment layout, see Patrick Favardin, "La Villa ou l'avènement d'un nouveau monde d'habitation," *Monuments historiques,* 102 (April 1979), 57–60; Donald Olsen, *The City as a Work of Art: London, Paris, Vienna* (New Haven, 1986). For the disposition and functional specialization of the rooms in a bourgeois home, see Jean-Paul Aron, *Essai sur la sensibilité alimentaire à Paris au 19e siècle* (Paris, 1967), 39–40; Roger-Henri Guerrand, *Les Lieux, histoire des commodités* (Paris, 1985); Georges Vigarello, *Le Propre et le sale, l'hygiène du corps depuis le moyen âge* (Paris, 1985). The issue of furnishings is discussed in E. Henriot, "Le Décor de la vie sous le Second Empire," *La Gazette des beaux-arts,* 5th ser., 6 (July-August 1922), 108; Colombe Samoyault-Verlet, "Furnishings," in *The Second Empire, 1852–1870: Art in France under Napoleon III,* exhibition catalogue, Philadelphia Museum of Art (1978), 74–76; Rémy Saisselin, *The Bourgeois and the Bibelot* (New Brunswick, 1984), 71.

3. Thérèse Moreau, *Le Sang de l'histoire: Michelet, l'histoire et l'idée de la femme au XIXe siècle* (Paris, 1982), 11.

4. Acollas, *Nécessité de refondre l'ensemble de nos codes et notamment le code Napoléon au point de vue de l'idée démocratique* (Paris, 1866), 32.

5. Léon Richer, *Le Code des femmes* (Paris, 1883), 292.

6. Cited in ibid., 172.

7. Clarisse Coignet, *De l'éducation dans la démocratie* (Paris, 1881), 12, 15–16, 332.

8. Pelletan, *La Famille: la mère,* 2nd ed. (Paris, 1865), 226.

9. Ibid., 36. See also Jenny d'Héricourt, *A Woman's Philosophy of Woman, or Woman Affranchised* (Westport, Connecticut, 1981; rpt. of 1st English ed., 1864), 263; Coignet, *De l'éducation,* 12, 279.

10. See the discussion in Karen Offen's pioneering article, "Ernest Legouvé and the Doctrine of `Equality in Difference' for Women: A Case Study of Male Feminism in Nineteenth-Century French Thought," *Journal of Modern History,* 58 (June 1986), 452–484.

11. Michelet's views on women and marriage are discussed in hair-raising detail by Moreau in *Le Sang de l'histoire;* D'Héricourt, *A Woman's Philosophy,* 287; Coignet, *De l'éducation,* 279.

12. See the speeches by Jules Ferry and Camille Sée, cited in Françoise Mayeur, L'Education des filles en France au XIXe siècle (Paris, 1979),139; Susan Groag Bell and Karen Offen, eds., *Women, the Family, and Freedom: The Debate in Documents, 1750–1950* (Stanford, 1983), 1.444. Sée's remarks were addressed to the Chamber of Deputies in 1880. He was speaking for a bill he had authored, providing for the creation of state-run lycées for girls. For all the talk of equal education, however, young women in the new high schools had a limited curriculum, which did not include classical languages. Without additional training, they were unable to sit for the baccalaureate, which until the twentieth century required Latin. See Offen, "The Second Sex and the Baccalauréat in Republican France, 1880–1924," *French Historical Studies,* 13 (Fall 1983), 252–286.

13. Remarks by Jenny Sabatier-Herbelot, *Congrès international du droit des femmes* (Paris, 1878), 164, 166; Pelletan, *La Famille,* 301–302.

14. Michael and Ariane Batterberry, *Mirror, Mirror: A Social History of Fashion* (New York, 1977), 230–234; remarks by Mme. Eugène Garcin, *Congrès international des femmes,* 30, 34.

15. Charles Blanc, *L'Art dans la parure et dans le vêtement* (Paris, 1875), 374–375.

16. Juliette Adam, *Mes Premières Armes littéraires et artistiques,* 8th ed. (Paris, 1904), 24–25.

17. Garcin, *Congrès international des femmes,* 34.

18. Pelletan, *La Famille,* 280.

19. Charles Letourneau, *La Sociologie d'après l'ethnographie,* 3rd ed. (Paris, 1893; orig. published 1880), 89–90.

20. Pelletan, *La Famille,* 280, and *La Nouvelle Babylone, lettres d'un provincial en tournée à Paris* (Paris, 1862), 84–85, 315.

21. See the discussion of prostitution in *Congrès international des femmes,* 114, 147, 149. For the abolitionist campaign, Alain Corbin, *Les Filles de noces* (Paris, 1982), 315–344.

22. Pelletan, *La Famille,* 326. See also Julie Daubié, *La Femme pauvre au XIXe siècle* (Paris, 1866); general discussion in Laurence Klejman and Florence Rochefort, *L'Egalité en marche: le féminisme sous la Troisième République* (Paris, 1989), 42–43.

23. Juliette Adam, *Idées anti-proudhonniennes sur l'amour, la femme et le mariage,* 2nd ed. (Paris, 1861), 72; Coignet, *De l'éducation,* 177ff; Jules Simon, *L'Ouvrière* (Paris, 1861).

24. Blanc, *L'Art dans la parure,* 373.

25. D'Héricourt, *A Woman's Philosophy,* 292.

26. On Cassatt and Morisot, see Griselda Pollock, *Mary Cassatt* (New York, 1980), 12, 15, 18–19; Anne Higonnet, *Berthe Morisot* (New York, 1990); Valerie Steele, *Paris Fashion: A Cultural History* (New York, 1988), 183–188; and, for general discussion, Griselda Pollock, *Vision and Difference: Femininity, Feminism, and the Histories of Art* (New York, 1988), 50–90, 208.

27. Pollock has remarked on this contrast in *Vision and Difference,* 80–81.

28. *Renoir,* exhibition catalogue, Hayward Gallery (London, 1985), 214; Steele, *Paris Fashion,* 124.

29. Henriette Caillaux, *Aimé-Jules Dalou* (Paris, 1935), 79; John Hunisak, *The Sculptor Jules Dalou* (New York, 1977), 53–56, 68.

30. Martyn Lyons, *Le Triomphe du livre: une histoire sociologique de la lecture dans la France du XIXe siècle* (Paris, 1987), 242–245.

31. Pelletan, *La Famille,* 316.

32. Ibid., 245; d'Héricourt, *A Woman's Philosophy,* 27.

33. Garcin, *Congrès international des femmes,* 34.

34. Pollock, *Mary Cassatt,* 7. See also Monet's painting, *Le Déjeuner* (1868–69), which depicts a mother, child, and servant having breakfast, with a copy of *Le Figaro* folded on the table.

35. Ix. (Mallarmé), "Chronique de Paris," *La Dernière Mode,* 20 December 1874.

36. *Congrès international des femmes,* 149. For general discussion, see Katherine Auspitz, *The Radical Bourgeoisie: The Ligue de l'Enseignement and the Origins of the Third Republic* (New York, 1982), 33.

37. D'Héricourt, *A Woman's Philosophy,* 291.

38. Gustave Droz, *Monsieur, madame et bébé,* 87th ed. (Paris, 1878), 125–126.

39. Cited in A. Parménie and Catherine Bonnier de la Chapelle, *Histoire d'un éditeur et de ses auteurs: P.-J. Hetzel (Stahl)* (Paris, 1953), 472.

40. Ernest Legouvé, *Les Pères et les enfants au XIXe siècle,* 16th ed. (Paris, 1878; orig. 1867), 242; Adolph-Charles Clavel, *La Morale positive* (Paris, 1873), 284.

41. Clavel, *La Morale,* 284; Coignet, *De l'éducation,* 95–96.

42. Coignet, *De l'éducation,* 95.

43. Legouvé, *Les Pères et les enfants,* 243.

44. Perrot, *Les Dessus et les dessous,* 8, 67n, and *Le Travail des apparences, ou les transformations du corps féminin, XVIIIe-XIXe siècle* (Paris, 1984), 175.

45. Blanc, *L'Art dans la parure,* 101–102.

46. Cited, with approval, by Adam, *Mes Premières Armes,* 373.

47. Linda Nochlin, *Realism* (Harmondsworth, 1971), 187–190.

48. See Giselle Freund, *La Photographie en France au dix-neuvième siècle* (Paris, 1936).

49. Legouvé in fact uses the English, "le *self-government.*" *Les Pères et les enfants,* 49.

50. Ibid., 201; also 5–10, 209, 211.

51. See the views of Eugénie Niboyet, cited in Strumingher, "L'Ange de la maison," 52; remarks by Eugénie Pierre, *Congrès international des femmes,* 66–69.

52. Morisot, on the other hand, hired a wet nurse after the birth of her daughter Julie and painted a canvas on the subject, *Wet Nurse and Julie* (1879). See the discussion in Linda Nochlin, *Women, Art, and Power and Other Essays* (New York, 1988), 37–56.

53. On the campaign for the Roussel bill, see George Sussman, *Selling Mother's Milk: The Wet-Nursing Business in France, 1715–1914* (Urbana, 1982), 122–128, and "The End of the Wet-Nursing Business in France, 1874–1914," *Journal of Family History,* 2 (Fall 1977), 242–243. Sussman demonstrates that the Roussel bill failed to discourage wet nursing, which remained a thriving industry into the first decades of the twentieth century.

54. Pierre, *Congrès international des femmes,* 65. See also Clavel, *La Morale,* 141. In all such arguments, of course, republicans were following in the footsteps of Rousseau.

55. Legouvé, *Les Pères et les enfants,* 75.

56. Droz, *Monsieur, madame et bébé,* 294.

57. Legouvé, *Les Pères et les enfants,* 193.

58. Droz, *Monsieur, madame et bébé,* 335.

59. Verne was elected at Amiens. In later years he soured on the republic and, at the turn of the century, could be found in the anti-Dreyfusard camp.

60. See the remarks by Antide Martin, *Congrès international des femmes,* 183.

61. Pauline Kergomard, *L'Instruction maternelle dans l'école,* 2nd ed. (1886; Paris, 1889), 65–66. Kergomard's book was intended as a manual for teachers in the new system of state-regulated kindergartens. In 1881 the

republic created a uniform administration for all child-care facilities, formerly called *salles d'asile* and now renamed *écoles maternelles.*

62. Crubellier, *L'Enfance et la jeunesse,* 209; Antoine Prost, *Histoire de l'enseignement en France, 1800–1967* (Paris, 1968), 285.

63. The notion of object lessons was first worked out by Marie Pape-Carpantier, director of an experimental *salle d'asile* in the 1840s and 1850s. Pape-Carpantier, who worked with Denys Cochin, the scion of a distinguished monarchist family, was not a republican. But the teaching practices she pioneered had obvious appeal to republicans who were interested in the pedagogical potential of spontaneous play. See her *Histoire et leçons des choses pour les enfants* (Paris, 1858); Prost, *Histoire de l'enseignement,* 282–284; Kergomard, *L'Instruction maternelle,* 99.

64. Kergomard, *L'Instruction maternelle,* 17–20,

65. See e.g. the criticisms in Crubellier, *L'Enfance et la jeunesse,* 220–221.

66. P.-J. Stahl (Hetzel) and Jean Macé, "A nos lecteurs," *Magasin d'éducation et de récréation* (1864), 1; also Stahl, "La Lecture en famille," ibid. (1868–69), 19–23.

67. Soriano, *Guide de littérature,* 477.

68. Crubellier, *L'Enfance et la jeunesse,* 359. For a thumbnail sketch of Ségur and her work, see Soriano, *Guide de littérature,* 477–482.

69. Sophie de Ségur, *Les Malheurs de Sophie* (New York, n.d.), 123.

70. Jules Verne, *Voyage au centre de la terre* (Livre de poche, Paris, n.d.), 249.

71. Vigarello, *Le Propre et le sale,* 223, 233; Jules Verne, *Les 500 millions de la Bégum* (Livre de poche, Paris, n.d.), 153; Jean Chesneaux, *Jules Verne, une lecture politique* (Paris, 1982).

72. *P.-J. Hetzel, de Balzac à Jules Verne: un grand éditeur du XIXe siècle,* exhibition catalogue, Bibliothèque Nationale (Paris, 1966), 55.

73. Charles Blanc, *Grammaire des arts décoratifs* (Paris, 1882), 2.

74. On Burty, see Nord, "Manet and Radical Politics," *Journal of Interdisciplinary History,* 19 (Winter 1989), 452–453.

75. Henry Havard, *L'Art dans la maison, grammaire de l'ameublement,* 2 vols. (1884; Paris, 1887). On the success of Havard's book, see Debora Silverman, *Art Nouveau in Fin-de-Siècle France: Politics, Psychology, and Style* (Berkeley, 1989), 141.

76. Burty, "Le Mobilier moderne," La *Gazette des beaux-arts,* 1st ser., 24 (January 1868), 43; Havard, *L'Art dans la maison,* 1.4–6. Zola pictured both locales in acid colors. In *La Curée,* the real-estate speculator Saccard is made to live in a Parc Monceau mansion designed in *"style Napoléon III,* that opulent bastard of all styles." The heavily draped richness of the mansion, Zola implies, constitutes a decorative analogue to the moral corruption of its inhabitants, who swindle and commit incest with equal abandon. In

Pot-Bouille, a decorative setting is again invested with moral value. The apartment house in which the drama takes place is populated by various representatives of a rising, pretentious, and adulterous middle class. Zola describes the vestibule and staircase as decorated "with a violent luxury": "At the foot [of the staircase] was a female figure, a kind of gilded Neapolitan, who carried on her head an amphora from which sprouted three gas jets encased in frosted globes. The wainscoting in white fake marble with rose borders spiraled regularly up the circular stairwell; while the railing, made of iron and mahogany, mimicked old silver." Emile Zola, *La Curée,* 27, and *Pot-Bouille,* 9 (Livre de poche, Paris, n.d.)

77. Havard, *L'Art dans la maison,* 1.3, 6; Pelletan, *La Famille,* 280.

78. Pelletan, *La Famille,* 280.

79. Burty, "Le Mobilier moderne," 44.

80. Blanc, *Grammaire des arts décoratifs,* 136–137, 147, 152–153. Blanc's comments on nature are in the 2nd ed. of the *Grammaire* (Paris, 1882), i–iii. Subsequent references here are to the 1st ed.

81. Ibid., 86; also 29–30, 59–61, 82–83, 94, 137, 240–245, 332, 336.

82. Renoir's proposal is reproduced in Lionello Venturi, *Les Archives de l'impressionnisme* (Paris, 1939), 1.128–129; also John House, "Renoir's Worlds," in *Renoir,* 12–13, 18n.

83. Burty, *Chefs d'oeuvre des arts industriels* (Paris, 1866), 170–171, 210.

84. Havard, *L'Art dans la maison,* 1.2; also 2.4, 10.

85. Ibid., 2.133; also 2.29, 31, 132.

86. Burty, *Chefs d'oeuvre,* 314.

87. Havard, *L'Art dans la maison,* 2.161–166.

88. Burty, *Chefs d'oeuvre,* 439–440, 555–556, and "Le Mobilier moderne," 27–28, 34, 36, 43–44; Havard, *L'Art dans la maison,* 1.72.

Acknowledgments

I HAVE BEEN fortunate in my colleagues at Princeton, past and present. David Bell, Nancy Bermeo, Natalie Zemon Davis, Gerald Geison, Peter Mandler, Suzanne Nash, Theodore Rabb, Daniel Rodgers, Carl Schorske, Jerrold Seigel, Christine Stansell, and Dror Wahrman, all have read one or more chapters of this book, and my work has been enriched by their comments. A number waded through the entire manuscript, none with greater care than Arno Mayer, who has been a mentor and critic over the years, unstinting of his time and acumen.

Academics are often overburdened, but many still find the time to read the work of friends and associates. I have profited from such gestures of collegiality time and again and want to return the favor now with an expression of thanks to Geoff Crossick, Rachel Fuchs, Peter Hall, Gerhard Haupt, Steven Hause, Anne Higonnet, Patrice Higonnet, Leila Kinney, Molly Nesbit, Karen Offen, Michael Osborne, Aron Rodgrigue, Peter Sahlins, Daniel Sherman, Michael Smith, and Peter Stearns.

French colleagues have been no less generous, sharing conversation and ideas, extending a hospitality that has made the pursuit of this project as much pleasure as work. I offer warm thanks to Maurice Agulhon, Christophe Charle, Patrick Fridenson, and Jacqueline Lalouette. Thanks as well to two scholar-archivists who, with patience and good will, rendered invaluable assistance: Philippe Landau at the Jewish Consistoire Central and Yves Ozanam at the Palais de Justice.

ACKNOWLEDGMENTS

I have had the opportunity to present portions of the manuscript to a variety of seminars and colloquia. The critical response was at times spirited but always acute and constructive. I want to express my gratitude to hosts and participants: Reid Andrews and Herrick Chapman, conveners of the Carnegie Mellon and University of Pittsburgh Conference on the Social Construction of Democracy; Jean-Philippe Antoine, Tony Judt, and the luncheon seminar at the Institute of French Studies in New York; Susanna Barrows and the Bay Area French History Seminar; Steven Kaplan and the Cornell Graduate Colloquium; Gene Lebovics and the New York Area French History Seminar; Patricia O'Brien and the University of California at Irvine Seminar on French Cultural Identity; Kent Worcester and the Social Science Research Council.

A large portion of this book was completed while I was a fellow at the Rutgers Center for Historical Analysis. To the center and its then director John Gillis, who has extended himself on my behalf many times, I owe a special debt. As I do to Gerhard Haupt (once again), Michael Müller, and Stuart Woolf, project directors of the European Forum at the University European Institute in Florence. It was in Florence as a visiting professor that my final revisions were completed.

An earlier version of Chapter 2 was published as "Republicanism and Utopian Vision: French Freemasonry in the 1860s and 1870s," *Journal of Modern History,* 63 (June 1991); Chapter 9 as "Republican Politics and the Bourgeois Interior," in Suzanne Nash, ed., *The Home and Its Dislocations in Nineteenth-Century France* (Albany: SUNY Press, 1993).

My children, Joseph and David, have helped me to keep my work on this book in perspective. Whenever I encountered difficulties, I turned first to my wife, Deborah, for her calming good judgment and critical counsel. I am never more myself, intellectually or otherwise, than I am with her.

Index

INDEX

Duranty, Edmond, 142, 160; journalistic career, 161; and salon system, 181, 182–183
Duret, Théodore, 131, 132, 184, 187; at Café Guerbois, 158; republicanism, 162, 163; at salons, 165
Durkheim, Emile, 46, 47
Duruy, Victor, 33–34; suspension of Renan, 35; and student unrest, 37, 38, 40

eclecticism, 32–33, 35; influence on aesthetics, 184–185. *See also* Cousin, Victor
Ecole d'Anthropologie, 41–42; neo-Lamarckianism, 43–44; state aid, 46
Ecole de Médécine. *See* Paris Ecole de Médécine
Ecole des Batignolles, 158, 160
Ecole des Beaux-Arts, 139
Ecole Libre des Sciences Politiques, 248
Ecole Mutuelle: membership, 20; support of education, 26; Clamageran in, 106; and cult of Voltaire, 196
Ecole Normale Israélite Orientale (ENIO), 77; republicanism, 81; faculty, 88
Ecole Normale Supérieure: in Second Empire, 36–38; republicanism, 45–47
Ecole Professionnelle de la Coopération, 26, 86
Ecole Rabbinique, 64
education: freemasons' support, 25–26; of women, 26, 27, 77, 79, 81, 221; UNCI's support, 58; rabbinical, 66; AIU's support, 80–81; ENIO's role, 88; role of liberal Protestants, 90, 106–107, 113, 210; Gambetta's support, 133; laicization, 136; in Second Empire, 210–211
elites: role in parliamentarism, 4, 5, 6–7; role in democratic transitions, 7, 9; in Second Republic, 10, 12–13; masonic lodges, 19, 20–21; Jewish, 66, 68, 90; Protestant, 90, 92. *See also* notables
Elwitt, Sanford, 2
encyclopedias, 36, 212–213
England, democratizing movements in, 4, 5

ENIO. *See* Ecole Normale Israélite Orientale
Erlanger, Michel, 76
Espinas, Alfred, 37, 46
etiquette, republican, 230
Eugénie, empress, 222, 229, 243
evangelicals, 91; in Paris consistory, 93–94; in regime of Moral Order, 94, 100, 101, 104; conflict with liberal Protestants, 94–106; in Société Biblique, 96; in national synod, 100. *See also* Protestants; Reformed Church
evolution, theories of, 42–43

Fabre, Charles, 99
Fantin-Latour, Henri, 158, 160; *Hommage à Delacroix*, 142–143, 144; *Studio*, 145, 164; at salons, 167; republicanism, 168; women subjects, 226
fashion, in dress, 222–224, 230, 243
Fauvety, Charles: as freemason, 18, 22; and workers' movement, 29; in ARU, 84
Favé, Ildefousse, 210
Favre, Jules: support of Ecole Normale, 45; in campaign of 1869, 87; as orator, 118, 119; as deputy, 120, 129; in Baudin affair, 132; and siege of Paris, 168
Favre, Mme. Jules, 110
feminism, 22, 193, 243; masonic support for, 27–28, 29; and marriage, 221; in Third Republic, 247. *See also* women
Feray, Ernest, 87
Ferry, Charles, 124
Ferry, Jules: legal style, 1; and elites, 4; as freemason, 16; positivism, 16, 133; political activities, 45, 128, 129, 133; and Conseil de l'Instruction Publique, 46; and Union de la Presse, 58; Protestant appointees, 90, 101; on Protestantism, 110; legal training, 122, 123; at Morisot salon, 124; role in education reform, 136, 221; abolition of salon system, 188; on Thiers' funeral, 200; European associates, 250
Figaro, 226, 229, 243
Flammarion, Camille, 25, 193, 209; in Ligue de l'Enseignement, 211; scientific publications, 213–214

INDEX

Floquet, Charles, 29, 60, 108; in Conférence Marie, 122; political activities, 129, 130; and Commune, 134; marriage, 197
Fontanès, Ernest, 96
Forain, Jean-Louis, 160, 174, 175
Fortoul, Hippolyte, 11, 33, 34
Fouillée, Mme. Alfred, 233–234
Franck, Adolphe, 66, 68, 177
Franco-Prussian war: and Grand Orient, 26; and Jews, 82; and new painters, 158
freemasonry, 251; in Second Empire, 13, 16, 17–23; in Third Republic, 14, 15, 30; of republican ministers, 15; radicalism, 16, 22–23, 30; allegiance to Second Republic, 17; elite lodges, 19, 20–21; dissident lodges, 19–20, 21, 23, 26, 101; republicanism, 21–22, 29; utopianism, 23–30; views on education, 25–26; and labor movements, 28–29; Jews in, 71, 85; and cult of Voltaire, 196; autonomy, 250
freethinkers, 40, 84; among academics, 44; among Jews, 70–71; among liberal Protestants, 102–103; and civil ceremonies, 197, 198; publication of, 208
free trade, 248; in Second Empire, 50; support of UNCI, 54–55
Froebel, Friedrich, 234, 237
Furet, François, 1, 4

Gambetta, Léon: oratorical style, 1, 126; and elites, 4; on new social stratum, 20, 48–49, 186; on freedom of association, 55–56; on *seize mai* crisis, 61; support of Jewish candidates, 88; nonconformity, 120; legal training, 121, 122, 123; at salons, 125, 164; in Baudin affair, 132; support of education, 133; as minister of interior, 134; in Chamber of Deputies, 135; and Burty, 162, 238; and *nouvelle peinture*, 165, 169, 170–171; and Bastille Day, 205; in Ligue de l'Enseignement, 211; military views, 247–248; European associates, 250

Gambettism: in Latin Quarter, 46; in UNCI, 49, 57, 62
Garibaldi, Giuseppe, 5, 168, 169, 193, 250
Garnier-Pagès, Louis-Antoine, 124
Gauche Républicaine (party), 115
Gauguin, Paul, 159, 161, 172
Germany, democratizing movements in, 4–5
Gervex, Henri, 198
Glais-Bizoin, Alexandre, 54, 162
Gleyre, Charles, 142
Goldschmidt, Salomon, 77, 78, 88
grand masters (freemasonry), 16, 20, 250
grand masters (university), 32
Grand Orient of France, 17–22; in Second Empire, 11, 16; constitution (1854), 19, 21; meetings, 19, 20, 21; lawyers in, 20; support of black emancipation, 25; in Franco-Prussian war, 26; and Commune, 27; and women, 27; republicanism, 29; reform faction, 85; lecture series, 193; and cult of Voltaire, 197
Grawitz, Charles, 97
Grenier, P. J., 39
Gréville, Mme. Henry, 110
Grévy, Jules, 58, 122, 127
Grousset, Paschal, 209
Guépin, Ange, 23, 25
Guéroult, Adolphe, 22, 25, 71
Guillaumin, Armand, 142, 158, 161; socialism, 173
Guizot, François: and public institutions, 10, 11; and Reformed Church, 12, 96, 98, 100; opposition to universal suffrage, 103

Habermas, Jürgen, 7
Hatet, Alexandre, 60
Havard, Henry, 238; on home furnishings, 240, 242
Havard, Joseph-Louis, 53, 54
Haviland, Charles, 167
Hayem, Charles, 177
Hendlé, Ernest, 85, 86, 87; in public office, 88
Hérold, Ferdinand, 58, 129, 205; and laicization of education, 136

INDEX

pacifism, 248; masonic views, 26–27, 30; and free trade, 55; of liberal Protestants, 105–106
Pagnerre, Charles-Antoine, 207, 208
painting. *See nouvelle peinture*
Pajot, Charles, 45
Paris bar, 116–120; suppression in Second Empire, 11–12, 13; organization, 116–117; code of conduct, 117–118, 128; constitution, 119; council elections, 126–128; and 1864 elections, 129–130; alliance with journalists, 132–133. *See also jeune barreau*
Paris Chamber of Commerce: suffrage in, 12; conflict with UNCI, 49–54, 61, 62–63; organization, 50, 54; franchise reform, 50–51, 54, 62–63; and labor unrest, 53; decline, 61
Paris Ecole de Médécine, 36; riots (1862), 38, 164; militancy, 38–41; freethinkers, 40
Paris municipal council, 135–136; beautification schemes, 197–198; and Clésinger's statue, 202
participatory government, theories of, 5–6
Pasteur, Louis, 37
Pauliat, Louis, 209
Paulin, Alexandre, 207
Paumier, Henri, 97
Pécaut, Félix, 90, 91; in UPL, 97; in public office, 108; on scripture, 111
Pédézert, Jean, 97, 98, 102
Pelletan, Camille, 166, 185, 198
Pelletan, Eugène, 113; *Tribune*, 130; as lecturer, 193; on marriage, 220–221; on courtesans, 222, 223; on women's reading, 226, 243; on fashion, 238
Pensée nouvelle, 34, 35–36
Pétain, Maréchal Philippe, 248
Peyrat, Alphonse, 132
Phrygian cap, symbolism of, 205
Picard, Alfred, 130
Picard, Ernest, 120, 121; as deputy, 129; journalism, 130
Pierre, Eugénie, 233
Piette, Ludovic, 159, 172
Pissarro, Camille, 141, 142; and Franco-Prussian war, 158; exhibitions, 159,

182; and Renoir, 164, 165, 173; republicanism, 171–173
Pognon, Maria, 29
Pointoise group, 159, 171, 173, 174
polygenesis controversy, 42
positivism: in Third Republic, 15, 16, 191; of freemasons, 23, 30; of Ecole de Médecine, 41, 47; and Judaism, 83; Ferry's support, 133; of republican publications, 212; of print culture, 216
Pouchet, Félix, 24
Pouyer-Quertier, Augustin, 55
Pressensé, Elise de, 111
print culture, republican, 205, 207–212, 216
private sphere, 218–220; role of women, 220–229; role of men, 229–234; home furnishings, 237–244; effect of political conviction, 243–244; reform, 251–252
Prix de Rome, 139
protectionism. *See* free trade
Protestant libéral, 96, 104, 105; on moral belief, 112
Protestants, political activities, 101–109. *See also* Consistory, Protestant; Reformed Church
Protestants, liberal: associational activism, 55–56, 109; and republican moral debate, 84–85; role in public education, 90; conflict with evangelicals, 94–106; presbyteral council, 96–98, 102, 103; voter registration, 101; freethinking, 102–103; and popular education, 106–107, 113, 210; in public office, 107–108; pastorate, 108–109; theology, 109–114; and Ecole Libre des Sciences Politiques, 248
Protestants, orthodox. *See* evangelicals
Proust, Antonin, 162, 170
public-library movement, 86, 106, 209–210
public sphere: in transitions to democracy, 7, 8; in Second Empire, 13; women in, 137, 217
publishing: republican, 207–212; for children, 209, 218, 235–237; and positivism, 212, 213. *See also* journals

[318]

INDEX

Quinet, Edgar, 1, 103; *Révolution*, 109–110; exile, 192; burial, 200; unitarianism, 214

rabbis: education, 66; liberalization, 67; authority, 79–80
racism, 245; scientific, 32, 44
radicals: journals, 22, 207, 209; student, 34–35, 37, 192; Jewish, 89
Raffaëlli, Jean-François, 160, 188; *Clemenceau*, 156, 174
Ranc, Arthur, 30, 169
Rappel (journal), 209, 211
Raspail, Benjamin, 205
Ratier (freemason), 20
rationalism: and freemasons, 23–24; and Jews, 82
Rault, Charles, 57
Rayer, Pierre, 38, 164
Raynal, David, 88
Read, Charles, 90, 93
Reclus, Elisée, 209, 215–216
Reformed Church: governing elite, 12; relations with AIU, 84; liberals in, 90; synods, 92, 99–100; and consistory, 93; schism, 94–101, 113; liberal agenda, 105. *See also* Consistory, Protestant; Protestants
Reinach, Joseph, 88
Reinwald (publisher), 207, 208
Renaissance par les Emules d'Hiram (masonic lodge), 19, 106
Renaissance (Protestant journal), 105–106
Renan, Ernest: inaugural lecture, 35; *Vie de Jésus*, 97, 186
Renard, Georges, 37–38
Renoir, Auguste, 142; *Mme. Charpentier*, 150, 224; exhibitions, 159, 161, 182; and Pissarro, 164, 165, 173; republicanism, 164–166; and salon system, 181; *Maternité*, 232; aesthetic views, 239
Renouvier, Charles, 22, 41; on liberal Protestantism, 110
Republic of the republicans. *See* Third Republic
Reuss, Edouard, 94
Réville, Albert, 95, 96; theological views, 104, 108–109, 111
Revolution of 1789, 1; legacy to Third

Republic, 3–4; in French political culture, 190, 191
Rey, Aristide, 35, 136
Riche-Gardon, Luc-Pierre: as freemason, 18, 22; scientism, 24; in Ligue de l'Enseignement, 25; support of feminism, 27, 29
Richer, Léon, 23, 25, 27, 193
Richter, Eugen, 4–5
Rigault, Raoul, 164
Rive gauche (student journal), 34, 35–36, 44
Rivière, Georges, 185
Robin, Charles, 38, 40, 46
Rochebouët, Gaëtan de, 59, 135
Rochefort, Henri, 45–47, 171, 200
Rodrigues, Hippolyte, 80, 83
Rognon, Louis, 103
Rothschild, Gustave de, 74, 76
Rothschild family, 66, 68
Rouart, Henri, 159, 161, 175–176
Roussel, Théophile, 232–233
Rousselle, André, 18, 20; support of feminism, 28; as lecturer, 194
Royer, Clémence, 28, 30

Sainte-Beuve, Charles, 37, 103
Saint-Simonians: freemasons, 16, 22, 23, 29; Jews, 71; artists, 176; educational activities, 201, 209
Saint-Victor, Paul, 75
Salle Frascati meeting (*seize mai* crisis), 59–60, 108
salon (Académie des Beaux-Arts): state control, 139; painters' opposition to, 141, 179–181, 187; inaccessibility, 158; critics' opposition to, 182–185; reform of jury system, 188
Salon des Refusés, 179–180
salons: radical, 22; political bias, 124–125; artists at, 164, 165, 167–170, 176; decor, 238, 239
Say, Léon, 95, 108
Schérer, Edmond, 95, 96
Schickler, Fernand, 106, 210
Schneider, Henri, 55
Schornstein, David, 87
science: republican doctrine, 31–32, 47; and student activists, 35, 36; human, 36, 41–44; at Ecole de Médécine, 38,